# A CHARACTER OF HUGH LEGARÉ

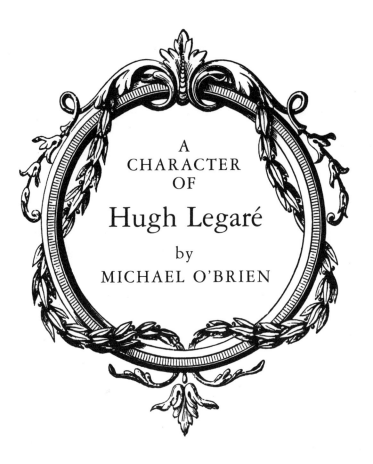

A
CHARACTER
OF
Hugh Legaré
by
MICHAEL O'BRIEN

THE UNIVERSITY OF TENNESSEE PRESS

KNOXVILLE

The paper in this book meets the guidelines for permanence and durability
of the Committee on Production Guidelines for Book Longevity
of the Council on Library Resources.
Binding materials have been chosen for durability.

*Frontispiece:* HUGH SWINTON LEGARÉ, by John M. Stanley, after Edward
Marchant (1858). Painted for the Gallery of Attorneys-General, this is the best
copy of the only portrait known to have been done from life. (Courtesy,
Department of Justice.)

*Library of Congress Cataloging in Publication Data*

O'Brien, Michael, 1948–
    A character of Hugh Legaré.

    Bibliography: p.
    Includes index.
    1. Legaré, Hugh Swinton, 1797-1843. 2. Statesman—
United States—Biography. 3. Intellectuals—Southern
States—Biography. I. Title.
E340.L5023   1985      973.5'092'4 [B]      85-3207
ISBN 0-87049-471-6 (alk. paper)

*For my wife
with love*

# Contents

# Illustrations

# Preface

It is fifty years since a study of Hugh Legaré was published. The lapse of a full half-century alone makes a reassessment necessary. New sources have come to light, perspectives have altered. Legaré was most remarkable in 1934 for his irrelevance and angularity to the issue of the day, the origins and nature of Southern literature.[1] Certainly it would have required a great detachment then to have found much life in Legaré's memory. He had the misfortune to be extravagantly praised in life and death, the more so for being a prodigy who died young, just forty-six in 1843. There was more bombastic eulogy heaped on the poor man's head than was customary even in the nineteenth century and in the American South, which had many occasions for remembering its dead. The critic can be forgiven for not having been able to distinguish between the worthy and unworthy dead. Legaré had become a ponderous, formal, and very stiff corpse. Plain Hugh Legaré had become "Hugh Swinton Legaré," the three names indissolubly brought out like a cold marble bust on a rusty trolley for ceremonial occasions.

This fate befell many nineteenth-century worthies, of whom a few have gained, and deserved, reassessment. Vernon Parrington tried it for Legaré, as he tried for many others, but the effort miscarried. It is time to try again, for Legaré was a remarkable man, and no antebellum southern intellectual better deserves the attention of historians. As only a moderately important politician and diplomat, he would not command the extended interest of posterity; as a thinker, engaged in affairs, he does, even if his achievement has an unfinished air. But it would be harsh to apply to him what he once said of Sir Philip Sidney: "It is obvious to observe that the hasty productions of one who died at so early an age, and was so deeply engaged in the affairs of active life, ought not to be brought into comparison with the master-pieces of professed authors. . . . We are, therefore, bound in fairness to look upon these remains with an indulgent eye—non enim, as Cicero has it, *res* laudanda, but *spes.*" Instead, Lord Acton's judgment that Legaré in his day was "the most accomplished scholar among American statesmen" seems more apposite, even as it invites a parallel of Housman's irony: Legaré was a greater scholar than Calhoun, a greater politician than Simms.[2]

I have argued elsewhere that the mind of the Old South needs a fresh look, without pleading its extraordinary achievement as an intellectual culture. But Legaré is a different matter. I do think his mind is of permanent interest and ought to form a necessary and accessible part of the American heritage. This will explain why I have paused in the narrative to consider his thought, at that moment in his life when he himself paused to set it down.[3] It is, I suppose, old-fashioned to write from such motives. Modern biographies tend to regard their subjects with suspicion, even disdain, as poor creatures to be stretched on couches, as though biography were a therapy for the dead. My motives may seem the more suspicious because Legaré was many things held now in little respect. For the little it matters, there are few things that Hugh Legaré believed that I believe. Sympathy, I take it, is not agreement, but respect for whatever qualities of tenacity, grace, and self-awareness he commanded and expressed.

Yet Legaré can never be a popular writer. He was too confessedly learned, too little disposed to flatter the ignorance of his readers. Few have been able to keep up with him, and so, with glazed astonishment, they have chosen between uncomprehending condemnation and bemused praise. I do not exclude myself from those who pant after him. To master Legaré, one needs to know much recondite and difficult matter, across a span of time and cultures. I do not pretend to such mastery; this study is necessarily a layman's guide to Legaré, written by a layman.

On one point, it is well to be clear. This is a book about Hugh Legaré, not the history of a Southern intellectual, or a slaveholder, or a classicist, or a lawyer, *sui generis.* Its intention is specific and modest, as I believe the genre of biography is obliged to be modest. As recent historical literature has grown ambitiously social, biography has been laid under tribute, sometimes with interesting results, sometimes not. This has compounded the familiar problem of the modern biography, that bloated and corpulent thing that waddles among us unread and unloved. To keep its integrity, biography must keep resolutely to the individual life, though that life, once documented, may become of service to other historians with wider concerns. One cannot explain a culture by a single life. Legaré himself offers his student a caution: "A history, written after the manner of Thucydides and Xenophon, does not suit us; we must have, not a mere narrative of facts, with such a development of their causes as may be necessary to a proper understanding of the events recorded, but withal ponderous disquisitions about political economy and national wealth, excursions on the march of intellect, and the state of letters and science. . . . So it is with biography. The life of an individual of any consequence is sure to present a succinct view, in two or three volumes, at least, of every thing connected with the history of the period during which he flourished, and perhaps, of some centuries before his birth." That I wished to resist these two vices of modern biography—annexation of the life by society and absurd length—may explain what one reader of the manuscript properly diagnosed as an austerity of form. Bearing this in mind, I have had recourse to an old phrase: this then is less a biography, more a character. "A character differeth from a picture," Halifax once explained, "only in this, every part of it must be like, but it is not necessary that every feature should be comprehended in it, as in a picture, only some of the most remarkable."[4]

# I

# TEEMING ANTICIPATIONS

# 1

# Youth

WHEN WALTER SCOTT had made a Highland past fashionable and given the lightness of romance to the trade of cattlethieving, the family liked to remember that Sir Alan Swinton had been noted in the chronicles of Froissart and turned up in the lines of Scott's "Halidon Hill" as a mace-swinging companion to Robert the Bruce. There was even a coat of arms, emblazoned with boars, a tree, and the uncertain dual motto, *"J'espère"* and *"Je pense."* William Swinton, descendant of Sir Alan, had come to the Carolinas as a surveyor and among his other duties laid out the site of Georgetown in the early eighteenth century. His children were to maintain a modest farm upon the Peedee and were most notable for a serious dose of Presbyterianism, though most famous when Francis Marion praised Alexander Swinton as one of his five best officers. [1]

The Swintons were earnest attendants of the Circular Church in Charleston, more properly "The Society or Church of Christian Protestant Dissenters of the Congregational or Presbyterial Form," a gathering that included many Huguenots, among them Legarés. The most romantic family legend, propounded by Mary Legaré Bullen after the Civil War to gild her brother's vanishing posterity, had it that the founder of the South Carolina Legarés, Solomon, had been dispatched by his mother to the colony in 1690 after the Revocation of the Edict of Nantes, to evade its persecution. [2] It made a pretty tale:

the mother sacrificing the closeness to the safety of her adolescent son,
who rose to prosperity in a foreign land, L'Egaré become Legaré,
pronounced in the transmuting manner of the South Carolina
Huguenots, "Luhgree." But the indefatigable genealogists of
Charleston seem to have demonstrated the legend false. Hugh Legaré
himself thought that his ancestor went first to Massachusetts and only
subsequently to the South, a knowledge shared and suppressed by his
sister Mary. A tincture of Boston was not convenient after Appomat-
tox. [3]

In fact a François L'Egaré had left Lyons prudently before the
revocation of Henry IV's grace and been naturalized in 1682 in
Bristol, the gateway to the green hills of Somerset and the slave marts
of West Africa. He was a goldsmith. His wife was named Ann and
they had three sons, François-Solomon, Daniel-James, and Stephen-
John, of whom two followed their parents to Massachusetts by 1688.
In that year they bought a house in Braintree near the coast, and three
years later the elder Legaré was admitted formally to the colony of
Massachusetts. Here matters grow dubious. One version has it that
François-Solomon, later called simply Solomon, who had been a
student at a French college when his parents decamped from France,
left Massachusetts for South Carolina much in the ill graces of his
father and was duly repaid for marrying against paternal wishes by
being expunged from his patrimony. This same Solomon died in
Charleston at an advanced age, said to have been ninety-eight. Another version, current in the 1840s and buttressed by quotation from
the South Carolina *Gazette* of 1760, has Solomon dying in that year at
the more meager age of eighty-seven, having arrived in the colony
sixty-four years earlier, in 1696. [4] A certain doubt is fitting. "L'Egaré"
does mean the misplaced or wandering one.

Solomon Legaré was a clockmaker, who kept his money in a chest
under a mound of old iron (care with money was a trait that descended
to Hugh Legaré) and did very nicely for himself and his two sons,
named, after family tradition, Solomon and Daniel. [5] Charleston
Legarés proliferated during the eighteenth century, often prosperous,
never especially conspicuous. Lack of ambition, Hugh Legaré was to
observe to his mother in 1835, was characteristic of the Legarés,
though Thomas Legaré, grandfather of Hugh, did sit in the provincial
assembly before the Revolution, as he sat in the state legislature after
it; and he was among the first to introduce to low-country planters the
seed of cotton. [6] The Legarés had, in the second generation, become
planters by the purchase of land on John's Island to the south of the

city and the Stono River. There the family seat was placed, and there
in the fourth generation a third Solomon Legaré married Mary Splatt
Swinton.[7]

Records are remarkably silent upon Solomon, the father of Hugh.
His son never spoke of him. Memorialists, eloquent about Sir Alan
Swinton centuries before, could find nothing remarkable about Solomon Legaré, dead only a few decades.[8] One infers that he was a
planter. What matters is that he married, bred six children (of whom
three died in infancy), seems to have reduced his patrimony, and then
died himself in 1799, aged twenty-nine, of a "nervous fever."[9] The
elder Thomas Legaré had divided a proportion of his wife's estate
among his three sons, Thomas, James, and Solomon. But, as Thomas
Legaré's will put it in 1801, "It having pleased God in his adorable
Sovereignty by a remarkable series of providences to deprive my
deceased Son Solomon of all that he possessed of it, I did and do think
it my bounden duty to make some provision for the maintenance and
support of his family." Provided Mary Legaré should not remarry, his
generosity was marked, even against the interests of his surviving
sons. She was to be given in trust for his grandchildren a portion of his
land, two-thirds of his cattle, a mulatto boy known as Prince, and
slaves named as "Smart, little George, big Will, Venus and her child
Lydia, Brutus, Carolina, long Cloe, Rinah and her daughter Maria
and Son Silver, old Stepney, young Stepney, Joe, Lucy, old Tom and
young Tom."[10] Many of these must have moved through Hugh Legaré's curious childhood.

The child had been born on the John's Island plantation on 2
January 1797. He became very healthy, rather large for his age, and
athletic. Edward Johnston was diplomatically to refer to him as
betraying "a marked and fine individuality." His sister Mary was more
blunt: "He was a very self-willed determined child apparently un-
governable—to strike him was to infuriate him, so that his mother
never strongly opposed him, or offered any thing like coercion—but
always addressed her disapprobation of his conduct, young as he then
was, to his self esteem," which then, as later, was considerable. He had
shown no very extraordinary signs of precocity, beyond learning to
speak with promptness. But he had not begun to read by his fourth
year and, one suspects, was fairly launched upon the usual career of the
handsome son and heir, until he fell seriously ill.[11]

Charleston, like other eighteenth-century cities, had habitually
suffered from the devastations of smallpox: the incubation of two
weeks, the feverish aching of three days, the swift pustular eruptions

that blistered, opened, crusted, and lost their scabs. Half of its victims died, and the rest survived with deforming scars. The principle of inoculation with smallpox virus had been known formally in England since 1714, though its record was mixed.[12] English doctors, persuaded that the wound needed to breathe and release its fluids, had taken to the lancet and opened great gashes. It was thought the patients required elaborate preparation and care, and this made inoculation expensive, a choice for the affluent. There was argument over the best sort of smallpox virus for injection, an issue bemusing to the blunt discriminations of medicine. An ingenious Scot from the Shetland Islands, known to his neighbors as Johnny Notions, took to drying smallpox matter in peat smoke and putting it underground covered with camphor, there to age like a good malt whisky; he would seal the scars with a cabbage leaf. The cure of smallpox distressed the religious, who condemned this violation of Providence as "Heathenish" and "Diabolicall." Yet more worrying was the real fear that the inoculation could occasion, as much as it mitigated, the disease.[13]

In 1796, Edward Jenner successfully vaccinated against smallpox with a virus of cowpox. He published his findings in 1798. *An Inquiry into Cause and Effects of the Variolae Vaccinae* reached Boston and Dr. Benjamin Waterhouse in 1799. In South Carolina the energetic apostle came to be David Ramsay, doctor and historian, who vaccinated his own son Nathaniel in February 1802, not in time to ensure the safety of young Hugh. "Charleston has abounded with cases of the natural small pox following the inoculated small pox," Ramsay recalled. The memoir of Mary Legaré notes, "When in his fourth year & just before the death of his grandfather, Hugh was innocculated [sic] with that direful disease the small-pox."[14]

He nearly died. The virus turned confluent and attacked his joints, which broke out in ugly impostumes, requiring constant redressing. For three weeks they were doubtful of his survival. The child, robust, surviving because of it, shrank. He became so skeletal, thin, and wracked that his mother carried him about upon a pillow, as his legs were weakened and his arms diminished. Stronger and needing air, he was taken still upon a pillow on his mother's lap in a buggy, the horse chosen carefully from his grandfather's stables for its ease of gait. It was three months before he learned feebly to walk again.[15]

Until the age of twelve or thirteen he was stunted. Then he suddenly grew as robustly as his first physique had intimated, but only in the head and torso. His legs and arms remained short and misshapen. One arm was stiffened, an injury later compounded when a kick from a horse dislocated his left elbow, and only with effort in later years could he learn to use it with grace in declamations. He limped a little. His eyes became subject to strain. Sitting, it was remarked with pity, he looked almost normal, even imposing; standing, the man was ill-proportioned, curious.[16]

One may infer the nature of Legaré's condition from the scattered evidence of symptoms. The likelihood is that a severe infection, occasioned by the virus, damaged his pituitary gland, which ceased the production of growth hormones. Later in his childhood the activation of prepubertal hormones, coupled with his recovery from the infection, recommended growth. That it was an uneven growth may have been because smallpox inflammation, settling in the joints as his did, can damage the epiphyses, the growth centers of the bones; lacking hormone stimulation, they can cease to function; that one arm was stiffer than another suggests an unevenness of epiphyseal atrophy. Smallpox infection not uncommonly occasions bone disorders, at worst osteomyelitis, even secondary inflammatory arthritis. In addition, such infection not infrequently damages the optic nerve, which may explain the eyestrain of which Legaré was often to complain. Technically, it might be possible to describe Legaré's condition as dwarfism, though a very mild case; the largeness of his head, often remarked upon, is characteristic.[17]

Whatever the causes, the results were profound. He was solitary at first, though he attained in later years a proud, austere, and reticent ease in general society. Even so, he preferred the company of close friends. He liked to walk, but alone. He sought the setpiece occasion, which he could orchestrate: to place himself impressively upon the chaise longue of the drawing room, to gather his frockcoat about his shortened legs if standing. He seldom rode a horse, the pride of any self-respecting South Carolinian, but went in carriages like a woman. Indeed he came to relish the company of women, with whom he could banter and flirt, because with men he was conscious of physical inferiority. He was absorbed by his health, fragile and ominous, a student of magnesium for his stomach, a connoisseur of the sulphurous liquids of watering places. He would confide to his journals and letters of his malcontent body, of whether he had slept soundly, or his complexion was ruddy, or his eyes were well. But he never spoke, even to himself with pen in hand, of his deformity. Rather he spoke of a lithe and graceful body that strolled and lounged like that of any man about town. He tried to dress like a dandy and no doubt conspired with his tailor to diminish his oddity—so much so that a

friend, advising him upon the proper appearance before the electorate
of Charleston, cautioned, "Remember . . . no whiskers, no rings, no
chain, no foppery, nothing but civility and common sense till the
election is over."[18]

Privately he brooded. He was given to sulking at nature and society,
which his friends would patiently bear because the moments would
pass, and he would return to his favorite habit of reading aloud from
the dramatists.[19] The nearest he came to mentioning his deformity
was in the relative anonymity of print, when discussing the clubfeet of
Byron and Scott, and the hunched back of Shakespeare's Richard III:
Legaré noted, with affected dispassion, how shy and sensitive, how
mortified at his lameness had been the young Byron, how the injury
accounted for the poet's morbid irritability and partially explained his
spirit of defiance at a dissembling nature that had cheated him of
feature and sent him into the world scarce half made up. He noted,
too, how Walter Scott, a more temperate man, had coped with a
similar disappointment by discipline and work. He praised Scott's *The
Black Dwarf,* absurd and fantastical to the unknowing but resonant
and masterful to the secret sharers of affliction. "It is vain to say," he
cautioned, perhaps himself, "that it argues a weak mind and an ill-
regulated temper to be so much affected by what is, in the eye of
reason, so trifling. Instinct, especially in youth, when character is
forming, is too strong for mere unaided reason. . . . The feeling, as
expressed by Lord Byron to a friend, is that 'nature has set a mark'
upon the sufferer—held him up to be a show and a laughing stock—a
thing for the vulgar to wonder at, point at, scoff at. Byron, we venture
to affirm, spoke only the language of all irritable and proud spirits,
under a similar misfortune, before time has reconciled them to their
fate, when he said, with so pointed an emphasis, what is ascribed to
him in the following passage. 'But the embittering circumstances of
his life—that which haunted him like a curse, amid the buoyancy of
youth and the anticipations of fame and pleasure—was, strange to say,
the trifling deformity of his foot. By that one slight blemish, (as in his
moments of melancholy he persuaded himself) all the blessings that
nature had showered upon him were counterbalanced. His reverend
friend, Mr. Beecher, finding him one day unusually dejected, endeavoured to cheer and rouse him by representing, in their brightest
colors, all the various advantages with which Providence had endowed
him, and, among the greatest, that of a "mind which placed him
above the rest of mankind." "Ah! my dear friend," said Byron mourn-
fully—"if *this* (laying his hand upon his forehead) places me above the

rest of mankind, *that* (pointing to his foot) places me far, far below them." ' "20

But Legaré's childhood was not all melancholy. He was denied, it was true, many of its pleasures; he could not run with other boys, climb trees, or have the fearful joy of a first pony. But he had tin soldiers, which he paraded before him on the floor, to be commanded with military precision and braggadocio. He had a pet pigeon that came at his call. He had a rolling Newfoundland puppy that roamed over the garden of his Charleston home. He had a doting mother. He had two sisters, the younger, Mary, especially tied to his side, in childhood as in maturity. He had children's stories: of giants and pygmies, of Tom Thumb and Jack the Giant Killer, of the Arabian Nights, of Gulliver and Crusoe; in later life he would discourse learnedly upon the superiority of such tales to the utilitarian children's literature coming into vogue. And he had Christmases on John's Island and visits to Richmond, Edward Rutledge's Cooper River plantation, which he remembered with particular fondness. Indeed his home and childhood were so cosseting that he fell an easy victim to the cult of domesticity that marked later Victorian years.[21]

He had a various schooling. At six he was sent to Mr. Ward, an Englishman plying his emigré trade as a tutor in Charleston, where the boy was run over the rudiments of English grammar, geography, and arithmetic. At nine he grew bored with this and importuned his mother, not often able to resist his wishes, to be taught Latin. She was able to oblige when, soon after, the Englishman went home and a substitute had to be found. A natural choice was the Reverend S.F. Gallagher, who ran a local academy. He was a Dubliner, a Roman Catholic priest but not a Jesuit, which offered much satisfaction to the family.[22] So the young Huguenot Covenanter went to school to the Papist and learned much, for Gallagher was the best teacher of the classics in a city fastidious about the literature of the ancients, "a man," as Bishop John England was to recall, "of extraordinary eloquence, of a superior intellect, and finely cultivated mind."[23]

Legaré was precocious. Ward had noticed it; Gallagher confirmed it. At ten he could recite from memory the principal events of Roman history, culled from Oliver Goldsmith's *Abridgement*. The child was eager, thorough, attentive, and grew to love the Latin of the Irishman, the cadences of the Church; later he had a marked aesthetic preference for "the imposing and gorgeous solemnities of the Catholic Church," the sensuality and incantatory grace of the Gothic and the complex. The Father was delighted with this and took especial care to transmit

Richmond, the home of Edward Rutledge, by Charles Fraser (1803).
COURTESY, CAROLINA ART ASSOCIATION/GIBBES ART GALLERY

not only the universality of the Church of Rome but the particularity of Ireland by instruction in the vehement oratory of Curran and the restrained reasoning of Burke.[24] Doubtless Legaré heard much of the imperial pretensions of the British, inescapable in a port alive with the masts and gossip of sailors in those days of the Napoleonic Wars and Jefferson's Embargo, of the recent Act of Union between Britain and Ireland bought with Pitt's gold, of the resistance of Grattan, Emmet, and Wolfe Tone. It was fit doctrine for a young American republican.

At home the child disputed with his elder sister, Eliza, at the family's round table about the niceties of words and grammar, while his mother knitted watchfully. There he was forthright and at ease. At school he was shy. The priest cautioned him that a great-man-to-be, who must learn the public arts of oratory implicit in the conning of Cicero, could not afford diffidence. The child dutifully tried and even learned a certain ease before his familiar schoolmates, but could be badly upset if his declamations were unexpectedly heard by a stranger in the classroom. Deformity fears the glance of a stranger.[25]

The priest died when Legaré was twelve, so transfer was made to the College of Charleston, then but a high school and under the charge of a young Scotsman, Mitchell King. King must have seemed romantic. Born in Fifeshire in 1783, he had gone to London in 1804 to seek his fortune; from there to Prussia, where he worked in a counting house; then to sea and Malta, where he saw in the harbor of Valetta the American squadron that Thomas Jefferson had sent, in the fullness of republican virtue, to chastise the Dey of Algiers. Returning to sea, King's ship was seized by a Spanish privateer and taken prisoner to Malaga. For ransom, the Scot was of little use, and he sat prisoner for more than a year. Doubtless his guards were unvexed when he escaped and found ship to Charleston. There he published a poem in a local newspaper, which attracted the eye of the Reverend Dr. George Buist, then president of the College of Charleston, who commissioned King a schoolteacher, possessed of "a dingy white hat with the crown like a sugar loaf & pinched up with much use, with which the rest of his habit accorded." Thereafter King rose to headmaster of the grammar school, then was admitted to the bar and, much later, became the eminent and very rich Judge King.[26]

Legaré was placed beneath a subteacher or usher, which proved unsatisfactory, for discipline was violent and indiscriminate: a transgression by an unconfessing child led to all of Legaré's class being struck for the crime. This offended the boy's pride, conscious of innocence and accustomed to leniency. He went at the midday break to his mother, demanded his withdrawal from the school, and could barely be soothed of his indignation. She went as emissary to King, who had not known of the incident but agreed to take Legaré, whom he did not think guilty, into his safer and especial care.[27] So King became a mentor and later a friend with an entertaining penchant for gossip. The incident is instructive. In manhood, Legaré was often to retreat in dudgeon from trespasses upon his sense of honor or propriety.

There is little evidence that the boy's education was significantly advanced at the college. Mary Legaré may have been made uneasy by the incident of the usher. The boy stood in danger of being spoiled by the twin threats of a home full of devoted women and attending slaves. King's resignation from the college to become a lawyer gave Mary Legaré the opportunity to push her peculiar son more brutally into the world. In the up-country of South Carolina there was a school not overfastidious of its inmates' peccadilloes. Moses Waddel had long known the Legarés, had settled his academy near Willington (a Huguenot settlement), had rapidly acquired a formidable reputation enhanced by the career of his brother-in-law, John C. Calhoun, and sounded a theme much upon the minds of South Carolinians: the resolution of tension between low-country and up-country.[28]

The Willington Academy was a natural choice, even a fashionable one, but scarcely welcome to the boy. He was wretched, for the school was a rough barracks deep in the woods. At its core was a large log hut, the academy proper, which served for prayers, assembly, courts-martial, and the Monday evening soirées of the teachers. Before this stretched an avenue, bounded by tiny log cabins, where the boys studied in plain discomfort. They lodged up to three miles from the school. They cut and hauled their own firewood. They dined upon cornbread and bacon. They studied by the light of pine torches. They were pounded by a fervid Presbyterianism, morning and night and all Sunday. Their recreations were bucolic: running, jumping, wrestling, games of town-ball and bull-pen, hunting for turkey and squirrel, possum and coon. The boys fought each other, as boys will, though often upon lines drawn between low-country and up-country, silk against homespun. Under these conditions and amid these amusements, Legaré was obliged to be wretched. His mangled body did not take well to such enforced crudity; his mind was not persuaded that he needed such overabundant cisalpine discipline; and he told his mother so, often and pleadingly in letters. It was her wisdom to ignore him.[29]

Over the barracks presided a man whose government, Judge Longstreet was to remember, "was one of *touching* 'moral suasion'; but he administered it in a new way. Instead of infusing it gently into the head and heart, and letting it percolate through the system, and slowly neutralize the ill humors with which it came into contact, he applied it to the extremities, and drove it right up into the head and heart by percussion."[30] Waddel did not at first take kindly to Legaré. The Doctor was never very fond of the effete low-country gentry and had partly designed his barracks to derange their inherited manners. This but added to Legaré's misery. Being a tyrant, Waddel suspected plots. A conspiracy was espied to set fire to the academy, low-country boys were cashiered, and suspicion fell upon Legaré, which—like the old blow of the usher—outraged him. Again he demanded withdrawal, and the Doctor was not ill disposed to grant the request, until an uncle, sent as emissary by Mary Legaré, quieted matters. The Doctor came to think better of Legaré, Legaré better of the Doctor. An armed neutrality ensued in which the enemies grew respectful of each other's powers. Waddel eventually got over the fact that Legaré had the virtues—love of the classics, discipline, method, rigor—that Waddel himself valued without the benefit of Waddel's suasion; Legaré came to understand that his education could be advanced even amid such discomforts, and came to appreciate Greek partly through the Doctor's instruction, which—while not profound—was correct and did not inhibit the speedy scholar to flatter the slow.[31] But it was a lonely time, a solitude fed by ambition. The Willington Academy was coming to induct a procession, led by Calhoun, of South Carolina's famous and some of Georgia's: William H. Crawford, George McDuffie, Augustus Baldwin Longstreet, James L. Petigru, Preston Brooks, William J. Grayson, Pierce Butler. This bent Legaré's thoughts towards fame and so to his books, where he was swift, not lame.

Waddel prided himself upon the thoroughness with which his pupils stood their college entrance examinations. Many went to Yale, as had Calhoun. Many more, especially those with inadequate patrimonies, went like Legaré to the South Carolina College in Columbia. Being so well prepared (not just on the Doctor's account), Legaré was admitted to the sophomore class in December 1811, when he was just fourteen, and took up residence after Christmas. He was six years older than the college itself, which was modeled upon New England colleges, had a Baptist New Englander, Jonathan Maxcy, for its president, took its religion fairly seriously, and had a regimen that even Waddel might have endorsed: students rose at six, went to chapel for prayers, returned to their studies until breakfast at eight, studied from nine to twelve, dined, studied until five, prayed, supped, and then were free until curfew at nine. Study consisted of private reading and recitations upon a strictly ordered system.

This, at least, was the theory. To be admitted, the applicant had to translate from Cornelius Nepos, Sallust, Caesar, and Vergil, as well as from the Greek of St. John the Evangelist; he had to bear letters of moral testimony, know English grammar and arithmetic "as far as the rule of proportion," spell and write in a legible hand. The freshman was set to the Greek Testament, Xenophon, Cicero and Vergil, Latin grammar and antiquities, as well as more English grammar, arithmetic, and elocution. From all this Legaré was exempted. As a sophomore, however, he was set to the *Iliad,* Horace, more Roman antiquities, Watts' *Logic,* Blair's *Lectures,* French, algebra, and the mathematics of fractions, decimal and vulgar. In his junior year there were the elements of criticism, geometry, theoretical and practical astronomy, natural and moral philosophy, French, Longinus, and Cicero's *De Oratore.* Lastly he advanced to Demosthenes, Millot's *Elements of History,* portions of Locke's *Essay on Human Understanding,* more abstruse mathematics, elocution, and oratory.[32] Some of these were to become a permanent part of Legaré's intellectual armory: Blair, Longinus, Cicero, and Demosthenes. And Maxcy did much to transmit Scottish common sense philosophy.[33]

This was a moderately progressive curriculum. Maxcy had made a point of diminishing the role of the classics by adding chemistry, moral philosophy, and French. He made little effort to make theology a part of the requirements, although by 1813 undergraduates were set to Butler's *Analogy* and Paley's *Evidences.*[34] The faculty was not then distinguished; its best days lay a decade off, when it boasted Thomas Cooper, Henry Junius Nott, and Robert Henry. In Legaré's day, apart from Maxcy himself, there was the Reverend B.R. Montgomery of Abbeville, a Presbyterian minister who dealt with moral philosophy and logic but was much distracted by his local church. There was Edward D. Smith of Charleston, who taught chemistry without distinction. There was Thomas Park, professor of languages and librarian, a mild man, easily harassed and gulled by his students. There was George Blackburn, who had come sternly out of Virginia to dispense the higher niceties of mathematics and in Columbia found only sloth and absenteeism. "It might be," he reproved, "that half of his class were very smart fellows, for he never saw them; but the half who attended his recitations were as laborious as oxen, but as stupid as asses." Thus goaded, his students eventually rebelled. Emboldened by liquor and disguise, they marched with drum and fife upon the library, broke in, damaged books, carried off and destroyed the college bell, and attacked the home of Professor Blackburn, who was rescued only by the intervention of the town militia. Upon this riot, Legaré—almost alone of the students—looked with interested detachment.[35]

A reputation for precocity had preceded Legaré, and with dedication he amplified the legend. He became a recluse, giving each day in his solitude seven hours to his prescribed studies, eight to his own, two hours to food and exercise, seven to sleep. Only to the Clariosophic Society, one of the debating clubs, did he give an opening for companionship. Alone he would practice declamation, gesture, intonation, resonance, in a study piled with books from the college's rich library, to pause at night if he heard under his window students returning from less Ciceronian revels.[36] Unsurprisingly, he was not liked. Later in life he was to quote with approval a passage of Bulwer Lytton's *The Disowned:* "His ill health, his long residence at home, his unfriended and almost orphan situation, his early habits of solitude and reserve, all these so calculated to make the spirit shrink within itself, made him, on his entrance at school, if not unsocial, *appear* so:—this was the primary reason of unpopularity; the second was that he perceived, for he was sensitive (and consequently acute) to the extreme, the misfortune of his manner, and, in his wish to rectify it, it became doubly unprepossessing; to reserve it now added embarrassment; to coldness, gloom; and the pain he felt, in addressing or being addressed by another, was naturally and necessarily reciprocal, for the effects of sympathy are no where so wonderful, yet so invisible, as in the manners."

Only later did Legaré manage any popularity, by becoming a learned mascot, a marvelous boy that the college could boast as its valedictorian in 1814, speaking fittingly—for one who had studied so much alone—on "the influence of imagination on human happiness." By his own testimony, his imagination had rioted. He thought himself on the Acropolis, in the Forum, in the debating chambers of Hell or eyeless in Gaza with Milton, circling Paradise with Dante, in philosophic exile with Machiavelli, trumpeted through Roncesvalles with Charlemagne, amused and instructed by Pope, edified by Clarendon. He found himself, as he later remembered, among sages, heroes, scholars, departed genius; in the generous community of the dead, which became his religion, the echo of his ambition.[37]

Yet he liked society and friendship, which makes his exertions in

Columbia the more remarkable. "My life is with respect to enjoyments a dead blank," he lamented to his sister. "I might as well be in a
cave for all the social intercourse I enjoy." But he contented himself
with his puritan intellectual vocation, with the begrudging admiration of his fellows, and with the debates then held in the chapel on
Saturdays. We have some record of his appearances. On 12 March
1812 he took the negative to the motion "Whether our extensive
territory is beneficial to a republican government." In the spring of
1813, he was arguing affirmatively the questions "If the provinces in
South America establish a republic is it probable it will continue
long?" and "Is it possible that a general congress of Europe and the
American States would at this time produce a lasting peace?" Debate
could be heated, and even Legaré uttered strong oaths in passion and
was threatened with expulsion for unparliamentary profanity.[38]

He graduated and returned to Charleston, there to postpone the
matter of a career. The law seemed sensible, appropriate in a republic
of laws and therefore lawyers, lucrative, and urged by Mitchell King,
who gave advice upon legal tomes that could be studied on the Legaré
plantation on John's Island. Alternatively, there was literature and
scholarship—intoxicating but not sensible. The decision could wait,
if not indefinitely. In the meantime Legaré could read until past
midnight, wake before dawn, and in winter have a slave light his fire
so that he could read on in bed until eight. He could walk about the
estate, stand on tree stumps and practice declamation. He could visit
the city.[39]

Charleston was then enticing, wealthy, influential. To the grace of
the eighteenth-century city was being added neoclassical architecture.[40] The difficulties of the Embargo and the War of 1812 surmounted, the city was ebullient, its streets clamorous with the
hammering of nails and the chatter of "factors in their jerkins upon
East Bay." The city's population, free and slave, English and Gullah,
was growing; its borders were expanding; its creeks were being filled
in. There was a new market, the better to disperse the products of its
hinterland, cotton and blacks. There were the amenities of Washington racecourse. In summer, citizens could retreat to Sullivan's
Island for breezes and sand, and the city resembled "a ship laid up in
ordinary, noiseless and deserted" until frost promised liberation from
the malarial miasma.[41] In winter, the theater offered the heritage of
Shakespeare, the Gothic inebriations of Monk Lewis and Kotzebue,
and the chauvinism of plays upon Revolutionary battles.[42] But not
only Otway's Venice was preserved in Charleston. The eighteenth

century was palpable, for one could tipple Madeira with Revolutionary veterans in rooms once billeted by the British. The precedent was intimidating, but elders were encouraging that the nineteenth century might outdo even the eighteenth. Charleston might be vexed by the old enemies of fire and hurricane, and by the new enemies of westward and northward economic competition, but the advantages of its intelligent elite and its wealth promised a mastery of the future.

Legaré's contemporaries belonged to the first Charlestonian generation to be indigenously educated and the last for more than a century to come of age in unmixed prosperity. His was an organizing generation, granted the opportunities of reform, not revolution, though some were to pine for the latter. They founded and reformed colleges and municipalities, deepened the professionalism of the law, established and wrote for new journals, sustained and spoke to literary and philosophical societies.[43] They were determined to take Charleston's heritage, a respect for which had been their weaning, and make it and themselves richer, materially and culturally. Among them the emphases of conservatism and change differed. Thomas Grimké, mild, diligent, famously charitable, was their most eccentric reformer, a pacifist who espoused the mild antislavery of the American Colonization Society, who demanded the removal of the classics and mathematics from school curricula, who insisted on practicing the phonetic orthography he preached. James Louis Petigru was their parvenu and Federalist wit, burly and scathing and kind, their best working lawyer, the inspiration for generations of anecdotes. Robert Young Hayne was their wonder, risen with astonishing speed from indigence to influential wealth and power by the inheritances of Langdon Cheves' law practice and successive marriages to a Pinckney and an Alston. And Hugh Legaré was their scholar, their critic, their elegist, most indecisive about his vocation, most easily bored, most alert to the texture of things around him. They were sure that they and Charleston would come of prosperous age together. By 1845 half were to be dead, others alienated, the city and the state entered upon an irreversible relative decline.[44]

Among the itinerant visitors to Charleston was James Ogilvie, Godwinite, orator pedestrian, late Virginian schoolmaster, who went to the South Carolina College in 1815 to give a three-month course of lectures and then to Charleston to superintend a ladies' academy sponsored by his fellow Scot, Mitchell King. Late in 1815, Ogilvie was visited by a former pupil, Francis Walker Gilmer of Virginia, brother-in-law and law student of William Wirt; he was traveling

with the Portuguese scientist, the Abbé Joseph Corréa da Serra, later
Minister to the United States. They were upon a botanical expedition,
an excursion eased by letters of introduction from that political
botanist, Thomas Jefferson. Naturally they met the young Charleston
set, among them Legaré, Robert Hayne, William Crafts, and Frederick Grimké. Gilmer took particularly to Legaré. Both were young
men of declared promise, trembling upon and at its fulfillment. Serra
himself was not unimpressive to Legaré: "He reminded me of a Greek
sage, travelling to distant countries in quest of knowledge, and
reducing it all to its very essence, and uttering it in aphorisms and
apophthegms."[45]

Legaré worked steadily through the winter and spring of 1816,
alone in the country, "cut off from all sorts of company and pleasure,"
with an imprudent and intellectual dedication of benefit to his mind
and danger to his health. His mother worried. His friend James
McBride urged relaxation and travel, so Legaré set out for the North
and Virginia. He followed a young lady to Saratoga and, amid his
devotions, surveyed the amenities of the spa. He fell in briefly with a
Virginian, James Skelton Gilliam, with whom on August 5, a sunny
Monday, he set out to visit the adjacent Ballston Springs in a most
excellent hack, only to have it break when bounced over a rut, leaving
them to walk to the Sans Souci Hotel. Legaré left about August 13 to
go back down to New York. By the 24th he was in Boston and about
to cross the Charles to Cambridge, where he proposed a few weeks of
reading French and Latin, and amplifying his Spanish.

In the meantime he fretted in letters to Gilmer about his future, the
choice between law and literature. Gilmer was newly a lawyer, ready if
not ripe to give advice. What was it like? How had his thinking
changed? Literature had the disadvantage that no one in America was
interested and purchasing; yet the law was bedeviled by details, the
quibbles of special pleading, the drudgery of an office. Law trained a
man in controversy and debate, to be sure, but also in sophistry? Did
not pleading incapacitate "those grand enquiries that are to develope
principles by the generalization of facts"?[46]

Gilmer answered that lawyering did not entirely paralyze the
brain, which Legaré conceded. The Charlestonian recounted his exertions and seclusion, the vexing competition between the present
pleasures of society and the all-too-remote chances of future eminence
implicit in study. "Indeed, it requires an heroic self-command" he
confessed, as much in sorrow as in pride, "a devotion something like
that of martyrdom, for a young man in such a state of society as ours,

without the spur of rivalship & competition, without any thing in the
estimate generally formed of his pursuits, either to direct or to
animate him, to abstain from the pleasures that are carrying away the
hearts of all around him, to refuse the intoxicating charm of the
eminence in society (however shortlived) which his talents can immediately command him, and to shut himself up in solitude for years—
& all too, for the renown which it is *not impossible* he may acquire in his
maturity or old age." Gilmer had replied that the active life was
better, because more useful. Legaré countered that early studies could
breed later and riper activity. "I see nothing to prevent a literary man
from taking part in national affairs. Intellect is ripe enough by the
time we are thirty five or forty years of age, and that is the period that
nature seems to have marked out for the management of . . . affairs."
This was the more so because studies had themselves been, of late, less
uselessly scholastic. "The learning that I would aim at is that of
Cicero—a learning that can be instrumental in promoting the purposes of active life, in elevating the man of business into the sage, and
the mere statement of wholesome truths, into sublime & touching
eloquence." And, he prudently added, if the world did not accept
these learned services, retirement could be embellished by refinement.[47]

Yet such dignified and anxious plans could be deranged. As Legaré
continued to read up to fifteen hours a day as he had for seven years, his
bluish gray eyes, always restless, rebelled at the endless prospect of
small print and flickering candles. Back from the North and into
1817, he was forced to a physician, who told him to stop reading or
else become not active like Cicero but blind like Homer. The advice
was easier to give than take, as Legaré's hand reached as naturally for a
book as it did for the pen with which he habitually marked striking
passages.[48] His perplexity can be imagined. It was to be relieved by
his younger sister, Mary. She was acquiring the usual adolescent
accomplishments, playing the pianoforte and sketching. Later she
would achieve a minor reputation as a painter. Mary was not pretty
and married very late in life, which was not all to the bad. Her sister
Eliza married in 1810 when sixteen, had twenty-one children, buried
eight of them, and was herself buried in 1842, fully needing the
zealous Presbyterianism that counterpointed her confinements. Mary
at least survived by dint of prolonged virginity. She volunteered to
read to her brother his formidable tomes in Latin and French and
Italian, not always comprehending, pleased and consoling herself that
apart from rescuing her brother's sight and future, it would improve

her pronunciation of Italian. For more than a year, through two winters, they kept this up until he was deemed safe. Thereafter, he was never seriously troubled by his eyes and did not need spectacles to read, although he was shortsighted and saw with difficulty across a street, even across a large room.[49]

But the doctors thought he would be foolish to plunge back *in medias res*. Mitchell King advised that it was time to enter the bar, Legaré having mastered enough common law to more than satisfy the exigencies of practice. Legaré demurred. He thought he might better study in Europe, particularly in Germany.[50] Perhaps at Harvard, then beginning to send its graduates off to Göttingen, he had heard of the virtues of German scholarship. Gilmer had been a friend of George Ticknor and conversed with the Bostonian in Philadelphia about the prospects of European study.[51] And South Carolinians had been sailing off to Europe for generations; Charleston was an Atlantic port that faced willingly to the east, reluctantly to the interior, a city that got its news more easily from Liverpool than from the uncivilized bowels of the continent. Europe was palpable to anyone who walked along the Battery, or looked out from a piazza upon merchant vessels bearing cotton and rice, or heard Mitchell King's Scottish burr, or wandered into the Charleston Library Society to find on its tables the latest *Edinburgh Review* or *Gentleman's Magazine*. There was Europe dead to be seen: Paris and the *ancien régime,* Rome and the Empire, the forests of Charlemagne's conquests. And there was Europe living: Walter Scott producing his astonishing novels, Talleyrand restored with customary flexibility to power, Byron *cavaliere servente* in Venice. Such a trip would not be easy, for the family did not have much money. They conferred, and he promised to be careful and keep accounts, as he always had. He pled the necessities of his health and said he was not ready for the bar. Education must be advanced by travel. He would profit. The state, in turn, would profit. The thing should be done. The thing, Europe, must be measured.

He left for New York in May 1818, leaving behind an anxious mother anticipating a separation of three years, whom he diplomatically and genuinely attempted to console. He reached Bordeaux and the Garonne after the gentlest of voyages of just thirty-four days— swift, considering they had sat becalmed in mid-Atlantic for a week. He stayed in Bordeaux for a week before traveling to Paris, for which he had made his usual laborious plans. He would consult doctors on his health. He would polish his French to the point where even the Parisian might approve, his foreignness betrayed only by his being too

Attic to be an Athenian. He would improve his Italian with a tutor, for he intended a visit beyond the Alps. He planned to find a drawing master, though disinclination and expense were to forbid. He expected to go on to Göttingen. As usual, Paris dissipated Puritanism; he was later to reproach himself for having seen and learned too little by *"lounging* and trifling" too much.[52]

He settled in lodgings and found for company William Campbell Preston, fresh from Edinburgh and rambles with Washington Irving over the Highlands upon routes dictated by Burns and Scott.[53] They were taken up, like many visiting Americans, by David Warden, an Irishman educated in New York whose dismissal from consular office—enforced by William H. Crawford, the American Minister—he jauntily defied by carrying a card emblazoned *ancien consul des États Unis*. Legaré and Preston wished to improve their fluency in French; Warden obliged by arranging that the young men dine with Madame D'Épinarde. She was a widow, a sometime poetess upon the merits of Commerce; her husband, carrying messages from Bonaparte to Murat in Naples, had been assassinated, which had given her a certain distinction and a pension. The Restoration had annulled the pension and, for income, she permitted visitors aspirant for Parisian elegance to dine at her table for a mere twenty francs daily. She had three daughters: Inez, who painted under Isabey; Osoma, who studied declamation with Talma; and Natalie, who was a musician. The table was open to many, Republicans and Imperialists alike. Talma came, before the theater, to relax with a friend. Benjamin Constant came, a relic of Madame de Staël, as were many. There were actors, actresses, swarms of journalists, pamphleteers, and Lady Morgan, liberally rouged, struggling to understand the French for literary sales in England.

In turn, Preston and Legaré went out to dine. Preston, at least, circulated splendidly and with the proud detachment of a Virginian: to a ball for the Duke of Wellington at the behest of Albert Gallatin's unpretending wife, to Lafayette's, to the Duc de Richelieu's. At the last, Preston had an exchange with Pozzo di Borgo, Russian Ambassador and Corsican, that seemed to sum up much of American history and European puzzlement at it. "As in leaving the table Pozzo di Borgo passed my chair, he said to me, as I rose to bow to him,— 'Vous êtes monsieur de la Province de Virginia.' 'No Sir, of the State.' 'Hah,' said he, with somewhat a doubtful smile, 'de l'état.' "[54]

Legaré took with most delight to the theaters and the art galleries. The Louvre had, it was true, been somewhat denuded of Napoleon's

William Campbell Preston in later life, by William H. Scarborough.
Courtesy, South Caroliniana Library

plunder, but the remnant of older booty was still ample. At the Comédie Française, Talma was rendering French tragedy into the antique, in costume and spirit, and Legaré was especially pleased by the "accuracy of costume" and the decorum of audiences not confined to the genteel. This was lofty, but Legaré, relaxing so far from home, also took with infectious jollity to the farce and the vaudeville. He was not himself witty, though he could be amusingly scathing towards incompetence and pretension, but he liked to laugh at the wit of others and, by laughing, amuse others. Almost above all, his youthful eroticism was fed in evenings at the ballet by "nothing half so voluptuous . . . as the sight of fifty of such girls, most beautiful of angels, crowned with jewels, covered or more properly *uncovered* with a light, floating drapery that seems to have been designed only to add to the exquisite grace of their forms, expressing in their looks & gestures, & by a thousand various attitudes the highest sensuality that is compatible with elegance!"[55]

Charleston was very remote and postponed save in one connection: a black named Jack. Jack had come to Paris from Charleston, his master a blind Jew, Sasportas. Jack had been turned off from his employment with just a month's wages and little French, more Macedonian than Attic. In the Palais Royal, Legaré and Preston bumped into Jack, who had known Legaré in Charleston. Jack took them up, followed them about, complaining of the gibberish of the locals and the inferiority of this Paris to his home. One early morning this improbable threesome, the newly dandified and limping Legaré, the graceful Preston, and the nostalgic Jack, walked through the Place Vendôme. Sunshine played on its "superb bronze pillar," illuminated the sweep of the apartments, and reached to the Tuileries beyond. Preston turned to Jack and demanded he acknowledge the peerlessness of such beauty. Jack admitted it was "all very pretty, but were you ever in Charleston, up towards Cooter Bridge?" Years later, in token of the incident, Preston and Legaré went up to Cooter Bridge, finding but a few shanties and a canal full of green water, but finding also Jack's birthplace and a memory of Paris.[56]

Legaré had planned Göttingen for his formal studies but heard it had closed, following civil war between town and gown.[57] Preston had been in Edinburgh, thought well of its university, and recommended the alternative. Edinburgh had a famous reputation, earned by the intellects of David Hume and William Robertson in the eighteenth century, and amplified by architecture well into the nineteenth. The Georgian grace of the New Town, rising beside the tall

and huddled medievalism of Knox's old Edinburgh, presented Legaré
with the embodiment of reasoned change, warmed by Walter Scott's
Tory nostalgia and salted by the wit of Scotch reviewers.[58] The
university was large and pell-mell, not yet settled into the grand
buildings proposed by Robert Adam in 1789 but still using decrepit
seventeenth-century buildings, some of them—not least the library—tumbling, propped by beams, and exposed to the blasting
weather. The university was intellectually past its best, even as the
city's society flourished. The medical faculty was plagued by nepotism
and rigidity. Professor Alexander Munro, the third of that name in a
century, was justly accused of plagiarizing his grandfather's lectures
verbatim but bore up manfully under the showers of peas from
students when he continued to observe, from the tattered text before
him, "When I was a student at Leyden in 1719." Medical examinations were still in Latin, lest abolition "open a door for the graduation
. . . of illiterate and impudent empyricks."[59] But the university was
cheap to attend, its entrance requirements nominal, and so it was
packed with 2,000 undergraduates. The student came, paid his fee,
and—if he cared—attended lectures as a distraction from the city's
ample taverns. J.G. Lockhart, Scott's son-in-law, lamented in 1819
that classrooms were contaminated by "the slovenly and dirty mass" of
students, and that "any young man who can afford to wear a decent
coat, and live in a garret upon porridge or herrings, may, if he pleases,
come to Edinburgh."[60]

Legaré studied under three worthies of the arts faculty: Playfair,
Leslie, and Irving. John Playfair, Professor of Natural Philosophy, was
then old, soon to die in 1819. As a mathematician he had expounded
the principles of geometry. As a natural philosopher he had been
energetic in popularizing the Vulcanist and Huttonian theory of
geological change, the principle of uniformitarianism later mastered
by Sir Charles Lyell. His devotions to ladies, and to rocks, Francis
Jeffrey was to summarize as "Philandering at the Needles" and Henry
Cockburn as "moral youthfulness." But he was admired and regretted
by many for his unobtrusive gentleness, the unvexed amiability of
nature's philosopher. On his deathbed, a relative offered to read to him
from Scott, of whom he was fond, but he declined, saying that he
would prefer the *Principia*. Legaré was to remember his praelections as
"more nearly up to our idea of the conversations of a Greek sage, than
any thing we have ever listened to in that kind. He was the very
personification of truth and science, in all their modesty, simplicity
and sanctity."[61]

John Leslie, who was to succeed Playfair in the Professorship of

Natural Philosophy just as he had in the Chair of Mathematics in 1805 (though over the protest of Presbyterian elders), had been in Virginia in 1789 as a tutor to the Randolphs. He taught mathematics as a duty but studied as a vocation the properties of heat. He was the first man to create ice artificially, an improbable achievement in Edinburgh's "sombre inhospitable climate." Fitting for an inhabitant of the North was his theory, held tenaciously against doubters from warmer climes, that cold had an objective existence apart from heat.[62] Such a proposition would doubtless have been conceded by Legaré, in the Forth Street lodgings he shared with Preston in the New Town, on a Christmas Day notable for being "gloomy & dark—no merriment, no songs of joy, no dancing & revelry."

Alexander Irving was a less weighty figure intellectually than Playfair and Leslie, being a local advocate, though a successful one. But in two courses upon the *Institutes* and *Pandects,* he did teach the civil law, a vital matter in Scotland.[63]

Scottish law was and is independent of that of England and markedly distinct: a special compound. Justinian was as natural to the Scottish lawyer as was Coke to the English, a taste created by the traffic between Scotland and Holland, and institutionalized by the commentary and reforms of Sir James Dalrymple, Lord Stair, whose *Institutions* of 1681 fashioned "an original amalgam of Roman Law, Feudal Law and native customary law, systematized by resort to the law of nature and the Bible, and illuminated by many flashes of ideal metaphysics." The reforms had been marked by civilian learning, mingled with a common sense that Scots were to make a formal philosophy in the eighteenth century. As Dalrymple observed, "We do always prefer the sense to the subtilty of law, and do seldom trip by niceties or formalities."[64] Legaré, becoming a student of Dalrymple, gleaned more than an enlarged enthusiasm for the civil law; he discovered an intoxicating precedent. American law, which he had so reluctantly been reading on John's Island, posed a problem analogous to that of Scotland. The United States, by revolution and constitution-making, had posed itself the problem of reconciling the common law of England with the reasoned invention of constitutional law, a problem bedeviled by the crosscurrents of federalism, which left unsure the crucial problem of *vires,* of sovereignty in a complex body politic.[65] Scotland, independent in legal form but united by politics and dynasty to England, faced similar ambiguities and made recourse to the civil law for answers. It was an enticing prospect, newly glimpsed, that would grow in Legaré's intellectual ambitions.

The civil law was exciting even if Irving was not, though Preston's "a man of small talent and moderate learning in his department" is too harsh. Classes were conducted in Latin, which pleased Legaré even as it rendered others mute and shuffling; and Irving was willing to debate with his students, a condescension not common in Edinburgh. Moreover, the reading was interesting, and the civil law had a special magic in Edinburgh, being regarded as "the noblest structure of human wisdom . . . involving in its study the whole of ancient history and literature."[66] There were the writings of Jacques Cujas, the sixteenth-century French jurist who had all but founded the historical study of the texts of the *Corpus Juris Civilis* and prepared critical editions of Ulpian and Paulus. Above all, there was Johann Gottlieb Heineccius, who had been Professor of Philosophy and Jurisprudence at Halle in the early eighteenth century, for whom law was a rational science, more philosophic than simple expediency. While Heineccius saw the law as arising from God's justice, it was a justice engraved upon men's hearts and embodied in their reason; thus the tendency of his thought was secular: the Bible offered no superior guide. He disapproved of Hobbes and, contributing to the debate on the origins of civil society later exemplified in Adam Ferguson, saw in primitive and advanced societies coequal opportunities for reasoned civility and viciousness. Yet as befitted a Councillor of State to the King of Prussia, he was a social conservative, seeing human equality diminishing in more complex societies, praising the necessity of hierarchy, approbating slavery while urging paternalism and damning decadent vanities.

Not all of this Legaré absorbed, least of all Heineccius' Prussian statism; he found most use for Heineccius as a historian and bibliographer of the civil law. Yet Legaré acquired a permanent taste, sufficient in his last year to contemplate a translation, into English for the edification of Americans, of a prose distinguished among civilians for its elegance, terseness, and erudition of Latinity. Heineccius had been for generations, earlier than Scott, earlier even than Boswell, the *vade mecum* of Edinburgh's civilians.[67] Later Germans were less regarded. Dugald Stewart was to observe that he had read with curiosity and interest some of the lectures of Friedrich von Schlegel, no admirer of the Scots, and looked forward to "English versions of the works of Kant, and of other German authors, from the pens of their English disciples." "Little more . . . is necessary, in this country," he tartly noted, "to bring down the philosophy of Germany to its proper level."[68]

Legaré was working hard. For Playfair and Leslie he did not read

The Civil Law classroom at Edinburgh, pencil sketch by James Hall (1819);
done while Legaré was in attendance.
COURTESY, EDINBURGH UNIVERSITY LIBRARY.

collaterally, but for Irving he gave sometimes ten hours a day to the civil law, with relaxation in reading the Tuscan of Dante, Guicciardini, and Machiavelli. On one occasion of intellectual absorption, celebrated by Preston in eulogy, "he found himself at breakfast Sunday morning, on the same seat where he had breakfasted the day before, having remained in it four and twenty hours." But there is scant reason for believing that in Edinburgh he was any less tempted by society than he had been in Paris and Charleston. "The Americans are taken into society here with extraordinary facility—which indeed is the case every where but in England," Preston noted. Legaré went, it is known, to the soirées of Mrs. Grant, one of the few women to exert social and intellectual influence in a city noted, unlike Paris, for the uproarious masculinity of its discourse. Cockburn's memorial is worth quotation: "Mrs. Grant, widow of a minister of Laggan, who had unfolded herself in the *Letters from the Mountains,* an interesting treasury of good solitary thoughts . . . . was a tall, dark woman, of very considerable intellect, great spirit, and the warmest benevolence. Her love of individual Whigs, particularly of Jeffrey, in spite of her amusing horror of their principles, was honourable to her heart. She was always under the influence of an affectionate and delightful enthusiasm, which, unquenched by time or sorrow, survived the wreck of many domestic attachments, and shed a glow over the close of a very protracted life. Both she and Mrs. Hamilton were remarkable for the success of their literary conversational gatherings. Their evening parties had the greater merit for the smallness of their houses and of their means." Legaré went, welcomed for his distinction by a hostess who struggled over his odd French name.[69]

With him went Preston and the other resident Americans: Joseph Cogswell, later to solicit Legaré's contributions to the short-lived *New York Review;* Andrew Govan, of the South Carolina College and later a congressman from the Orangeburg district, who had been traveling with Preston in Italy, elegant, athletic, "more studious of his physical accomplishments than of his mental," who had once wrestled with a Neapolitan officer near Herculaneum and been nearly transfixed by a stiletto for his initiative; and George Ticknor, in Scotland collecting literary scalps with his usual assiduity, with whom Legaré contracted a long friendship, one shared by Cogswell, who had been with Ticknor in Venice and met Pius VII in Rome.[70]

The Scotland around offered interest. Legaré traveled across to Glasgow to listen to the vehement oratory of Dr. Thomas Chalmers, Presbyterian preacher and later in 1843 a leader of the schismatics, who founded the Free Church of Scotland. While Legaré had formally subscribed himself a Presbyterian at South Carolina College, he wore his sectarianism lightly and was confirmed in that resistance by the bleak Calvinism around him, the "censorious and talkative Fanaticks" who had long hovered around the university. Chalmers, however, so attracted him by force of speech that Legaré owned him the first orator of Europe. "What struck him," Preston recalled of the excursion, "as the great peculiarity, and as one of the elegancies of his speaking, was the vehement involution into which he seemed to be hurried by his impetuosity and fullness, and the admirable dexterity with which he extricated his sentences."[71] Legaré was to imitate the celerity, if not the involution. As was to be observed of his own stump oratory, "Whole chains of reasoning were linked up in brief sentences, and flung out with an exhaustless rapidity." Chalmers taught the lesson that oratory could overcome physical disadvantages, for the preacher was famous for his pale, coarse, and melancholy face, his square and jutting forehead, his provincial burr, his uncoordinated gestures, but famous too for "the sheer pith of his most original mind . . . . [his] wonderful talent for ratiocination, and . . . an imagination both fertile and distinct."[72]

Legaré went for rambles into the Highlands. In April he was at Loch Lomond, to the northwest of Glasgow, looking upward to Ben Lomond, then covered in snow. This he was to remember in 1836, passing the Brockenberg, the seat of Faust's witches, also snow-covered. But a Scottish spring offered only tepid release for a Carolinian. Writing to his family, gentled by warm breezes, he felt nostalgia in the midst of his entertainments and reflected upon Charleston's "heavenly winter climate," considered sententiously that he had been sufficiently regaled with the pomp and magnificence of great cities, and wished a reprise of "my own wild woods & the sweet simplicity of our country."[73]

Nonetheless, Edinburgh did provide amusements. There was the old Theatre Royal, barnlike and not too comfortable, rough compared to Paris, but offering in 1819 a dramatization of *Rob Roy*. By 1818 the city had grown grander and was divided into New Town, in whose "draughty parallelograms" the gentry had gone to live, there to venture out less, and Old Town, nestled amid the reek of nightly hurled slops. The Old Town was still served, before the coming of piped water, by watercaddies, who brought a cask of water up the endless stairs at the cost of a penny. Its cuisine was ample and cheap, most distinguished for its seafood: herring, turbot, haddock, and cod, but also salmon from the Highlands and oysters and lobster. The fish market and the flesh market were famous, not alone for their smell. The vegetable market was less noxious, save for the smell of gin from the college of women who met upon stools and tables around the Tron Church. Taverns like Ambrose's or the Lord Nelson were ubiquitous and crowded, not only with the populace but with Edinburgh's inventive drinking clubs. There was the Friday Club, to which Scott, Sydney Smith, Playfair, and Dugald Stewart belonged, which early drank a rum punch ("a very pleasant but somewhat dangerous beverage," Brougham observed), moved on to claret, and, amid prosperity, "soared above prejudice, and ate and drank everything that was rare and dear." To this Legaré might have gained guest admission, which could not be said of the exclusive Wig Club, limited to twenty-five members and devoted to Twopenny, the native ale; it was a bibulous democracy that voted in a ballot box carved into the figure of a naked man, which was, as James Grant noted, "unnecessarily proportioned." And the city boasted many booksellers: on the High Street, Constable's for the Whigs and Messrs. Manners & Miller for the bluestockings and "literary beaumonde"; on the Prince's Street, Blackwood's for the Tories; and hard by the college, Laing's for the classical scholar, the place where Legaré could best seek his Aldines and Elzevirs.[74]

All this was engaging, and it is doubtful that, as Legaré assured his mother, far off and worried about her perambulating son, "I have rid myself of some bad habits." For Washington Irving remembered Legaré, "who used to play snake at his window ogling and 'charming' a bevy of sewing girls in an opposite house." More plausible was his filial claim, entered in February 1819, that "the coming to Europe has made me, in every respect, a better and—if I ought to use such a term when speaking of one who is so much inclined to melancholy—a *happier* man than I was. My longings will have been gratified; my restless disposition will have subsided into some sort of quiet—at least for a considerable time; and I have seen so much of the vanities of life, that I really believe I am beginning to be a little philosophical in practice, as I have always pretended, you know, to be in speculation . . . . I have learnt to be *an American,* to feel an interest in my country, and to be proud of my privileges as one of its citizens." The lesson of philosophical dedication was reinforced by the sight, later to become an insistent memory, of Walter Scott "diligently hobbling up to his daily task in the Parliament House at Edinburgh . . . for hours seated down at his clerk's desk, with a countenance of most demure and business-like formality," a man accepting "the dullest realities of existence . . . a falcon trained to the uses of a domestic bird." In this spirit, Legaré resolved, "My ambition . . . to make some figure in her [America's] history has been greatly excited of late; and I shall sit down to what is to be the business of my life, if not with the most hearty zeal possible, at least with a great deal of resignation and good will."[75]

But there were yet a few months before Legaré sought his hood and jesses. He traveled south into England, making excursions and reaching London in the late spring of 1819, there briefly to see the usual sights. He had occasion to meet Thomas Gaisford, Regius Professor of Greek at Oxford, when the latter called upon Preston. Feeling slighted in the conversation, Legaré amused himself by bamboozling the scholar for an hour with puzzling and erudite questioning upon Greek verbs. "There," he remarked to Preston, "I think he will not take me for a noodle next time." He crossed to Paris in early June with absorbing and chance companions: the Syrian Catholic Archbishop of Jerusalem, Mar Gregorius Peter Jarweh, and his Italian priest, a pleasant young man who chatted to Legaré in Latin. The Archbishop was clad in Oriental costume—the very dress of the apostles, as he proudly informed the American—and acted with becoming humility and piety. "He pulled out from time to time, a venerable old breviary, or something of that sort," Legaré noted, "in Syriac & read from right to left in a low whisper with great devotion & as many crosses as he judged sufficient." His mission in England had been worldly, the raising of cash, and the Archbishop's mind seemed to run much upon money. The East, he complained to Legaré, was more hospitable. In the West it was different. *"Sempre pagare* (always pay) would he say in the most pitiable tone, when a chamber-maid, a waiting-man, a *boots,* a commissioner, a custom house under strapper, a coachman, a *conducteur,* etc. successively demanded, or as they call it *requested,* any return he might be willing to make them for the services they tendered him. He was besides very much molested with the curiosity of the natives at Calais who crowded around him wherever he went, crying out *'La barbe'.*"[76]

Legaré dallied in Paris, while he planned Italy and a year in Germany. But news from South Carolina was worrying. His mother's plantation was faring ill and needed management. Money threatened to become scarce, and so he, disciplined hedonist as he was, embraced the imperatives of duty and abbreviated his plans. Italy and Göttingen were sacrificed, the latter without too much agony, the former

with uncertainty. It is curious that so avid a classicist twice declined
the opportunity to visit Italy, once in 1819 and again in the 1830s.
His usual fussing about money was decisive on both occasions, as he
could not undertake a sufficiently munificent and lengthy tour. Yet
the reluctance may have run deeper. Rome being so alive in his
imagination might only have been impoverished by the sight of its
ruins.

Instead he went eastward in August to Antwerp, then northward to
Amsterdam and Utrecht before striking south to the Rhine, Cologne,
and Bonn. He was not much impressed by Cologne, though the fertile
plain around was beautiful, not least for the tobacco plants he
nostalgically spotted. Then for a day and a night he took a *barque* to
Mayence—slowly, as the flat-bottomed boat was cajoled against the
stream by horses, poles, and sail. They reached Bonn after two the
first afternoon, and he took a quick look, noticing chiefly the Russian
Cossacks, still in occupation after the Napoleonic Wars. Back on the
Rhine, he passed underneath ruined baronial castles, a pleasant thing
for a young man steeped in Byron and most fond of *Manfred*. They
went by a convent, saved from suppression by the Empress Josephine:
"As we passed by the bell tolled six. The evening was heavenly: & so
were my feelings." The associations were rich and savored: the Sept
Monts, the spot where the armies of Europe had crossed the river in
1814 to finish the defeat of Napoleon, the ruins, the convent on a
willowed island, the tranquil stream, the soft sunshine of evening,
then the *coup de théâtre,* a nearly full moon reaching over the hill.[77]

He returned to the United States during the early winter and to
Charleston via Washington and the stage, meeting on his way the
young John Tyler, then taking a respite from the House of Representatives. Legaré beguiled the passengers with stories of his travels, an
incident that was to grow in Tyler's none-too-precise memory. By
1856, the ex-President was remembering Legaré descanting on visits
to Rome and Venice, standing in awe and veneration in St. Peters,
viewing the gaberdine of the Rialto. No doubt an ex-President must
remember with advantages.[78]

The strongest memory Legaré brought back was of Antwerp. In its
great cathedral he had had an epiphany, one recollected in unease
fourteen years later on the same spot. In 1833 he stood before the great
altar pieces of Rubens for two hours, while music resounded and bells
rang: "I endeavoured to *recall,* but in vain! what I had felt, standing
upon the same flag-stone as long ago as the summer (August) of 1819.
I went to the Cathedral one evening & was present at the touching

Antwerp Cathedral.

service of that time of the day. I was all alone, with my feelings, naturally inclined to melancholy & devotion, tho the wicked world has sadly perverted them, still more awakened by that solitude, the distance from me of all I loved on earth, & the affecting associations that throng about the gloomy recesses of one of these majestic monuments of the *Past* & seem to speak, in its echoes, the mysterious language of prophecy. Then I was young—not much beyond the threshold of manhood—& mine was *such* a youth, so full of romantic fondness & sensibility & teeming anticipations of the future. I never was more moved in any scene of life, & I have often said if I were allowed to recall one hour of all that I have lived, it should be that I passed at the Vesper service in the Cathedral of Antwerp in the summer of 1819. Why is it that, altho' I enjoyed the painting of Rubens this time with more assured & accurate connoisseurship, there was no longer a spell in the air of that noble cathedral, which I admire more than ever?"[79]

2

Politics

As he had expected, Legaré came back to unwelcome duty. His mother's plantation on John's Island had been damaged by crop failures, low prices (the Panic of 1819 having tightened credit), and mismanagement. So Legaré reluctantly became rustic, which was in his interest though not to his taste, a planter buying and tending to slaves, considering the cotton harvest, overseeing the overseer, discussing the weather. For he preferred a gentleman's countryside, offering "sweetness and repose," "wild flowers, to regale . . . wearied senses with their freshness and perfume," not work. Yet even in that spring of 1820 he found consolation in "some Italian Quartos . . . all that Macchiavel wrote, together with Cicero (16 vols) Tacitus, Sallust etc." Charleston society he kept at a distance, full as he was of the pride of the returned European traveler, dressed in the latest from his tailor in Bond Street, pained to discover his old Italian master penurious for lack of employment. "I hate the sight of most of those one commonly meets with in the streets of this city," he told Henry Middleton, still in Edinburgh and sympathetic to the cosmopolitan's disdain for home, "& it is a real violence to me to be obliged to listen to the jargon of the little knots & circles of rustic planters, half *bred* physicians, ill-*fed* lawyers, & above all, those wretched things that our facetious fellow citizens have agreed to nickname men of fashion." He sighed for London, "that great university of vice and pleasure," for

"Edina's palaces and towers," for "a young lady in Paris." He toyed with quitting "the mere vulgarity and ignorance" of Charleston for Philadelphia. Yet duty proved to have compensations. "Business and Blackstone," at first appalling because he found all business "*vulgar* & abominable," yielded "an ample field for the exercise of the most vigorous & exalted understanding." "The harmony of . . . [the common law's] principles is perfect," he told himself with genuine surprise, though with the traditional logic of Sir Edward Coke. But Legaré was a republican, a good citizen, and so resolved to become a lawyer. In 1822 he sold out the plantation, moved back to Charleston and his old home at 30 Bull Street, close by the college he had attended as a child, and began to practise.[1]

Legaré came condescendingly to the bar and more than equipped, which made him an object of suspicion. Many, like James Louis Petigru and Mitchell King, old friends and tending admirers, did not mind this, even understood it. But many thought him too learned, over-elaborate, needlessly assassinating minor game with heavy artillery. A little Blackstone, a faint dash of Coke was the usual staple even of the accomplished lawyer at the accomplished bar of Charleston. What was the point of all this Grotius and Vattel, Heineccius and Pufendorf? Who, in God's name, were Heineccius and Pufendorf? Legaré would explain to those who cared to listen, but even the explanation might bemuse. What did it have to do with settling wills and penetrating internecine legal feuds? Did it bring in extra business? He had to confess that it did not. Business came slowly at first, "thin and sometimes rather as a benevolence," natural enough for a young lawyer, however brilliant his parts. When he was melancholy, Legaré worried about the disadvantage of learning in a lawyer's society, fondly practical and "empyrick." "Nothing is more unquestionable," he complained in 1829, "than that there is a deep rooted prejudice against *bookish men* all over this country. It has cost me years of labor, anxiety & mortification to overcome it here . . . . I suppose I have been thrown back 10 years in life by my miscellaneous studies & at 31 only acquired the consequence as a public man & a barrister which I might easily have had at 21." This was the fate of the black-letter lawyer, as Justice Joseph Story was to note in 1843: "It is a most singular circumstance, that eminence in general literature should, in the public mind, detract from a man's reputation as a lawyer. It is an unworthy prejudice . . . . But the prejudice exists." When he was wryly jocular, Legaré could say, as he did to Edward Johnston: "Sir, do you ask how I get along? Do you enquire what my trade brings me in?

James Louis Petigru, by Thomas Sully (1842).
COURTESY, CAROLINA ART ASSOCIATION/GIBBES ART GALLERY

I will tell you. I have a variety of cases, and, by the bounty of Providence, sometimes get a fee: but in general, sir, I practice upon the old Roman plan; and, like Cicero's, my clients pay me what they like—that is, often, nothing at all."[2]

Still he found business and reputation from his office on Broad Street. He became solicitor for the Bank of South Carolina, was the trustee of several great estates, and had no lack of trade.[3] His learning had usages; studying the classics proved not only academic but practical. His analogy with Cicero, made to Gilmer in 1816 and much repeated later, was not idle. Cicero had been a lawyer, as was Legaré, deploying the art of rhetoric, the intelligent manipulation of words for intended results. Antiquity had given much hard thought to this business of speaking: how to train and use the voice, how to mask or exemplify knowledge, how to persuade, how to decide what human nature was capable of understanding and therefore of yielding. Cicero's treatises, the extant speeches of Demosthenes, the manuals of Quintilian were guides, direct and usable. Legaré understood the shift of historical context, that he stood in courts in Charleston or Georgetown before juries and judges, not in the Forum. That shift modulated technique. "The Bar," he observed in 1828 after seven years of practice, "does not admit of the most sublime eloquence," but was a place for eloquence disciplined to business. John Locke, Adam Smith, and Hugh Blair had argued that the plain style was the fate of the moderns, and nowhere should it be plainer than at the bar, where eloquence should be "of the calm and temperate kind, and connected with close reasoning."[4] Art was for disguise, not show; a lesson lost upon the fustian school of congressional and valedictorian oratory that Legaré so deprecated. In eulogy, eloquence might be an end; in law (and in politics), it was a means.

Writing in 1828 of forensic oratory among the ancients, Legaré spoke indirectly of his own method: "The truth of the matter is, not that we possess an art in extemporaneous debate, which the ancients did not: but that we have never compassed the higher art of writing and delivering speeches so well as to give them the appearance of arising immediately and exclusively out of the subject under discussion. Their most studied orations were the most perfectly *ex tempore*, that is best suited to the time and the occasion. They aimed here, as every where else, at the Beau Ideal, but it was the Beau Ideal of the *business speech*. They expected the orator to do all he could, by his eloquence, to accomplish his end, and he was not to lose sight of it for a moment. Every thing merely rhetorical, every thing, however slightly irrelevant or unsuitable as a means to it, was censured with more or less severity. They had not taste for an artificial speech as such; on the contrary, ease, simplicity and nature they rigorously exacted; but they knew that it was in this, as it is in every other department of genius, things done by great masters with most art, appear most natural to the connoisseur—they are refined into simplicity and elaborated into ease. I have taught him, says Boileau, speaking of Racine, *à faire difficilement des vers faciles*: and the saying is of universal application." Yet it was a quality, the use of "idiomatic turns of expression . . . colloquial ease and freedom," that he found "rare in our American writing." So he must have been pleased when Henry Nott reported of reaction to a Legaré speech in Columbia: "They [the undergraduates] were amazed to find that eloquence could be so much like common sense, common feeling & common talk."[5]

Thus Legaré's courtroom appearances were noted not for wilder flights of fancy but for studied casualness, ease, colloquial grace, as though he were at leisure with an intimate friend. He took the judge, the jury, the audience with him on a tour of his subject, pointing now at this, now at that, mocking the follies of the opposing counsel, mentioning the obscure to flatter an audience previously ignorant but pleased to be thought knowing. He was not above dramatic tricks of emotional manipulation if the occasion warranted, not above invoking the destitution of widows and orphans, but that was not his mark. Story was to remember Legaré's appearances before the Supreme Court as "wrought in a style, beautiful and chaste, but never passing from the line of the argument, nor losing sight of the cause. His argumentation was marked by the closest logic; at the same time he had a *presence* in speaking, which I have never seen excelled. He had a warm, rich style, but no declamation; for he knew that declamation belongs neither to the jurist nor to the scholar." Brilliancies "were always recognized as sparks from the working engine, not fire works for mere show."[6]

There was pride in this, even vanity, which his critics did not fail to indicate. Legaré was of his age. Fame was an honorable pursuit. Applause was wanted, noted when it happened, puzzled over when it did not. Pride was the gift of ambition, as criticism was its price and evidence. Hearing applause, he could be satisfied that it was merited, not just given. On the other hand, as an observer noted: "When the case was one of absorbing interest, and when much was expected of him, we have known him to tremble before the court and jury with the weakness of a child: not, as he has been heard to say, from the dread of falling below expectation, but lest he might not reach the standard of excellence stamped on his own mind." Pride was an engine that he tried to master and use.[7]

The position of a lawyer brought responsibilities, minor but useful obligations to the smooth working of Charleston and low-country society. Legaré became a trustee of the South Carolina College. He was commissioned to purchase for the state legislature's law library. In 1825 he became a member of the Charleston City Council for the Fourth Ward. He gave a course of lectures before the Charleston Forensic Club. He served on the Book Committee of the Charleston Library Society. Above all, as he had long planned and expected, he went into politics.[8]

When still a resident of John's Island, he was nominated and elected without canvass or opposition to represent St. John's, Colleton in the lower house of the state legislature. The parish was a gentlemanly rotten borough, on an island itself scattered with just 190 whites and 2,666 unfranchised slaves. His friends were pleased to extend this courtesy to such a rising hope of the stern and unbending, and he diffidently to accept. Legaré did not have to proclaim a party, though he was "by birth & connection properly a member" of the Federalists (a taste that was to survive in his reiterated admiration for Alexander Hamilton), while by choice he was a Republican. Parties were not the strong suit of South Carolina politics, once Federalist, now vaguely Republican, and soon to be mercurial. Parties were little; kinship and faction were nearly all. The duties of the legislator, in the relatively quiet times of Monroe, were not onerous; he went for a month in late November and early December to Columbia. The state capital, although recent, was more than amiable, especially during sittings of the legislature. Legaré's friend Henry Junius Nott, who taught French at the South Carolina College to students and witty allegory to the world, was content with its amenities. "After all," he reminded Legaré in 1831, "it is not a bad country where one can, on an average twice a week throughout the year, eat Scotch salmon, pâté de foie gras and tranches de chevreuil moistened with Champaigne, Chateaux Margaux, Johannisberger, not to mention such common things as Amontillado & Sercial. On inspecting my journal for the last three months, I note not less than some forty or fifty dinners en règle; & during the legislature, the service is still more active—for a Batchelor I confess there is something still wanting. You, however, with true philosophy have always taken the goods the gods have provided you. And like Desdemona 'fattened on a Moor' in absence of better pasturage."[9]

Legaré took care to be respectful, working efficiently but unaggressively. He was on the Committee on Internal Improvements, at a time when the state was undertaking many roads and canals, at great expense and little profit to trade or comfort. In 1828 he was to refer to the scheme as "a system . . . wasteful and injurious," though his views in 1820 are not known. He sat upon three committees charged with considering pressing issues of the day: the Missouri Compromise, the Bank of the United States, and national tariff policy. The last of these had been given a set of resolutions condemning the tariff; the committee responded unanimously by deprecating the practical inequities between industrial and agricultural regions created by the tariff, but granting the competence of the federal government to legislate such laws. But in 1820 such issues intimated, rather than demanded, urgency, Legaré, novice legislator, was more interested in making his discreet mark in Columbia. He made the contacts necessary to a politician, and a particular friend in George McDuffie, who was heard to predict great things for this new member. McDuffie was a natural ally. He had been to the Willington Academy and to the South Carolina College, from which he had graduated a year before Legaré, his equal in precocious reputation. He had been patronized by the Calhouns, whose nationalism Legaré had early imbibed. But as to temperament, it was an improbable connection. McDuffie was excitable, given to dueling, ugly, silent in company, rustic in manners, ill dressed to the point of having holes in the elbow of his coat. Yet he had the gift of oratory. True, it was not Legaré's style. McDuffie was vehement, emotional; he waved his arms, paused melodramatically for emphasis, thumped the podium. Still they made their alliance. [10]

McDuffie published in 1821 a vituperative repudiation of essays in the Milledgeville *Gazette* by "The Trio," supporters of William H. Crawford (another Willington graduate in this smallest of political grounds). McDuffie, "One of the People," was energetic: these were dangerous and designing demagogues, bent only upon their own advancement, shamelessly exciting the morbid passions of the electorate, clinging to a foolish states' rights position now exploded by the arguments and policies of Calhoun. To this, in substance though not in tone, Legaré gave his endorsement in a commentary in Jacob Cardozo's *Southern Patriot*. The distinction of tone may have been fortunate. McDuffie was called out for the violence of his manner by Colonel William Cumming, the outraged leader of "The Trio." There was a duel; McDuffie's shot managed only to strike the earth, while his opponent lodged a bullet near McDuffie's spine. McDuffie nearly died (in the long run, the bullet was to enfeeble both body and brain), but he was game, if imprudent. A few months and he rose again, dueled again, and lost again—this time at the price of a shattered arm.[11]

Removal to Charleston in 1822 disqualified Legaré from his St. John's constituency. He was nominated for a Charleston district, St. Philip's and St. Michael's Parish, but made a respectable rather than a successful showing. Most notable in the next two years was his first major political oration. Charleston had its share of patriotic societies—the Palmetto Society, the Revolutionary Society, the Order of the Cincinnati, and the '76 Association—which would meet on the anniversary of America's independence, hold parades and banquets, give toasts of loaded meaning, and listen to the ritual assessment of independence's significance. It was an honor for a young man to be asked to speak, a badge of approval and a test of competence. The city had no more sacred mystery than the Revolution, rendered more holy by exegesis. James Louis Petigru was to speak himself in 1834 and, sending a copy of the speech to Legaré, observe: "Pray, don't laugh at the pious defence of our planetary system, which custom has made so reverend. Think of your own case and be careful of quizzing people that may have things to tell." For Legaré it was a delicate task. The Revolution, in the person of its survivors, was palpable; Thomas Pinckney, for one, whose love of the classics had so influenced the younger Legaré, lived on. Cicero's name was the very first word of the oration, and Legaré was later to observe how deliberately Cicero had mythologized the Roman republic. Certainly Legaré's generation was energetically intensifying its own charter myth, the Revolution, the better to berate or inspire themselves. Alexander Garden had just published his *Anecdotes of the Revolutionary War,* and William Johnson a biography of Nathanael Greene. Few undertook the task with more self-conscious and anxious wistfulness than Legaré. Yet intellectual pride required an original interpretation of a genre more notable for bombast than analysis.[12]

He attempted the bombast. "What were the victories of POMPEY," he asked his willing listeners, "to the united achievements of our Washingtons and Montgomerys and Greens—our Franklins and Jeffersons and Adams' and Laurens'—of the Senate of Sages, whose wisdom conducted—of the band of warriors, whose valour accomplished—of the 'noble army of martyrs', whose blood sealed and consecrated the Revolution of '76?" But his heart and style were not in it. Such panegyrics, he admitted after a paltry few minutes, "however interesting in themselves, and eminently well

Thomas Pinckney, by Charles Fraser.
COURTESY, CAROLINA ART ASSOCIATION/GIBBES ART GALLERY

fitted for the purposes of popular declamation, are become so trite that
it would be difficult, by any art of composition, to bestow upon them
the graces of novelty." But what was left, if panegyrics were dis-
claimed? There was an attempt at defining the causes and character of
the Revolution, one not lacking in patriotism but also not barren of
insight.[13]

He claimed, what was scarcely original, that the Revolution was
the expression of free men desiring freedom. A principle had been at
stake, yet not one motivated by extravagant oppression. Legaré did
not expatiate upon the horrors of George III, which he termed minor,
an admission that might have raised eyebrows in his audience: "In
accounting for our declaration of independence, it is quite hyper-
bolical to speak—as it has been too common to do—of the tyranny of
the mother country, and the evils under which the Colonies laboured,
as too grievous to be endured." There were grievances, but nothing
swingeing, no atrocities, no royal outrages, no patrician insolence, no
religious persecution, no proscriptions. "Even the right of taxation
against which they were contending was a prospective and contingent
evil, rather than an actual grievance, and nothing can be more just
than the quaint metaphor of BURKE, that 'they augured misgovern-
ment at a distance, and snuffed tyranny in every tainted gale.' " Hint
of tyranny altered consciousness. Thus the Americans "argued—
refined—distinguished—explained, with all the learned ingenuity of
the schools. But if they reasoned about their rights with the subtlety
of doctors—they were prepared to maintain them with the constancy
of martyrs, and, for the first time in the history of civil society, a
metaphysical dispute resulted in the creation of a great empire."[14]

Thus, for Legaré, it was a subtle Revolution, wrought in men's
minds. This belief required him to fashion a new explanation. Take
away encroaching Hanoverians and bloodthirsty Hessians from the
conventional wisdom, and what was left? There were the gains of
philosophical reason that the eighteenth century exemplified. There
were the social components of a heterogeneous immigrant population:
Huguenots, escaping not poverty but proscription; Pilgrims, seeking
the rights of conscience; "the unfortunate, the persecuted, the adventurous, the bold, the aspiring of all clime and conditions, congregated
and confounded in one vast asylum." There were the reforms of the
colonial period that bred a habit of change: "For it is very important to
observe that the whole history of the colonies is a history of successive
revolutions in their municipal government and administration, and it
is only by a figure of speech that we confine that term exclusively to

the declaration of independence." There was the absence of entrenched and armed abuses—of feudalism, as Tocqueville was more than a decade later to remark. The revolutionaries "had no inveterate prejudices to encounter here—there was no inheritance of abuses come down from remote ages—there were no grievances established by custom—no corruptions sanctified by their antiquity." There were the opportunities of reform that revolution, once commenced, offered: the times "gave our fathers, who were great reformers, an opportunity of purifying the fountains of society—of forming the character and controlling, in some degree, and directing the destinies of the infant commonwealth, by such principles as philosophy and experience had shewn to be best, although they had no where else been fully admitted in practice."[15]

Thus had been created, by logical but peculiar circumstances, a novel experiment, a continental and imperial republic. Upon the term "republic" Legaré was insistent, for this was no democracy. The tenor of his speech was Federalist, not least in the claim that most men, in most ages, had endured more onerous and vile social conditions than Americans, and so the new republic was distinguishable as a lonely trial that might not succeed. The possibility of failure was raised, to be ambivalently rejected. Legaré was aware that classical and Italian precedents for republican longevity were not encouraging; he had read his Machiavelli, his John Adams. He knew that an imperial republic was especially to be suspected; no reader of Cicero needed reminder. Why should the United States turn out differently? Legaré mentioned Providence, although not with confidence. He asserted with more assurance the fluke that America was founded in the years of Europe's enlightenment, not its feudalism, and so the new country's lifeblood was relatively uncontaminated. It was probable that virtue and the experience of freedom bred further virtue and freedom. Whatever the future, the American present was singular and blessed, a reproach to a Europe riddled by the Holy Alliance, and a Philhellene inspiration to Greece, fighting the Alliance for independence. All this was illustrated by quotation from Byron's "Ode on Venice," in praise of an America increasingly alone in a world diminished of liberty. This was vigorous and traditional; the tails of lion, bear, and double-headed eagle were meant for American twisting.[16]

Yet at the core of the oration, at the moment of customary uplift where the speaker was supposed to promise his listeners the future, was not Legaré fudging? "To conclude," he had said, "our institutions have sprung up naturally in the progress of society. They will flourish

and decay with those improvements of which they were the fruit—
they will grow with the growth of knowledge—they will strengthen
with the strength of reason—their influence will be extended by every
advance of *true* civilization—every thing that has a tendency to make
man wiser and better, will confirm and improve and adorn them. If
humanity was not endowed, in vain, with such noble faculties, many
ages and glory and freedom are before us—many nations shall learn,
from our example, how to be free and great. The fortunes of the
species, are thus, in some degree, indentified with those of THE
REPUBLIC—and if our experiment fail, there is no hope for man on
this side of the grave." In the pleasantness of a Fourth of July, wine
gone and coming, fireworks and cannon thickening the ear, this must
have seemed brave enough. In the colder light of restrospect, a
Charlestonian would have seen careful phrasing. If man advanced, if
reason were strengthened, if knowledge grew, the republic was safe
and exemplifying. Yet "if" was not "because." The future was not
predestined; it was postulated. Did Legaré believe in the postulates?
On this he was silent. Later he was to be scathing towards the "march
of mind" and to remark after the shock of nullification: "I almost
despair of the Republic. I am afraid mankind are too wicked &
depraved for such a government as the Washingtons & Jays established." Later still he was to descant on the blessings of the steam
engine. Silence may have been mandated by uncertainty. [17]

The year 1823 in Charleston was not without uncertainty. The
preceding year had seen the conspiracy of Denmark Vesey and Gullah
Jack: the arsenal, the guardhouse, a store packed with musket and
powder, major roads into the peninsula, stables for a slave cavalry were
all to have been seized; ambush and surprise were to have conquered
the city before the victors escaped to Saint Domingue. But there had
been rumor and confession. The militia, commanded by Legaré's
friend Robert Hayne, had scotched the revolution a scant two days
before its planned bloody amazement. Charleston saw thirty-five
hangings and thirty-seven exiles, and felt a persistent trepidation.
The precedent of Haiti had been intimated. Those who wished, and
could bear the recitation, could listen to the aging refugees of Saint
Domingue still living in the city, and reflect that the future had its
postulates. The Legaré family itself had eleven slaves living with them
in Bull Street, cooking, cleaning, tending the horses, oiling the new
books brought from Paris, brushing the frockcoat that masked
Legaré's deformity. [18]

The state legislature had been alarmed by Vesey. In the last month of 1822 it decreed that any free black sailor docking at the port of Charleston should be imprisoned for the duration, lest he disturb local slaves by loose talk of freedom and the wide world. The British government protested violation of a treaty guaranteeing mutual and free access to ports. With less abstract motive, Harry Elkison—free black of Jamaica, sailor, and temporary resident of a Charleston jail—protested and asked William Johnson, Justice of the Supreme Court and South Carolinian, for the courtesy of a writ of habeas corpus. Isaac Holmes, Legaré's friend, and Benjamin Hunt argued before Johnson that South Caroline's need for self-preservation took precedence over a treaty that violated the Constitution. Johnson demurred, arguing that South Carolina was not sovereign but the United States was, and both treaty and Constitution concurred in abominating this law. However (in small consolation to Harry Elkison), the same Constitution forbade the federal government the jurisdiction of habeas corpus over state prisoners; though the law might be wrong, its effects would stand. None of which satisfied the British government; or John Quincy Adams, the Secretary of State; or William Wirt, the Attorney General. In 1824, Adams sent to the governor of South Carolina a copy of Wirt's opinion—arguing that the law violated the treaty and the commerce clause of the Constitution—with the polite but firm request that the state legislature remedy this "inconvenience."[19]

The matter came before the Committee on Unfinished Business, of which Legaré was chairman. Upon the same committee sat Benjamin Hunt, who had not been idle since the original case but energetic in the press. The issue was delicate and emotional, moving in crosscurrents with the volatilities of the day: states' rights and slavery. On states' rights, Legaré had been moving away from the stance of his *Southern Patriot* letters and towards particularism. On slavery he was then, as later and preferably, owlish. He was fretfully aware of the threat of a servile war, yet reflected that slavery was ruinous but inescapable. His expectations were dismal. Indeed Thomas Grimké warned Legaré that so much gloomy thought ended in vague indecision. Slaves like Gracie, John, Josey, and Boatswain the coachman were his convenient servants, and Legaré did care for his comfort, his lit fires and decanted Bordeaux. But in the legislature, comfort became fraught with meaning. He would turn to brief advice, to a moderation of language that, if it did not solve the problem, would diminish the confusing abundance of portents. Logic and dispassion must serve, lest illogic and passion destroy: the burden of the mangled but disciplined experience of Legaré. So he stood before the state legislature to advise it upon the Elkison case. Benjamin Hunt might speak of heats and prejudices, and invoke the fresh memories of Denmark Vesey, "the dangers that stalk by night: violence, murder and rape." Legaré would have none of it. He was a lawyer and so would speak only on constitutionality. He was a worried slaveholder and thus still would speak only on constitutionality. "With the other matters which have been so largely expatiated upon in the course of a very angry controversy, I desire to have no concern."[20]

Hunt had been foolish enough to invoke the precepts of Vattel and international law to defend the Negro Seamen Act, which was to play into Legaré's hands. Sarcasm at the expense of other's ill learning was Legaré's strong point. "Vattel is gravely cited to prove that 'a nation consists in the duration of the political association of which it is formed,' and that 'if a period be put to the association, the nation or state no longer exists, though (which is really astonishing) the individuals who compose it still exist,!!! that is, when the association ceases, it ceases! . . . [Hunt] asks with an air of triumph What nation ever disputed the right of the Chinese to protect themselves from the contagion of European manners by a sort of universal non-intercourse act. Why, who ever did? or who disputes the power of the U. States to do so? Altho, unfortunately for Mr. Hunt's far fetched illustration, the same answer would scarcely be given to the question whether the Legislature of So. Carolina could do as much." The logic was clear. Once South Carolina had been independent and sovereign; by subscribing to the federal union, she had abandoned that sovereignty and in all matters "relating to peace & war, commerce, etc., retains no more sovereignty than if she had never existed at all as an independent commonwealth." Hence the law of 1822, being inconsistent with the commercial treaty between the United States and Great Britain, was inconsistent with the Constitution and so null and void.[21]

Legaré's opinion was not dominant. The Senate passed by 36 to 6 a resolution announcing that the duty of guarding against servile insurrection involved the right of self-preservation, a thing "paramount to all Laws, all Treaties, all Constitutions." The House was less extreme, noting in resolution merely that the 1822 act had been a measure of "domestic police absolutely necessary to insure the safety of the citizen." The season expired without these two resolutions being reconciled. The next year, 1825, saw some amendment of the statute: free black sailors were obliged to remain aboard their ships, which were to anchor at least 150 yards from the dock. Yet free blacks were still imprisoned, and the British and federal governments continued to protest, all to little avail. In time, the Attorney-General of Andrew Jackson decided the South Carolina law was not, after all, repugnant to Constitution and treaty. Even Lord Palmerston was obliged to notice an embarrassing clause of the treaty, which declared freedom of commerce "subject always to the laws and statutes of the two countries respectively," so protest from London grew less unequivocal. This dispute over race, unlike most in these antebellum years, grew fainter and murkier.[22]

On the Elkison case Legaré had ranged himself with John Quincy Adams, William Wirt, and William Johnson in asserting the competence of the federal government. The assertion was particular, not general. In the mid-1820s Legaré was moving cautiously towards strengthening the prerogatives of the states because of the tariff, that catalyst of constitutional reassessment. In the same session of 1824, in which the governor had sent to the state legislature the protests of Washington over the Negro Seamen Act, John Lide Wilson had also transmitted a message expressing concern over the drift towards federal consolidation. The state Assembly had appointed a special committee, headed by Samuel Prioleau and including Legaré, to examine the matter and recommend policy. The Senate had its own committee, which heeded the resolutions of Stephen Miller, follower of the states' rights faction of William Smith. The Miller resolutions, strict constructionist, denouncing the tariff and internal improvements as unconstitutional, were sent to the House, where they were tabled. The Prioleau committee produced contrary resolutions: power derived from the people, who made separate delegations of authority to state and federal governments; the people had not given the state legislature power to challenge the actions of either the federal government or the Supreme Court; the people, if displeased with Washington, could act directly upon their delinquent representatives; the state legislature had no power to suggest amendments to the constitution but merely to petition Congress to summon a general constitutional convention; liberty would be endangered if either state or federal legislatures exceeded their delegated and respective powers. These Prioleau resolutions were, like those of Miller, tabled by the House.[23]

But 1825 was a different matter. The United States Congress had increased the level of its appropriations. Discussion about slavery's status in the Union had heated. Ohio, endorsed by several other Northern states, had proposed a national scheme of emancipation, freeing all slaves over twenty-one who reached that age after the law's passage and agreed to their foreign colonization. Rufus King had requested of the United States Senate that public land revenues be used to fund emancipation. There was derangement in the cotton market. John Quincy Adams had become President, Henry Clay his Secretary of State. So Legaré changed his mind and was in a position to make the alteration moderately influential. Prioleau was no longer in the House; Legaré succeeded him as chairman and so became one of the floor leaders for the Miller Resolutions, rechristened the Smith Resolutions, since William Smith was now in the state House. The irony did not go unnoticed, even or especially by so close a friend as Alfred Huger, who informed Joel Poinsett (then Minister to Mexico): "The House of Representatives are at this moment engaged in discussing Prioleau's Resolutions which remained among the unfinished business of the last year. Judge Smith & Hugh Legaré are anxious to render to the State that service which they think would accrue from the adoption of our disgracefull sentiments expressed the last session, how they will succeed I do know not." They succeeded well enough, the House endorsing the Smith Resolutions by 73 votes to 28, over the protest of Calhoun's faction.[24]

In his own speech, Legaré had been at pains to elucidate his change of emphasis. The federal government might be compared to the trustee of a great estate. "The government of the United States . . . is a government of sovereign but limited powers. These limited powers are conferred upon the government to enable it to perform certain trusts. These trusts are defined with the utmost precision, in an instrument called the Constitution, but which is neither more nor less than the great Trust Deed between the States and the United States." It followed, therefore, that "a government of limited powers has no greater right to divert the funds of the government beyond the enumerated objects—because it has an unlimited Power to appropriate for the general welfare—than a trustee, who has an unlimited power of deed to raise money on the trust estate, has to divert those funds to any other purpose of the estate than are expressed in the different trusts." The tariff, though technically legal, was an abuse of trust; the use of its revenues for broad social purposes, such as expansive internal improvements or the emancipation of slaves, was more so. Thus it was proper, by these resolutions transmitted to Washington, to protest and ask a redress of grievances.[25] Here Legaré stopped, as did everyone else in 1825. The step from protest to nullification wa a few years off, the doctrine of state interposition a discredited, half-forgotten memory of 1798.

Fleetingly, in 1827, South Carolina's contentious politicians were to endure a moment of consensus. Most stood for Andrew Jackson (whom Legaré was to dub "one of the most exalted & heroic characters that ever existed"), then the ally of Calhoun and the patron of states' rights against Adams. There was agreement that the tariff and internal improvements had gone too far, an agreement underscored willingly and triumphantly by the faction of William Smith, sullenly by the Calhounites. There was agreement upon the necessity of protest to Washington. The Smith Resolutions had been repassed in 1826, and Legaré reintroduced them in 1827 with their central contention that "all the acts of Congress, known by the name of Tariff Laws, the object of which is neither the raising of revenue or the regulation of foreign commerce, but the promotion of Domestic Manufactures, are violations of the Constitution in its spirit and ought to be repealed." They passed after perfunctory discussion. The immediate response from the Washington of Adams and Clay was unencouraging, but there was a presidential election coming, and Jackson bid more than fair to be elected. A redress of grievances seemed likely, especially with Calhoun as Jackson's vice-president, his probable and anxious heir.[26]

But consensus was fragile. Disagreement and bitterness would ensue when the tariff of 1828 precipitated the splintering of words into varying strategies of action. Controversy demanded scrutiny and elicited publication, in the press and in pamphlets. Robert Turnbull's *The Crisis,* which deployed Legaré's metaphor of the federal government as accountable trustee, though emboldened and passionate beyond Legaré's ability or willingness, riveted attention in 1827. But what was lacking, the grandees of Charleston decided, was a quarterly, that very nineteenth-century and progressive organ of enlightened and learned opinion. The Whigs of Edinburgh had had one to register their witty discontent with the Tories of London, and prospered through it. That was common knowledge, reinforced by the experience of Legaré, who had lived among those very Whigs. The Bostonians had their *North American Review,* succored by Legaré's friend Ticknor. Baltimore had *Niles' Register.* Perhaps the politicians of Charleston might fare as well in protesting the oppressions of distant Washington. They met at the home of Robert Hayne to plan, consider a prospectus, appoint an editor, procure promises of contributions, nominate trustees to guard against financial irresponsibility.[27]

The immediate purposes of the *Southern Review* were political, expressing that fleeting consensus and proclaimed by its advertising prospectus of 14 September 1827. The press, they declared, "once so

humble, so insignificant, known only to the closets of the studious, of
the privileged intercourse of the learned, addressing itself to the few
in ancient and exclusive language, has in modern days, in consequence of the wide diffusion of education, been directed to the great
mass of society with decided effect, and now exercises an almost
despotic control over the opinions of mankind." Public opinion, in
turn, was powerful upon affairs of state; a quarterly, by influencing the
public and giving the alarm of dangerous trends, might analyze and
dispel dangers, not least by refuting any publication with contrary
opinions. Thus "it shall be among our first objects to vindicate the
rights and privileges, the character of the Southern States, to arrest, if
possible, the current which has been directed so steadily against our
country generally, and the South in particular; and to offer to our
fellow citizens one Journal, which they may read without finding
themselves the objects of perpetual sarcasm, or of affected commisera-
tion." Above all, "it shall be our care faithfully to point out these
encroachments, and strenuously to resist that consolidation of all
power in a national head, which, whatever may be the impressions of
the moment, or the views of the agents in each act, must lead
ultimately, perhaps rapidly, to discord and disunion."[28]

Yet the choice of an editor was not a political act. To have chosen a
partisan editor among supporters, agreed for the moment but frag-
ilely so, would have been difficult. Stephen Elliott, the presiding
spirit of Charleston's intellectual life, had the virtue of being as close
to nonpolitical as a man could be in a city dedicated to the observance
of politics, though he had been decades before a Federalist and was
now president of the state bank, a matter not uninvolved with
controversy. But it was Elliott the botanist, the man Serra had praised
as "the first man in his walk of science in America," whom the
launchers of the *Southern Review* now preferred: the Professor of Botany
and Natural History in the state's new Medical College, the founder of
the city's Literary and Philosophical Society, the man who read so
insistently and widely, who loved to converse of ideas, who knew
everyone and was respected by most, especially for a gentle humility.
He had, Legaré was to remember with affection, "the simplicity and
modesty, nay bashfulness of a girl."[29] But Elliott had also the practical
acumen, patience, and intellectual eclecticism that made the *Southern
Review*, beyond its prospectus, the home for a various critical discourse
and a forum for political controversy after the consensus of 1827
vanished in great public meetings, Expositions, Protests, memorials,
conventions, test oaths, social rancor. Important as politics was in the

launching of the quarterly, it did not overwean. Instead, the *Southern Review* became a crystallization of the intellectual judgments of Charleston especially and of Columbia secondarily.

Charleston had been an intellectual but not a writing city. Men had read, had talked together, had even delivered learned or light discourses before societies and colleges, but few had thought it crucial to publish thought. Thought was a social matter, an accomplishment necessary to standing in society but less a public thing. David Ramsay, it was true, had written his histories of South Carolina and the Revolution, and done credit to the city. Elliott himself had published two volumes upon the botany of North and South Carolina. William Crafts had published verse, about whose virtues local opinion was dubious. Thomas Bee, bearing a reputation for brilliance endorsed by an English education, had made a mistake in publishing and so ruined his reputation for wit and learning.[30] But mostly, thought had vanished in the drawing room or decayed in the perishable columns of the press. Legaré himself had, by the end of 1827, reached thirty without more than a handful of letters to the press, occasional printed orations, speeches to the legislature; half of them forgotten, half closely tailored to a local occasion. The opportunity for permanence had been wanting. That occasion the *Southern Review* was to provide. Willingly because he wished to write, and unwillingly because others did not and he was required to supply their place, Legaré entered a period of extraordinary productivity, the distillation of his years of reading and reflection.[31]

In writing, Legaré clarified his position. He was to become estranged, marked off by the intensity of his erudition and the severity of his criticism. In thought as in politics, he did not grasp the usefulness of party. Yet he had friendships, alliances, enemies, a place.

Legaré tied himself to the past, thinking it pertinent to the future. His regard for the Founding generation of South Carolina was filial, as though 1776 could stand godparent to a fatherless man, yet his admiration was textual and abstract. The men of flesh and bone who inhabited the Charleston of his youth are remarkable for their absence from his letters and writings. David Ramsay, Charles Cotesworth Pinckney, Charles Pinckney, Henry Laurens, Henry Middleton were all but silent influences, being almost too close to require exegesis. Only Thomas Pinckney, whose death occurred while Legaré was writing a manifesto for the new *Southern Review*, elicited a tender appraisal. Among his contemporaries Legaré was most at ease with those who deferred to continuity, suspected radicalism, and modulated a Federalist vision: James Louis Petigru, Stephen Elliott (the elder and the younger), William Grayson, William Elliott, Alfred Huger, Charles Fraser, Mitchell King. This taste transcended locality, for up and down the eastern seaboard he had connections with such moderate men, turning acid at the times: John Pendleton Kennedy in Baltimore, George Ticknor in Boston, Joseph Cogswell in New York, William Cabell Rives in Virginia.[32]

There was nothing unfitting in Legaré's honorary Columbia University degree. It came more naturally than his election to the Georgia Historical Society, because he played no role in spreading Charleston's influence westward in the South and hardly thought even to visit this new empire.[33] Upstate in Columbia, he was close to Henry Nott but not to Robert Henry: the one whimsically jaundiced about man's frailties, the other too zealous in his religion. Thomas Cooper he admired for intellectual eclecticism, though not for a Jeffersonian past and nullifying present, and not for a suspicious rapidity of scholarship. David McCord had been a close friend, but the politics of a nullifying Columbia Junto had separated them into bare formal politeness.[34] But to have been Legaré's friend in childhood and youth meant much, because he made new alliances and friendships awkwardly; his stock tended to dwindle with the depredations of adult contention. His loyalties were social and political, firmer when the two combined.

Legaré never aspired to an intellectual or literary coterie, its boundaries policed by aesthetic orthodoxy. The *Southern Review* never had a party line except in its suspicion of the merely belletristic, of those who leaned to the model of *Blackwood's Magazine* instead of the *Edinburgh Review.* So he invited young men like Jesse Burton Harrison and Edward Johnston to write, in the mode of himself or Sydney Smith, but never reached out to the young William Gilmore Simms. Legaré was willing to judge the coming school of Bulwer Lytton and James Fenimore Cooper but had no interest in patronizing it. Admirers Legaré was to acquire in large numbers: Thomas Caute Reynolds was to study in Heidelberg and dedicate his thesis to Legaré; George Frederick Holmes was fierce in his devotion to Legaré's scholarship; Francis Lieber, though unhappy with South Carolina, admired Legaré upon the ancients; Edgar Allan Poe reproached James Russell Lowell for neglecting Legaré; Paul Hamilton Hayne felt Legaré the best of the old regime of Charleston.[35] Yet these were admirers, not disciples. Legaré discouraged the young from his own model, knowing that what he had tried to hold in unity, scholarship and politics, was coming to be separated. Not encouraging loyalists, he was to lack a school that would perpetuate his legacy.

Legaré's was a lonely achievement, which seemed a justification for his melancholy temperament. But he did fit idiosyncratically into the times. He was important as an interpeter of Romanticism, rendering it into American and Southern terms. As a bulwark of the *Southern Review*, he helped to found a model of critical discourse that was to be persistently emulated in the region. He modernized the case for the classics, against indigenous opposition, by assimilating German scholarship and thereby preserving a context for Basil Gildersleeve and the professional classicism to come. One among many, he reinterpreted the republican tradition for new circumstances. As a judge of American and European literature, he tried to fashion a usable amalgam of American nationality and the riches of the European intellectual tradition, and so budge his contemporaries from the euphoric cultural separatism of David Ramsay and Noah Webster.[36] He forcefully represented the cause of the civil law to a time that deceptively promised its growing influence in America.[37] He stood for slavery, though in a grim Burkean voice, at odds with those who rested the racial cause of the South upon transcendent morality, religious sanction, and ethnological necessity. He clarified a note of elegy that, translated from the instance of South Carolina to the debacle of the Confederacy, was to inform the Lost Cause.[38] He pragmatically endorsed the political economy of laissez faire, more technically examined by Jacob Cardozo.

But these influences were piecemeal. His single underlying vision faltered because—being "shy and particular"—Legaré ruthlessly guarded its privacy, even as he pined to belong.[39] He was perhaps the best of the old Charleston, come into awareness and confidence but a shade too late. While Legaré did not choose to defy his times, they gently then abruptly alienated him; the historian would be puzzled to imagine a Hugh Legaré in 1860, puzzled to know whether he would have cheered Edmund Ruffin shelling Fort Sumter, been a dissenter with Petigru, or even been still a Charlestonian. Legaré's misfortune was that he was insufficiently a romantic to admire the usages of alienation, to appreciate the modern pride in singularity and dissent, to share the modern passion for specialist concentration. By our terms, he essayed too much. By his own, he only succeeded too little.

# II

# HOOD AND JESSES

# 3

# Manner

THE PERIODICAL ESSAY dissipated coherence. It was published anonymously, even though in the small world of Charleston and South Carolina, many readers could guess or knew the names of authors. It appeared intermittently and sat among the essays of others, its standpoint put out of focus by the passage of time between issues and the conflicting styles and perspectives of its companions. It was a flexible form, short or long, light or heavy, defensive or aggressive, admirable for eliciting thought but weak as a device for thought's reconsideration of itself. Not only could the reader lose sight of the author, but the author could lose sight of himself. The tradition, now firmly established, of publishing collected essays was weak, and weaker in the South. Only the accident of death compelled the issuance of Legaré's writings in 1846. That it was done by a sister and by friends not especially sensitive to Legaré's own perspectives impoverished the book. Legaré did not have the chance—and it is not clear that he would have wanted the chance—of arranging, winnowing, and understanding his own work. He was denied the shock of recognition and discovery that is common to the author collecting the fugitive pieces of his past years.

The *Writings* of 1846, compounding the incoherence of the original periodical form even as collection diminished it, has been virtually the only mode by which Legaré has been available to later generations and so stands between him and us. It is in two volumes. The first begins with a biographical notice by Edward Johnston, itself identified only by Johnston's initials: a piece necessarily eulogy rather than assessment, though full of invaluable information from a man who was never especially close to Legaré but who made an honest effort to assemble a web of fact and anecdote fit for decorous gilding in a memorial edition.[1] There follows a printing of the diaries that Legaré kept in Brussels and on his German travels. They are badly transcribed and mildly bowdlerized—a matter of some moment, since the "Diary of Brussels" is no longer extant, and the "Journal of the Rhine" (so called by Legaré's sister Mary with no authority from the manuscript, and inappropriately for a travel diary that ranged far beyond the Rhine) exists only in fragments.[2] The Brussels diary begins on 16 May 1833, where Legaré resumed the habit of keeping a diary, but abruptly terminates the following October 3, with no indication whether Legaré himself or the editor ceased. Next, there are two sections of Legaré's correspondence: the first, of his diplomatic dispatches to the State Department between 1832 and 1836; the second, of various private letters. The former are erratically edited, with the dates of dispatches occasionally misconstrued and all but one of the State Department instructions missing, so that the nature of Legaré's diplomatic mission in Belgium becomes opaque.[3] Because publication followed so swiftly upon his death, and only Isaac Holmes and Alfred Huger gave Mary Legaré letters to be printed, the latter are oddly selected, arranged in no very logical pattern (even with respect to chronology), and somewhat edited in substance; as reflections of the nature of Legaré's private letters, they are very inadequate. Then come seven orations: two 4th of July addresses (1823 and 1831), plus five speeches from Legaré's term as a United States representative. Nothing was chosen from his early career in the South Carolina legislature or his later as a conservative politician, and nothing from his forensic career or his opinions as Attorney-General. The volume closes with three essays—upon the "Constitutional History of Greece," Demosthenes, and Roman legislation—written for the *New York Review* between 1837 and 1841. Thus the reader is confronted with the later work, which significantly amplified and redirected Legaré's thought, before having had the chance to discover the earlier pieces.[4]

The second volume of the *Writings* consists entirely of Legaré's essays for the *Southern Review*. Sixteen articles are reproduced, out of a canon much larger: "Classical Learning," "Roman Literature," "Kent's Commentaries," "Crafts' Fugitive Writings," "Travels of the Duke of Saxe-

Weimar," "The Disowned—Tales of the Great St. Bernard," "Cicero de Republica," "Hall's Travels in North America," "Early Spanish Ballads—Charlemagne and his Peers," "Sir Philip Sidney's Miscellanies," "Lord Byron's Character and Writings," "Byron's Letters and Journals," "Jeremy Bentham and the Utilitarians," "Codification," "The Public Economy of Athens," and "D'Aguesseau." These are arranged, with one exception, chronologically by original publication ("Kent's Commentaries," published in August 1828, is inexplicably placed before "Crafts' Fugitive Writings," published in May of the same year). This has the merit of a consistent plan but the disadvantage of scrambling subject matters, thus preserving rather than modifying the incoherence of the original periodical form. Omitted are essays of considerable substance and importance. Legaré's "Roman Orators" was intended to stand with his "Roman Literature," though the latter is reprinted and the former not. "Hoffman's Legal Outlines," a natural companion of "Kent's Commentaries," is excluded. "The American System," perhaps Legaré's most important venture into contemporary political criticism, is left out, possibly for that very reason, as the *Writings* was published at a time when South Carolina was eager to heal the wounds of nullification, the controversy to which that essay had been addressed. The most useful, almost the only, editorial help given the reader is that the marginal notes made by Legaré in his own set of the *Southern Review* are included to amplify the text. Most regrettably, no definitive list of Legaré's writings is given, an omission that has complicated later scholarship.

In short, the thing was botched. Incoherence was confirmed rather than dispelled. Paul Hamilton Hayne, who unsuccessfully attempted a new edition of Legaré's works after the Civil War, was driven to complain, "[These] cumbrous volumes, must be characterized as simply *execrable!*—execrable in general arrangement; execrable in print and binding; execrable in the style of annotation; and, worst of all, most imperfect . . . . we never take the disjointed volumes in hand, without involuntarily regarding them as a species of sepulchre in which the bright genius of Legaré lies buried!"[5] It was an ironic fate for Legaré, notable for clarity and devoted to fit proportion, to have been jumbled and crowded into obscurity and misunderstanding.

Nonetheless, Legaré took the essay as his form. He never wrote a book. He was said to have remarked of his diplomatic mission to Belgium that he had enough materials for a volume but did nothing with them. There are hints that he looked forward to writing his memoirs, and at his death he had been toying with a translation of a volume of Heineccius. But he was candid in saying to Jesse Harrison, "I do not myself like a literary life strictly so called. I prefer the bar & the public contest."[6]

Mostly he wrote as the occasion took him, and the motives for his various essays in the *Southern Review* were miscellaneous. His first, "Classical Learning," was a conscious manifesto and presage of the critical positions he would develop over the life span of the journal. His two pieces on Byron seized upon the important publication of Moore's *Letters and Journals of Lord Byron* to express and lay to rest an old fascination with the poet. His essays on Roman literature and oratory, to which that on Cicero's *De Republica* forms an appendix, were a conscious series to which he had planned to add a third, on the Roman historians. "Codification" has the marks of being a speech delivered to the South Carolina legislature, possibly modified for the purposes of the *Review* but reprinted several years after the fact and so probably a filler when other contributors failed him. "Kent's Commentaries," "Hoffman's Legal Outlines," and "Law of Tenures" were critiques of the most recent legal literature by the periodical's most accomplished jurist. As a traveler he was interested in the accounts of his own culture by the Duke of Saxe-Weimar-Eisenach and Basil Hall; in the latter case, he seems to have been responding to local pressure, for it begins, "Our only motive for reviewing this book is the general expectation that we shall do so."[7] The essay on medieval Spanish literature had no very plausible contemporary reason beyond Legaré's own long-standing interest in the subject. His piece on Sir Philip Sidney had the excuse of a 1829 English edition of Sidney's *Miscellaneous Works* and a desire on Legaré's part to make more widely available the "Defense of Poesy," which he thought too little known. "D'Aguesseau," though it spoke to an old passion for the French Chancellor, appeared in the expiring issue of the *Southern Review*; it was probably fashioned in haste to fill the need for a bulk of prose. "The American System," on the other hand, was a conscious move in the South Carolina political game. Most casual of Legaré's writings were his commentaries on contemporary American and British literature, with which he seems to have been loosely charged by the *Review*—a mission he apparently did not take too seriously save in the cases of Byron and Scott.

As an exponent of the essay form, as a student of its compact niceties, Legaré was not extraordinary. He did rise to shaping his argument; to stating, developing, digressing, restating, concluding; to bearing the reader along a fashioned and abbreviated path. But while he accused the nineteenth century of being an age of prosing dissertation, he was not innocent of his own charge. His mind crowded with thoughts; often conscious of a destination but tempted into overelaboration, he would rush forward until, realizing that page had succeeded page without describing the arc that led to a summary final paragraph or an unsettling last sentence, he would stop. "We have not space to say anything more of these interesting tales," one final paragraph begins. Another starts, "But enough of Utilitarianism."[8] An impetuous mind must often use a brake abruptly.

Legaré was conscious that the review was not always a review but an occasion. After a particularly savage demolition of the Latin scholarship of George Featherstonhaugh, he observed, "We should make our readers an apology for troubling them so long with this very minute examination of a worthless book, but for one reason. We have recently heard great complaints made against the form and style of the periodical criticism of the present day. Reviews, it is said, are mere set dissertations, in which, the work *nominally* censured, is only mentioned at the head of the article, in a sort of *ac etiam* clause to found the jurisdiction upon. We have been ourselves, more than once, guilty of this heinous offence againt primitive manners and models, and have, therefore, endeavored to atone for our past sins, by this specimen of a legitimate critique, which, we trust, will be graciously received as a sufficient expiatory sacrifice for them all." In fact, for his time, Legaré was remarkable for keeping his focus upon the book or author in hand. "To return to our text" was a characteristic phrase.[9] Sometimes this virtue became a vice, especially in reviews of poetry and novels, when he was inclined in lazy moments to extensive quotations (though this was the practice of his time). Mostly, attentiveness was a merit, though it is one of the reasons why his writings have not better survived. He entered into a close dialogue with the views of the author in hand, exposing faults, praising virtues, worrying out the merits of the case to a strict conclusion conformable to Legaré's own standpoint, itself duly explained. It is this intimacy which, now remote in both time and scholarship, has made Legaré inaccessible to later readers and helped to make a writer of energy and firmness seem dull and pedantic. Critical debates having changed in focus and principle, this intimacy has become a handicap to the reader unwilling to undertake the labor of reconstructing the context of its nuance. Writing for a particular audience, with that audience now vanished, Legaré's voice comes strangely to those who no longer care whether the American law should heed the elegancies of the civil law, or whether Cicero offered fit counsel to an American statesman, or even whether Byron was classic or romantic.

Yet, contexts recovered, Legaré becomes especially interesting for this closeness of scrutiny, for the spectacle of a thinking man meditating upon others thinking. Everywhere in his prose is this tactile intimacy, whether the subject was a friend like Thomas Grimké or Demosthenes or himself. Principles and men danced together, flesh and blood and ideas. Legaré was especially careful to define personality, to realize the author or event before him, nowhere more than in his two essays on Byron, which were firstly a meditation upon Byron the man. And he was equally careful to implicate his readers, to make them feel the Charlestonian sitting down to his critical task, to understand that the reviewer too was a man of curiosities, views, prejudices, and history.

He explained his motives, as in beginning a review of *The Fair Maid of Perth*: "We did not read the first series of these tales [*Chronicles of the Canongate*], but the disappointment so generally expressed in relation to them, on this side of the Atlantic, excited our curiosity as to the present volumes to the highest pitch. We were impatient to see and feel for ourselves, whether the author of "Waverley"—like the great captain, whose fortunes he had so lately recorded—were about to astonish mankind as much by his fall as by his triumphs and dominion over them—whether the wand of the enchanter were indeed broken, and the sources of what has always appeared to us an almost superhuman inspiration, had been, at length, exhausted, like those of the Delphic tripod, by too much use or by time, or, in short, by the departure of the god." The reader engaged, the image of Legaré critically circling Scott is deepened with further confession: "For some two or three hours, we had sad misgivings in the present instance. We found the first hundred pages of the novel excessively heavy—partly, no doubt, because the reader does not well perceive the author's drift in them until he has made considerable progress in the story, but still more certainly, because this part, in fact, is very unequal to the rest of the work, and especially to some passages of it to which we shall, hereafter, more particularly, call the attention of our readers. But just as we began to sink under the combined effects of weariness and the heat of a summer's evening [the review was published in August], we reached a point in the narrative at which a new prospect opened before us, and from which we pursued our way to the end with a still increasing interest and alacrity, amidst such scenes as no hand can conjure up but Sir Walter Scott's."[10] Three elements artfully combine:

the situation of the reviewer, piqued, bored, then absorbed; the interests of the reader, whose care Legaré bears in mind; the objective judgment of the book, whose early pages do not merely seem to be bad, because of the reviewer's dullness or the enervations of a Charleston summer, but are actually so.

Legaré employed personal anecdotes to convey general truths, less for confession than for instruction. Thus, addressing Basil Hall's penchant for being irritated at the vagaries of democracy, he summoned his memories of Paris: "It is the French way of criticising Shakspeare. They have no conception at all of the comprehensive unity of design which harmonizes these apparent irregularities. They acknowledge no genius that is not every where stately, decorous and elegant. It is in vain that you appeal to nature—that you dwell upon all that makes the peerless bard a standing intellectual miracle. They answer your eulogies upon Hamlet, by a jest upon the grave-digger's buffoonery, and think of nothing in Macbeth but the absurdity of a plot concocted in a witches' cauldron, and consummated by the march of a forest to take a castle by storm! The best of it is, that England— *cette isle,* as Bossuet sublimely expresses it, *plus orageuse que les mers qui l'environnent*—is treated by continental philosophers, precisely as we are by her own. We remember that, in 1819, the wise men at Paris were confidently predicting the speedy wreck of her whole system, because the Manchester rioters had to be put down by the yeomanry, and Lord Russell and others of the whigs were pelted with brickbats at the hustings in Westminster! They are utterly unable to comprehend that queer compound a *tête Anglaise.*"[11]

He addressed his readers often and with sympathy, conscious that the critic bore a responsibility in molding the taste of his time and community. "We earnestly exhort our readers to consider the state of the question as we have put it" is typical Legaré. Writing of William Crafts, he bore self-consciously the mingled responsibilities of severity and kindness for the sake of Charleston: "We here close our observations upon the character and writings of Mr. Crafts. We have discharged our duty, we trust, with candor and fairness. Where we thought his example calculated to do harm, we have spoken with the freedom, and even the severity of criticism; but none, we are persuaded, entertain a higher opinion than we do of his natural endowments, and the gentleness and kindness of his disposition, or are less inclined to dwell upon recollections which charity should bury him with in the grave." Legaré, like any good orator, modulated his emphases with his audience. He could address Charleston alone, or

South Carolina chiefly. He could speak to the South, although for an author in and progenitor of a *Southern Review*, he was notably uninterested in developing a solidarity of sentiment in the region, save on slavery. He mainly wrote as a South Carolinian and an American, within his own rather special definition of nationality, which embraced as an intellectual imperative the merits of the cosmopolitan. [12]

Legaré showed little interest in influencing European opinion, in marked contrast to the Charlestonians of the eighteenth century for whom a kind word from a European was a ticket to local esteem, and to his Bostonian contemporaries who—though they spoke with rapture of American intellectual independence—felt justified by the praise of Carlyle for Emerson or of Hallam for Ticknor. Legaré was vain enough to notice any compliment, but recognition in *The Times* or praise from an old acquaintance of Byron had no special *frisson*. [13] Ticknor hunted out the intellectually distinguished of Europe as a pig hunts truffles, trained to it. But Legaré was notable in Europe for his diffidence. If he met Brougham, it should be in the normal run of social affairs, one gentleman and thinker coming across another. He did not enter Abbotsford with letters from Jefferson, or haunt the deathbed of Madame de Staël for an anecdote. Europe was a place to learn, not a pilgrimage. "We have too much national vanity, and too little of the far nobler feeling of national pride," he explained, long before Emerson. "There can be no true greatness either in individuals or in multitudes without self-reliance. Enthusiasm must be too intense to quail at ridicule, genius must soar above criticism, or there is no hope of excellence. We must learn to think only of truth and nature in what we do and say, and be contented with the applauses of our own people. Instead of slipping and paring away our energies to suit ourselves to the taste of foreigners, let us give them free scope, and trust to the sympathies of our neighbours, our friends, our brethren." [14]

Bearing the responsibility of the critic, he was unsparing and confident in his judgments. He disdained the "dainty, mincing, priggish" style of an Edward Everett. He admired boldness and reproved even Terence for peddling only the "perfectly genteel thing." "Since we must needs speak, we shall even speak out" was his motto. The reader should be in no doubt. The critic was advocate, hauling many unambiguously before the bar, invoking others as judges or character witnesses. Thus, in a review of the American translation by John Neal of Dumont's French edition of Jeremy Bentham's *Principles of Legislation*, the matter is forthright: "The style in which the author [in a

biographical notice] tells his story is full of a quaint pedantic affectation of simplicity. . . . He talks to his reader as if he were writing an
epistle to one of Jeremy's private secretaries, and as if the world had
nothing to think of but the 'High Priest of Legislation and the Lord
Bacon of the age.' The excessive importance which he attaches to every
thing connected with the Reformer and his dogmas redounds, of
course, upon his humble self. But he does not trust to distant
inference for his share in the honours of the school. His self-conceit is
fully commensurate with his admiration of his betters, and he takes
care to garnish his panegyric upon his master with an abundance of
garrulous egotism." The more weighty Thomas Moore was similarly
ticked off: "We certainly expected, from such a man, something
different from the awkward, glozing, parasitical apology, which he
has given to the public under the equivocal title of 'Notices of the Life
of Lord Byron'—to say nothing of a determined propensity for book-
making which appears in it." Bulwer Lytton's unhappy *Siamese Twins*
was swiftly dispatched: "We can scarcely help gaping even now, when
we think of the dreary and dismal waste through which, from a sheer
sense of duty, and with great effort, we have made a most tedious
journey. It is inconceivable, how so clever a writer as the author of
'Pelham,' should so completely have mistaken his walk, or have failed
so utterly to accomplish what he had in view. He has published two
hundred pages of satire without point, buffoonery without gaiety, and
doggerel without drollery or quaintness—the stupidest, without
exception, and most vulgar variety, of what is so expressively called in
French, *platitude*." The mighty were not exempt. Montesquieu was
condemned for "random epigrams."[15]

While it would be idle to claim Legaré as an intellectual radical,
nonetheless he had no small taste for the intellectually angular and
underprivileged. He tried to rehabilitate Aeschines against Demosthenes; he preferred Hector to Achilles; he dismissed Augustus as a
despot; he scorned "Napoleon's guilty and little ambition." Power,
especially its glamor, he mistrusted. Even his preference for settled
order was tinged with the heterodox, for he believed order to be
fugitive and endangered, the underdog of history.[16]

To those with a taste for intellectual butchery, a company that has
dwindled in modern times, Legaré offers pleasures. Irony was his
weapon, used not for insinuating self-doubt but by the accomplished
critic annihilating in an unequal contest the unaccomplishing author.
By quotation laced with commentary, he could demolish pretension.
Among many examples, his description of John Neal's first worship-

ping visit to Bentham is especially notable. This précis of the Duke of
Saxe-Weimar-Eisenach's naively documented travels is an example of
sustained irony: arrived in Boston, "His Highness established himself
at the Exchange Coffee-house, kept, we are informed, by a man who
had been 'a volunteer colonel in the last war, and who, according to
the custom of the country, still retained his old title, without feeling
himself above his present business. ['] Here he found himself in
excellent quarters, and soon began to experience those polite and
hospitable attentions for which our good friends in Boston are so
justly renowned. 'He had imagined that no one would take the least
notice of him in America.' We are not informed how he came to
conceive this extravagant notion, but it gives us great pleasure to
state, in his own words, that 'he soon found himself agreeably
disappointed.' " This is sly: "Mr. Grimké's assertion that the ancients
did nothing in ethics, struck us as one of the boldest (and that is
saying much) in his whole discourse." This upon Bentham is con-
clusive: "His nomenclature or terminology is a study of itself—as
complicated, if not quite so systematic, as that of the chemists. This
wrapping up of plain matters in the mysteries of artificial language,
which Hobbes destested so much, is Jeremy's great title to the
admiration of the world. He is the Heracleitus of the age." [17]

Strength of conviction made Legaré's expression strong, more than
supple. He had a variety of tones and a capacity for modulation, but
he tended to extremes. The blood of his victims must not merely flow;
it must spurt. The thing must be decisive. Legaré's prose inhabited a
vivid world, with the brightness of colors he so loved in Raphael.
Still, he was capable of delicacy, as in this gently ambivalent compliment, a bow fit for the deft acid of the drawing room, by which he
ended an attack upon Thomas Grimké: "Mr. Grimké's speculative
opinions we think utterly erroneous—his excellent example cannot be
too closely imitated—but it is unfortunately easy for all to repeat the
one, while few have the industry and perseverance to follow the
other." His prose failed most notably in its upper registers. He
admired and aspired to the sublime, but not successfully, as is
pointedly exemplified in this apostrophe to it: "It is spread over the
whole face of nature—it is in the glories of the heavens and in the
wonders of the great deep, in the voice of the cataract and of the
coming storm, in Alpine precipices and solitudes, in the balmy gales
and sweet bloom and freshness of spring. It is in every heroic achievement, in every lofty sentiment, in every deep passion, in every bright
vision of fancy, in every vehement affection of gladness or of grief, of

pleasure or of pain."[18] This was naming, not evocation. Legaré was strongest in logical exposition, not in inspiration. As he properly suspected of himself, he was a Cicero, not a Demosthenes; a baritone, not a tenor.

That he had trained as an orator before he practiced as an essayist might have been fatal had he not been an easy colloquialist. As it was, he brought from the podium to the study mixed blessings. He was betrayed into overreaching, overestimating the capacity of his prose to stir the emotions and effect the sublime. Rhetoric had begun with the spoken word, and it was logical that a theory of moral manipulation should have been fashioned by the Sophists, for in the pace of oratory the hearer is crowded by sound and gesture and impetus into yielding assent. Even as practiced by Legaré, oratory retained the ambition to invoke and use the sublime and the subliminal. But written prose is a colder medium. An author can achieve more complex and delicate lines of persuasion, but a reader has the prerogative of leisured reconsideration. Oratory's greatest gift to Legaré was the awareness that words have a sound and a rhythm, echoing in the head, tumbling in disharmony or held in balance. At its most trivial level, this explains a peculiarity of his writing: the frequency of his commas, which marked breathing pauses. Hastily glanced at on the page, his writing has a misleadingly fractured density. But Legaré wrote not for the eye but for the ear. Sounded, the labyrinth of punctuation vanishes in the nuances of emphasis and aside, in the intimacy with which he addresses the reader.

His prose, like his temperament, was a mixture of reason and passion. He could compose sentences of the utmost clarity and balance, as in this upon William Crafts: "He was more remarkable for the grace than the dignity, for the beauty than the strength of his person, and there was something effeminate in his exquisitely touching and melodious voice." He could also write with Gothic complexity, ideas and phrases elbowing their way into the sentence, disciplined only by the saving grace of an insistent habit of balance. This upon feudalism is sufficient evidence: "The revenues of kings at that time—all that did not spring out of their own domains—were merely the fruits and incidents of tenure. Such an income (stinted as it was), together with the obligation of every vassal to serve forty days in the year, might enable them to carry on war, according to the fashion of the times, when war looked more like a border foray and lifting of black-mail, or a sanguinary tournament and a gorgeous pageant, than (as we see it) a vast scheme of national ruin, concerted with the pro-

foundest calculation, and combining and commanding all the resources, with which wealth and science have armed the destructive
passions of the species."[19]

The mingling of complexity and simplicity was a conscious rhetorical strategy. He liked his prose to be seamless, with an overlapping
density that makes it hard to quote briefly or to compress. The logic of
the reader has difficulty breaking in upon the logic of the author.
Legaré's prose is hard to plunder or manipulate, which is part of the
reason why he has been so little *used* by later generations. The most
notable feature of writing upon Legaré is its evasiveness, its generality
of praise and indefiniteness of outline. The force of the mind and the
prose cannot be denied; yet its character yields only to patient
reconstruction of the simplicity of logic within the density of exposition. This difficulty is compounded by his easy use of languages and
information inaccessible to most. Yet he was an unpretending writer,
however much he tossed in quotations from Latin, French, Spanish,
and Greek. He used them with the freedom of his native tongue, and
thought such erudition the fruit not of difficulty but of effort available
to anyone.[20] He was seldom interested in seeming profound; his
ambition was to give ease to the complex. Legaré was the embodiment
of the mission of the nineteenth-century periodical: popularization.
He looked outward to the world, and few are less responsible for the
Alexandrianism of later years.

His mind ran to images, often of landscape, and he was best at the
elegiac mood. He was struck, because it was so opposed to his own
habit, by Byron's use of images drawn from human qualities to
describe natural phenomena. Legaré confessed himself "a man of
woods and streams," though his was the interest of the visitor, seeking
the energies of the wild for his moral imagination, rather than the
necessities of the agriculturalist. The exuberant disarray of nature was
the useful backdrop of human society, a corrective and a caution.
Once, in Brussels—vexed by the struggles of nullification of which he
heard so persistently in the letters of his Charleston friends, and
saddened by the news of Thomas Grimké's premature death—he
paused to reflect upon Grimké, Stephen Elliott, and John Gadsden,
all dead. So doing, he turned by instinct to the imagery of landscape
mated to elegy: "The worst of it is that, as such persons have never
been produced any where else in America than in the low country of
South-Carolina, so that soil is now worn out, and, instead of these
oaks of the forest, its noble original growth, is sending up, like its old
fields left to run to waste, thickets of stunted loblolly pine, half

choked with broom grass and dog fennel. Take it all together, there are few spectacles so affecting as the decay of our poor parish country, which I often think of, even at this distance, with the fondness of disappointed love."[21]

Most often was the image drawn from literature or history, as in this comment upon a passage of James Kent: "We regarded, with indulgence, the natural disposition of a mind much addicted to certain studies, to overrate their importance, and make their application as universal as possible—like the musician in Cicero, who explains every thing by the principles of harmony, and the dancing master in Molière, who considers his own art as the foundation of all the sciences." Most striking was the frequency of imagery drawn from disease, as when he compared slavery to syphilis, or observed of a bad translation of the *De Rerum Natura* that it was "Lucretius in the last stage of the dropsy, bloated even to suffocation, and utterly deformed." The motive for such language lay in hard personal experience. But pain was balanced by the benign imagery of South Carolinian nature, observed both nakedly and through the prism of literature. When Legaré wrote to Jesse Burton Harrison in 1828 in his elegiac mood, "Alas! Sir, I know how to sympathize with you & have the very same sort of objects to excite my feelings: decaying *Chateauxs*, once magnificent gardens & groves dilapidated & grown up in weeds & forests—old elegance and hospitality departing," he saw his native state through the eyes of Oliver Goldsmith. When he wrote of loblolly pine and dog fennel, he saw it through his own.[22]

He had a sensibility poised between convictions of fixity and change: part of him believed in the stability of human nature, part in the mutability of things; part was classic, part romantic. It was a dilemma characteristic of his times, which gave ample resources from which to ponder the tension. Legaré had been young in a South Carolina versed in the sensibility of the eighteenth century. He was mature in a world that tampered, albeit gingerly, with that sensibility. Choosing like most first-footing romantics, he opted for both and so became a sharpened critic of each.

On the side of order he committed a naked sense that human nature was unchanging, and morality an unprogressive and simple discipline. "Human nature being the same in all ages," he wrote, almost casually, it followed that "the science of morals has very properly been divided into two distinct kinds. The one contemplates man as an active being, having duties to perform and obligations to fulfil, approving good and disapproving evil, pursuing happiness and avoiding misery and pain. The other regards this moral constitution itself, as an object of inquiry and analysis, and aims at explaining its phenomena . . . in the same way as Natural Philosophy arranges and accounts for those of the material world. The former is obviously practical—the latter altogether speculative and metaphysical." As Adam Smith had acknowledged and anyone looking into Plato's *Dialogues* or Cicero's *Tusculan Questions* would discover, the ancients had arrived at a sufficient understanding of morality. Yet the moderns had made interesting and growing discoveries in the physical and intellectual motives for morality, perhaps with progressive effect, although Legaré was inclined to see changes in speculative philosophy as fashion, as much as advancement. "Hobbes had his day," he observed, "and a brighter one than any has had since, and is forgotten—then Locke followed—then Berkely and Hume—then Drs. Reid and Beattie—then Dugald Stewart (who is still at it)—and now we think that Kant is likely to take possession of all who will not be prevailed on to abandon the inside for the outside of the skull, and to study the *organic* philosophy." He noted, but did not take seriously, the accounts rendered by the nascent discipline of anthropology, for his imagination confined itself to European and American culture. Tartars might eat their fathers, Babylonian women might once in their lives become prostitutes, Zoroaster might enjoin incest, but these were to Legaré "the fee-faw-fum of misunderstood or apocryphal history . . . the horror-breathing figments of travellers—with which it is so easy to embellish a book of the 'sketches of man.' "[23]

In moral philosophy "the field of discovery" was "excessively confined and completely preoccupied," since there were no discoveries left in the heart, no "*terra incognita* in the mind of man." In mechanical philosophy it was otherwise, for experiment and demonstration made boundless the astronomer's or chemist's analytical researches. As Hume had said, philosophers tended to become grammarians disputing with words rather than profound controversialists over substance. For "the rules of morality are few and simple. Follow nature, as the oracle said to Cicero. Love your neighbour, and indulge, without fear of consequences, the promptings of an honest heart. The duties of life are, generally speaking, plain and obvious to any man of common capacity, and woe to those who consider them as problems, as matters of recondite and perplexing science, which all the powers of algebra are required to settle!" Morality followed from "pursuing happiness and avoiding misery and pain," a logic closer to the Epicureanism of Thomas Jefferson than to the embrace of alienation and pain by the gloomier romantics. By sentiment and allusion, this was Scottish and commonsensical. The Scots had bequeathed the most lasting monument of the American Enlightenment, reinforced for Legaré by his education at home and abroad. Elsewhere, doubting Winckelmann's environmental explanation of Greek cultural superiority, he observed with skepticism at himself: "For our own part, we are content to explain the phenomenon after the manner of the Scottish school of metaphysicians, in which we learned the little that we profess to know of that department of philosophy, by resolving it at once in an original law of nature: in other words, by substantially, but decently, confessing it to be inexplicable." This was a shrewd hit. The virtue of the Scots was to render the inexplicable self-evident, to diminish complexities and offer a usable circularity of logic.[24]

It followed that Legaré doubted the significant improvement or perfectibility of man. He was especially uncomfortable among those, including South Carolinians like Thomas Grimké, who proclaimed a dizzy future for Americans and mankind. This turned upon the old dispute between the ancients and the moderns. In seventeenth-century England the argument had hinged upon natural science, not morality or social progress, with the proponents of the ancients insisting that scientists need look no further than the texts of Aristotle or Hippocrates to fathom the stars or cure their patients. Bacon and Newton had annihilated that thesis, leaving an admission that Legaré and the eighteenth century had to make. No Charlestonian would sensibly look to an Aristotelian to cure him of the yellow fever, but however large this concession, it left ample grounds for contention in morals, politics, and literature. Here Legaré was inclined to stand with the ancients and against euphoric Americans. "It is curious to observe the revolutions in opinion," Legaré noted. "It was quite fashionable about 200 years ago, to compare the moderns, in their intellectual relation to the ancients, to a dwarf mounted upon the back of a giant—seeing further, indeed, from the advantage of position, but no more to be compared with the mighty being under him, than any other dependent, with him on whose bounty he subsists. In these times the picture is exactly reversed. The giant is mounted upon the dwarf, and is to go on, it seems, increasing in dimensions, until his stature shall reach the skies. The *superstition* of Europe believed too much of the past—the *enthusiasm* of America expects too much from the future." Grimké had prophesied that "in this autumnal age . . . a nation had arisen, European in language and descent, which has laid the foundations of literature broader and deeper than ever nation did before,—in the nature of man, in the character of universal society, in the principles of social order, in popular rights and popular government, in the welfare and education of the people." Legaré thought this nonsense.[25]

It seemed nonsense for various reasons, firstly that the Grimkés of America had not thought the problem through, so much knowledge being alien to them. Legaré was conscious that knowledge could grow obsolete, that "the erudite ignorance as Voltaire calls it" of scholasticism was as skillful and laborious as "the Science of Newton and La Place," yet still it had become "absolutely good for nothing either in practice or in speculation."[26] But no knowledge or insight was redundant by simple reason of age or distance. What Grimké lacked and Legaré possessed was an absence of mystery about the recondite. All was accessible: Homer, Boccaccio, Hobbes, Racine, Calderon, Greek, Latin, German, French—all could be handled by a sensible man of labor and intelligence. All was alive and tangible, even the dustiest folio vivified by the author's talent and the reader's caring intelligence. Nothing died but the incompetent.

This sense of accessibility was the gift of Legaré's view of human nature. Not needing to apologize for knowledge or empathy gave his discourse verve and freedom to roam. His mind and prose swarmed with men, books, events, the consciousness of time, in marked contrast to the mellifluous unallusive seamlessness of William Ellery Channing, whom—for all the difference—Legaré admired. Those with less stamina or care found pedantry in such tripping, and gagged at Legaré's recipes for education, given unselfconsciously though modeled on himself. "All we ask," he prescribed, was a thorough grounding for a boy between eight and sixteen in the ancient languages, which entailed "the principles of universal grammar," history, geography, "the chronology of all antiquity," and "a vast fund of miscellaneous literature besides." Imagination kindled, critical faculties disciplined, curiosity fired, the boy and so the man would "find himself in possession of the golden keys, which open all the recesses where the store of knowledge have ever been laid up by civilized man. The consciousness of strength will give him confidence, and he will go on to the rich treasures themselves and take what he wants, instead of picking up eleemosynary scraps from those whom, in spite of himself, he will regard as his betters in literature." The sentiment, "go on to the rich treasures themselves and take what he wants," was characteristic Legaré.[27]

Critical ecumenicalism bred cosmopolitanism. Latin in the early nineteenth century offered only the dregs of the humanist community of Erasmus' century. The cosmopolitan was now the master of vernacular languages. No incident is more evocative of this than the hours Legaré spent in 1819, crossing the Channel with the Archbishop of Jerusalem, conversing in Latin and Italian as the prelate read Syriac and was taunted in French. Cultures were instances, not bastions.

The strongest expression of cosmopolitanism was Legaré's passion for the civil law, a practical discipline learned chiefly through the Latin of the Pandects, Cujas, Heineccius, Grotius. Here Legaré's antique tastes threatened modernity. He wrote often that with the internationalism of commerce and manners, the civil law would become increasingly necessary and influential. "When we read a foreign author of our own day, we occasionally, indeed, remark differences in taste, in character and customs; but in general, we find ourselves *en pays de connaissance.* Modern civilization, of which one most important element is a common religion, is pretty uniform." Though "systems of positive law may differ," the civilians sought out the similarities that were growing with universal rationalization, the elimination of technical and arbitrary rules. "This tendency is, of course, increased by the progress of commerce and the intercourse of nations. Thus the *Lex Mercatoria*—the great body of the law merchant, is strictly *juris gentium*—and there would, at the present day, be very little discrepancy between the decisions of a French and English, and an American court, upon any commercial question." What was the *jus gentium?* It was not, as many misunderstood, the law of national peculiarities but the law of human nature. Convergence was plausible, because the underlying structure of human uniformity permitted, even required it. This proposition was reminiscent of Adam Smith, who also had been antique enough to intimate the modernity of a laissez faire political economy. For the Scottish Enlightenment had been nurtured by the humanism of the civil law, the eminent domain of Latin. Adam Smith had sought to define an economics to fit the natural law of Grotius and, especially, Pufendorf.[28]

The foregoing denotes the Legaré who preferred fixity and timelessness, by a restful instinct for the essential. This was only half of him, perhaps not the more important half, though the half whose stolidity and contempt for progress has puzzled and outraged scholars who have found him out of joint with his American times. But there was also Legaré the romantic.

Most notable was his historicist sensibility, a care to define how time and place varied, how context mattered. "There is not a more common error," he once observed of commentators upon Magna Carta, "than to ascribe our own notions to those who have gone before us, and to suppose that in politics, the same words always mean precisely the same things." One virtue of studying the originals, including the classics, lay not in asserting the similarities of ancient and modern but in measuring the distance. "Compare the knowledge," he asked, "which a scholar acquires, not only of the policy and the *res gestae* of the Roman emperors, but of the minutest shades and inmost recesses of their *character,* and that of the times in which they reigned, from the living pictures of Tacitus and Suetonius, with the cold, general, feeble, and what is worse, far from just and precise idea of the same thing, communicated by modern authors. The difference is incalculable. It is that between the true Homeric Achilles, and the Monsieur or Monseigneur Achille of the Théâtre Français at the beginning of the last century, with his bob wig and small sword. When we read of those times in English, we attach modern meanings to ancient words, and associate the ideas of our own age and country, with objects altogether foreign from them." So Legaré took great pains to jar his reader out of a modern complacent understanding, to see the past without anachronism. "We are in quite a new world," he wrote of ancient Greece. "Manners and customs, education, religion, national character, every thing is original and peculiar. Consider the priest and the temple, the altar and the sacrifice, the chorus and the festal pomp, the gymnastic exercises, and those Olympic games, whither universal Greece repaired with all her wealth, her strength, her genius and taste—where the greatest cities and kings, and the other first men of their day, partook with an enthusiastic rivalry, scarcely conceivable to us, in the interest of the occasion, whether it was a race, a boxing match, a contest of musicians, or an oration, or a noble history to be read *to* the mingled throng." Here he dissented from the Scots who, though they spoke of and wrote much history, were too absorbed in defining the principles of human sympathy to seek out and celebrate the discontinuities of time and cultures. On the other hand, it was not unsurprising that a man versed in the scholarship of the civil law should have had an instinct for historicism. The legal scholars of the French Renaissance, men such as Jacques Cujas and François Hotman, by meditating upon the mutations of Roman law in medieval France, by struggling with texts by ingenious philology, by adapting the traditions of Italian humanism, had arrived at an intimation of historicism flawed less by theory than by weak technical accomplishment. With these Legaré was very familiar, and he consistently paid tribute to their improvement and critical reinterpretation of a corrupted civilian tradition. The Abbé Terrasson, a later exponent, he had occasion to observe, had been among the first to attempt a reconstruction of the Law of the XII Tables, an attempt to be perfected by Barthold Georg Niebuhr in the nineteenth century.[29]

Changing between time and place, and mattering deeply in Legaré's thought, was national character—the spirit of culture— whether expressed in literature, jurisprudence, or politics. Literature, especially among the Greeks, "springing out of their most touching interests and associations—out of what would be called, by German critics, their 'inward life,' " was itself a social force, not inert like the classical learning of bookworms but interwoven into the very frame and constitution of society. For Legaré the chief recommendation of recent scholarship was to transcend pedantic antiquarianism and come to terms with "the true genius and spirit of laws and institutions" in a way more satisfactory than "the random epigrams" of Montesquieu because more systematic and philosophical. Political forms and legal systems were indeed influential and more than worthy of analysis, but their evolution was dependent upon the spirit that created meaning. For example, "Magna Charta was the means of bringing back the feudal aristocracy to its first principles—one of the worst governments upon the whole, as a practical system, that ever existed—yet, Selden and Coke and Hampden, regenerated the government of England by bringing it back to the principles of Magna Charta, as explained in an enlightened age. So pliable are all political forms—so absolutely do they depend upon the spirit which animates them, and the sense in which they are interpreted. So fortunate was it for the people of England, that by a series of events, the bold and proud character which was at first peculiar to her barons, became common to her whole people."[30]

So powerful was this spirit of national character that it could be expected to remold and reform political institutions, even after constitutional debacle. Once, contemplating the possible breakup of the United States, Legaré speculated, that while the Union was perhaps "the cause of all our liberties" and "its dissolution would make their duration far more uncertain," all would not be lost. New England would retain its popular institutions. In other states, "peculiarities in their situation," would make matters less clear, "but we have no reason to despair of any. The first, almost the only question in such matters is are the people prepared for free institutions. It is the national charac-

ter that is to be looked to when we talk of constitutions—it is the
national history that is to regulate our conjectures about the future."
So crucial was national spirit that patriotism amounted to a moral
obligation. That Byron had been disloyal to England was one of the
gravest charges Legaré could think to bring. "Except the admirable
lines on Childe Harold, in which he describes England as the 'invio-
late island of the sage and free,' we do not, at present, remember one
syllable in all his works, from the *spirit* of which, it could be fairly
inferred that he was even a citizen, much less a hereditary counsellor,
lawgiver and judge—one of the privileged and honoured few—of that
famous commonwealth. Yet England had done nothing to injure him
. . . . And even if he had suffered injustice at her hand—could he
have suffered more than Dante, or, suffering less, might he not have
blushed to contrast, in this respect, the writings of that immortal
victim of persecution with his own?" True to this, Legaré mistrusted
his own pleasure in visiting Europe and reminded himself that
expatriation was no virtue, and that Byron's self-characterization of
"citizen of the world" betrayed vice.[31]

Such emotional nationality echoed Legaré's view of the imagination
and man's capacity for access to the sublime, which it was not the
business of education to stunt by narrow concentration upon utility.
Education was meant not mainly to produce "druggists and apothe-
caries, or navigators and mechanists" but "to form the *moral* character"; not to kill with "barren precepts" but to fashion the sensibility by
"heroical models of excellence," warmly inspiriting. For what was the
object of a liberal education but "to make accomplished, elegant and
learned men—to chasten and to discipline genius, to refine the taste,
to quicken the perceptions of decorum and propriety, to purify and
exalt the moral sentiments, to fill the soul with a deep love of the
beautiful both in moral and material nature, to lift up the aspirations
of man to objects that are worthy of his noble faculties and his
immortal destiny"? And what was poetry but "an abridged name for
the sublime and beautiful, and for high wrought pathos[?] It is, as
Coleridge quaintly, yet, we think, felicitously expressed it, 'the blossom and the fragrance of all human knowledge.' " Such poetry was
pantheist, "spread over the whole face of nature." It lay in every
human deed or passion that created "the deep, the strictly *moral*
feeling, which, when it is affected by chance or change in human life,
as at a tragedy, we call sympathy—but as it appears in the still more
mysterious connection between the heart of man and the forms and
beauties of inanimate nature, as if they were instinct with a soul and a

sensibility like our own, has no appropriate appellation in our language, but is not the less real or the less familiar to our experience on that account." These mysteries were important because moral, instructive by making man conscious of his smallness in the scheme of things; they taught resignation and submission; they expressed ambition and made failure tolerable; they served, in short, many of the usual purposes of religion.[32]

Religion itself played a small part in Legaré's cosmogony, an offshoot of these mysteries rather than their cause. Religion was poetry, and so Legaré preferred Milton, whose verse he carried *vade mecum,* to the scriptures. The Bible was of use in discussing whether Hebrew poetry could be made to fit modern critical theories, but theology was Whiggishly useful even if intellectually limited: "Take this very principle of utility for an example. In the hands of Paley, it is quite harmless—it is even, in one point of view, a beneficent and consoling principle. It presupposes the perfect goodness and wisdom of God; for the rule of moral conduct, according to that Divine, is His will, collected from expediency. This—whatever we may think of its philosophical correctness—is a truly christian doctrine, christian in its spirit and its influences, no less than in its origin and theory." Thomas Grimké had insisted that Christianity, especially that of the Reformation, had rendered the ethics of the ancients supererogatory, but Legaré was cagey. He quoted Grimké, with sly parenthesis, " 'that in every department of knowledge, whether theoretical or practical, where thinking and reasoning are the means and the criterion of excellence, our country must, if there be truth and power in the principles of the Reformation (and that there is, no man entertains so little doubt as Mr. Grimké) surpass every people that ever existed,' " and he could suggest that disquisitions on the Garden of Eden were less than riveting, though they were becoming the stock-in-trade of romantics for whom the Fall was a potent allegory of man's alienation. The Huguenot could not cry havoc on Christ, nor would he have wanted it. Did he not politely note that revealed religion was "by far the most serious and engrossing concern of man"? So Legaré conceded the point, with irony sufficient to indicate that the concession was something to keep his sister and mother happy. "We have been always accustomed to think, that if those [ancient] refined ages have left us anything, in any department of knowledge, of which the excellence is beyond all dispute, it is (after the Greek geometry, perhaps) their moral philosophy. We presume it will not be considered as derogating from their merit in this particular, that they did not by mere dint of reasoning, *a priori,* make themselves partakers in the benefits of the Christian Revelation. Neither do we conceive ourselves responsible for certain strange customs and heathenish practices, into which they occasionally fell, in their conduct and way of living . . . . We concede, therefore, to save trouble, that their morality—that for instance of Rome in the time of the first Punic war—would not be good enough to stand the *severe* censure of London, of Paris, or of New-York." "The grand idea of Religion," Alexander Everett was to marvel, "which lies at the bottom of the whole, does not seem . . . to have made any impression upon him."[33]

Yet religion hinted at mystery, as did poetry and the music of Handel and Gothic cathedrals and great waterfalls, the more sublime for being inexplicit. So Legaré found deism not intellectually mistaken but emotionally thin. He spoke partly of himself—though only partly—when he wrote to the editor of the *Southern Literary Messenger* in 1838 and commented on a shared quality of modern writers: "They almost all *feel* the want of *faith,* as they love to call it—faith in religion, faith in morals—*faith* in political doctrine, faith in men & women. There are proud blasphemies, there are wild ravings, there is demoniac phrenzy & moonstruck madness, but they believe & tremble—or what comes to nearly the same thing, they tremble that they do not believe. There is a craving void left aching in the hearts of the present generation. They are rebuilding the temple which the 'march of mind' had demolished, & putting away their proud philosophy to become as little children before their long desecrated alters. . . . The age of sciolists, called Age of Reason, is past with them."[34]

This sense that reason merged emotion with rationality gave Legaré's social understanding an instability. Emotion, being mobilized, could be wayward. Politics could not, as David Hume had hoped, be reduced to a science. "The springs and causes which operate in human events are so mysterious, so multifarious, so modified by the slightest circumstances, the most subtle and shadowy influences, that nothing is more unsafe than a political theory. The test of accurate knowledge in matters of inductive science, is to be able to predict the effects of any given cause . . . . But a politician should avoid prophecy as much as possible. Hume exemplified this in the instance of Harrington, who thought he had found out the secret of all government in the arrangements of property, and, on the strength of his discovery, ventured to affirm most confidently that monarchy could never be re-established in England. The words were scarcely written before the prediction was falsified by the restoration." Little wonder that Legaré was fond of Edmund Burke and, like so many contemporaries, used the French Revolution as a great fund, illustrating the dangers of speculation and the vagaries of life.[35]

Legaré's intellectual generation gave him a great debate on which to make these perspectives turn: the dispute between classicism and romanticism. He followed the controversy with care and interest, noting both its origin and its usefulness. He judged that its chief source was Germany, in those days when one could with justice say (August von Schlegel had immodestly made the claim himself), "The Germans are, of all nations that ever existed, the fairest in their criticisms upon others. Their studies are too enlarged for bigotry, and excessive nationality hás never, we believe, been numbered among their faults." And he judged correctly both the motive and the nature of these studies in a passage worth extensive quotation: "Since the beginning of that struggle, which resulted in the deliverance of German literature from the bondage of French authority and a servile imitation of foreign models, a new order of researchers, and almost a new theory of criticism have been proposed by scholars. It has been discovered that there is no genuine, living beauty of composition which springs not spontaneously, if we may so express it, out of the very soil of a country; which is not connected with the history, animated by the spirit, and in perfect harmony with the character and opinions of its people. It has been found that all imitative or derivative literatures are in comparison of the truly primitive and national, tame, vapid and feeble—that Roman genius, for instance, did but dimly reflect the glories of the Attic muse, and that, even in the *chefs d'oeuvre* of the Augustan age of France, replete as they are in other respects with the highest graces of composition, the want of this native sweetness, this 'color of primeval beauty,' is universally complained of by foreigners. The German critics, therefore, and, after their example, many others have, within the present century, busily employed themselves in tracing the history of modern literature up to its sources, with a view to show its connection with national history and manners. The repositories of antiquarian lore have been ransacked for forgotten MSS. The oldest monuments—the most scattered and mutilated fragments have been brought to light, and collated and compared. The simplest traditions, the wildest fictions, the superstitions of the common people, the tales of the nursery and the fireside, legend and lay, and love-ditty and heroic ballad, have been all laid under contribution, to furnish forth such pictures of national manners, and 'to show the very age and body of the times' which produced

them, 'its form and pressure.' " This was to discriminate against the
not inconsiderable claim of the Scots to have been the progenitors of
historicism.[36]

Legaré read and pondered the latest literature and scholarship:
Goethe, Herder, the Schlegels, Savigny, Niebuhr, Wordsworth, Coleridge—these and many others. He pondered as far as his taste would
take him, which was short of the most abstruse of German metaphysics. Schelling, Fichte, and Hegel, even the precedent Kant, were too
cloudy for him. "Nothing is more possible," he confessed, "than that
we are ignorant of the understanding of these writers, instead of
understanding their ignorance, according to the distinction of an
ingenious admirer of the philosophy of Kant [Coleridge, in the
Biographia Literaria]. Be it so. We do, however, for our own part,
cheerfully resign these thorny and unprofitable studies to those who
profess to comprehend and to read with edification such things as the
Theaetetus of Plato or the cloudy transcendentalism of the German
school." And he added, in rueful footnote, "We really debated with
ourselves a long time whether we should venture to encounter those
awful personages, the Metaphysicians," and by way of commentary
quoted from the Aeneid about the Underworld, of "Gods whose
dominion is over the Souls, Shades without sound, Void, and you,
Burning River, and you, broad Spaces, voiceless beneath the night."
This indifference to epistemology extended even to Legaré's discrimination of the Scottish Enlightenment, for he was as uninterested in the
formal psychology of common sense philosophy, exemplified by
Thomas Reid, as he was absorbed by the social meditations of Hume
and Stewart. He was to react with irritation when the American legal
commentator David Hoffman felt it necessary to preface law with
metaphysics, a discipline "in the last degree unprofitable as a science."
Moreover, Legaré's indifference, since it scanted an epistemology that
struggled mightily with the problem of man's place in nature, meant
also his neglect of the racist anthropology that was sketched in the
speculations of Lord Monboddo and Lord Kames and became so vital
in the thought of many Southerners.[37]

The critic Legaré heeded most was August von Schlegel, the
accessible popularizer of German Romanticism. The poet he wrestled
with, as casting most light upon modern times and upon Legaré
himself was Byron. It was in an essay on Byron, with a digression on
Schlegel, that Legaré most considered the controversy of classic and
romantic.

"The distinction . . . originated in Germany," he began. "It was

August Wilhelm von Schlegel, after Adolph Hohneck.

seized by Madame de Staël with avidity, as well adapted to her
purposes of metaphysical, mystical and ambitious declamation, and it
has since been entertained, with more respect than we conceive it
deserves, in the literary circles of Europe. A.W. Schlegel, in his
valuable Lectures upon Dramatic Poetry, makes it the basis of all his
comparisons between the ancients and the moderns in that art." Both
accuracy of scholarship and the German philosophical temperament
in Schlegel induced, by a comparison of Greek and modern drama, a
belief that "in all the arts of taste, the genius of modern times is
*essentially* different from that of the Greeks, and *requires*, for its
gratification, works of a structure totally distinct from those which he
admits to have been the best imaginable models of the classic style."
Schlegel explained the distinction by religion. The "gay, sensual and
elegant mythology" of the Greeks "addressed itself exclusively to the
*senses,* exacted of the worshipper only forms and oblations, and confirmed in him the tranquil self-complacency or the joyous spirit
which the face of nature and the circumstances of his own condition
inspired." But in Christianity, to quote Schlegel, "every thing finite
and mortal is lost in the contemplation of infinity; life has become
shadow and darkness, and the first dawning of our real existence is
beyond the grave. Such a religion must awaken the foreboding, which
slumbers in every feeling heart, to the most thorough consciousness
that the happiness after which we strive we can never here ob-
tain. . . . Hence the poetry of the ancients was the poetry of enjoyment, and ours is that of desire; the former has its foundation in the
scene which is present, while the latter hovers between recollection
and hope . . . . *The feeling of the moderns is, upon the whole, more intense,
their fancy more incorporeal, and their thoughts more contemplative.*"[38]
     To much of this, Legaré was "disposed to assent . . . . We think
that Modern Literature does differ from that of the Greeks in its
*complexion and spirit*—that it is more pensive, sombre and melancholy,
perhaps, we may add, more abstract, and metaphysical—and it has,
no doubt, been 'sickled o'er' with this sad hue, by the influence of a
religious faith which connects morality with worship, and teaches
men to consider every thought, word and action of their lives as
involving, in some degree, the tremendous issues of eternity." But
this was as far as Legaré would go. "The *spirit* . . . is changed . . . but
does this alter, in any essential degree, the *forms* of beauty? Does it
affect the *proportions* which the parts of a work of art ought to bear to
each other and to the whole? Does it so far modify the relations of
things that what would be fit and proper in a poem, an oration, a

colonnade, a picture, if it were ancient, is misplaced and incongruous now? In short, has the philosophy of literature and the arts, the reason, the logic . . . undergone any serious revolution?" Schlegel was convinced that it had, but Legaré was unsure.[39]

For one thing Schlegel was inclined to compare like with unlike, ancient sculpture with modern painting, or ancient melody with modern harmony. In architecture, for instance, modern taste hinted at a preference for the Gothic. No doubt, Legaré admitted, with a memory of Antwerp in 1819, "a Gothic cathedral has its beauties . . . . The origin of the style was in a dark age; but it has taken root, nor is it at all probable that, so long as Christianity shall endure, the modern world will ever be brought to think as meanly of these huge piles, as a Greek architect (if one were suddenly revived) possibly might. Still, there are very few builders of the present age who do not prefer the orders of Greece—and, even if they did not, how would that prove that future ages would not?" In so arguing, Legaré was disdaining to accept a central point of Schlegel, that the classic had separated genres, while the romantic had mingled them.[40]

One needed to distinguish between essential and accidental, form and associations: "Suppose the object described to be twilight. If the pictures were confined to the *sensible phenomena,* it is obvious there *could not be* any variety in them, as any one who doubts what is obvious to reason, may convince himself by comparing parallel passages in the ancient and modern classics—e.g., Milton's lines, 'Now came still evening on, and twilight gray', Virgil's beautiful verses on midnight, in the fourth Aeneid, Homer's on moonlight in the eighth Iliad. The exquisite sketches . . . are all in precisely the same style, and, if they were in the same language, might easily be ascribed to the same age of poetry." This was essence. There were, to be sure, contingent associations of ideas or circumstances that would make a very material difference. "For instance, Dante's famous lines on the evening describe it, not as the period of the day when nature exhibits such or such phenomena . . . but by certain casual circumstances, which may or may not accompany that hour—the vesper bell, tolling the knell of the dying day, the lonely traveller looking back, with a heart oppressed with fond regrets, to the home which he has just left—very touching circumstances no doubt to those who have a home or have lived in Catholic countries, but still extraneous, and it may be, transitory circumstances." Thus spirit and associations could vary, but "ideal beauty, with which human nature, that never changes, will rest forever satisfied," could not.[41]

Yet it was a historical fact that the ancient and classical differed from the modern and romantic. The classical had unity of purpose, simplicity of style, and ease of execution. The romantic was the less as art for not having these qualities. "The superiority in their [the ancients'] exquisite *logic* of literature and the arts . . . is, we fear, a lamentable truth, nor will it help us much to call our deformities, peculiarities, and to dignify what is only *not* art with the specious title of the 'romantic.' " In short, Legaré conceded the historical point to Schlegel but bridled at the implication that classic and romantic might be coequal, or the romantic superior.[42]

This discussion Legaré applied to Byron. For "Lord Byron's speculative opinions in literature, were . . . all in favour of the classical models. His preference to Pope is owing to this. . . . But," and this was a crucial "but," for Legaré as for Byron, "theory and practice are unfortunately not more inseparable in literature than in other matters, and of this truth there is no more striking example than the author of Childe Harold." Nothing more exemplified the conflict between theory and practice, classic and romantic, than Byron's *Manfred,* which Legaré deemed to be the poet's flawed masterpiece. Manfred's situation was classic, the lone hero struggling with the Fates. Yet the treatment was romantic, for the burden of Manfred's anguish was the internal demons of his moral imagination. "The *spirit* of Manfred is strictly modern or romantic. The air of abstract reflection, the moral musing, the pensive woe, which pervade it, are a contrast to the sensible imagery and the lively personifications of the Greek play [the *Eumenides* of Aeschylus]. Yet its *frame and structure* are strictly 'classical.' "[43]

As Legaré confessed, *Manfred's* special interest, for him as for Goethe, lay in Byron's "conception of Manfred's character and situation." The effect was religious: "We never take it up but with some such feeling as we conceive to have possessed of old the pilgrims of Delphi and Dodona, or those anxious mortals, who, like Count Manfred himself, have sought to learn the secrets of their own destiny, by dealing with evil spirits. The book contains a spell for us, and we lay our hands upon it with awe." What satisfied Legaré's aesthetic ambitions about *Manfred* was classical. Yet what drew him to the poem was romantic: the internal monologue, the tangle of remorse, "not self-condemnation for a mere crime or sin committed" but the exemplification of Byron's ruling idea. "That idea is that, without a deep and engrossing *passion,* without *love,* in short, intense, devoted love, no power, nor influence in the world, nor genius, nor knowledge, nor Epicurean bliss, can 'bestead or fill the fixed mind with all their toys;' and that a man may be completely miserable for want of such a passion, though blessed, to all appearance, with whatever can make life desirable."[44]

In this definition lay much of Legaré's melancholy, his struggles with ennui, his dissatisfaction at his own ambition even when fulfilled, his sense of "that dreariest of all solitudes, the utter loneliness of the blighted heart." And why should *Manfred* be more evocative for Legaré than *Childe Harold?* "The style of Manfred is more sober and subdued . . . is, indeed, remarkable for a degree of austere and rugged force." It embodied a spirit of resignation and submission to untoward forces, which Legaré felt himself to possess. For Byron usually lacked the morality of the disciplined and impartial spectator, that lauded by Adam Smith, which, "instead of consecrating the absurd conceits of vanity, the bitter moodiness of despite, the wild sallies of vengeance, the spirit of rebellion against restraint; the pride, envy, hatred, and all uncharitableness, which are the accursed brood of this concentrated *égoisme* . . . inculcates upon the aspirant that there can be neither happiness nor virtue where there is not resignation, and that it is not more the lot, than it is the duty and the interest of man, to acquiesce in the order of nature and of society."[45]

4

# Antiquity

WHEN LEGARÉ WAS YOUNG, American classicism was not learned but omnipresent and chiefly political; it traced itself in a Constitution defining republicanism, boasting a Senate, and inhabiting Greek temples. The eighteenth century in America produced no classical scholar, certainly no philologist, worthy of the name, but it had in abundance men who liberally mined the classics—mostly in translation—for precedent, maxim, and edification. The United States was too remote from the sites of antiquity to foster antiquarians, the *érudits* whom Gibbon used for their collections of texts, coins, inscriptions, bits of marble, vases. But the new nation, a lone republic in a world filling with imperial monarchies, was too close to the political forms of Athens and early Rome not to foster men who scoured Tacitus for illustrations of tyranny, Seneca for stern morality, Polybius for advice on political forms, and Plutarch for the encouragements and warnings of individual greatness.[1]

Legaré had in Thomas Pinckney the model of a classicizing Founding Father; at once soldier, diplomat, and Hellenist, he had been the best Greek scholar of his year at the Westminster School and carried a pocket edition of the Greek poets on campaigns. Pinckney was, Legaré remembered with fond but tempered praise, "the very best Hellenist (of a young man) that any part of America has ever had to boast of." Pinckney could read and translate Greek and had a usable library of the classics, but his knowledge was limited even when richer than those who knew of Cato only from Addison. Skeptically, Legaré grew up in this tradition, whose core was a belief that the classics were useful for the man of afffairs and should be undertaken with the high seriousness of the accomplished amateur. [2]

Aside from politics, the classics had flourished in the American eighteenth century only as fumbling pedagogy and scholarship. Nothing in this Legaré found usable. His dismissal brooked no appeal. "Professors of Greek and Latin in our numerous American colleges, in possession of comfortable livings, and discharged from all other duties and engagements, have dozed over their sealed volumes in . . . stupid unaspiring ignorance." A student got a "worthless smattering of classical literature," despite long and extensive years. At best he could turn into "uncouth or nonsensical English, the most exquisite beauties of poetry and eloquence, without so much as the remotest idea, of what it is that has recommended to the admiration of all ages, those 'Delphic lines,' whose unspeakable harmony he utterly destroys by a barbarous pronunciation." The abuse was so great that it became a puzzle how so practical an American race paid so much for so little. "Classical studies are good for nothing unless they be elaborate and critical. Better a thousand times that they were altogether exploded—that a boy should never so much as look into a Greek or Latin grammar—than waste upon the acquisition of such an imperfect knowledge of them, as for any practical purpose, just amounts to no knowledge at all, eight or ten of the most precious years of his life." No American scholar who fell beneath Legaré's eyes escaped a similar dismissal save George Ticknor and those few who lived in the immediate vicinity of Boston, "our Western Florence." [3]

Ticknor, as Legaré had intended to do, had studied the classics in Germany, an experience that compounded an appreciation of America as the classical dunce, standing in the corner of Western culture. Yet Germany could paralyze the classicism of Ticknor, Cogswell, Bancroft, and Everett as readily as it inspired. Germany was a torrent of new editions, ingenious emendations of familiar texts, great and dusty scholars, yet propounders of a new world view filtered through the old. So fresh was Germany that the spring of American classicism, English scholarship, came to seem muddy and useless, the titanic Richard Bentley aside, to whom even the German paid homage. [4]

Germany in the eighteenth century, like the United States in the nineteenth, had confronted a crisis in its scholarship of antiquity. While America's classicism was inept but politically relevant, Germany's had been erudite but sterile. The Old Humanism had tried to prolong classical literature by imitation but by 1650 had failed, to decline into the barren erudition of Halle, only partially vivified by Heineccius. "The School of Göttingen, as represented by Gesner, found a new use for the old literature," Sandys has explained. "Thenceforth, in learning Greek (as well as Latin) the aim was not to imitate the style, but to assimilate the substance, to form the mind and to cultivate the taste, and to lead up to the production of a modern literature that was not to be the mere echo of a bygone age, but was to have a voice of its own whether in philosophy, or in learning, or in art and poetry. The age of Winckelmann, Lessing and Goethe, was approaching." This was the New Humanism, first the use of the classics to stimulate the spirit of a vernacular national literature, then the unexpected ideology of a Germany fallen asleep upon the laurels of Frederick the Great's love for French culture but annihilated into regeneration by Napoleon. At the focus of *Neuhumanismus* was a new emphasis upon Greece, the center of sunlight and beauty. Greece was the more useful as an exemplar of nationality because Greek was the weaker legacy of a German Middle Ages, in which Latin had been the language of Germany's servility to powers spiritual and temporal beyond itself. Herder took Winckelmann's rapturous defense of Athens and turned it into a polemic against Rome. "*Latin* was from the first the enemy of German, which might have resisted it, had not Charlemagne and the monks let loose upon us the barbarous deluge of *Latin* literature, *Latin* religion, and *Latin* speculation. O that we had been an island like England! . . . *Latin,* being considered an end in itself, is ruining our education . . . . We must begin our reform by giving up Latin,—not as a learned language, but as a means of artistic expression and as a test of culture."[5]

Legaré was sharply aware of this intellectual revolution and shared its perspectives. He damned the "men of the sixteenth and seventeenth centuries, the Scaligers, the Casaubons, the Salmasius', the Gronovius' " as erudite and uncritical, "as ignorant and prejudiced as their vulgar contemporaries, who spoke no language but their mother tongue." He praised the new scholars who "have poured out a flood of light upon every controverted point . . . shaken many an established dogma, and exposed many a consecrated error." The need was for a philosophical and enlarged knowledge of antiquity. The historicist task was "to re-construct the fabric of Greek society—to give the body of those times its very form and pressure—to enable us clearly to perceive how far their institutions and opinions agreed with our own, or differed from them—to reveal to us the secrets of their thoughts, to translate the very language of their affections into our modern tongues, to make them objects of sympathy, and examples for conduct to us—in short, to bring their little world before us, not as an empty pageant, or a wild phantasmagoria, having neither relation nor resemblance to the things about us, but with all the force and impressiveness of a sober and ascertained, yet vivid and living reality."[6]

*Neuhumanismus,* to make its way, had had to fashion an apologia and thereby created a genre, the defense of the classics. In the twentieth century the genre became circumscribed, the protest of dons when scientist and sociologist moved upon the entrance requirements of ancient universities and were rebuffed, or not, with epigrams from Martial. In Legaré's day the genre was young, blocking out its tactics, persuaded that the defense was not small (that of the academy) but large (that of society). One had only to look at the new University of Berlin, the centerpiece both of Prussia's recovery and of the *Neuhumanismus,* to know that the stakes could be great. In Charleston the challenge came mainly from Thomas S. Grimké, Legaré's friend and rival, who held that the classics might be dumped from curricula without loss to sensibility or society. Legaré's response was a summary and restatement of the three traditions that converged upon him: the political classicism of America, the literary controversy of ancients and moderns inherited from England, and *Neuhumanismus.*[7]

Certain things seemed so obvious that he was pained to observe the necessity even to mention them. Yet Grimké was not an isolated case of Philistinism but the symptom of a "grievous malady . . . rapidly becoming epidemical." So it was needful to assert that the distinction between civilization and barbarity was worth preserving, that a utilitarian education was not even likely to be useful if it neglected the necessity of firing the imagination, that literature both ancient and modern was morally instructive. These were general considerations, as relevant to Milton as to Sophocles. But the ancients had special recommendations, made clearer by German scholarship. Greece was a special instance, a "lonely brightness" exemplifying a harmony of thought and action, style and substance, possessed of a rich and extraordinary language as near to perfection as man had contrived. It was no small matter that the classics were so embedded in Western literature that ignorance of the ancients would render even the vernacular unintelligible; that the ancients were crucial to the formation of Western religion; that the civil law made no sense without a knowledge of the antique. It was of some moment to an American that the classics inculcated a spirit of liberty, the same republicanism that Milton of the *Areopagitica* had learned: "Much better to imitate the old and elegant humanity of Greece, than the barbaric pride of a Norwegian or Hunnish stateliness; and . . . despise that slavish and nauseating subserviency to rank and title, with which all European literature is steeped through and through. If Americans are to study any foreign literature at all, it ought, undoubtedly, to be the Classical, and especially the Greek." It was not inconsequential that the English language itself was formed so largely by Latin that no one could feel the shape of his own idiom without the comparative understanding granted by studying the alien.[8]

It was for comparative learning that the classics were most useful because most relevant to grasping the modern, a point that Montesquieu and Dugald Stewart had not neglected. "A literary man should be master of various languages . . . to make him distinguish what is essentially, universally and eternally good and true, from what is the result of accident, of local circumstances, or the fleeting opinions of a day. That most invaluable of all intellectual qualities—which ought to be the object of all discipline, as it is the perfection of all reason—a sound judgement, can be acquired only by such diversified and comprehensive comparison. All other systems rear up bigots and pedants, instead of liberal and enlightened philosophers." Every school having its mannerism, and mania, only "constant access to the models of perfect and immutable excellence, which other ages have produced, and all ages have acknowledged" offered a cure. The contrast of individual peculiarities was mutually correcting. "If the tendency . . . of the modern or romantic style is to mysticism, irregularity and exaggeration—and that of the classical, to an excess of precision and severity, he would be least liable to fall into the excesses of either, who was equally versed in the excellences of both . . . . It is thus . . . and only thus, that sound critics, sound philosophers, sound legislators, and lawyers worthy of their noble profession, can be formed." This comparative instinct, with the belief that cosmopolitanism was the only foundation for an intelligent nationality, was the core of the last days of the *Aufklärung* and the first days of German romanticism, the essence of Goethe's conception of *Bildung* and the rationale of Ranke's bold assertion that all nations and ages were equidistant from God.[9]

Legaré had resisted romanticism as a canon of taste but not as a historical typology, partly because it had been anticipated by the Scottish Enlightenment. Adam Ferguson, in his *Essay on the History of*

*Civil Society,* had seen history as the growth cycle of human nature. Yet Ferguson had influenced not only other Scots but Herder; so Legaré mingled Edinburgh and Weimar when he argued that history had progressions and rhythms, in which antiquity had participated, in parallel with the progression of the modern European mind out of medieval darkness. The logic lay in human nature, in "the invariable progress of the human mind from a state of complete ignorance to that of the highest refinement. The first efforts of genius are . . . the spontaneous effusions of nature, uttered without any idea of rules, or pretensions to excellence, or fear of criticism. Out of the fulness of the heart the mouth speaketh. This is the whole sum and substance of the rhetoric and poetry of rude ages." The savage was graceful because he had a "consciousness of perfect equality" with his fellows. "No man is either sheepish, or stately and affected, until he has conceived the idea of a degree of excellence to which he feels that he has not attained, or of the terrors of a criticism to which he is apprehensive of being exposed. In this . . . . the day which condemns him to feel his inferiority robs him of (more than) half his grace and power." This general problem was exemplified historically in Europe. "The age of creative genius, of passionate eloquence, of vast and profound and adventurous imaginings came on early. It was immediately after—nay, rather coeval with—that of legends and troubadours—the daybreak, as it were, while twilight, with its spectral imagery and shadowy wonders, still lingered in the vale and the wood. It is such an age that produced Dante and Chaucer. Then came a long period of sterility and blank vacancy—the era in Italy, of the Filelfos and Poggios and Politians— of plodding, pedantic mediocrity, oppressed by its own acquirements and embarrassed by its own art, with just talent enough to perceive and to avoid the dangers of originality. A still more advanced age generally brings back the simplicity of nature, because it restores the confidence of genius—the Ariostos and Macchiavellis take the place of the Dantes and Boccaccios, and . . . the perfection of discipline and the absence of it . . . may be said to meet." This was the archetypal romantic rhythm: early naive grace, later formal pedantry, final complex simplicity. History had often swung through the cycle, possessed by the internal logic of a language and people. Homer became the Beowulf of the antique, Racine the debased modern Euripides. [10]

This typology hovered around and through Legaré's understanding of the ancient world, knotting the antique into the problem of the modern, directing but not mandating his discriminations. Legaré had special perspectives as a politician and lawyer. Schlegel had analyzed from the standpoint of dramatic literature for the needs of the modern German stage, mediated through the antique and Shakespeare. Legaré's various needs—law, politics, literature, ethics—could not be jammed into a single rhythm, and he made the effort only fitfully, as when he observed that Homer lived in a primitive society and the *Iliad* approached "the unaffected narrative style of an old border ballad," or compared Greek literature to that of Sismondi's Southern Europe, or saw in the Roman mimes the form of the commedia dell'arte, or designated Voltaire's and Goldsmith's styles as Attic. [11]

The American eighteenth century had preferred the Roman; the Germans had discriminated in favor of the Greek. Legaré gave his heart to the latter, his good sense to the former: the Greeks were extravagantly admired but scarcely to be emulated; the Romans were indifferently respected but accessible. Yet both offered models. As has been observed of Legaré's classicism, "antiquity was not something you received or enjoyed only; it was something you did." Legaré's strongest need for antiquity lay in his political and legal career as an orator. So at the center of his Greek and Roman worlds were Demosthenes and Cicero. [12]

Why was Greece preeminent? Why were "the thoughts of all men with curiosity and wonder, [fixed] upon the barren little peninsula between Mount Cithaeron and Cape Sunium, and the islands and the shores around it, as they stand out in lonely brightness and dazzling relief, amidst the barbarism of the west on the one hand, and the dark and silent and lifeless wastes of oriental despotism on the other[?]" There was the Greek language itself; rich, precise, unspeakably charming, flexible, "equally adapted to every variety of style and subject—to the most shadowy subtlety of distinction, and the utmost exactness of definition, as well as to the energy and the pathos of popular eloquence—to the majesty, the elevation, the variety of the epic, and the boldest license of the dithyrambic, no less than to the sweetness of the elegy, the simplicity of the pastoral, or the heedless gaiety and delicate characterization of comedy." This language of a race of marvelous boys Winckelmann had tried to explain by talking "very learnedly about a fine climate, delicate organs, exquisite susceptibility, the full development of the human form by gymnastic exercises, &c." Legaré was unsure of the causes but certain of the fact. For a man fond of mysteries, instructive and beyond reasoned analysis, this particular cultural mystery was gratifying. [13]

The core of Legaré's fascination with Athens (which, as was typical

Socrates' Last Interview with his Friends,
by Charles Fraser (1801); this belonged to Mitchell King.
Courtesy, Carolina Art Association/Gibbes Art Gallery

of his generation of classicists, was nearly all of his Greece)[14] was his belief that it was a peculiarly unified society. Style and thought were indissoluble; thought was tied inextricably to action. Grimké had tried to dissociate Greek style from Greek thought, a project Legaré deemed absurd. The Greeks were "more fastidious in regard to style than the moderns," yet style implied substance, both "chaste and natural" for a people "to whom any thing like the ambitious ornaments so much admired in this philosophic age, would have been an abomination." Likewise, thought and action were coequally esteemed. Along with Thucydides and Pericles, Sophocles was a general, one whose *Antigone* had gained him command of the Samian expedition. And the "verses of Euripides softened even the bitterness of hatred and hostility, and saved from butchery, in a war of extermination, all who were fortunate enough to be able to repeat them."[15]

At the focus of this unity was Demosthenes, ruled and ruling by force of language and action, and apogee of a unique race at its moment of greatest peril, severe to the point of austerity, channeled and morally sublime, vehement but polished, sinking the rhetorician's vanity in the statesman's obligations. Above all, Demosthenes melded man and nation, his power felt "rather than seen," speaking "more to the heart than to the ear." He came to embody, as Aeschines complained, "the Parthenon and the propylaea . . . the ancient achievements and the hereditary glory of Athens." Longinus founded upon Demosthenes' practice the *Treatise on the Sublime*. The Athenian's orations were "an experimental proof to us that . . . the effect of the highest order of speaking is not persuasion only, but rapture and ecstacy." Imagine "a union of the lofty declamation of Lord Chatham with the close, business-like, vehement and rapid debating of Fox," to guess at Demosthenes.[16]

For Legaré, Athens formed a nation, primitive and original, rooted in a place sanctified by religion and blood, alive with the "fountains of nature," popular mythology and "the exaggerated traditions of an heroic ancestry." This nationality was shared between lesser and greater, between "men of genius" and "even the populace," who absorbed "the same passionate love for that ideal beauty which is the object of the arts, and with somewhat of the same aspirations after excellence . . . an instinctive perception, or feeling rather, which enables them to discern and to enjoy it with all the delicacy and the sensibility of a refined taste." So unifying and primitive was this *Zeitgeist* that it antedated the invention of the private, the notion of personal property and natural rights. Greece had neither the advan-

tages nor follies of "society," and so could produce no students of
manners such as Molière: "Among the Greeks, there was very little of
what is known among us by the name of *society.* They had no home—
no family circle with its unreserved intercourse and social discipline,
no tea-parties, and tertúlias or soirées, and conversazioni. Your Greek
gentleman did not value himself very highly upon the exploits of the
drawing room or the amiable frivolities of our modern dandyism.
They lived for the public, and in public—in the streets, the prom-
enades, the *agora,* the porticoes, the gymnasia, and the theatres.
Their whole existence was a part which they played before the people,
as their tragic heroes acted theirs before its representative, the chorus." In this description, Legaré was following the sociological logic
of the "new rhetoric" that had come of age with Adam Smith and been
popularized by Hugh Blair: audiences of a special social nature created
the possibilities for the efficacy of words. [17]

This special unity was the secret of Demosthenes' sublimity and the
reason he could not be emulated. The orator was gifted with an
audience, in "every way better fitted at once to task and to animate, to
chasten and to restrain the genius of the orator . . . . this advantage
was twofold; first, as the Athenian audience was more thoroughly
democratic: second, as it was more refined." For the Greeks were the
most severe and wayward of critics: "The only thing in modern times
that affords any parallel is the love of the Italians for music, and their
skill as connoisseurs in it." It was a hard school, in which even
Demosthenes had at first failed. They howled when he mispro-
nounced, so he corrected. Yet this precise taste belonged "to the
wildest democracy that ever existed—a tumultuary and excitable
mob, wayward, fitful and refractory, alternately slave and tyrant—
now a passive instrument of the demagogue, then 'like a dev'lish
engine back recoiling' upon the rash hand that aspired to direct it."
And the orator was in the midst of events, a man who "might be said
to legislate with a halter around his neck . . . . A Turkish vizier is not
more deeply interested in the success of his policy and conduct, than
were the Athenian orators. We may judge what were the comforts of
such an existence—what 'joy ambition found' amidst the most splendid triumphs of the Bema—from the experience of Demosthenes
himself, who declared in the bitterness of his spirit, that had he his life
to live over, and there were only two roads before him, the one leading
to the public assembly, and the other to instant destruction, he
would, without hesitation, pursue the latter." It was a mixed compliment: that a social force, "all the elements of commotion, disorder

and excess" that Legaré so deprecated should produce the very eloquence he so admired, that the society he labored to prevent should create the sublimity he desired. The taste in his mouth, as he sat in Broad Street or Bull Street or on John's Island and wrote such words, aware that Charleston was eddying with political passions that it was his effort to restrain, must have been bitter.[18]

It was a resentment that applied not just to Athens but, by extension, to the situation of Legaré's generation, successors of an American Revolutionary generation to whom had been granted the sublime events that alone could create transcendent eloquence: focused, chaste, and important. The halter that had sat around the neck of the Athenian orator had, after all, sat around the necks of rebels against the sovereign majesty of George III. "The highest order of eloquence can no more be displayed except on occasions calculated to shake and to agitate the human soul, than heroic courage, which emanates from the same source, and is nearer akin to it than is commonly thought . . . . It is when a universal consternation prevails—when even the brave are mute with astonishment, and 'each in other's countenance reads signs of his own dismay,' that he who stands forth unmoved, and points out the means of deliverance, or leads the way to a noble self-devotion to honour and duty, is eloquent even without the aid of laboured language. This is the true account of Patrick Henry's reputation," as it was of the Declaration of Independence, that "immortal paper," that "bare recital of facts . . . wisely considered as the highest and the only eloquence which was consistent with the character of the occasion."[19]

If Legaré romanticized Greece, the rapture was limited to matters of poetry, taste, and political eloquence. About the society that underpinned Demosthenes, he had grave doubts. He admired its products; he had few illusions that he could wish to live near the Parthenon. In this he was cooler of historical judgment than many, even Herder, who had striven to give each culture sovereign rights over its own time and place but who took the metaphor of Greek cultural adolescence so seriously that he had the Greeks leaping and dancing with jollity amid the sunshine of the Agora. For Legaré, as for Thucydides, the popular assemblies of Athens were heartless, especially in the moments of their greatest power, for they confounded decrees with laws, executive with judicial powers, "the very definition of tyranny under every kind of polity" but "more intolerable in a popular than a monarchical or aristocratic form." The ancient philosophers who abominated democracy "saw that, as Burke expresses it, 'a mob has no heart,' for the same reason that a corporation is said, by Lord Coke, to have no soul. It retains only the harshest features, the most fearful and repulsive energies of the individuals that compose it." The Bema presaged Babeuf. Other ancient states arrived at mixed polities, but Athens lurched bizarrely between extremes. The ancient world in general, and Athens at particular moments, was overly inclined towards aristocracy or oligarchy. "Thus Plato and Aristotle both consider . . . the exercise of any mechanic art, as altogether inconsistent with the character of a freeman and a good citizen . . . . Every profession, of which the object is to make money, was regarded as illiberal—*their* word for ungentlemanlike. Thus, merchants were proscribed by Plato . . . . These opinions may be considered as the great vice of antiquity, and one among other causes of the superiority of modern institutions—that is to say, where feudal principles and notions have been exploded. What would Harrington ["who learned his republicanism in a good degree from these doctors"] have thought of our first Congress—of that truly Roman Senate, which declared our independence, and which carried us through the war of the Revolution? To speak disparagingly of professional men and tradesmen, as the founders of a commonwealth, in the country of Henry and Rutledge, of Franklin and Sherman, of Laurens and Morris, would be to advance a paradox not worth the pains of refutation."[20]

Antiquity had other vices, including no real sense of liberty. Here Legaré touched upon delicate ground. "The institution of domestic slavery, and that principle of their *jus gentium,* which doomed captives in battle to perpetual bondage" underlay the ancients' hierarchial views. "It is taken for granted . . . that Greeks were created to conquer and to control barbarians. Aristotle, in a grave inquiry, whether slavery be consistent with the law of nature, decides that it is so where one race is by nature inferior to another, and even justifies war, if it be necessary to subject the predestined bondman to his chains . . . . Liberty, in short, was rank and nobility among the ancients; and inspired the same sentiments for good and for evil. It was considered as the birthright—the hereditary dignity of certain races—but the idea that it was part and parcel of the law of nature and nations—that it was due in common justice to all mankind, seems to have occurred to very few, and to have been acted upon by nobody." Elsewhere he was undemonstratively precise about ancient slavery. Most South Carolinians would have shuddered to observe that Athens was defended by "a city-guard of from three hundred to twelve hundred public slaves (for the number varied at different periods), who lived in tents in the market-place, and afterwards on the Areopagus, and kept watch and ward over the peace of society." This even tone, the musing dryness of the parenthesis, "for the number varied at different periods," was at marked odds with the eager plundering of classical history and thought by proslavery writers, and stemmed from his historicism. Antiquity, for Legaré, was evidence, not proof. He knew that modern domestic slavery differed sharply from the ancient, not least in the connections between war, plunder, and slavery.[21]

Nonetheless, he did make sociological inferences between ancient and modern practice. Ancient slavery was more various in its recruitment, for "in an age of perpetual war, the slave-market was always well supplied, and the range of choice presented to a purchaser in it, was as great as the distance between ignorance and brute nature, and the highest cultivation of taste and talent." Yet it shared one effect with the modern. The omnipresent slaves of the wealthy reduced by competition poor freemen to dependence and into "the ready instruments and accomplices of unprincipled demagogues." "The same effect upon the labouring classes is noticed by Tacitus, at Rome, and it was mainly to remedy this very evil—which seems inseparable from the institution of domestic servitude, under certain circumstances— that the Gracchi undertook their 'reforms.' " The inference was unmistakable, for this last came in the final number of the *Southern Review*, when nullification politics was most tumultuous, when Unionists and nullifiers alike were cajoling the buyable poor into meetings and polling places.[22]

Legaré looked to the Greeks for grace, but not because he was indifferent to the violence that soaked the world of Demosthenes. His is a strikingly brutal vision of Greek society: its taxation mere plunder, its war ethnocentric and predatory, its life harassed by the conflict of rich and poor, its state all-engrossing and selfish, its political economy intolerable to the modern American. His devotion to Attic grace lay precisely in an astonishment that such sweetness of voice should have emerged from so wretched a social context.[23]

While he was disposed to see merit in ancient morality, especially in Roman *gravitas*, he found little of use in Greek philosophy, though he acknowledged Hellenic superiority over the imitative Romans, as so close a student of Cicero well might. For Aristotle, Legaré had great admiration but little service. The Categories were a miracle of comprehensiveness, acumen, originality, and copiousness, beside which the achievement of Hume was paltry. "Yet after all, for any one *substantial* purpose in literature or in life, of what use is all the logic of Aristotle? It is a question we have asked ourselves over and over again, after toiling for three or four hours together over his Analytics, and taking immense pains to possess ourselves of his whole train of thought. Every thing is admirable to look at—but *materiam superabat opus.*"[24]

As with logic, so with rhetoric. It was well to know the names of tropes or figures, but that was but a preliminary to action. And what Legaré most admired in the Greeks was the interpenetrations of thought and action. Left with Greek thought alone, he grew bored. But Greek ethics was another matter. He took pleasure in many of Plato's Dialogues, and read the Epicureans with interest if skepticism. Plato "thought that the great desideratum of moral discipline was, not to shew what are the duties of life, but to dispose men to perform them, and rather to make them enthusiasts in the love of virtue, than casuists and cavillers about the subtleties of doctrine . . . . His philosophy, therefore, has poetical colouring. It is delivered in a lofty and glowing strain, and addresses itself to the imagination, which it inflames and elevates with visions of perfection and hopes of bliss." This was visionary, useful in ethics but dangerous in politics. Plato's *Republic* was as pernicious as the *Meno* was uplifting, for its "mere vision" soared above the mundane, beyond even the utopias of Harrington and Sir Thomas More. "Compared with it, Telemachus, though a mere epic in prose, is didactic and practical." The best of Plato the social theorist was not the *Republic* but the *Laws.* For the rest, Plato was a good Sunday sermon: "When we read the writings of St. Paul, we are struck with the resemblance they bear . . . to the dialogues of Plato." This was not entirely a compliment.[25]

But a chief legacy of Greece was literary and dramatic. The orator was necessarily interested in the actor, and Legaré in Paris had haunted the stage, as he did the Chamber of Deputies. Greek comedy he judged inferior to the modern, because the most subtle of comedy flourished in the contradictions of private and public codes, and the Greeks had no private world. So the Greek drama, not only comedy, had fewer resources and thus fewer plots and characters, whereas "in the works of Molière, for example, we see the impress of a cultivated age. It was a period when manners were reduced to a system which was regulated by its own code—and that a most rigorous one—of usages and laws, and were infinitely diversified by the various tastes, pursuits and conditions of a very advanced stage of society. The perpetual intercourse of the *beau monde*—of the opulent, the educated, and the witty—for the sole purposes of pleasure and conversation, made it the study of every individual to approximate as nearly as possible to the approved standard of character and conduct, however arbitrary or artificial, and the exquisite sense of propriety, in reference to that standard, which was thus acquired, enabled them to detect the slightest deviation from it, and to expose it to an unsparing, though polished and elegant ridicule. The same state of things has continued ever since. Modern comedy has thus an unlimited range for the choice of its subjects and materials." But Greek comedy was a Tom and Jerry business, often amusing, often disgusting, especially in its Roman imitators, Plautus and Terence. For the convenience of curious male readers, he considerately provided references to scabrous passages. They were "*sui generis* . . . poems in the nature of comedy, (to borrow a phrase from the bar) rather than . . . comedies." Aristophanes was not subtle, not a "painter of individual character or . . . of private society" but "a severe satirist of public abuses—a vehement and relentless enemy of great state criminals, whom he thinks it quite fair to hold up to derision, even by the exaggerations of buffoonery and caricature, and to overwhelm with the most bitter and unmerciful mockery."[26]

Yet Greek tragedy endured undiminished, for it required not social nuance but poetic force. Aeschylus and Sophocles were incomparable, the distillation of the frightening unity of Greek culture turned upon itself. "Turn from the Oedipus Tyrannus to the Oedipe of Voltaire, which has always been considered by the French critics as one of that author's happiest efforts, and by some of them, we believe, as decidedly superior to the original. The difference between the Greek name, and the French mutilation of it, (bad as that is) is not, by any means, so great as between the things themselves. Even Racine, with all his admirable talents for this department of poetry, has fallen far short of the Greeks, whenever he has attempted the same subjects, as we think is clearly made out by Schlegel, in his comparison of Phedre with the Hippolytus of Euripides."[27]

The effect of Legaré's admiration for Greece was thus ironic. Those things he admired, the political oratory and the tragic drama, were beyond reach, locked in a vanished time and society. Rome too was gone. But the distances between Charleston and the Forum for an American republican were smaller, as the Romans were less grand, more accessible, less original, less decided, and so able to speak not to Legaré's loftiest sensibilities but to his common sense. Demosthenes was one at whose feet he could only stand in wonder; Cicero was a man to have to dinner. Demosthenes was God; Cicero was the local bishop, albeit of Saint John Lateran.

The romantics had tinkered with the reputation of Rome. Niebuhr had shifted attention towards the early days of the Republic and Savigny toward the later days of the Empire, when Roman law was about to vanish in complicated ways into medieval law. Something of a vacuum had appeared at the center, filled by Herder's polemics against the military imperialism of the Empire, the destroyer of populist worlds. Legaré took this modification of traditional views with more skepticism than he took the changes in Greece's reputation. For an American the practical consequences of a Romanizing constitution included a freezing of the eighteenth century's preferences, which had been already wary of Rome the despot, the shadow behind the enactments of George III. The Roman political theorists—and their modern interpreters, Machiavelli and Harrington, whom the Founding Fathers had consulted—were precisely those who resisted or reflected upon the brute power of the Julio-Claudians and spun a fine web of discourse about the virtues of a mixed polity and the old republic.[28]

Legaré had occasion to examine the early history of the republic, especially its literature, and was unenchanted. Its literature was too imitative of the Greek, and imitation was not a word of approval in Legaré's vocabulary (in which usage he was distinctly unclassical). "It was five whole centuries after the building of the city, before that nation of sages and warriors could boast of a single author. During this long period, there is no vestige of any thing that can be supposed to have been a regular composition in verse, except a sort of Pythagorean poem of Appius Claudius Caecus, mentioned by Cicero. The only history that can be given of their literature during all that interval . . . consists in the progress and improvement of the Latin language." Arrived, its literature was exotic, inferior, and servile. Indeed, many of the early authors of Rome, such as Livius Andronicus, were Greek slaves. The genius of early Rome was at war with literature, the Romans being a practical people suspicious of mere literary pursuits, devoted to *gravitas* and power. To have preferred the triumph of art to that of war would have marked "a despicable effeminacy and poorness of spirit in a young man." Yet such an "aversion from literary pursuits" stemmed from a systematic and enlightened policy. "Their scheme of conquest had been organized with profound wisdom, all the departments of their government were filled with consummate skill and ability, and in every sense of the word, 'there was nothing barbarous in the discipline of these barbarians.' " Thus Cicero was diffident of his philosophical writings and "felt the studies of Plato to be somewhat unworthy of himself," Virgil designated his pursuits " 'studia ignobilis otii,' and there is a remarkable passage in the life of Agricola, which shews that, even in his time, the dignity or the duties of 'a Roman and a Senator' did not permit him [Agricola] to be very profoundly versed in philosophy and learning."[29]

Therefore the early history of Rome did not, like Homer's Greece or Dante's Tuscany, excite a literary interest. The Etruscans were obscure and probably deserved to be, and it was with amused disdain that Legaré considered the various ingenious antiquarian and philological theories accounting for their origin and influence upon Rome: "Judging from our own distaste for antiquarian researches, we suppose our readers to be as little inclined to receive, as we are to furnish, a detailed account of the various hypotheses, or rather wild guessing, to which this puzzling question has given rise." The Etruscans were variously held to be Lydians, Celts, Phoenicians, Egyptians, Pelasgians, Canaanites, or simply aboriginal (according especially to Lord Monboddo, who had a fondness for aborigines and anthropophagi). More important than origin was influence, the transmittal to Rome of a military precedent and "divination, which seems to have been taught in Etruria as a regular system or science—a sort of art for the interpretation of natural signs—and of which, the mysteries or occult doctrines and ceremonies were confided only to some privileged families." This mysticism, Legaré believed, was a significant underpinning of the Roman state. But the literature of pre-Augustan Rome was most interesting when extant only in fragments, as with Ennius, and of doubtful worth when available, as with Plautus and Terence.[30]

Catullus and Lucretius were more worthy. Yet Catullus was commendable because "most of a Greek, not by study and imitation, but by nature. His lively wit, his voluptuous character, his hearty affections, his powerful imagination, seem naturally to overflow in verse. . . . His amatory poetry is less tender than that of Tibullus— and less gay and *gallant* than that of Ovid—but it is more simple, more cordial, more voluptuous than either. A modern reader would be very much disappointed if he expected to find in it that delicacy of sentiment—that *culte des femmes*—that distant, mysterious, and adoring love which inspired the muse of Dante and Petrarch, and which ever since has characterized the amorous ditties of our sonnetteers. The passion of Catullus had not a particle of Platonic abstraction in it—it was as far as possible from being metaphysical. It is deeply tinged with sensuality . . . . It is that 'drunkenness of soul' of which Byron speaks." Most especially was Catullus notable for the Galiambic ode, which even Julius Caesar Scaliger, who usually disdained the poet for vulgar ribaldry, had been obliged to praise. There can have been no such resistance in Legaré, for its theme—the eunuched priest of the Idaean Goddess, running for the night with the Gallae and the Maenades in Bacchanalian revelry, only to awake on a perfect morning to the desolate appreciation of his final and multilated physiognomy—matched precisely the Charlestonian's melancholy sense of self.[31]

Lucretius was remarkable for making poetry out of such unpromising material, doing justice to both the atomic philosophy of Epicurus and the felicity of verse, offering "the most beautiful strains of inspiration and harmony" even "in the midst of a concourse of jagged or polygonal atoms," to "blossom forth like wild flowers." As with Lucretius, so with Virgil in the *Georgics,* a poem often dear to the heart of classicizing Southerners. Yet for Legaré its "high-wrought and studied elegance of which it is scarcely too much to say that no writer was ever so great a master as Virgil," arose despite an agricultural theme. "The wonder is how the poet was able to reconcile his genius to his subject—how he could describe a plough for instance, without either sinking down into prose, or elevating his style so far above the matter, and how he has contrived to throw a sort of Epic dignity and animation without any air of burlesque, into his pictures of the Bee-hive. . . . the perfection of the Georgics is unapproachable in Didactic poetry, and were it not that we have that work and Lucretius De Rerum Naturâ before our eyes, we should even doubt whether the very phrase 'Didactic poetry' were not somewhat of a contradiction in terms."[32]

The Augustan age was most admirable because the roughness of Roman practicality was most softened by an effective admiration for Greece, thus permitting "that perfect civilization and full and dazzling development of literary genius, with which . . . a cruel reverse of fortune has forever identified the fame of a usurper and a despot." For Legaré's Latin tastes were Greek; the involuted complexities of which Latin was capable were repellent. Lucan he had never been able to read through. Tacitus he admired for republican sentiments and portraits of imperial horrors, but not for intimidating brevities and wanton idiosyncrasy. "Lucan, Statius, Silius Italicus, and *tous ces garçons là*" betrayed mere "turgid imbecility—the stuffed and painted decrepitude of a superannuated and declining literature." Legaré's Latin tastes were Roman chiefly in politics. The Roman state was less sublime than the Greek in the eloquence it inspired, but it was more sensible. No doubt it shared vices with Athens—a preference for aristocracy, class warfare, contempt for trade—and had one of its own, suspicion of philosophy. Yet Rome had happier and more sustained periods of constitutional stability. Between 202 B.C. when Scipio Africanus Major defeated Hannibal at Zama, and 133 B.C. when Scipio Aemilianus took Numantia and completed the conquest of Spain, the republic was most successful in war and most balanced between "the stern morals of a primitive, and the graces of a polished age." "At the same time the voice of civil discord was mute—the tribune almost forgot how to pronounce his *veto*—the very name of Dictator was falling into desuetude. From the beginning of the fifth century, when the Plebeians may be considered as fairly relieved from all constitutional disabilities, until the seditions of the Gracchi . . . the history of the Republic is one bright record of virtues and achievements, almost too heroic for the infirmities of human nature." It was this moment that Polybius studied and Cicero looked upon with nostalgic and fitting regret, especially in the *De Republica,* freshly discovered by Cardinal Mai in a Ligurian palimpsest and published in 1822. Cicero upon the state was the happy mean, less fanciful than Plato, less cold-blooded than Machiavelli. For Machiavelli "had no *sentiment* and very little imagination. His unrivalled excellence (for unrivalled he is) consists in a cold, calculating, 'long-sighted and strong-nerved' reason—seasoned, as is proved by Belfagor and Mandragola, with a good deal of vivacity and wit . . . . He was a heartless Italian diplomatist, who had learned to be a *speculative* republican—where Milton, and Sidney, and Harrington afterwards imbibed their more sincere love of liberty—in the schools of antiquity, and whose head was full of the notion, so rife at that time in Italy, of the superiority of the antique over the gothic model, and of the Pseudo-descendants of the Romans over the whole race of Ultramontane barbarians." Yet the *Discorsi* were "the best work of the kind extant—less metaphysical than Aristotle's Politics—more philosophical and comprehensive than our own Federalist—and not to be degraded by a comparison with the random epigrams of Montesquieu."[33]

Cicero admired a mixed polity guided by an aristocratic spirit. Antique philosophers had abominated the simple forms, democracy even more than kingship. Happily, the United States had learned that lesson, but could not entirely avoid the type of Aristotle's Parasites, "those 'firm and undeviating republicans, *par excellence,*' those exclusive 'friends of the people,' who deafen us with their self-proclaimed virtues and obstreperous humility whenever there is a scramble for place in the commonwealth," for whom government was "a great state lottery for the distribution of office to indigent patriots," men who inflamed excitements, complied with prejudice, suppressed truth, propagated falsehood, adhered to no party that was not triumphant, cringed to every apparent majority, and sacrificed scruple to promote some worthless popular leader. What Rome in its republican heyday had understood was the same appreciated by the Revolutionary generation: "True liberty, like true eloquence, is founded on the most elevated moral sentiments, and is incompatible with any other. C'est le culte des ames fières, as Madame Roland nobly expressed it. But it requires something more even than this sublime spirit, rare as that is. Liberty is law—liberty is truth—liberty is reason. . . . It is of the very essence of republican government, that the laws, which all are free to choose, should be implicitly obeyed by all. And as law has been defined to be 'reason without passion,' so those who administer and execute it should partake of the same unblemished nature. It is in this respect that Washington stands without a similar or a second. He was living law—the very personification of the purest, the sternest, the most dispassionate, the most sublime republicanism."[34]

The lesson of Rome was *gravitas,* and the problem of democratic assemblies was that a crowd could not possess it. Cicero's *De Republica* became Burkean. Legaré quoted the Irishman, that "great man— whose speculations have exhausted this subject, and occur to us whenever we have occasion to contemplate it," upon the Revolution in France and observed, "Cicero would have felt the whole force and beauty of the following period [of Burke]." For "Cicero . . . thought that he saw in the constitution of his country, as it existed during the happy and glorious period before alluded to, the best of all possible schemes of government—a perfect model of the well-tempered and balanced polity, imagined by philosophers in their visions of perfectibility, but never successfully reduced to practice by any other great people. He was willing to take it with all its imperfections on its head—with all its apparent anomalies, irregularities and defects . . . . He knew, that the *mores,* the manners, opinions and character of people, are by far the most important part in every political problem, and that no constitution can be either stable or efficient which is not in harmony with these." Rome, America, and the Paris of Babeuf melded instruction. Lares and penates mattered.[35]

Cicero was central, for both living in and documenting the republic. Legaré the lawyer looked upon Cicero with incestuous affection, aware of the advantages Cicero relished and the disadvantages he endured. Demosthenes was, on balance, the greater orator, but Cicero's was the more various accomplishment, in oratory, in popular eloquence, in philosophy, in elegance, in "all the studies of a refined humanity." "Wonderful that he should have combined in the oratory of the Forum and the Senate, the vehemence and force of Demosthenes (which he sometimes equalled) with the sweetness of Isocrates, and the majesty and copiousness of Plato—that his dialogues on ethical and metaphysical subjects . . . should be inferior to nothing that Athens produced . . . and, that even his familiar epistles, thrown off, generally, without the least premeditation, often in haste, in sickness, in sorrow, under some of the severest trials and vexations that man ever encountered, should afford the most perfect model imaginable of that engaging species of composition! Still more wonderful that he reconciled the highest excellences of the speculative character, with the greatest ability and success in active life, and had a right to boast as he did in 'the Philippic of divine fame,' that while he had never neglected any duty, either social or political, private or public, he had employed his leisure in adding so much to the literary monuments of his country, and in promoting by his works, not less than by his precepts and example, the studies of her youth."[36]

Yet Cicero was accessible, a man to be fond of, a man of amiable foible, of occasional naiveté, of bad puns, of vanity, of sometimes misplaced discursiveness. His oratory served the "political aggrandizement" but also the finished education of an accomplished character and a Roman. Yet "this speculative notion of his art had a decided effect upon his manner of speaking, giving it in a slight degree a scholastic and artificial air," extending even to self-indulgent *concetti* in his harangues, "altogether at variance with the exquisite purity of his taste in all his other writings." This was a forgivable fault, suggestive of an analogy between beauties in different artistic genres. "No description which we could give of the manner and the merit of Demosthenes, as compared with those of Cicero, could afford so just and lively a conception of them to a mere English reader, as the remarks of Sir Joshua Reynolds, in reference to the two styles in painting, called the *grand* and the *ornamental,* and the effect of a mixture or composition of both. For Raphael substitute Demosthenes, and it presents a perfect picture of the austere simplicity and grandeur of his manner: but it would be degrading Cicero to talk of him with Tintoret or Paolo Veronese, or even with Corregio, though he belongs to a somewhat similar class." Yet Cicero had talents greater than Demosthenes. His inferiority lay in matters beyond his control: his audience was Roman and not Greek; he had fewer unifying crises, his being precipitated by Roman upon Roman, not by external enemies; he had to deal too much with ordinary events. Even the impeachment of Verres was mediocre stuff, lent importance by Cicero's eloquence rather than lending sublimity. In short, Cicero lived in a lesser age, doing his best with it by extraordinary talents. Legaré, living in the shadow of the Revolution, looking about him to a national oratory bloated and Asiatic, to "the volubility of mountebanks and pettifoggers," could see a parallel. "As to that vulgar faculty of speaking a whole day about nothing, without stopping to breathe or even to think, we have the ample evidence of experience in this country that it may be infallibly acquired by practising a few months in any piepowder court or country circuit."[37]

The moral was clear. Even Cicero's slim chances were grown slimmer, for "the age of chivalry—the heroic age—of eloquence, as of every thing else in this degenerate world, is gone." "The voice of . . . that mighty eloquence which once shook whole democracies" was gone with the simple society that fashioned "the shout of Stentor, or the blast of the dread horn of Fontarabia." Instead, the press had destroyed the orator, just as "the invention of gun-powder is represented, in the pathetic lamentations of Orlando and Don Quixotte, to have [destroyed] . . . the knight-errantry of Europe—a mighty leveller of all distinctions, and the means of advancing the mass at the expense of the individual." Cicero, confronted with too patient audiences, inspired only by mediocre circumstances, hedged around by the suspicions of a people wary of philosophic learning, had only himself to hold himself to himself. Cicero might be weary, indifferent to honors, and melancholy about his country, yet choose consciously to fashion the legend of a heroic past. But the strain was too great; the failure, however splendid, was evident. For Legaré, who saw and would live to see himself praised for inferior eloquence, touted for what was ill comprehended, condemned for what was ill understood by audiences who committed a crime in asking too little of Legaré's exertions, ready to be unstinted, the implications of Cicero and Rome were sharp and sympathetically depressing.[38]

# 5
# Belles
# Lettres

L EGARÉ WAS FOND of the medieval romance rather than impressed by it. The *Morte d'Arthur, El Cid, Amadis of Gaul,* the *Song of Roland*— all these he read with pleasure but a marked sense of wandering in agreeable but improbable country. "We pity the man," he observed, "who can read a genuine old Spanish *romance,* and not feel 'his heart,' in Sir Philip Sidney's phrase, 'more moved than with a trumpet.' For these artless lays are the very language of nature, at once heroic and simple—the living record of what the most 'renowned, romantic' race of modern men, under circumstances the most peculiar and the most interesting, did and suffered." His tone was relaxed and slightly amused, as though recounting the exploits of a remarkable young nephew. He was almost apologetic, conscious of a "secret charm." Cicero mattered, spoke to Legaré's needs and ambitions, but *El Cid* was a Sunday picnic, the amusement of a passing hour with not even the engagement of serious wooing. While antiquity was real, and Legaré showed no interest in its mythology save as an obfuscating nuisance to be removed by the researches of Niebuhr and Boeckh, medieval mythology was engaging. That he took matters so lightly, for a man whose generation saw great importance in early prodigies and portentous nationality, was because he was never very much interested in origins. Where Etruscans originated was not of great moment; that they were the Etruscans was. Equally, "whatever diver-

sity of opinion may exist about the source from which the Romances of
Chivalry were derived, there can be none as to their principal subject-
matters." And their world was not real, but even then a dream: "The
heroes who figure in them . . . exist no where else but in them."[1]

But he delighted in their luscious and almost Charlestonian relaxation, reminiscent of his "balsamic, soft south." "There is something
exceedingly brilliant and captivating in these pictures of Moorish life.
The splendor of oriental imagination is there—the soft and bewitch-
ing voluptuousness of those bright climes, where the earth is ever gay
with flowers and the whole air loaded with perfumes, and the sky
lighted up with a cloudless and tranquil glory. The dreams of that
'delightful londe of faerie' where the fancy of Spenser lingered so
fondly, seem to be realized in these sunny regions." It was a garden
with no serious serpent, or—as in the martial epics of the medieval
imagination—with dangers galore but sure to be vanquished. Indeed,
matters were so assured that such as the ballads based upon Turpin's
Chronicle tottered upon the "burlesque and caricature" of Cervantes.
"So true is it that in this tragic-farce of human life . . . there is but a
single step from the sublime to the ridiculous, and that the most
heroic devotedness and the loftiest aspirations of man are excellent
game for the wit of the satirist, or the scoffings of the misanthrope." It
was the dubious virtue of those with a romantic imagination, formed
not by Cervantes but by Boiardo and Ariosto, to "sit down to read a
book of fiction [and] consent 'to become as little children,' and make
it a merit to believe, like honest Tertullian, because 'the thing is
impossible,' rather than indulge their 'reasoning pride,' at the expense of their best interests, in scepticism and profane mockery."
Legaré was divided between moments content with the dream and
moments permitting a sense of absurdity. The latter is best exemplified in his own dry burlesque of the duel between Orlando and
the giant Ferracute.[2]

Underpinning the literary character of the romance was a special
sociology, a precommercial society that had less motive to inhabit
imagination. As Sismondi had insisted and Legaré quoted, "Ce n'est
pas aux lois les plus sages aux temps d'ordre et de prospérité, qu'est
réservé le plus grand développement de l'imagination chez un peuple." This was the medieval side of the equation that had lauded the
earliest efforts of the Greeks. France, from the eleventh to the fifteenth century, was early dominated by "the character and pursuits of
the *seigneurs de chateaux*," later by the commercial spirit of the towns.
"The lawless Baron, who held only his sword, and, submitting to no

sovereign, scarcely deigned to acknowledge a superior—Che libito fe' licito in sua legge—and whose castle was an emblem and epitome of the existence which it protected . . . . if not himself a Troubadour, like Coeur de Lion, or Alfonso I., was at least the natural friend of the Troubadour. This simple, but pleasing and peculiar poetry, accordingly flourished under their favour and cultivation. Under the influence of the commercial spirit, on the contrary, it died away—men at arms yielded to men of business—the useful supplanted the agreeable, and the *aerugo et cura peculi,* of which Horace speaks, produced the same effect in France as at Rome."[3]

Spanish literature was less interesting than Italian, partly because the latter had been more firmly fixed in the typologies of literary criticism and seemed to lead into English literature, into Sir Philip Sidney, the votary of Petrarch. But the Spanish dissipated, though triumphantly, in the auto-da-fé of Cervantes' satire. Spain's "old national poetry is second to none," but her later classical productions "have ever appeared to us, as to the majority of mankind, incomparably inferior to those of her neighbours . . . . we venture to say that, in spite of Schlegel or Cervantes, it will be long before Calderon, or Herrara, or Garcilaso de la Vega, shall rival Dante, and Ariosto, and Tasso, in the estimation of the world."[4]

Of the Italians, Legaré put Dante above all, now a conventional judgment but then heterodox. The early eighteenth century had elevated Petrarch and Boccaccio, Dante being too medieval and thus too barbaric. Voltaire had sneered at the Florentine. Thomas Warton, English Poet Laureate until 1790, found some power in Dante but more rawness and, above all and improbably to later generations less neoclassical, whimsicality. Sismondi, the Schlegels, and Pierre Louis Ginguene had nudged Dante's reputation into a more romantic era, and Hazlitt in the *Edinburgh Review* had suggested that love was not so comic a passion as Voltaire and Warton had found it. Henry Hallam, in his *View of the State of Europe in the Middle Ages* (1818) had been judicious, and Macaulay in pieces for the *Quarterly Magazine* in 1824 followed Sismondi in making the magic connection between Dante and Shakespeare. But these efforts did not add up to a wave of reappraisal in Dante's favor, so Legaré showed independence when he observed, *inter alia,* that "it is not disparaging any poet to say that he is not equal to Dante—one of the most extraordinary of men, whose 'soul was as a star and dwelt apart' from the whole species—far above the highest, brighter than the most shining." Romantically, Legaré saw in the vanished cosmogony of the *Divine Comedy* the poetry that

preceded modern science, the mists of obscurity that modernity had
been so eager to dispel at the expense of the muse. "In the progress of
knowledge, the idols of fancy and the forms of enchantment that once
covered the whole earth, have disappeared one by one. Look at the
effect of modern improvements in geography. Take the discoveries of
Columbus and Vasco da Gama for an example; what have they done for
the muse? So long, indeed, as a mist still hovered over the shores they
had touched upon, so long they afforded scope for the marvellous, and
haunts for fiction. Accordingly, the first adventurers of the Portuguese gave us the Lusiad . . . . But now that the sea and the land
have been so thoroughly explored . . . what is become of the
poetry?"[5]

Legaré repudiated with circumspection the tradition of putting
Petrarch above Dante. Sismondi and Gibbon had had doubts about a
poet who merely composed love ditties. But Italy had consistently
idolized Petrarch, and Gibbon had cautioned that the foreigner who
flouted national opinion must do so with grave reservations. Thus
Legaré temporized that one should "award . . . all the praise which
the best critics among his own countrymen have bestowed upon his
sweet and elegant muse." He was not a poet of the very highest order;
he was unequal to Tasso and Ariosto and vastly inferior to "his mighty
master and precursor, Dante," who exceeded even in eroticism, in
such a masterpiece as the sonnet beginning, "Tanto onesta e tanto
gentile pare, la donna mia." "But, with all his faults—with all the
forced and frigid conceits and the puling sentimentalism that have
been imputed to him—there is enough of tenderness and beauty in
the verses of [Petrarch] . . . and especially of elegance both in thought
and expression, to have given immortality to any poet in any age—
especially to one who, in the fourteenth century, could anticipate in
his style all the refinement and politeness of the sixteenth."[6]

Legaré made little of Boccaccio—oddly, since the Italian had been
held by the eighteenth century to be, althouh admittedly below
Petrarch, greater than Dante. He praised Ariosto and Tasso as greater
than Petrarch but was skeptical of Metastasio and Alfieri, eighteenth-
century poets whose heroes were "*too* godlike," with language swollen
into "rhodomontade and extravagance," "so very Roman, that they
cease to have human feelings, or to excite human sympathy." In this
criticism, Legaré paralleled his view of the achievement of *Paradise
Lost,* great but diminished by its lofty and inhuman chilliness.[7]

But the Italians led to the English, even more than did even the
early English. The formal achievements of medieval English literature, not excluding Chaucer, were less regarded by Legaré than *El Cid*

or Dante. In this he was of his time. The enthusiasm for Anglo-Saxon, for Beowulf and the sagas, was a mid-nineteenth-century phenomenon, though intimated by the late eighteenth century's passion for the spurious Ossian, the more popular and plausible for being not *very* medieval, for being rather the eighteenth century's impression of the more attractive side of the barbaric Middle Ages. That first passion for the Middle Ages had centered largely upon the "Celtic" fringes of English culture, the more admissible to even the Enlightened sensibility because the more remote, not touching the core of civilization that had descended, through the Roman cultures, from Greece and Rome to modernity. Indeed, it had been widely believed the Celtic muse had been inspired by the troubadours through Armorica to the Gaels, so there was no contradiction between a taste for *El Cid* and the tales of Arthur's Round Table. Legaré, presented by Thomas Percy's *Reliques of Ancient Poetry* with a purely Scandinavian theory for the origins of English medieval romance, was inclined to doubt and prefer Warton's contention that amid "the gloom of superstition, in an age of the grossest ignorance and credulity, a taste for the wonders of Oriental fiction was introduced by the Arabians into Europe, many countries of which were already seasoned to a reception of its extravagancies, by means of the poetry of the Gothic Scalds, who perhaps originally derived their ideas from the same fruitful region of invention." Thus Legaré fondly discussed Geoffrey of Monmouth in the same breath with the medieval Spanish romance: "We owe to Geoffrey, a Welsh Benedictine, sometime Archdeacon of Monmouth and Bishop of St. Asaph, all that has come down to us in so many various and wonderful tales of King Arthur and his faithless Guenevre or Gwenhwyfar, of Sir Kay, Sir Launcelot, Sir Gawain, Sir Tristam, and, above all, of that first of seers and sorcerers, the mad eremite of the Caledonian Forest, the enchanter Merlin." Chaucer and Gower he did admire, but English poetry was after them largely silent and needed Sidney's defense in 1581 against having become, "from almost the highest estimation of learning . . . the laughing-stock of children." "It is certain that, through a long tract of time, her voice had been almost mute in England. With the exception of Surrey, Wyatt and Sackville—meritorious, but still inferior poets—two centuries had passed away without producing a single name worthy to be had in remembrance by posterity. Chaucer and Gower . . . had hitherto found as few successors as Dante and Petrarch; while, in both countries, the national literature, after this period of darkness, 'burst forth into sudden blaze' about the same time, or at no great interval."[8]

Horace Walpole had done much to discredit Sir Philip Sidney, below the praises of Spenser, Young, and Samuel Johnson, which had been much influenced by the union in Sidney of the gentlemanly man of affairs with the poet and theorist. Legaré himself, only an occasional and private poet but a writer in and of the world, dwelt with pointed emphasis upon Sidney the statesman, while admitting that Walpole had treated "the reputation of Sidney as a *hum* of the first magnitude." It was as a theorist of poetry, not as a poet, that Legaré was inclined to defend Sidney, though in both instances praise was tempered by an awareness of Sidney's youth: "It is obvious to observe that the hasty productions of one who died at so early an age, and was so deeply engaged in the affairs of active life, ought not to be brought into comparison with the master-pieces of professed authors. It is not very common to see men of business or men of fashion—and Sidney united in himself both these characters—even in this age of universal authorship—leaving behind them, in the maturity of their faculties, any thing that may challenge the attention of posterity. We are, therefore, bound in fairness to look upon these remains with an indulgent eye—non enim, as Cicero has it, *res* laundanda, sed *spes*." The poetry was inferior, too much in the school of a Petrarch himself flawed, with Sidney more successfully imitating the Italian's vices than his virtues in being affected, strained, all "cold imitation and abortive effort—without any life or soul."[9]

But Sidney's defense of poetry touched a Legaré restless to find weapons against the utilitarian Philistinism of Thomas Grimké. The enemies of poetry were, historically and logically, the Puritans and the utilitarians. The Puritans, no doubt, had made invaluable contributions to the history of political liberty, in the Long Parliament and by reforms in the English Constitution. "It is no serious objection with us, as it seems to have been with Hume, to Hampden, Vane, Pym &c., that their leisure moments were devoted to the worship of God, after their own fashion, however uncouth that fashion, instead of being employed, as such moments were wont to be by Brutus and his compeers, in literary studies or elegant social converse." But their views of human nature and imaginations were too marked against "the abominations of idolatry in those 'gay religions full of pomp and gold,' from which they were desirous of purging England." So they demanded in church and life "simplicity of forms, and the severest spirituality." "In this vale of tears, how absurd, how criminal was it to be gay! How could a being, accountable for every idle thought, indulge his fancy, with impunity, in vain and chimerical figments, in foolish dreams of what he never could expect, or should never wish to see realized! When every imagination of the thoughts of his heart was evil only, and his whole being was so infected with the taint of original sin, that a life of ascetic abstinence, uninterrupted devotion, and penitential tears, could not, without the influences of His grace, restore his fallen nature—amidst the temptations of the world, the flesh and the devil—was it *safe* to inflame the mind with visions of pleasure and beauty, and to stimulate the senses by the soft delights, the syren melody, the false enchantments of poetry and song?"[10]

But the modern utilitarians too waged war "against poetry, as *proving* nothing—as leading to no *practical* results—as doing nothing to advance the 'greatest good of the greatest number.' " These erred in treating man as a mere machine and in disregarding the innate sensibility of beauty. "According to this theory, taste, and the sense of beauty and of melody, were given us in vain. Imagination is no part of our original nature, but a consequence, rather, and proof of its corruption. Nature is lovely in vain." Worse, the utilitarian "tends to harden, and, consequently, to corrupt the heart, by perverting the understanding. . . . Those who exact a reason for every thing, destroy reason itself." To these, resistance was offered by poetry, the "voice of nature appealing to the heart with its utmost sublimity and power. Its precepts differ from those of philosophy only in their effect. Instead of teaching merely, it persuades, elevates, inspires. It excites a feeling where the other leaves only an opinion or a maxim." As the defender of poetry thus conceived, Sidney deserved honor.[11]

Legaré hinted at the Elizabethan explosion of literature, reveled in it, without feeling the need for explication. Shakespeare he placed beside Dante, an opinion ordinary enough on Shakespeare's side not to require defense and firm enough to permit the occasional doubt on details, such as a low if fond opinion of Shakespeare's buffoonery. Once, quoting Bottom, he noted, "Those blackguards of Shakespeare *are* so taking, one never loses sight of them." Legaré absorbed Shakespeare instinctively into his prose and shrank from assessments that would be trifling beside the massive achievement. Spenser was lesser though great, on a par with Byron—high praise from Legaré. What mattered, however, what constantly recurred to Legaré's mind, was Milton, the poet whose verse he carried on his travels. Shakespeare defied all categories, but Milton embodied that of the moral sublime.[12]

Milton exemplified Legaré's preferences in style, the containment of complexity within simplicity and ease, the more remarkable in Milton because the complexity was so vast and the simplicity so stern.

"Even Milton," Legaré wondered, "who has drawn together his materials from a greater variety of sources than any other writer, and whose mighty genius is for nothing more remarkable than the apparent ease with which it appropriates and applies, and melts and moulds into new and original combinations, the most multifarious learning that ever fell to a poet's lot, is still distinguished by an antique and severe simplicity, even in his boldest and vastest conceptions." And Milton offered that combination of classical learning and religious sensibility that so appealed to Legaré. He also embodied hard Puritan religious belief, something Legaré acknowledged more than he relished. [13]

As Frederick Porcher was to observe, Milton was more praised than read, a monument decorous and massive whose inscription need not be scrutinized. Legaré read the inscription often, with a grave sense that here was a vision beyond mere humanity: *Paradise Lost* did not deal with "this wicked, but interesting world, with its pursuits and passions, its weaknesses, its tears and its agonies, its hopes and fears, its joys, its sympathies, its love, its madness"; it inspired amazement at a "solemn and austere moral grandeur" that was cold and desolate. "The burning lake, the Archangel ruined, but still rebellious, Pandemonium with its infernal council, the starless darkness which involved the realm of Chaos and Old Night, the battle of the Angels, so improbable and even worse—these daring conceptions are all bodied forth with infinite power of language and imagery, and such as it is not possible for poetry to surpass—but there is nothing there for the heart of man to sympathise with." Its very greatness destroyed intimacy. Heaven and hell were best as extensions of human graces and sins, and so men tended to bypass Milton as a grand irrelevance. Yet "Milton's is the creative power. His flight is as sustained as it is lofty. He soars 'upon the seraph wings of extacy' through height and depth, through the Empyrean and the abyss, and his ample pinion never for a moment flags. . . . His whole poem is a creation. Design is evident in every part of it—design projecting, composing, combining, harmonizing all." Milton was therefore a poet for the scholarly connoisseur who knew whence the combinations came: "Master of every branch of knowledge, but especially of ancient literature, he turns all he knew into poetry, and this unequalled and astonishing union of a daring creative genius, operating upon materials drawn from every quarter of the universe, and from every repository of learning, is what constitutes at once his peculiar excellence, and with a view to popularity, one of his capital defects." If Demosthenes was the god who looked towards the practical life of the sublime statesman, Milton was the god who looked towards not-too-Christian sublimity and served quite conveniently as a substitute for God Himself. Why carry the scriptures when one could carry Milton, so properly reminiscent of the epic strain of Homer and Vergil? Milton integrated and embodied tastes dear to Legaré, not least because Milton was the greatest of commonwealthmen, defending liberty, the "godliest heritage of man."[14]

Milton towered over the seventeenth century, certainly over the "gross ribaldry" of Rochester. He bore comparison rather with the neoclassical strain of French literature, of Racine especially, for whom Legaré had a respect born of many evenings in the Comédie Française. By its own choice, the traditional French theater had asked comparison with the antique and had come out in Legaré's eyes less badly than many, like Victor Hugo and the Schlegels, thought. French comedy in Molière's hands may have been better than the Greek, but French tragedy was inferior. To be sure, there were buffooneries in Molière as there were in Shakespeare, and stiffness in Racine. Nonetheless Racine, like Milton, had earned the right to "strike the harp of the Prophets and the Psalmist." "Paradise Lost, and the Choral odes of Esther and Athalie, preserve that sublime and somewhat stern simplicity, that awful grandeur, that comes up to our conceptions of the divine power and majesty. Their raptures are as of those who have been admitted, if it may be said with reverence, to the glories of the Vision Beautific." Legaré liked to tell of how *Athalie*—first dismissed as a tedious, unfashionable, and puzzling play "of a Jewish High Priest, a forgotten child, a furious beldame, surrounded by a host of Levites, preaching in the vestibule of the Temple of Jerusalem, through five mortal acts"—was rescued because a gentleman of fashion was exiled for a social transgression to a few hours of ennui, to be compounded by the reading of the play. To his astonishment, he found the play a treasure and emerged to proclaim his discovery. Legaré felt *Athalie* to be "a work, with which, in our opinion, nothing that modern genius has produced in the same kind can be compared." Even though it teetered always upon the preposterous because it was resting upon a byzantine network of social niceties, there was a high seriousness and stateliness in the age of Boileau that fed satisfactorily both solemnity and ridicule, both Racine and Molière. It was preferred to what followed. For example, "D'Aguesseau was educated in the school of Boileau and Racine. His taste was pure and classical; his mind was deeply imbued with the love of the beautiful, and he aimed, in his compositions, at perfect excellence, and in his studies, at profound erudition. This is, in short, the character of an Augustan age, such as that of Louis XIV. But when genius has had its day, that of *esprit* succeeds—a sort of brilliant, lively, second-rate order of mind—and the master-pieces of eloquence and art with all solid learning and exact science, disappear, to make way for things better adapted to a frivolous and fastidious age." Racine yielded to Voltaire.[15]

Voltaire fretted Legaré as "half eagle, half ape." The prose of Ferney was admirable, even Attic in its graceful simplicity. Yet the man was a philosopher, not an *érudit*; he knew so little, ignored so much, failed to undertake the high difficulty of disciplining the intractable into simplicity, was the precursor of a "folio-hating age." He was a symptom of that decline in classical learning that characterized the French eighteenth century, so much so that Voltaire could stand as a metaphor for indifferent criticism. "If we were called upon to exemplify the difference between sound criticism and the petulant and presumptuous dogmatism of prejudice and ignorance, we should refer to W. Schlegel's course of dramatic literature for the one, and Voltaire's strictures upon the Greek tragedies, in his various prefaces, commentaries, &c., for the other." Voltaire, like Byron later, lacked that "*limae labor,* which entitles a work of genius to be classed among perfect specimens of art," did not bother with those "corrections and improvement . . . the true secret of the *curiosa felicitas* in all times and tongues." And Voltaire stood for the French eighteenth century, years which—lacking profundity and emotional intensity—were left only with adeptness. This opinion was not uninfluenced by the Huguenot in Legaré. He acknowledged once, after seeing Meyerbeer's *Les Huguenots,* the ambivalent heritage of the "deep, fervent, solemn & sublime tho' withal severe & stern, fanaticism of our fighting & praying Calvinistic fathers," and was inclined to see in the draining of that spirit from French life after 1685 a reason for the lightened tone of eighteenth-century French discourse.[16]

The transition from the Augustan period to the eighteenth century in England was less dramatic. Pope and Dryden were less stately than Racine, Samuel Johnson less frivolous than Voltaire. And England led not to Babeuf, the product somehow of Voltaire's glibness, but to Burke, who kept his eyes riveted upon the concrete difficulties of human nature and aspiration.[17]

Dryden, Legaré admired for a "vigorous and bold pen" and used occasionally for observations upon classical literature, but Pope was closer to his heart—and not only for belonging to that odd community of the talented malformed: Byron and Pope, Scott and Legaré.

Among the many views of Byron with which Legaré disagreed, the defense of Pope was not to be included: "We venture to back him in this—his chosen vocation of critic and champion of injured genius—against any Aristarchus of the schools from the first downward. We would willingly reprint all that he has said upon this subject . . . to aid in the circulation of so much excellent sense and good writing." Indeed, Pope was Byron's superior as a satirist. "His defence of Poe, against the modern Grub-Street . . . had been worthy of all praise, had he gone a little farther and only gibbetted a few of that great man's detractors in another Dunciad, as an offering to his offended manes. Having tried his own hand at satire, with some degree of success, Byron was the better able to appreciate the matchless excellence of Pope, in his peculiar walk." Byron could not match Pope's "condensed and sententious elegance," but then Byron had dissipated in genre, whereas Pope had concentrated, though not in the highest realm of poetry where Milton dwelt. Pope was, "in spite of his extraordinary merits . . . in some degree, a mannerist, and so far, falls short of absolute perfection." Remembering what Legaré had observed of Tintoretto and Veronese, one can see in this term the identification of a lower order of things, a splendid doodling. And in classical scholarship Pope was unimpressive, deserving Bentley's gibe about the translation of Homer, even if faring better as not a translator but an imitator of Horace. [18]

Many in Charleston were fond of Addison. Legaré liked Sir Roger without being unduly impressed, merely giving lightness its due. Addison's successor in tone was Goldsmith, of whom George Croly's *Tales of the Great Saint Bernard* was later to excite a reminiscence: "It bears a strong resemblance to the Vicar of Wakefield, and is not altogether unworthy to be mentioned in connection with that charming novel, not only for the general drift and structure of the fable, but for the simplicity of its style, the candor and *bonhommie* with which the hero tells his story, and a certain sly and quiet humor that pervades it throughout." Amusement was the main resource of the English eighteenth century for Legaré—the better when unpretending, the worse when too frivolous, as with Chesterfield's *Letters*. Horace Walpole amused by perversity: "this Iconoclast by profession—this wayward and opinionated sceptic whose perverse delight it was to doubt where others believed, and decry what all the world admired," no more to be taken seriously than Strawberry Hill. Boswell amused by anecdote: "the invaluable Omnium Gatherum of that first of biographers and of boobies, the incomparable Bozzy." Young amused by lugubriousness: " 'a death's head with a bone in its mouth' . . . . a hum-drum monotony of lamentation . . . . though . . . full of healing religious consolation for those who are wrapt in a settled and pensive grief." Cowper amused by sentimentality: "not a man of genius—but . . . much talent, a ready command of language, and of an easy, flowing versification, and above all, the most perfect purity of heart, and a tenderness and sensibility which overflow in love for all mankind, nay, for all created beings, and which, united with great simplicity, and tinged with a pleasing melancholy, makes his verses the delight of sentimental and philanthropic, and especially of pious readers."[19]

Samuel Johnson, Legaré took more seriously. He first read *The Lives of the Poets* when traveling in Germany in 1836, a reading that belies those who would make Legaré "the great Cham of Charleston literature." Dr. Johnson was "a horribly bad writer," artificial, pompous, insupportable, a sensible critic but incapable of comprehending the sublime or the pathetic. "Nothing can be more unworthy of the mighty theme, than his way of treating Milton except his superficial notes on Shakespear." And he was an indifferent Latin student, and "*no* Greek scholar at all," as could be judged from his praise of Pope's Homer and "his absurd remarks on 'Samson Agonistes' and Greek tragedy." "His talent is colloquial—ingenious argument, quick turns of thought, ready, pointed, witty repartee, clothed frequently in metaphor wh. looked like reasoning and does often bear a great abundance of maxims and of moralities, uttered with oracular solemnity, even when rather trivial—but withal a taste for elegance, tho' false and a lively but not a sublime fancy—these qualities aided by very considerable, and various literature and by an invincible confidence in himself and a most dogmatical superciliousness in regard to other people account for his prodigious celebrity in that day of *talkers* and *clubs* and will secure to him a certain (greatly curtailed, no doubt) reputation with posterity. But he is in his true element when he speaks of Dryden—Milton was above his pitch. He had not as much heart as head, and not as much soul as heart and is *never* either very original or very profound."[20]

There are two lacunae in Legaré's English eighteenth century. Oddly, for a man so fond of the sarcastic annihilation, Swift he barely mentions except to refer later to his "mischievous irony," scarcely a sensitive characterization. Gibbon, the greatest literary figure of the century and, next to Bentley and Porson, its most various classicist, Legaré scanted. He did recur to Gibbon's opinion that the foreign critic must have reservations when challenging national estimates of literary greatness. He did occasionally refer to opinions of "that great master" with respect, and praise chapter 44 of the *Decline and Fall* as a comprehensive and satisfactory précis for the "general reader" of the Roman law. Yet for a man so interested in the fate of the civil law among the wreckage of the Roman Empire, Legaré seldom used Gibbon, though the balancing ironies of that pudgy squire can occasionally be heard in Legaré's own prose. His only extensive citation from Gibbon, significantly in a footnote, gives a clue to the omission. Legaré was discussing the romance of Roncesvalles and felt it necessary to append this: "The only notice which Gibbon bestows upon an event so important in the History of Fiction, is the following:—'After his Spanish expedition, his rearguard was defeated, in the Pyrenaean mountains; and the soldiers, whose situation was irretrievable, and whose valor was useless, might accuse with their last breath the want of skill or caution of the general.'—*Decline and Fall*, c. 49. To this is appended the following note—'In this action, the famous Rutland, Rolando, Orland, was slain—cum pluribus aliis. See the truth in Eginhard (c. ix. pp. 51–56) and the fable in an ingenious supplement of M. Gaillard, (tom. iii. p. 474). The Spaniards are too proud of a victory which history ascribes to the Gascons, and romance to the Spaniards.' A totally different version of this affair is given by Beuter in the Cronica de Valencia, p. 158, as quoted by the translator of the work before us [Thomas Rood]." Much of Legaré's attitude can be gleaned from this apparently artless citation: his pleasure in Gibbon's prose, for it is quoted at length, not merely cited; his disapproval of Gibbon's lack of interest in romance; his respect for Gibbon's scholarship, for Legaré does not challenge Gibbon directly or even explicitly, instead leaving combat to the editor Beuter. Gibbon was best respected but not used. Gibbon stood for Rome over Greece, interest in decay over pleasure in achievement, ironic contempt for Christianity over wary secularization of the sublime. Yet Gibbon, unlike Voltaire, more than embodied the legacy of the seventeenth century's *érudits*, and his work could not be dismissed as mere ignorant presumption. So Legaré left him alone, lest he be ensnared by the perspective when employing the materials. Silence betokened respect.[21]

The *Southern Review* had given French literature to Henry Junius Nott and German literature to Robert Henry, so Legaré's views on contemporary continental writers were little published. He did not learn to read German until he was chargé d'affaires in Brussels, so he made little of German literature, itself not occupying a vast space in literary history. He read, as has been seen, the German critics and Goethe in translation. The Germans shed light upon other literatures, pointed outward rather than inward. He used Goethe when commenting upon Byron's Manfred, Schlegel when speculating on Horace. The Germans interpreted and defined romanticism and were themselves interpreted by Madame de Staël.

France itself offered mostly riveting memoirs of the Revolution, whose chaos had postponed the collapse of neoclassicism even beyond Legaré's own time in Paris. But France had had Rousseau, used by Legaré more as a presage of revolution and romanticism than as a contemporary of Voltaire. Rousseau, with Byron, was to be judged unflatteringly as a moral animal, a vain parvenu intoxicated by "the extraordinary elevation to which he so suddenly attained, at a rather advanced age." "He never felt at home in the great world—his immense reputation and popularity did not sit as easily upon him as a suit of livery. He was, accordingly, the victim of a morbid vanity—always doubting the sincerity of the worshipper, even when he was suffocated with the fumes of his incense, mistaking his best friends for assassins, and every social circle for a conspiracy against his reputation, which, of course, entirely engrossed the thoughts of all mankind. Byron has been frequently compared with this 'inspired madman'; and not without reason. But we do not know any trait in which he resembles him so much, as his morbid and jealous vanity. The difference between them is, that Rousseau had none of that gloomy and insolent pride which made the vanity of the poet so peculiarly bitter and odious." Such self-love was the stuff of metaphysical politics and ambition, leading in Byron to a sympathy for tyrants like Sulla and Napoleon, implicitly leading in Rousseau to the creative narcissism of the French Revolution.[22]

Nothing could offer a clearer contrast to Rousseau and Byron than the businesslike imagination, solid and Tory, of Walter Scott. Here Legaré stood in his own time and experience, reaching a literature where canons of taste were still forming, tumbling piecemeal and contemporary from the latest reviews and from what chanced to catch his eye and fancy. A Swinton could not help liking Scott's early border ballads, although a Legaré noticed "an immense falling off in the later poetry of Sir Walter Scott." "In truth, that to call things by their right names, he had begun to indite insufferable doggerel." Fortunately, Scott had turned to prose, and Legaré felt the power of the enchanter's wand, summoning forth not only engaging stories but a portentous

genre, the historical novel, by "an almost superhuman inspiration."
Scott could be uneven. Legaré found the early pages of *The Fair Maid of
Perth* slow and heavy, his earlier novels superior to his later, his
Scottish novels better than his medieval romances, his heroines flat,
his denouements predictable. Nonetheless, the achievement was extraordinary, not sentimental but tough, far from the tinseled romanticism that indifferent critics of Scott and the South have since
celebrated to condemn.[23]

As has been observed, Legaré had a special reason for reading Scott:
the novelist's infantile paralysis and permanent limp. In Scott were
nuances of frustration that eluded or bored others but were seen by
Legaré in *The Black Dwarf,* and even in *The Fair Maid of Perth*. The
former taught more than *Richard III;* it was based upon a real dwarf,
David Ritchie of Peebles, whom Scott had visited in 1797. The story
itself tells of Elshie the Dwarf, who appears—sudden and mis-
anthropic—upon Mucklestane Moor, spurning company and sympathy, having various escapades, saving a fair maiden though in
violation of his solitude, turning out to be an aristocrat with an
ancient grudge against a society that had despised and imprisoned
him for manslaughter of the enemy of a friend—a friend who went on
to marry the dwarf's espoused. As Legaré admitted, and later criticism
has thought, the novel "appears a piece of fantastic extravagance to
superficial readers," but to the Charlestonian it seemed "a profound
and masterly conception, which nothing but such a genius, instructed by personal experience, could have formed." Whereas Shakespeare had made of Richard a mere unsympathetic villain, Scott had
penetrated into the unreasoning tangle of proud mortification in
Elshie. "It is the interest of human nature," Legaré reflected, "to show,
where those who have, in some respects, adorned and exalted it most,
have gone astray, that their errors may be accounted for, if not excused,
by sufficient reasons, and that the highest gifts and accomplishments
of man have not been, as if in mockery, thrown away upon *monsters.*
There is deep sense as well as pathos in [Byron's] lines on Sheridan—
'ah! little do ye know / That what to you seems vice might be but
woe!' "[24]

Luxuriant melancholy was offered by passages such as this, in
which Elshie explained his feelings: " 'I am . . . . a poor miserable
outcast, fitter to have been smothered in the cradle than to have been
brought up to scare the world in which I crawl . . . . look at every
book which we have read, those excepted of that abstract philosophy
which feels no responsive voice in our natural feelings. Is not personal

Hugh Swinton Legaré, by Henry Bounetheau, after Edward Marchant;
a posthumous portrait by a Charleston contemporary.
Courtesy, Carolina Art Association/Gibbes Art Gallery

form, such as at least can be tolerated without horror and disgust, always represented as essential to our ideas of a friend, far more a lover? Is not such a misshapen monster as I am excluded, by the very fiat of Nature, from her fairest enjoyments? What but my wealth prevents all . . . from shunning me as something foreign to your nature, and more odious by bearing that distorted resemblance to humanity which we observe in the animal tribes that are more hateful to man because they seem his caricature?' "[25]

Quite naturally, Legaré drew a parallel between Scott and Byron as victims of physical deformity. In this he chanced upon a sympathy that Byron himself had felt. The poet's half-sister, Augusta Leigh, suspected that Byron had written the pseudonymous novel, and Byron, reading the book in Rome in 1817, then wrote to John Murray, "I have read [it] with great pleasure—& perfectly understand now why my Sister & aunt are so very positive in the very erroneous persuasion that . . . . [it] must have been written by me—if you knew me as well as they do—you would have fallen perhaps into the same mistake."[26]

Scott mattered in flashes for Legaré. Byron mattered entire. To no other writer did Legaré give such focused attention. Legaré's literary criticism of moderns tended to be his worst writing, done to fill up a space in the *Southern Review* and notable for indifferent padding by long and undistracting quotation. He would give his opinion—with surprised enthusiasm for Robert Pollok, with dismissal for Robert Montgomery—and leave the reader to wade through précis and quotation. This was laziness and perhaps a theory that modern writing, just off the boat, needed summary and explication more than works long known or knowable to his readers. But Byron was a serious matter, familiar to all, contemporary yet prematurely available for assessment as a guide to the age because dead so young and splendidly, the object of immediate reminiscence and legend. And Byron had been the literary idol of Legaré's youth, the counterpoint of his fevered and ambitious adolescence. "We well remember a time—it is not more than two lustres ago—when we could never think of him ourselves but as an ideal being—a creature, to use his own words, 'of loneliness and mystery'—moving about the earth like a troubled spirit, and even when in the midst of men, not *of* them." Now Byron was dead, like youth, and needed assessment for the sake of maturity's sanity and ease.[27]

The occasion was the publication of Thomas Moore's *Letters and Journals of Lord Byron*. Legaré regarded Moore, with amused contempt, as a necessary if ridiculous satrap, most useful when most out of the way of Byron's generously reprinted and somewhat censored papers. Such papers, combined with Byron's verse, invited an assessment balancing literary and ethical considerations. Legaré did look upon literature as an ethical venture, though not baldly so. Addison, La Rochefoucauld, Johnson, Fénelon—these were useful, for "there is always room for eloquence and poetry—for the drama, the novel, or the essay—for vivid descriptions of life, and impressive exhortations to duty." But ethics alone and naked were of a lower order of literature, for morality consisted in fidelity to human nature, not in blinking before unpleasant and depraved facts. "It is no objection to the instructive and salutary moral tendency of . . . [a] novel, that it does not distribute what is called 'poetical justice' among its chief personages. We have always thought that nothing was, at once more fallacious in a philosophical point of view, and more at variance with the analogy of nature and of human life, than such a principle." Thus Legaré regretted the craven destruction of Byron's memoirs by Moore, Hobhouse, and Murray, and was happy to see the record of Byron's salacious life placed before the public. "We need not say that the life, of which the secret *post-scenia* and deepest recesses are thus unexpectedly laid bare to the gaze of the world, is that of a man of pleasure— dashed, it is true, with the gloom of a complexional melancholy, or more brilliantly diversified by the mingled glories of genius and literature, and abruptly and prematurely terminating in a high tragic catastrophe—an atoning self-sacrifice, and a hero's grave. A book of this character, it may very well be conceived, will in spite of its attractions, or rather in consequence of them, find a place in the *Index Expurgatorius* of the sterner sort of censors—along with the "Mémoires de Grammont," and the "Amours des Gaules" of the Comte de Bussy-Rabutin. Yet it is fit and desirable that such truths should be told. They are passages in the book of life which all would and some *should* read, and, although the example of such a man as Lord Byron is, no doubt, calculated to do much harm to minds of a certain stamp, we must only take care to deny it to such people, as edged tools and dangerous drugs are kept out of the way of children, and adults who are no better than children." So Byron offered the best of ethical opportunities, the chance to study, to learn, and to judge.[28]

Autobiography mingled with verse, yet it was possible to distinguish between the two in making judgments, by form if not by motive. Much could be said against Byron's verse. His later poems, their "wanton, gross, and often dull and feeble ribaldry . . . broke the spell which he had laid upon our souls; and we are by no means sure that we have not since yielded too much to the disgust and aversion which follow disenchantment like its shadow." He could be bombastic, too hasty in composition, exaggerated and strained, too uniformly despairing, absurdly vain, unable to define the variety of woman, blustering, discursive, limited in inventiveness both of style and subject: a formidable indictment. What could be said in his favor? Byron was revealed in his letters as a master of English prose, almost unequaled in any language. Perhaps Thomas Gray or Lady Mary Wortley Montagu had more grace and elegance, perhaps Madame de Sévigné had more of "that inimitable, ineffable *bavardage*," but Byron's letters "fully rival the best of them in spirit, piquancy, and, we venture to add, *wit,* while, like the epistles of Cicero, they not unfrequently rise from the most familiar colloquial ease and freedom into far loftier regions of thought and eloquence." He could surprise a smile, a broad laugh, "by some felicitous waggery, some sudden descent from the sublime to the ridiculous," the mark of "the hand that drew Childe Harold."[29]

But there were virtues in Byron the poet. Some were external. He wrote often about subjects especially resonant. "Madame de Staël ascribes it to his good fortune or the deep policy of Napoleon, that he had succeeded in associating his name with some of those objects which have, through all time, most strongly impressed the imaginations of men, with the Pyramids, the Alps, the Holy Land, &c. Byron had the same advantage. . . . His early visit to Greece, and the heartfelt enthusiasm with which he dwelt upon her loveliness even 'in her age of woe'—upon the glory which once adorned, and that which might still await her—have identified him with her name, in a manner which subsequent events have made quite remarkable." Then, he had the advantages of position and temperament, being a lord among wits, with a distance from mere book making, a man both in and of the world. Legaré briskly dismissed, as a professional to an amateur, Byron's claims as a statesman and parliamentarian, yet it mattered that Byron was no cloistered spinner of insubstantial gauze. But most of Byron's strengths proceeded from his weaknesses, the fascinations of a poet of feeling mining himself, eking out his self-love in autobiographical verse. "His whole being was, indeed, to a remarkable degree, extraordinary, fanciful and fascinating. All that drew upon him the eyes of men, whether for good or evil—his passions and his genius, his enthusiasm and his woe, his triumphs and his downfall—sprang from the same source, a feverish temperament, a burning, distempered, insatiable imagination; and these, in their turn, acted most powerfully upon the imagination and the sensibility of others." Even in metaphor, feeling dominated Byron's language: "With regard to figures of speech, in general, Byron is the most anti-classical of the romantic poets. Instead of drawing his similes, &c., from the natural world to the moral, as the ancients uniformly did, he does just the reverse. Thus, a lake 'is calm as *cherished hate.*' Zuleika was 'soft as the memory of buried love.' The cypress is stamped with an eternal grief, 'like early unrequited love.' " In short, Byron had turned moral vice into poetic force, picturing—"to borrow a quaint phrase of Madame de Staël—the very 'apotheosis' of self-love. They were considered as grovelling and degraded, these selfish passions, better suited for comedy than ode or epic, before they were raised to a 'bad eminence' by his verse. But he has lifted them up to the height of his great genius."[30]

This accomplishment was dangerous, as many felt and Legaré particularized. He embraced Byron without stooping to celebrate the Byronic. Macaulay, reviewing the same volumes, later was to do likewise: "The number of hopeful undergraduates and medical students who become things of dark imaginings, on whom the freshness of the heart ceased to fall like dew, whose passions had consumed themselves to dust, and to whom the relief of tears was denied, passes all calculation . . . . There was created in the minds of many of these enthusiasts a pernicious and absurd association between intellectual power and moral depravity . . . . a system of ethics, compounded of misanthropy and voluptuousness, a system in which the two great commandments were, to hate your neighbour, and to love your neighbour's wife." Legaré concurred: "Nothing can be imagined more utterly subversive of all sound principle than such a system. The end of moral discipline is the very reverse of these notions." The idea should be laid decisively to rest, for the sake of both children and historical veracity. "That it can be laid down as a general rule that genius is inconsistent with the most sacred duties, and the sweetest affections of life, we cannot admit." Men of genius could "draw blanks in the great lottery of matrimony, as well as the common herd of mankind." And there were so many others, "exemplary men" like Scott, Schiller, Wordsworth. "Perhaps there never was a more affecting and beautiful picture of 'wedded love,' in all its holiness and rapture, than is presented in the biography of the most sensitive of this imaginative race of beings, poor Mozart." Even Pope was "the most devoted and affectionate of sons." "In short, men of genius have, in general, strong passions, but there is no reason in the world, why they should not have sound principles, and where this is the case, the evil, in the course of a few years, infallibly works its own cure. The progress of a warm and vigorous mind, under the discipline of experience, reminds us of that of the sun in this climate, at a certain season of the year—when, if he generally rises in mist, he always melts it away by noonday, and goes down in cloudless and serene brightness." While it was justice to admit that Byron was a great poet, it was duty to insist that he was "an unprincipled and bad man" and fashion lovingly a catalogue of his vices.[31]

Yet Byron did raise important issues of morality, of literary form, of sensibility. Through him could be made to flow the great controversy of classic versus romantic. In him could be traced Legaré's greatest fears, though not his sharpest wishes, for Byron looked too resolutely inward to satisfy a man with public and forensic ambitions. Seeing his fears most clarified, Legaré saw Byron as too "uniformly the *dark* sublime he drew," despite the sunshine of the poet's letters. "The truth is that his whole poetry is steeped—dyed, through and through, with these feelings [of selfish passion]. They obtrude themselves upon him in the deepest solitudes of nature—they discolor to his eye the most glorious objects of contemplation—they turn the sun into blood and the moon into darkness, and earth into a charnel house, and a den of wild beasts, and a hell before him." *Manfred* thus stood at the center of Legaré's Byron, its darkness and desolation touchingly softened by melancholy and "relieved by gleams of beauty and freshness, ever and anon, breaking forth, the more striking as they are unexpected." Manfred was "a mind in which neither sorrow nor pain, nor even despair itself, [had] . . . been able to quench the deep love of nature." The second scene of the first act opens with Manfred alone on the cliffs of the Jungfrau as dawn illuminates the Alps, "upon which his desolate soul must no more gaze with rapture." He is doomed "to see 'undelighted all delight'—to know that what he looks upon is beauty, to feel it even, but just enough to make him conscious of the curse that is upon his soul, the blight that has seared his heart, and deadened and destroyed all its capacities of enjoyment."[32]

Byron had accompanied youth and clarified maturity. Other writers both English and American were interesting but not crucial. Chief among the English was Bulwer Lytton, in his first Regency incarnation before the many-named lord tacked before every available literary breeze. Lytton in *Pelham* had defined the world of Beau Brummell with wit and awareness, a world that interested and repelled Legaré.

In *The Disowned*, characterization had been sharpened and pathos deepened, even though morality had become so tidy as to become implausible. In *The Siamese Twins,* the author had wandered into a genre unfitted to his talents and repulsive to taste, and so produced "a wretched failure . . . . satire without point, buffoonery without gaiety, and doggerel without drollery or quaintness." But Lytton showed English literature at a low point, just as Legaré haphazardly and indifferently took up his reviewing pen. Many were gone or in decline: Byron, Wordsworth, Coleridge. Many more were yet to come: Thackeray, Dickens, Trollope. Jane Austen was still a secret name. Pollok, Lytton, Montgomery, Croly, Disraeli—these were inconsiderable names, inconsiderably judged, even if not quite deserving Legaré's later view that they were "beneath contempt."[33]

American literature too was indifferent, with little past, not much of a present, and only the promise—often weighed—of a future. Here Legaré was resolved to be unsparing, not because he thought ill of that future but because he cared and did not wish to see it falsely announced and trumpeted. True, he did observe that " 'the influence of America upon the mind,' (to borrrow a convenient, though somewhat pedantic phrase)" would come chiefly in politics and law. "We are not aware that any new and peculiar sources of poetical enthusiasm have been revealed to us, nor have we as yet seen any thing in our history and condition, to justify the belief—so confidently inculcated by many of our prophetic fellow-citizens—that some great revolution in the abstract sciences and in speculative philosophy is to be reckoned among the probable consequences of the declaration of independence." There would be an American national literature, but it would embody an instance of culture, not its transformation. The key lay in pride and self-reliance, not in the vanity of "a nation of systematic self-flatterers." After all, "what Frenchman expects to be admired at London, or cares a straw about the opinions of English and Scotch censors? For him the whole world lies between the Alps, the Pyrenees and the ocean." Population alone favored the United States, for it would offer within fifty years a "theatre more vast and imposing, if not altogether so brilliant as that of the parent country. At the end of yet another half century it will be said of England, with truth, *pars minima est ipsa sui.* Her language will become a dialect. It will be to the great Anglo-Saxon tongue, spoken on the banks of the Missouri and the Hudson, at best, what the Attic was to the Hellenic or common Greek . . . . what does it signify to us whether that language shall be intelligible and agreeable or not to a foreign ear[?]

Happy the men who shall lead the way in the formation of a national literature—who shall strike the chord to which so many millions of American hearts shall vibrate forever, and leave a name to be re-echoed 'With a shout / Loud as from numbers without number, sweet / As from blest voices, uttering joy.' " This was the principle.[34]

Practice was spotty. Legaré bothered to review only two contemporary American poets or novelists, James Fenimore Cooper and William Crafts. He caught Cooper in an off moment, *The Wept of Wish-ton-Wish,* and found the novel a failure, an unnecessary extension into a full-length tale of an incident scarcely enough for a short story. The American was inferior to Scott, but he usually managed better than this and deserved praise. "There are interspersed through all his novels, graphic pictures, which the imagination retains with delight. The panther hunt and the burning mountain in the Pioneers—the escape of the prisoner in the Spy; the chase on the lake in the Mohicans—the crossing of the river, and the burning plains in the Prairie—the irruption on the farm in the work before us—all, once read, are never forgotten; and the unique splendour, we had almost said powerful poetry of his ocean scenes would redeem a thousand failures—but 'Infelix operis summa, quia ponere totum / Nesciet.' " Except in Leatherstocking, his common sailors, and his Indians, Cooper failed in the delineation of character, because he was "rather an admirer of external nature, than a close observer of human conduct in society," inspired "in the solitudes of the ocean and the wilderness." "Hence the well represented romantic attachment of his seamen to their vessel, Tom Coffin's love of his harpoon and Leather-Stocking's of his dog and rifle—the greater ease and intimacy of his Indian friendships and his comparative coldness to his white associates, the genuine poetry of his aversion to the clearings and of his affection for the trees, and the other accompaniments that impart a wild interest to his solitary life." Legaré was especially fond of Leatherstocking, "a creation which proves that Shakspeare has not exhausted the new world if he has the old." Otherwise, Cooper's drama was melodramatic, not tragic; his humor not playful; his wit not exquisite; his imagination not ethereal and lacking "the tempering guidance of instinctive taste." "There is truth in the scenery, but it is brought to the mind's eye as by the *camera,* with not enough of the exclusion and heightening of art, and even in the most graphic and spirited of his sea pictures, there is occasionally a rawness and feebleness of execution, a want of repose, and a jejuneness of effect—an absence of boldness in the outline—and of those evanescent touches in the colouring, the unbought graces and poetical hues—the sylphs that hover around the pencil of a master, and distinguish his finished magic, from the mere skill of the correct draughtsman—and yet all other sea pictures are tame to Coopers's!"[35]

Cooper was severely criticized and warmly praised because Legaré respected the New Yorker and wished for better. William Crafts posed a very different problem. He was a Charlestonian, personally known to Legaré and his readers, and dead. Obituary criticism suggested gentleness, yet Legaré chose severity, an explosion of Crafts' reputation from which the poetaster was never to recover. Partly this was Legaré's normal instinct, for he always went for the jugular. Mostly it was that much in Crafts' career as lawyer, politician, amateur author, and Charlestonian paralleled Legaré's own. He wished to draw the line between them, to distinguish the serious from the flippant, Legaré from Crafts, and so prevent Legaré from degenerating into Crafts.

Legaré conceded much, the more to point the moral. Crafts was amiable, gentle, and suave, and (an unexpected impression from his memorially published writings) he had "an air of pensive sadness—a tone of settled, though subdued melancholy, and of meek resignation under misfortune." He had had a brilliant beginning, at Harvard and in Charleston: "Man, woman and child, ran after Mr. Crafts' society, repeated his brilliant sallies, and laughed at his witty jokes." But success ruined him. He acquired much legal business, then lost it. He dissipated influence and reputation. Facile at the bar and in writing, he came to pride himself upon mere speed. He began to disdain the plodder and the thorough scholar, to neglect the work that might sustain his voracious appetite for fame. "Those coruscations of a lively fancy which had delighted and dazzled in the youth, seemed to be out of place in the senator of mature years—his little stock of knowledge, acquired almost exclusively by his early studies, was exhausted—his exertions as an advocate ceased to be called for, because his opinions as a counsellor were not respected, and, at the age of thirty-five, Mr. Crafts had already survived his hopes, his popularity and his reputation." This was a failure of exertion and duty, not of raw intelligence. The tragedy and the lesson was that Crafts could so readily, though not so easily, have prospered. This lesson needed pointing because Crafts' nonchalant example "prevails among our young barristers to a most pernicious extent."[36]

In his verse nonchalance sometimes served. "His most hasty and careless compositions, often happened to be his best; while those he took the most pains with, were sure to be written in his worst taste.

He set most value upon such of his compositions as were overrun with metaphor and exaggeration, with antithesis and epigram—while there were simple effusions—spontaneous beauties—which flowed from his pen without his knowing it—which, to borrow a very pretty thought of Sir Walter Scott's, his fancy yielded him with as little effort as a tree resigns his leaves to the gale in autumn, and which he appreciated as men are apt to do, whatever costs them least." The style was late Byron, *Beppo* and *Don Juan*—a dangerous inspiration, as Byron had required genius to put substance into a style superficially nonchalant. Otherwise, one just wrote "away at random with visible and invincible determination to transmute doggrel [*sic*] and absurdity into the rarest wit in spite of Minerva." There were odds and ends in Crafts' verse worth a moment's attention, the "Raciad" and "Sullivan's Island," but not much. Still less could his oratory be recommended, for it was undergraduate stuff worsened by a taste for festival declamation, itself the worst American speaking. "We do not suppose that it would be possible in any other country under the sun, or at least in Christendom—not even excepting Spain—to make such a collection of vapid bombast and rhodomontade, blended with every vice of style for which grammar or rhetoric furnishes a name, as might easily be got up in any single city in the United States under the title of 'American Eloquence.' "[37]

Crafts was dismissed over the pained protest of his friends who had put together the "little volume," only to see it instantly annihilated. Legaré chose stricture over silence. He cared for Charleston, respected the stern intellectual duties of the knowing critic, and did not care to permit prostitution even at the cost of domestic comforts. How could he respect his own pronouncements on Dante if he flattered William Crafts? Proportion mattered in criticism as it did in Greek porticoes. Yet it was cheap game. It is sound counsel that if you strike at a king, you must kill him. But only if you strike at a dandy whom you suspect of being yourself need the wound be fatal.[38]

6

Society

LEGARÉ PROPERLY FELT HIMSELF to be no professional in his studies
of antiquity and literature. In Berlin in 1836 the Prussian Foreign
Minister was politely to observe that Legaré was known for cultivating
Greek. Legaré noted in his diary, "I answer, rather confused, as I
always am, I know not why, when allusion is made to my studies of
*that kind*—that I am a mere amateur, and amuse myself in that way, in
my leisure moments." But he was a professional as a lawyer and
politician, and so his expositions of the law and the state are more
technical, more extensive, and more finely honed. [1]

At the basis of society was the law, not as an icon but as the most
concrete of influences upon history, embodying and influencing the
workings of human and social nature. Following Dugald Stewart,
Legaré was inclined to see the law as the most exact of the moral
sciences (with the caveat that no moral science was very exact), a kind
of mathematics, uncertain because exposed to the world but similar in
being a series of axioms, defined and maintained. In this Legaré was
following Stewart's unacknowledged master, Hobbes. For "in all other
sciences," Legaré explained, "the propositions, which we attempt to
establish, express *facts*, real or supposed, whereas in mathematics (and
we may add, in jurisprudence also) the propositions which we demon-
strate, only assert a connection between certain suppositions and
certain consequences. . . . Our reasonings therefore, in mathematics

and in law, are . . . to trace the logical filiation of consequences which follow from an arbitrary hypothesis, and, if from this hypothesis we reason with precision, the evidence of the result is of course irresistible." Stewart went too far in considering the law as precise as geometry, but "the logical method of the Civilians, is not mere formal parade and idle affectation."[2]

Virtue, being a thing invented and applied, explained why Byron could be designated an unprincipled man. "He alone can aspire to the reputation of virtue, who, besides having good impulses, and what is called an amiable character, lays down settled rules for the government of his conduct, from which it is possible to calculate, with some approach to certainty, what that conduct will be, from day to day, under given circumstances." Wayward charity, though benevolent, was not "strictly virtuous." So "prudent men often do charity, where they are doubtful about the claims of the object, merely that their own good habits may not be broken in upon, and their principles supplanted by caprice." Yet bad men might have inflexible rules, so principles must be good, "must be such as arise out of and confirm the better impulses of our nature, the social and benevolent affections . . . . the feeling and the principle ought every where to co-exist." A father might be virtuous without being amiable, without inspiring or feeling love. "Nay, it is very possible that an exemplary man, instead of being blessed with such impulses, should be visited by feelings of the very opposite character; yet, if he resisted them so successfully as to act up to the standard of nature and right reason, he would still deserve the reward of virtue, for virtue consists in *action*." Adam Ferguson had emphasized the paramountcy of habit over instinct, but here Legaré echoed more closely the socially conservative logic of William Paley, for whom utility and habit were the true tests of virtue; he was resisting the coming perfectionist theology which was to emphasize the centrality of sentiment.[3]

Law bore the same logic. The state extracted axioms from the benevolent dispositions of human nature and provided the mechanism by which they might be enforced; observance of the mechanisms of these axioms, not heartfelt approval or disapproval of them, was the morality of law and society; consent to the invention, not sentiment, mattered. Yet axioms had to be modified by experience. "An imaginary code of laws may be formed—and every possible variety of cases to which its principles would apply, be anticipated and decided, and a whole ideal *corpus juris*, with the *responsa prudentum*, and the equity of the praetor to explain and to temper its positive rules, be arranged and systematized. . . . Suppose this fictitious code to be, in all respects, conformable to the dictates of right reason, and we have a perfect system of natural law." Yet even if a liberal despot, a Dionysius of Syracuse, should provide a laboratory for the experiment, "very great changes would have to be made in it, in order to accommodate its principles to existing circumstances. In other words, the law of nature will inevitably be modified by the policy of society."[4]

Law moved between these polarities, invention and experience, axiom and history. Their embodiments were the civil law and the common law. Social thought resolved itself primarily into squaring the circle of these two systems and bringing to bear upon the reasoning clarity of the civilians the untidy experience of Westminster Hall and the Supreme Court. Law became the working-out of Legaré's poised sensibility, logical yet tactile to circumstance.

But the law was functional. Legaré read Homer without wishing to become an epic poet, and Byron without desiring to indite ribald verses. But he read Hugo Grotius and John Marshall to understand and come to match them. His ambition was great, though eclipsed by early death. There is a tenseness in Legaré upon the law, because he felt an intimation of influence, the American law being plastic, with Legaré the possible philosophic molder. "Nature, which is explained by philosophers and imitated by the artist and the poet, is every where the same, and it is not impossible that our literature and science, to however an exalted a pitch of excellence they may ultimately attain, may never exhibit any strictly national peculiarities. But the case is very different with the civil and juridical institutions of a country. There are, in a great degree, the work of man, and may be moulded, and have been moulded into endless varieties of form to suit his occasions or caprices." While the greatest molding had of necessity been done by the Revolutionary generation, much remained both of creation and digestion, remolding and understanding what others had molded. Thus Legaré took special care to note moments of change or philosophical comprehension in the history of the law. More, he took great pains to observe his own society, not only its constitutional law and politics but its nuances of social behavior, how Americans thought and acted, chose their dinner or their adjectives. For he was convinced that the burden of history, the influence of society upon law, lay in national character, and the lawyer was nothing who did not master its genius: "We believe that no constitution in the world is worth a straw but public opinion and national character."[15]

What of the civil law, his special passion? Its main attraction was elegance. "In comparing what the Civilians have written upon any subjects that have been treated of by English text writers, or discussed in the English courts, it is, we think, impossible not to be struck with the superiority of their truly elegant and philosophical style of analysis and exposition. Their whole arrangement and method—the division of the matter into its natural parts, the classification of it under the proper predicaments, the discussion of principles, the deduction of consequences and corollaries—every thing, in short, is more luminous and systematic—every thing savors more of a regular and exact science." Yet Legaré was wary of this aesthetic pleasure because conscious of the need for the law to be practical and aware of the instructive history of the civil law itself.[6]

He was no idolator of the ancient forms of the civil law but prized it most as a modern creation, fitted for the deployment of a modernizing world. The great lawyers of antiquity were great philosophers, but this fact meant that their "disquisitions, their dicta, their very definitions, all smack of the schools." This spirit grew in the Roman law with arbitrary rules, from which were "deduced, by an over-refined and captious logic, conclusions more subtle than sound, which gave to that jurisprudence the same technical and artificial air that strikes us in the writings of the bulk of our common lawyers." Such rules were modified by the praetors, evaded by the jurisconsults, and abolished by the emperors. One could discern in the Institutes and the scholarship of Heineccius improvements by the Caesars and by Justinian, "of which the object was to substitute rational for arbitrary legislation, and to give to the law a simplicity, at once elegant in theory and convenient in practice—the *simplicitas legibus amica*, as Tribonian happily enough expresses it." The third century was the Augustan age of the civil law, though "its great luminaries Papinian, Paulus, Ulpian, Modestinus, Julianus, Caius, and others, were not worthy of all the admiration which their immediate successors awarded to them and which still lives in a general tradition and consent of mankind." The Justinian Collection, though its principles either were "perfect as rules of right, or have been pregnant with lessons of improvement and usefulness," was not well done. "On the contrary, there are many learned men, who have thought, as Jortin bluntly expresses it, that Justinian did more harm than good to the civil law, by his slovenly and unphilosophical method of compilation, and by substituting, in so many instances, the language of his own degenerate and barbarous age, for the elegance of a more fortunate era." After all, Justinian had mingled with the barbarians, who had "made one blot" of the Western world, broken its spirit, narrowed and enfeebled its taste. All three parts of the collection—the Code, the Pandects, and the Institutes, were unsatisfactory: the Code was garbled; the Pandects had been absurdly jammed together in the space of three years; the Institutes, though more rationally disposed, were but elementary.[7]

The main achievement of the civil law lay in the modern era. This misled many English and American lawyers who learned of the civil law "not from the original text, but from modern commentaries and versions, especially from the writings of Domat and Pothier." This was the most favorable medium through which to view Justinian. Of Jean Domat, "it has been well remarked . . . that whoever has made himself master of what he has written, would be if not the most learned of jurists, at least the soundest of judges." Of Robert Joseph Pothier, "we have no language to express our admiration. The highest compliment that can be paid him is to state that the *rédacteurs* of the French code have generally followed his opinion in cases, where there is any difference of sentiment among jurisconsults, as the Roman emperor enjoined it upon his judges to abide by that of Papinian."[8]

The common law had a marked prejudice against the academic world. That a judge should be a man of business and not a scholar was a recommendation in the Inns of Court, as it was to Legaré's personal knowledge and occasional discomfort in the piepowder courts of the United States. The civil law had no such prejudice, leaned too much the other way: "It has been made, in every part of Europe, a branch of academic education, and enthroned, with philosophy and learning, in the most venerable seats of science. Paris and Padua, and Bourges succeeded to the honors of Rome, Constantinople and Berytus—the most erudite professors, men who devoted their whole lives to the science, with an intensity and enthusiasm, of which this degenerate age can scarcely form an adequate idea, have collated, criticized, expounded and *arranged* its principles—and, since the revival of the study in the twelfth century, so many editions, glosses, commentaries, paratitla, systems, abridgments, abstracts, have been published, that as many camel-loads of lumber, of all sorts, have been created by the work of Justinian, as it is said to have superseded and sunk."[9]

Much was useful, some not. The civil law was notoriously Caesarist, an underpinning for absolutism, an inconvenience for an American recommending its utility. So Legaré was careful to point to civilians like D'Aguesseau who were aware of this and skeptical, and to indicate the superiority of the common law in this respect. An American must reproach continental lawyers for "a servile spirit, a repugnance, not to say hostility, to all institutions favourable to public liberty which they confounded with license and anarchy." He should beware an imperial law, upon which in Constantinople was impressed "the image of oriental despotism" where "the will of the Prince was recognized as the only true source of legislation." Kings of Europe had employed such lawyers gradually "to undermine the power of the feudal barons." "In this important particular our common lawyers boast a glorious superiority over the civilians."[10]

But the civil law had made most useful distinctions: those between the *jus naturale*, the *jus gentium* and the *jus civile*. By the *jus naturale* was comprehended that "common to the whole animal creation, such, for instance, as the union of the sexes, the procreation and education of offspring, &c." By the *jus gentium* was meant that law common to the human species, "those things which are so manifestly reasonable and proper, or so agreeable to the general condition and exigencies of society, as to have found their way into every system of laws." The *jus civile* embraced that "part of the municipal law of every country, which arises from arbitrary legislation and peculiar customs, and which therefore, cannot be classed either with the *jus naturale* or the *jus gentium*." Legaré was especially interested in the *jus gentium*, for it seemed of growing relevance in modern society, where the "peculiarities of positive law are gradually effected by the intercourse of nations, and each code approximates more and more to the standard of that— quod naturalis ratio apud omnes gentes constituit. In this respect it will be found to be with the laws as it is with the characters of different peoples; they appear, at first sight, to be infinitely diversified, but very little examination is necessary to convince us that they resemble each other much more in the great, eternal principles of a common nature, than they differ in respect of local or national peculiarities."[11]

The *jus gentium* was not identical to international law, though it might embrace that. The civil law had, as a consequence of its earliest Caesarism, found little place for international law. The political and legal system of the Caesars "was calculated for perpetual success: they did not contemplate the possibility of their wanting the protection of such a code. As soon as a Roman citizen fell into the hands of an enemy, he was *capitis minor* and dead to the commonwealth. . . . Their *jus belli et pacis* was excessively simple—extending no further than to the fair interpretation and religious observance of *treaties*, and to such other obvious and necessary usages as must exist even among barbarians and outlaws, as for example, the immunity of ambassadors." Only in the seventeenth century was a systematic body of international law engrafted into the civil law by Grotius, "that extraordinary man." Bentham might scoff at the works of Grotius, Pufendorf, and Burlamaqui for being all things, "political or ethical, historical or judicial, expository or censorial." Legaré saw "much truth in this criticism . . . more, if possible, than its author would demand." Like D'Aguesseau, Legaré had never been able to finish reading Pufendorf's fat book. "But it is impossible to reflect upon the era at which Grotius wrote, in the midst of the horrors and atrocities of religious persecution and of civil war—calamities, of whose utmost bitterness he had himself been compelled to taste—without acknowledging that his treatise De Jure Belli et Pacis, in which enlightened reason, refined humanity, immense learning and elegant scholarship, mingle their winning and varied attractions, and where strong sense and convincing argument are rendered still more persuasive and venerable by the authority of great names, was at once a most noble monument of that day, and the herald of one yet brighter and more auspicious." No doubt half of the treatise could now be erased as "cumbersome and superfluous." The law of nations was then young. "Those intimate relations, commercial and political, which have since bound up all Christendom in one great society, and, as it were, family union, were just beginning to be formed and consolidated." The principle of the balance of power, "familiar to mankind in all ages," was not yet "a standing rule of conduct on a grand scale." So treaties like that of Westphalia were clothed with the authority of law. "Since Grotius wrote, two centuries more fruitful by far of great events, and magnificent improvement than any equal period in the history of mankind, have been continually adding to the number of such principles and confirming and consecrating them as they have been ascertained."[12]

There were the virtues and vices of the civil law, of whose relevance to the United States Legaré was sure. It was in the nature of American independence that the law had been forced into self-conscious reasoning by the break with England and Westminster Hall, though the divergence had commenced before 1776 and helped to explain the rupture. "All that was local and customary—all that, in England, was preserved because antiquity had allowed it, or prescription turned it into property, was discarded; and wherever these and such like changes left any chasm in the system, it was filled up by positive legislation, or by judicial decisions, founded upon the analogies of the constitution and the laws." Original speculation and reasoning were enforced, for in every case one had to decide "first . . . what was the law in England, and secondly, whether it were applicable here. The latter question it was impossible to answer without going into the true grounds and reasons of the law; and Burke's lawyer, who was at a loss, 'whenever the waters were out,' and 'the file afforded no precedent,' would often find himself as much embarrassed in an American court of justice, as in our deliberative assemblies." It was natural that, seeking reason, the lawyers should seek out the civil law. The career and writings of James Kent of New York, "that venerable and learned man," was an instance of "the use that may be made in our courts of the enlightened equity of the Roman jurisconsults."[13]

Legaré's praise of Kent, whose *Commentaries* marked a scholarly epoch in American law, matched those eulogies he tendered to jurists such as D'Aguesseau and Mansfield, struggling between traditional law and reasoned reform. Of D'Aguesseau, Legaré was insistently fond. "His mind and his heart were equally and perfectly well disciplined. He had received the sort of education which metaphysicians have mentioned as the best practical fruit of mental philosophy. All the powers and capacities of his intellectual and moral being seem to have been cultivated with a view to its highest perfection. His was that harmony of character, the music of the well attuned soul, in which the Platonists in their dreams of that perfection make it to consist." As Avocat-General for sixty years, as Procureur-General of the Parlement of Paris for sixteen, as Chancellor of France, he had displayed mastery of the feudal complexities of a French legal system that was, "so far as jurisdiction went, a mere confederacy of independent states." Honest, influential upon and resistant to the Regent, he had yet "inculcated the necessity and, so far as it was practicable at that time, set the example of reform in the law, with the double purpose of making it more perfect in itself and uniform throughout France. . . . That his reforms were not complete and radical—that he did not project such a code as has been since completed, under the auspices of Bonaparte—must be ascribed to the situation of France. Such a scheme . . . would have been quite chimerical at any period anterior to the sitting of the Constituent Assembly."[14]

The works of D'Aguesseau, model of the elegant and wary modifier, offered a bleak caution, for "the customary law of France . . . has been obliterated forever by the Five Codes." Only an antiquary could pore over "volumes—rich with the spoils of time—which were once useful to advocates and judges—such as the Capitularies, the Establishment of St. Louis, the Assizes of Jerusalem, the Anciennes Coutumes de

Beauvoisis by Philip de Beaumanoir, the Somme Rurale of Bou-
thillier, the Decisions of Jean Desmarés, and even Bracton and Lit-
tleton, the latter edited by M. Houard, as a repository of the old
Norman law." It was "appalling to reflect how much of the knowledge
of a lawyer, whose studies have been principally confined to matters of
positive legislation and local custom, may be swept away by a single
repealing clause." Yet scattered through D'Aguesseau's volumes were
enough natural equity and immutable truth to console the accomplished jurist. "We are firmly persuaded that jurisprudence is destined to attain, in this country, to a much higher degree of perfection,
both in theory and practice, than is compatible with the situation of
things and the character of the profession in England; but, long before
the dawn of philosophic light, which we believe to be opening upon
us, shall have brightened into perfect day, the name of D'Aguesseau,
with the kindred names of Domat and Pothier—his contemporaries,
his friends and even his *protégés*—will be as familiar to us as those of
Mansfield and Hale."[15]

The name of Lord Mansfield suggested a bridge between common
and civil law. Mansfield had founded a new method of jurisprudence,
simplifying and pointing out "connections where none had been
before observed." "He did much to perfect the harmony and con-
cordance of the law, and to shew that its seemingly arbitrary rules
generally coincide with the dictates of right reason," and in this he
was "indebted . . . in no small degree, to the writings of the civilians." "They were his masters and his model. In every branch of
commercial law, they furnished him not only with ascertained principles. but even with express precepts and established precedents—and
. . . even in laying down the rules which govern the action for money
had and received, he adopted not only their doctrines but their very
words."[16]

On the common law, Legaré's feelings were mixed. He traced the
legal history of feudalism with relief that it was not more relevant to
American law. He resisted the myth of liberty-loving German tribes
and Magna Carta, so energetically canvassed by his revolutionary
forebears. He even retranslated Tacitus to clear up ambiguities in
evidence cavalierly adduced by Blackstone. "The seeds of the feudal
system were sown . . . in the character and policy of the ancient
Germans, but the full development of it was owing to causes that
began to operate subsequently to the first settlement of the Northern
hordes in the countries which they over-ran. Those causes are to be
sought for in the violence and anarchy of a dark age, when not only

every kingdom, but every dutchy, every county, every district, was subject to the incursions of its enemies—when, in short, there was a war of all against all." A developed feudalism was only presaged in the early days of Tacitus' Germania, when fiefs were distributed arbitrarily by the spoils of war and not transmitted to heirs by agreed conventions. Feudalism did not arrive in France until Charles the Bald, if Montesquieu could be trusted. In Germany it took another two centuries and the reign of the Emperor Conrad, begun in 1054. "In England, although some writers fancy they perceive the origin of tenures in the Thane-land and Reve-land of the Saxons, it is not probable that any general and systematic establishment of feuds took place before the Norman conquest." In origin feudalism was a military system, the holding of territory and the reward of arms, and so it was confined to land; from this arose the "wide difference between real and personal estate in all their legal incidents and qualities, which pervades the whole system of English jurisprudence, and is almost wholly unknown to the civil law." In time feudalism lost its peculiarly military character, becoming a varied and complicated system of obligations. In France, under the weakening hold of Charles the Simple, it produced "an almost total extinction of all consolidated political government, and the substitution in its stead, of a disjointed and rickety confederacy of barons, if we do not abuse the name of a confederacy, by applying it to that never failing source of disorder, hostility and blood." In the midst of this period, the condition of the people was necessarily abject, "every fief, as it is strongly expressed by the Abbé de Mably . . . one vast prison to its inhabitants." Property, privilege, right were unprotected. This French system collapsed before "the energetic despotism of Richelieu," but its decay was prepared in courts staffed by clerics accustomed to Catholic traditions of hierarchy and obedience, where the civil law, "so excellent in questions of contract and property, so detestable in matters of public law and political rights," came to hold the field. Royal courts became the tribunal of last resort. "Thus it happened in this as in other instances, that the right of interpreting the law, conferred the power of altering it—that a court of justice became the mightiest engine of usurpation."[17]

In England, by contrast, the royal authority neither fell so low nor rose by reaction so high. The resistance of barons to king, and of conquered Saxons to conquering Normans, awakened a spirit of resistance that became in time English liberty. But Legaré was very careful to argue that, "in that age of barbarism and violence, it . . .

[was] next to impossible that any idea of well-regulated liberty should have been entertained by a whole class of men, and more especially by a body of petty tyrants, like the barons of England. . . . Men had not yet learned the meaning of the words nation, constitution, society, the people." Magna Carta was not even so "favourable to popular rights, as the charters extorted from Henry I., in the iron age of Norman despotism." It expressed "no *idées libérales*, as the constitutionalists in France express it—no platonic love of liberty in the abstract"; was instead "a mere treaty, extorted 'by the brute and boisterous force of violent men,' from a cowardly and feeble tyrant, whose pretensions came in conflict with their own, and whose arbitrary exactions, under colour of feudal dues, were likely to ruin their estates." Only later, transformed by a new spirit, could Magna Carta inform liberty. But feudalism, still a potent influence on English law, was almost imperceptible in American law, "thanks to the good sense and the favorable situation of our ancestors," just traceable, though indirectly, in "remainders, escheats and a few other like subjects."[18]

The merits and vices of the common law opposed those of the civil law. The civilians were elegant and scholarly, the common lawyers rough men of business. "The Common Law of England, as it has been generally studied by the practitioners of Westminster Hall" was the enemy of elegance, literary acquirement, philosophy, and "liberal and enlarged views of science and of society." "Polydore Virgil is represented as having pronounced the jurisprudence of that country a mingled or chaotic mass of foolishness and captious subtlety, and Erasmus breathes a sigh over the fate of Sir Thomas Moore, constrained by circumstances to devote his elegant mind to the study of a body of laws, than which nothing, in the opinion of the Dutch scholar, could be more *illiterate*." Mansfield and Eldon fell "miserably short of that elegant and finished model upon which the distinguished civilians seem to have formed themselves." Even Blackstone, the Ulpian of the Common Law, whose *Commentaries* deserved "Horne Tooke's remark, that 'it is a good gentleman's law book, clear, but not deep,' " was no "original or philosophical thinker," and did "nothing more than fill up the outline sketched by Sir Matthew Hale."[19]

Where the civil law was tidily and philosophically arranged and collated, the common law was obscure, inaccessible, judge-made. "The citizen who ought to know the rules of his civil conduct, as well as those of morality and religion, is forever in danger of doing what he ought not to do, or leaving undone what he ought to do, from sheer ignorance, and *that* incurable ignorance," of profit to lawyers. Yet contrary to some opinion, the common law offered a splendid training by "the subtle and rigorous logic" of its pleadings, almost geometric in their precision. The ill-trained or uncomprehending young lawyer's "ignorance may escape detection in the haste and confusion of a Nisi Prius scramble, and he may even be pre-eminently successful in the management of his cases before juries; but his want of that exact and scientific knowledge of legal principles, of which good pleading is at once the fruit and the test, must make itself glaringly manifest in every argument before the higher tribunals." For the common law was "the application of common sense, disciplined and directed by certain established principles, to the affairs of men."[20]

But the greatest defense of the common law was its contribution to social and political liberty. A confederacy of feudal lords had forced the treaty, Magna Carta, in which "the primitive spirit of Teutonic liberty was confirmed." "Stubborn bigotry . . . wholly excluded the Civil, and very much restrained the Canon Law" in England. Its lawyers, though "deformed by the technicality of the profession," protected liberty "with all its practical ability, its shrewd skill, its adherence to the forms of popular trial, its zeal for 'common right' and the good old customs of the realm; and even its religious, and, it may be, superstitious veneration for established precedent, has contributed not a little, at once, to fortify their conquests against the throne, and to save them from the opposite and not less formidable perils of a mere revolutionary levity." Taken all in all, the common law had a "justly conceded pre-eminence, as . . . a scheme of practical liberty."[21]

But the polarity of common and civil law was more apparent than real, as became clear when South Carolina became concerned during the 1820s with the issue of legal reform. Codification was a national movement, given especial prestige by Edward Livingston's reworking of Louisiana law. There were obscurities in the law of South Carolina, of a piece with the difficulties of the common law. John Lide Wilson, urging the legislature in 1827 to codify, stressed that a simple collation would save the lawyer the difficulty of tracing down every principle of common law. Thomas Grimké wished to save lawyers from the years of labor involved in establishing what portions of English law still had authority in South Carolina. Thomas Cooper did not like lawyers, laborious or not. "I almost incline to think with Barlow" he observed in 1824, "that when a man applies to a lawyer, he is like a hero of the eastern tales, who boldly mounts the back of a griffin, and takes all the risks of his temerity, in complete ignorance of the course he is to be carried."[22]

Legaré successfully opposed codification. His objections were simple: "Why not codify it? We answer simply because it will cost a great deal to do so, and because, in the present state of our law, it can do very little good, and may do much harm." His reasons were subtle: "The difference between written and unwritten law—or, to use less ambiguous terms, between statute and common law—consists not in the shape in which they ultimately appear, so much as in the manner in which they originate." The history of Roman law was illustrative. Its bedrock had been the XII Tables, but they were soon modified by the Senate, plebiscites, and the edicts of praetors and aediles to produce "what is properly called the *jus civile*, or common law." Statutes were "commented on and applied . . . to particular cases, by the learned jurisconsults whose authority was binding upon the judges." So "whereas our statutes are engrafted upon the common law which they derogate from, or change or control, *their* common law grew up out their statutes." Any law was condemned to hermeneutics, being the mirror of social experience, the child and father of process. Whatever its origins, it was obliged to converge on the varying needs and changes of society. As society was difficult, so was the law. As philosophy could not be reduced to a few settled rules of utility after the manner of Bentham, so was the law various, its truth often inaccessible. "But then the common law—the common law—with its antiquated trumpery—and its technical jargon—and its quaint subtleties, and its black letter, and its Norman French, and its scraps of bad Latin, and its Egyptian mystery, and its fictions, and its formulary! Verily she hides her truths at the bottom of a deep well, and her ways are past finding out! And so does all truth lie at the bottom of a well." The argument was characteristic of Legaré, who believed that mastery lay in learning and so belonged to the few, heeding the many. His discriminations between civil and common law were of a piece with his temperament: the former embodied elegant clarity; the latter, untidy experience. Law, like self, was the compound.[23]

What of society, which interpenetrated the law? Legaré was that unusual creature, a philosophical politician eager to extract general truths from particularities. Alexander Everett was only a little hyperbolic when he noted in 1840, "Legaré is the only man whom I have met with in the United States who was willing to converse upon the theory of govt. or who, if he undertook it shewed any interest in the subject."[24] He aspired to detachment even as his headlong temperament willed engagement. So he wished to define that partly new thing, American society.

Of the American mind of his day, he had no high opinion. He threw off indictments of wretched congressional and festival oratory; he protested at the indifference of legal pleading; he condemned weak literature; he mocked ignorant classicism. Above all, he was wearied by the inadequacy of American education. Too little had been done, because so much American education in the eighteenth century had been expatriate. "There are very few men of science and still fewer scholars among us—we speak, of course, in reference to the European standard." A few accomplished young men had studied in England and "true to the spirit imbibed in the writings of the ancients, contributed greatly to the independence of their country." "We are far, very far, from disputing their merit—they were an honor and blessing to the State, and they formed a society far superior, in some interesting respects, to anything that has succeeded it in any part of the Union. But the system was essentially aristocratic and exclusive, as the improvements it led to were altogether *exotic*." The wealthy were educated in England, but nothing was done at home, "no seminaries of science . . . endowed in the Provinces," nothing "provided by the government for people of moderate fortunes." Education had been badly organized and wasteful, though matters had improved. "What can be more magnificent, than the liberality which Harvard has experienced from the opulent merchants of Boston? And where can any society be found more entirely devoted to liberal pursuits, than that of the city just mentioned? The same spirit has prevailed in every part of the country—even where circumstances have been far less favorable to its development. This State, for instance, appropriates annually much more than a tithe [more accurately a sixth] of its whole revenue to the instruction of its people. She has founded at great expense a college . . . and furnished it with a most excellent library." Education should be indigenous, and it would therefore follow that Thomas Jefferson had erred in launching his University of Virginia with foreign scholars. Yet investment in education did not seem to work, because the speed of American social mobility and opportunity was so great as to distract energies away from learning. And the learned encountered prejudice. "There can be no doubt but that, throughout the Southern States at least, and, perhaps, throughout the whole country, a taste for literary studies (much more any serious or continued application to them) stands very much in the way of a young man in the pursuits of active life. It raises a presumption among worldly people, that he can never become *practical*, and such a notion when it has once taken root in the public mind, is, beyond all comparison, the most formidable obstacle a man of talents can encounter in such a state of society as ours." Thus "the more democratic the education of boys, the better."[25]

American thought had a marked and depressing characteristic, which to denote was the first act of Legaré's writing for the *Southern Review*. "We Americans take nothing for granted—except, indeed, as it would appear from the tone of some recent publications—the immeasurable superiority of those who have lived to see this 'Age of Reason,' over all that have not been so fortunate. . . . We take up all questions *de novo*, and treat every subject of general speculation and philosophy, no matter how frequently and fully discussed, or how solemnly decided elsewhere, as what is called at the bar *res integra*, that is to say, as fair game for criticism and controversy." Congressmen "from one of the more enlightened, because less *ancient* and prejudiced States" prefaced speeches on the colonial trade with "a 'brief' account of Columbus and his discoveries"; politicians discussed "the most casual and ordinary questions of commerce and finance" by spouting volumes of political economy. Once, having waded through the prefatory chapters of Hoffman's *Legal Outlines*, which rambled on in the manner of the nineteenth century ("the age of dissertation; every thing runs out into prosing common-place, and takes the shape of a scholastic diatribe") with pronouncements on the distinctions between animal and vegetable, instinct and sensation, sensation and perception, Legaré wearily remarked, "We grieve that Mr. Hoffman has given the sanction of his example to this crying sin against good taste and common sense, which is, indeed, becoming an intolerable public nuisance." It was not that Americans were impractical. To the contrary: "Call upon an American for action, and you are sure to find him ready, skilful, decided and efficient. . . . the patent-office—that great repository of Jonathan's practical cleverness—is already overcharged." But American theory was "nothing but rigmarole or rhetoric."[26]

This fault extended too seriously into politics itself. Legaré saw around him, in legislatures and on hustings, men fatally inclined to subtle distinctions, for the shape of the American state compelled men into metaphysics. There was too much complacency, an "unbounded faith in forms" and in "a written constitution as a sort of talisman, which gives to the liberties of a nation 'a charmed life.' "

Political discourse, unrestrained by a fear of failure, had become "wild and visionary," "addicted to abstractions." "It is really curious to look into the debates in Congress, when measures pregnant with important consequences are the subject of discussion. The University of Paris, in the heyday of scholastic divinity, never excelled them in the thorny, unprofitable, and unintelligible subtleties of dialectics. Our statesmen are, in general, any thing but practical men—a fact that may be, in some degree, accounted for by the vast predominance of mere professional lawyers (not of the first order) and the fact, that we have a written constitution to interpret by technical rules."[27]

Issues were decided less upon the bald questions of right and wrong, expedience and inexpedience, than upon the more abstract question of constitutionality. Legaré summarized the dialectic with a precision worth full quotation: "A measure is proposed, revolting to the moral sense and the common sense of mankind—unequal and oppressive, inconsistent with the cardinal objects and the whole genius of the government. It is opposed by those upon whom it bears hardest as *unconstitutional*—that is to say, as unfit to be adopted by the rulers of a free people, because it is unjust, and is not *bona fide* intended to fulfil the purposes of the federal compact. Immediately a metaphysical disputation ensues, and if by such jargon as has immortalized the angelical and seraphic doctors, the constitutionality of the scheme be made to appear *very doubtful*, it is at once assumed by the majority as demonstrated, and, perhaps, acquiesced in by the minority, because the question, if it should be thought sufficiently important, can be tried again before the Supreme Court. The responsibility of those who pass the law is shifted upon those who interpret it; and thus the former venture a great deal farther upon the questionable ground than they would were their decision entirely without appeal. If, again, when the law comes before the Supreme Court, that judicatory, from some defects in its constitution or its administration, will not or cannot pronounce it void—the will of the majority is at once considered as sanctified—its act is of course lawful, is just, is reasonable and proper. The people at large, after a few unheeded murmurs, submit to this imposing authority, and think that their discontents must be unreasonable, because their understandings have been puzzled by sophisters, and awed by the learning of the bench! In short, the constitution is made to have the effect of an *estoppel* (an odious thing in law) upon their just complaints, and they are expected to suffer, like poor Shylock, any hardship which a subtile interpretation can deduce from their 'bond.' "[28]

So Legaré felt himself not a learned scholar among rude "empyr-icks" but a commonsensical man among imprudent metaphysicians. As he reserved some of his most bitter remarks for "speculative" politicians, it was a mark of no small unease in his attitude toward the United States that he denoted its political class as metaphysical, not just by private inclination but by the pressure of institutional and social necessities. Extravagantly as he admired the prudent Revolu-tion of 1776 and the Constitution of 1787, it was precisely his devotion to a political framework he deemed a moderate conservative government of restricted and enumerated powers that gave him a sharpened motive for pondering his loyalties to the Constitution as it had evolved in 1830.

For the Constitution was not identical to the social compact, Legaré being at pains to resist the tendency to replace political thought with constitutional thought, to make thinking about the Constitution of 1787 identical with thinking about the state and society. "What constitutes the identity of a state?" he asked in 1829. "What is a revolution in the government, and how far does it affect the rights and duties of the body politic towards other bodies politic, or towards individuals?" This could not be decided by abstract philosophy or the claims of a French Revolution born from an age of reason, in which the "popular definition of well-regulated liberty seemed to be that every body might do as he pleased with respect for his neighbours, and all obligations, moral or political, natural or civil, were regarded as inconsistent with the rights of man." One read such "impracticable speculations . . . as Voltaire pleasantly says of them, for the same reason that we keep in our houses the portraits of individuals whom we never saw and never expect to see." The nineteenth century had brought soberness.[29]

Upheavals in the constitutional world affected only the constitu-tional, not the social compact, especially in America where it was "one of our favourite national amusements to pull down and put up our governments." For republican political orthodoxy was like Roman Catholic orthodoxy, only "the decree of an ecumenical council—the voice of the majority, which is infallible, because it is paramount." Right in civil wars adhered to the successful. "The people of these States—that is to say, the majority in the name of the whole—declared, on the fourth of July, 1776, that they owed no allegiance to the British government—that it had been *ipso jure* extinguished by the infractions of the political compact there set forth—and the object of the declaration was to announce this indisputable *fact* to the world. . . . all who were parties to . . . the *social* compact, as contra-distinguished from the constitutional—owed a natural allegiance, not to the *government*, but to the *body-politic*, of their respective States, and are presumed to have assented to the separation which the majority of that body-politic declared to exist."[30]

In revolutions men did not return to a state of nature, there obliged to begin again. Society survived even when the state was deranged. "We admit the principle of Locke in our declamations, and lay great emphasis upon its reasonableness and equity. But when we come to put it in practice, we then for the first time discover, that it is *casus omissus* in all our constitutions—that it is in direct conflict with the maxims of our common law—and that without mentioning the speculative difficulties that surround it, the common sense of mankind and the uniform practice of society, (our own included) are altogether irreconcileable with it." The will of the majority was but the right of the strongest in society, however much disguised by "the technical and mystical jargon of lawyers and publicists. . . . under such sounding and learned appellations as the Eminent Domain and the Original Compact." It was as idle to speak of a state of nature as it would be for a court to "tolerate a fanatic raving about the kingdom of the saints on earth, or discharge a Don Quixotte from arrest for his tavern-bill, on the principles of the most ancient and venerable institution of knight-errantry." However much Legaré was the good commonwealthman in his preferences for "that *instinct* of liberty, which characterizes the controversial reasoning of the great fathers of the English constitution—the Seldens, the Sidneys, the Prynnes—and their worthy descendants and disciples, the founders of our revolution," his reasoning upon the state was Hobbesian, just as he echoed Hume's Tory and anti-Lockean insistence that men entered involuntarily into the social compact.[31]

But Hobbes predated the doctrine of nationalism. If constitutional compacts might come and go, social compacts were, if not eternal, then sufficiently permanent. The American people, perhaps with republicanism, would survive even if the compact of 1787 did not. "It is the national character that is to be looked to when we talk of constitutions—it is the national history that is to regulate our conjectures about the future." This was so because the American was "not a race of barbarians, whose character was yet to be formed or developed," but a continuous development from European experience, refreshed by American circumstances. Colonists had "the manners, the knowledge, and the modes of thinking," of an advanced European society with all its historical recollections, hereditary feelings, literary associations, and philosophical tenets, even its "religious doctrine and discipline." "Nor was there any thing in their situation here, to sever these strong ties—to give a new impulse to opinion in matters of philosophy and learning, or, in short, to influence, in any material degree, their own intellectual character and pursuits—much less to produce a sensible effect upon the general condition of the human mind." Part of that inheritance was an instinct for liberty. "Our experience on this subject is exactly as great, that is to say, the very same as that of England. We both date from the Petition of Right, two hundred years ago. The parent country never knew the *placidam sub libertate quietem*, until she got rid of the Stuarts. Her history, until 1688, full as it is of high and heroical examples of patriotism and devotion to the great cause, is very far from encouraging. On this side of the Atlantic, the love of liberty is unsophisticated and virginal. The children of the Puritan and the Huguenot have never ceased to breathe the spirit which animated the first Pilgrims—the spirit of Naseby and Marston-Moor, of Montcontcour and Ivry."[32]

Equally, the American Revolution was a continuous development from the colonial experience. As he was to remark to August von Schlegel in 1835, on a visit to Bonn: "[We] speak also of M. Tocqueville's recent book on the democracy of the U.S. Tell them I have not read it and so get off without giving a general opinion of the subject. Add that from some observations on it in the *Débats*, he seems to have seen things in a truer light than foreigners usually do—e.g. he dates our republicanism, not as people on this side the Atlantic absurdly imagine, from the Revolution, but from the very foundation of the colonies which I explain, adding at the same time, that nothing could be more widely different than such a revolution, and one (like that of '89, for instance) where every thing had to be pulled down and set up again." The Revolution was "one, not of desperate necessity or excited passion, but of pure, in one sense, almost, of speculative principle," that led to "no violent innovations, no popular commotions." Likewise, the confederation was fashioned with "a gravity, a deliberation, a critical examination, a comprehensive discussion of the exigencies of the times and the situation." This frame of mind created that "defence of rational liberty, and so ["though God forbid we should ever have to make the experiment"] the republican institutions of the States would not necessarily perish even with the present general government."[33]

Yet continuity implied no insignificant shift from English forms.

Legaré felt of American politics what he had insisted of American law, that circumstances had compelled a difference from before 1776. "Our founders could not, if they would, be imitators. They could bring with them from the mother country only the general principles of government and jurisprudence—the great outlines of a free constitution, and the invaluable maxims of the common law. But its institutions were more or less inapplicable to their present circumstances, and their civil polity had to be recast and built up anew from the very foundation." So this independent civil polity, while it could learn immensely from the stores of European knowledge and experience, had no need to imitate European social forms or heed European criticism of American society. It was with amusement that Legaré examined travel books written by the likes of Mrs. Trollope and Basil Hall, praising them when accurate, reprobating them when in error, never taking them too seriously. Despite his European travels and the inclinations of his passion for scholarship, Legaré was no Anglophile or Francophile. Whatever his discomforts and dissatisfactions with American society, and they were many, he believed himself morally bound to the essential forms of American life, and was content and pleased to be so. Nationality was in his marrow, sufficient to permit the cosmopolitan.[34]

"To us, peculiarly situated as we are, to be by a foreigner looked at with any thing like impartiality seemed rather to be desired than expected," he once observed when reviewing the American travel account of that engaging patron of Goethe, the Duke of Saxe-Weimar-Eisenach. The country was "felling its forests, laying out towns, and providing itself with the necessaries of life," and it needed indulgence. Travelers "have exacted of youth the maturity of age; of poverty, the splendour and magnificence of hereditary wealth." They were irrelevantly offended by "the spirit of equality under a democratic government," manifested in northern servants insisting upon being treated and addressed as "helps." Such "vulgar cits and adventurers of no character," "travellers of the Cockney school," the Fauxs and the Fearons, were not worth "the wrath which condescended to break such insects upon the wheel." But even the shrewder visitor failed of insight, and "it will be a long time before we can expect perfect justice—not to speak of favour and indulgence—from British writers of any class."[35]

Americans took criticism with an ill grace, but Englishmen dispensed it with little sensitivity. "Even when they roam through countries strictly foreign—that is of a different origin and language—

they rarely do more . . . than tolerate their peculiar usages and manners. Still they do make some allowances on this score. . . . But with us nothing escapes their observation, and everything is tried by false weights and measures." In particular, they were inclined to attribute to the innovation of democracy all differences and all error: the defective education of the wealthy, lax domestic discipline, bombastic congressional speeches, rough roads, stagecoaches with hard seats and no doors, the gobbling of dinner in a trice, eating in a country inn or a cheap boarding house in town "with a broad-sword, nicknamed a knife, instead of a silver fork, and without any napkin."[36]

The misunderstanding between England and America was, he admitted, reciprocal. Legaré found English society as distasteful as Basil Hall found American. Americans naturally abominated the English polity; for "all the admirable characteristics of her people, which have raised England to such a pitch of glory and power," there was nowhere to be found a society "so artificial, exclusive and disagreeable . . . so widely at variance . . . with the *jus gentium* of polished life." They were obsessed with "the merest minutiae of dress and manners . . . regulated by a most arbitrary and fluctuating standard," bemusing to the uninitiated. Legaré's horrified amusement in Lytton's *Pelham* lay just in its burlesque of this brainless dandyism. "Brummel seems to have studied profoundly the character of fashionable society in England. He saw that it was not founded, as it had formerly been in France, on the mere love of elegant conversation and refined pleasures, which a truly polite noblesse did as much as they could to promote, by admitting without reserve into their circles, all whose talents and accomplishments were fitted to delight and adorn them. He perceived that the disease—the all-devouring, epidemic disease—of the *bonne compagnie* in England, was *vanity*." His "vacant, listless, yawning existence" could only be abrogated by ostentation, Almack's, the attainments of the lion. The problem was not so much that England was aristocratic—eighteenth-century France had been that—but that it sanctified the parvenu by making fashion a substitute for rank or accomplishment. "The classes condemned to what is technically called 'climbing,' are far more extensive in England, than on the continent of Europe." The parvenu and the man of fashion formed an unholy alliance to "wage a war of extermination against all pretenders to 'gentility,' who have been up and are going down, or who, being down, are struggling to get up." This was vicious and perverted, at variance with self-assurance and liberality, at odds with " 'the old and elegant humanity of Greece'—or even of that exquisite, though more artificial and effeminate refinement in France, under the ancient *régime*, so winning, so gentle, so accessible, so unpretending." The sin of the parvenu was not inferior birth but a passion for advancement that made him pinched, self-absorbed, without "ease and freedom."[37]

This was a sharp reproach from Legaré. Certainly South Carolina had bred him to a quasi-aristocracy markedly fluid in recruitment and origins. But it may speak of rebuffs in England unrecorded for the historian. As one obituarist was to remember, "He paid scrupulous attention to his dress; but its only merit was its niceness. In its selection and putting on, he was frequently so far forgetful of the good taste which regulated him in other respects, as to appear eccentric. We have known him, for instance, on a great and prepared occasion, deliver an address in white silk stockings and pumps, with pants not over long, buckled down with straps; and this too after he had done his day's marketing, with six or eight huge and dusty law books under his arm. He lived and died a bachelor, which is, perhaps, the best apology we can offer for such pardonable trivialities." Legaré was a man to fret over appearances. When in Berlin in 1836, asked to dinner by the Foreign Minister of Prussia, he put into his diary: "First put on boots according to our fashion at Brussels; but fearing lest there might be ladies and a different rule here and being an entire stranger—think it safer to go in shoes. Do so and repent, no womankind and everybody in boots." In London in 1834, he was given the coveted ticket to Almack's and did not bother to attend, whether from indifference or trepidation.[38]

Yet dislike of a dandy's society did not mean approval of pell-mell. Legaré censured Northern society for a want of ceremony and manners. Unlike many contemporaries, he saw no intrinsic vice in the mannered artificialities of civilization, or especial strength in the rude directness of folk cultures. Like David Hume, he preferred, as was demonstrated by praise of eighteenth-century France, a discourse regulated by decorum and softened by the influence of women. It was a defect of the ancient Greeks that "their virtuous women were condemned to a sort of oriental seclusion. . . . The exclusion of females from the society of the other sex, is a decisive proof of a state of manners savoring of rusticity and barbarism. We may judge from our own parties of brawling politicians and professed wine bibbers, from which the charms of female conversation are so rigorously shut out, what such a system leads to, even under the most favorable circum-

Hugh Swinton Legaré, by Thomas Sully;
a "society" portrait, done posthumously.
COURTESY, CAROLINA ART ASSOCIATION/GIBBES ART GALLERY

stances." Rude wassailing killed "the delicacies of a chastened wit and raillery that make French society so delightful." So it was natural that Legaré preferred the lightness of the supper and regretted its surrender to the weight of the dinner, migrating in the nineteenth century through the afternoon into the evening. Nothing compared to *"petits soupers* arrayed in all their appropriate charms of delicate wit, delicate wines, and delicate viands." One could settle "the never-ending controversy about the comparative merits of the ancients and the moderns" by pointing out that the main meal of the ancients was supper. Dinners by candlelight were not the same thing, "no more than a 'fashionable' man's residence, in what he is pleased to nickname a 'cottage,' makes him taste the pleasures of a true 'Cotter's Saturday Night.' " This was the lament of a man with a delicate stomach, who preferred sherry to port, Johannisberger to Bordeaux, vegetables to meat, who stood appalled at the advancing and multiplying stodg-iness of the Victorian dinner. It was also the cry of a man who, having spent much of his life alone with mother and sister, was thrust with evident unease into a rude man's world.[39]

The mutual incomprehensions of England and America were struc-tural, implicit in their varying social orders. Nonetheless, passing events could further deepen mistrust. Basil Hall had traveled in the United States during the election of 1828, an unedifying spectacle to the American, let alone the English sea captain. He saw "disgusting and disgraceful abominations which have made the late presidential election forever memorable—may it be forever unparalleled—in our history." He saw rancorous hostility, atrocious calumnies, systematic misrepresentations, "the violation of every decency of life" proceeding from party warfare. He saw a daily press of "ribaldry and falsehood," shaming and loathsome. "He heard of eaves-droppers reporting con-versations—of friends publishing the letters of their correspon-dents—of guests violating the rights of hospitality, and the sanctity of the fireside and the festive board. He saw this ruthless and unprin-cipled warfare carried into the very bosom of domestic life, and even female sensibility and honour assailed by remorseless ruffians, appar-ently with the countenance of men who ought to have blushed at the bare idea of such an alliance." Such corruption alarmed and made anxious "any good citizen." It reversed "the fundamental maxim of republican government" by sacrificing principles to men. The press needed reform; the politicians needed correction for their partisanship and for believing "success the only test of merit, and failure the only sort of dishonour worth avoiding."[40]

Yet Legaré was a supporter of Andrew Jackson. Democracy could mean many things to different men. Legaré's democracy was of the late eighteenth century: it should be an influence upon the body politic, not a guiding principle. He reproved his own distaste for 1828 when he noted, "It is a shrewd observation of Machiavel, that those who find fault with the tumults occasioned by the differences between the nobility and the commons at Rome, quarrel with the main cause of all her freedom and power. . . . The great maxim of all popular government is *ex fumo dare lucem*. It is a mighty maze, but not without a plan." It was an energizing confusion, and the "test of excellence in politics, is the same as Paley's in morals—utility in the long run." "A well-balanced popular government" produced "a greater sum of happiness and improvement than . . . any other kind of polity, a greater number of people [were] made, 'in mind, body and estate,' what their Creator intended them to be." The commonwealth of citizens interacted with the republic of genius to produce a messy but durable state. The people were a powerful adviser, though not a sovereign, in a body politic with no sovereign but the law. So the congressman should not be an instructed delegate, although "through the frequency of elections, the people exercise a greater control over their representatives here, than they do in any part of Great-Britain, and so much the better." Hence Legaré had thought the House of Representatives within its rights to elect John Quincy Adams over Andrew Jackson in 1824, despite Jackson's having the greater total of popular votes, and in 1838 he was to ignore an instruction from the South Carolina legislature to vote for the Sub-Treasury.[41]

Naturally, Legaré viewed with suspicion innovations that transformed a popular republic into a simple democracy. In particular he was sensitive about alterations in the judiciary, for he viewed the bench as the necessary guardian of the Constitution, the more to be held to a high standard because it was of necessity virtually irresponsible. Here the English had been wiser, by giving judges liberal salaries, tenure, and pensions. But the American people were stingy and "will not spend money without a present and palpable *quid pro quo*. . . . Extinguish the light of a Kent or a Spencer—submit to the drivellings of dotage and imbecility—nay, even resort to the abominations of an elective judiciary system—anything rather than adopt the plain, manly, and only sure means of securing the greatest blessing, but liberty, which civil society can attain to, the able administration of the laws!"[42]

Unlike Basil Hall, Legaré objected to universal suffrage as tending to oligarchy and throwing an "immense weight into the scale of wealth." As yet it tended the "other way, because the population of the country is so thin," and scarcity promoted the dignity of labor. But in time, the cities swollen, it would be otherwise. Ultra-democracy would "operate as a check upon the *real* democracy of the country." "We shall not complain of it, however, if its tendency be, as some affirm, to postpone this result to a later period than might otherwise be assigned for it, by elevating the feelings of the poor and habituating them to the exercise of a practical independence."[43]

Danger to the republic came not from a licentious democratical mob but from the imprudent tinkerings of the politicians and the innovations of Marshall's Supreme Court, which were turning a limited republic into a simple consolidated government. The conjunction of *McCulloch* v. *Maryland* and *Fletcher* v. *Peck* was especially ominous to Legaré, the one sanctioning the federal government's power to create and regulate corporations, the other making the motives of a legislature opaque to the judge unless the lawmaker chose to avow them. Of John Marshall himself, Legaré had a high opinion, even as he doubted the decisions of his court. That political prophecy was unwise could be exemplified by comparing the Constitution of 1787 and *The Federalist* with the recent analyses by Chancellor Kent of constitutional jurisprudence, Jackson's first inaugural address, and the congressional session of 1828. "The government has been fundamentally altered by the progress of opinion," no longer one of "enumerated powers and a circumscribed sphere, as it was beyond all doubt intended to be . . . confining itself in time of peace to the diplomatic and commercial relations of the country," but one "interfering in the domestic concerns of society," threatening very soon "to control, in the most offensive and despotic manner, all the pursuits, the interests, the opinions and the conduct of men." In this was the hand of the Supreme Court, "which has applied to the constitution—very innocently, no doubt, and with commanding ability in argument—and thus given authority and currency to, such canons of interpretation, as necessarily lead to these extravagant results." This modified Constitution offered no barrier in theory to congressional omnipotence. Yet in practice it was restrained by "the vigilance, the wisdom, and the firmness of a free people."[44]

Legaré was here vexed by the matter of slavery, quite beyond the case of the tariff. Such a drift more than hinted that "the rights of the weaker part of this confederacy may, to any extent, be wantonly and tyranically violated, under color of law (the most grievous shape of oppression) by men neither interested in its destiny nor subject to its control, without any means of redress being left it, except such as are inconsistent with all idea of order and government." Slavery's standing in the Union compelled wariness upon the Southerner, made him the reader of entrails. "The task of a Southern politician is full of difficulty," he lamented. "The other parts of this country, with a good judicial system to regulate the transactions of individuals, could get along for some time to come almost without any administrative government. But *we must* be vigilant, and wary and provident. We must ask our watchman continually 'what of the night.' We must look at the seeds of future events, and the causes which have not yet begun to operate. Time, which is the wisest of all things, and the greatest of innovators, may possibly convince us, at a future day, that some changes ought to be made. And we are satisfied that, if we do not spoil his work by our presumptuous and precipitate interference, all will yet go well."[45]

Slavery was a burdensome inheritance which—like malformation—must be borne, an evil especially in the form of the slave trade. Legaré insisted that slavery had been foisted upon the South by the traders and merchants of Europe and the North: they, the panders, were as guilty, more guilty, than the libertine slaveholders. And pressure upon slavery was so new, "one of the most extraordinary revolutions that has ever occurred in the history of the human mind." Once "a few philanthropists" had complained "amidst the busy hum of a prosperous commerce, pleading for the victims of that infernal traffic." Virginia had even tried to stop it, to no avail. "It was decreed by those who had our destinies in their hands that the Southern regions of America should be crammed with this barbarous and abominable population—the commercial navy of the whole world vomited it forth upon us by hundreds of cargoes—every capitalist embarked in the profitable speculation—every insurance office greedily snatched at the premium paid for indemnity against the chances of this traffic in blood and tears—and, in the most rational department of modern jurisprudence, the question was seriously entertained whether 'these beings with immortal souls' might not, in case of necessity, be flung overboard like any other merchandize according to the *Lex Rhodia de Jactu!*" The profit of colonies implicated the whole world in the guilt of this commerce, this "conspiracy of all Europe and the commercial part of this continent, not only against Africa, but, in a more aggravated sense, against these Southern regions." How absurd then that England and New England should be "coolly lectur-

ing *us* upon the sin of keeping our fellow-men in bondage! . . . A
father, whose vices had entailed disease upon his offspring, and who
should cast him off with this hereditary uncleanliness, presents something like a parallel—the only one we have been able to imagine—to
this instance of prodigious effrontery."[46]

The image of slavery as syphilis hinted at no "positive good" theory.
The only morality Legaré accepted was historical: slavery was a
Burkean problem. "Whether slavery is, or is not reconcilable with
what is called by philosophers the law of nature, we really do not
know. We find the greatest theoretical publicists divided upon the
subject, and it is, no doubt, a very good thesis for young casuists to
discuss in the college moot-club. We shall not undertake it, for we
have no taste for abstractions. We will not quote Grotius or Huber. It
is enough for us that, when the Southern people consented to receive
the African race into their territory, it was upon the express condition
of perpetual service, and that this condition was then as lawful as any
other arrangement of civil society." Slavery had conformed to ancient
law, the modern law of nations, and Christian law. The New Testament, if read in the original Greek, made it clear that Christ enjoined
loyalty upon slaves, not merely servants. No doubt the world was
changing its opinion, abandoning the old link between war and
slavery, holding to the greater crime of war while blushing at the lesser
of slavery. "This may be all very well for some people; but *we* must be
allowed to hold on to the old logic a little longer." The issue was
historical necessity, for a Southern people in the midst of necessity.[47]

As a practical rather than metaphysical problem, slavery must be
decided by those, the Southerners, most implicated, not by distant
philosophers. Danton, *l'ami du peuple,* at least paid upon the
guillotine for the temerity of his doctrines and knowingly risked his
fate. "But when Brissot came out as *l'Ami des Noirs*, an ocean rolled
between this canting hypocrite and the frightful scenes occasioned
soon after, by the application of his doctrines." This was the just
complaint of the slaveholders of the English West Indies. "Men were
declaring war, without peace, truce or quarter, against them; whose
persons, assuredly, were never to be exposed to the dangers of war, and
whose appetites for their dinners would not have been in the smallest
degree, affected by the intelligence, that every slave-holder in the
world had been exterminated." While Legaré was disposed to think
that attacks upon slavery within the United States betrayed a "very
becoming degree of forebearance," the special constitutional status of

the District of Columbia boded ill, and much would depend upon the spirit of the coming debate.[48]

A slaveholder, Legaré sympathized with the slaveholders. He did express regret at the "unmerited sufferings of the poor negroes," but it was fleeting. Indeed, he thought the practical deficiencies of the institution of slavery stemmed not from harshness but from "its tendency to produce in process of time, laxity of discipline, and, consequently, disorders and poverty in a country, by the excessive indulgence of careless or too scrupulous masters. In the course of a generation or two, the family relation, the tie of a sort of *homage ancestral* between master and slave, becomes so intimate, and so affecting, that the sternness and rigor absolutely necessary in the management of men, not under the spur of necessity, sensibly abate, and with them there is a corresponding falling off in the cheerful and ready obedience, and of course, in the happiness as well as the usefulness of the slave." Nonetheless, he was conscious of just such a comfortable intimacy in his own household, had reproached himself with having once broken up a slave family, preferred to have slaves reared at home rather than bought on the auction block, and was to look forward from Brussels to settling himself in their care. "This circumstance [of intimacy]," he observed to his mother, "is after all some & even a great compensation for the unquestionable evils attendant upon the institution of slavery." Nature obliged men to extract good out of evil. "Was there no exultation, no heroism in the Vendean, or the Spanish patriots, because they were priest-ridden and degraded, and so blind as to fight for despotic princes? Was the Celtic Clan less devoted to its chieftain, for his exorbitant powers, and his occasional freaks of tyranny?" Subjection and misery were intrinsic to the human condition, for the working population of England as much as for the slave, whose fate was at least regulated by paternalism. "Such a frightful mass of evil as now exists in England—so much bodily suffering and mental anguish—so many crimes prompted by the desperation of utter want, and punished with the unrelenting rigour of a stern and necessary policy, shew that, even under the most propitious circumstances, a large portion of mankind are doomed to servitude and misery. We are sincerely sorry for it, but so we are for all the evil, moral and physical, in the universe, and can only bow with deep humility before the inscrutable wisdom which orders or permits it."[49]

Legaré feared precipitate schemes of emancipation, though not because Denmark Vesey had hinted at the duplication of Haiti. Whites would win a servile war "unless it be complicated with some other kind of war." "Let the *loyalty* of the slave not be disturbed by jacobinical lectures on the wrongs of which he has never been conscious—and he will not conspire at all. Let his conspiracy be unaided by foreign power, and it will be easily suppressed. Let it break out into open rebellion, and he and his whole race will be exterminated." It was in the slave's interest not to brook an interference that would lead to "discontent on the one side, and systematic cruelty on the other— to what Burke admirably characterizes as the 'merciless policy of fear.' "[50]

Legaré upon slavery was candid. He did not doubt the right of the institution, though not for religious or racial reasons. Of the religious proslavery argument he was sparing in his use; the racial, he did not employ at all. He was a racialist, although the anthropological case for slavery was as yet underdeveloped. He wished the institution gone, not for the welfare of the slave (for whom he anticipated only a transformed subjection) but for the welfare of the slaveholder shackled to an impoverishing regime; yet he could see no method decently to effect its abolition. Slavery was part of the burden of history and human nature, softened by affections but rooted in brutal necessities in which the slaveholder participated. Slavery was not an exception to the record of human life but an instance. Honor obliged that the honorable man, saddled with so vexed an inheritance, transmit it with as little a stain upon his own and his society's conscience as possible. "Upon the *right* of our Southern States, in all good conscience, before God and man, to uphold their hereditary institutions, we have not the shadow of doubt in any view of the question. Of their *duty* to do so, against any foreign interference, we have still less. They are called upon to maintain them by every thing which can bind a man to his ancestors and to his posterity—by everything which makes him feel that he has a country, and that he is bound to stand by her to the death, in all times of peril and difficulty." The social compact mingled right and wrong; more it did not exempt man from the realities of his condition but taught him understanding and resignation as the final human values. Moral discipline, Byron had occasioned Legaré to observe, meant to mortify, to control, to do all but extinguish self-love: "It inculcates upon the aspirant that there can be neither happiness nor virtue where there is not resignation, and that it is not more the lot, than it is the duty and the interest of man, to acquiesce in the order of nature and of society."[51]

# III

# EXILE

7

# Centrifugal
# Tendencies

Nullification was the crisis of Legaré's adult life. He was unsure that he had met it squarely, though he never doubted that he had analyzed and worried it through. It broke the South Carolina that had allowed him to proceed from success to uninterrupted success; it instigated the weary progress of Legaré the "thorough-faced Charlestonian" to Legaré the migrant expatriate, Legaré the survivor upon federal patronage. Years later he was to observe with the melancholy that was his mark, "The South Carolina in which & for which I was educated, has some how or other disappeared, & left a *simulacrum* behind of a very different kind—which I don't understand, neither am understood by it." His puzzlement and alienation had many sources, political and intellectual, but it started with the affair of nullification.[1]

Matters had begun bravely enough, with the election of Jackson and the launching of the *Southern Review*. South Carolina prided itself upon resolving divisive and threatening issues by hammering out a new consensus, a harmony for which the state was famous. Legaré was to remember the mood of 1827 and his own motives: "During that summer, the tone assumed by northern prints in regard to the (then) contemplated So. Review—the enormous pretensions of the Clay & Adams party and administration—the Harrisburg convention &c.— the *supineness*, as I thought of the whole South—the fact that what I considered as the strong, at least plausible & important ground of the unconstitutionality of the tariff was not so much as defended by *our own* members of Congress—the conviction that Mr. Calhoun was disposed to barter Southern interests & constitutional principles for his own purposes (right or wrong so I then thought)—the hue & cry raised in Charleston by the Clay party, and even by many of our Jackson friends against the fear of us who were endeavouring to catch the public attention to the importance of such subjects—a strong persuasion withal . . . that the opinion of the people in the non-slave-holding states was so decidedly against us as to lead necessarily in a few years to direct interference between master & slave & other causes did excite me to a very high & as I now think, an inordinate pitch of jealousy & indignation against them."[2]

But 1827 did not yet bring the challenge of nullification. Only in July of that year did Thomas Cooper suggest calculating the value of the Union, and only in 1828 did the strategy of nullification receive a serious airing, especially by Calhoun. It was to a Protest drafted largely by Legaré that, unwanted, Calhoun was unofficially and secretly to append his Exposition. The following year was quiet. Jackson dithered over the tariff, alternately offering encouragement and frustration to South Carolina. In the lull, Legaré traveled to Washington to plead successfully two cases before the Supreme Court, earn the good graces of John Marshall, Joseph Story, and Daniel Webster, and witness the presidential inauguration. The Jacksonian did not look with favor upon the Jacksonians who massed into the White House: "blackguards, thieves, women of ill fame, negroes &c., crammed into the splendid rooms without order or restraint, pêle mêle, with fair ladies & gentlemen. I never witnessed such a scene, but I hope it will never be repeated."[3]

In 1830, those persuaded of the merits of a nullifying strategy had begun with unexpected professionalism to organize for the elections. It was in this context that Legaré spent the summer of 1830 analyzing and refuting both nullifiers and tariff supporters, albeit anonymously, in a long article for the *Southern Review* in August entitled "The American System" and in eight pieces for the Camden *Journal* between July and September (written under the improbable pen name, "A Plain Man"). It was easier to attack—and better politics—than to defend, more advisable to shred the logic and historical reasoning of Clay and McDuffie than to explain why the Unionist position should be continued, even when palpably unsuccessful.[4]

The nullifiers were the easier intellectual game and the greater anonymity of the Camden *Journal* gave Legaré freedom to rail. The burden of his case was that nullification was inefficacious and revolutionary, the harbinger of "disunion, revolution and civil war." The calling of a nullifying convention would be *ipsa re* a revolutionary act, since there was no provision for such a body in the Constitution either of South Carolina or the United States. It was idle for the nullifiers to argue that the prerogative of a state veto was implicit in the language of the Constitution, for the novelty of the doctrine had astonished all by its "subtile and farfetched" reasoning. The right of revolution itself was not in doubt. Tyranny might oblige a dissolution of the political compact, and Legaré conceded the right of secession. But short of secession, a state was bound by the agreed terms of the Constitution, and nowhere could nullification be sensibly located within them.

The process of nullification would impose intolerable strains not just upon the Union but upon the individual citizen, who had of necessity a dual allegiance to the state and to the federation. If the state should nullify a law, what should the citizen who did not agree with the abrogation do? Would he go with state or Union? Even grant the logic of nullification; what would be its effects? The nullifiers insisted they would be peaceful. Legaré insisted they would restore the anarchy of the old Confederation, whose imbecility the Constitution of 1787 had expressly been designed to cure. Each state would become its own man, going its own way. Congressional power, even upon matters established as its prerogative, might be paralyzed by the shadow upon its deliberations of potential nullifying conventions. Yet ironically, the veto of the nullifiers was not a real veto; it did not even provide a remedy to tyranny, for the nullifiers argued a veto was efficacious until three-quarters of the states voted to disagree. This would supplant the tribunal of the Supreme Court with another of the states, as likely to tyrannize.

The theoretical logic of the nullifiers made no sense to Legaré. They claimed that the states had in the eighteenth century lent their sovereignty, which could be reclaimed at any moment. This was true in the case of secession, but nothing short of it. The United States was not a league of nations but a distinctive political compact. While Legaré did not agree with Daniel Webster that the people of the United States had formed the Union, he did think the thirteen distinct peoples of the states had done so, and thus the Union was a new body politic, a nation by consent. While it was federal (not national) in origin, it was national (not federal) in action. The constitution, solemnly agreed by the states, had vested in the federal government the powers of a supreme law, overriding all local jurisdictions and giving to the United States the right to punish resistance to its will as treason. These prerogatives went far beyond the legal powers of a mere alliance of sovereignties. Nor was there adequate precedent for nullification in the Kentucky and Virginia Resolutions. After reexamining them, Legaré had concluded that whatever the heated language of the moment, Jefferson and Madison had intended no more than the usual constitutional mechanisms of petition and protest; 1798 had been a matter of words, not action, least of all the revolutionary action proposed by the nullifiers. And the words of Jefferson, however to be respected, could not be regarded as holy writ superior to the legal terms of the Constitution itself.

This was to attack the nullifiers. Yet years before, Legaré had begun by attacking the proponents of the tariff. It was crucial in the politics of South Carolina that the Unionist continue to attack the likes of Henry Clay; to do otherwise would be to yield all serviceable political ground to the nullifiers. Thus it was necessary also to dissect the American System, the more delicate task. Nullification was a new speculation with very few historical antecedents. The tariff was an old issue, once endorsed by South Carolina—and Legaré—and rendered more complicated because, in the aged form of James Madison himself, the Founding generation had pronounced the constitutionality of tariff measures. In a political atmosphere increasingly apocalyptic, Legaré's difficulty was to lend drama to the dry metaphysics necessary to a refutation of the American system.

He began in chastened mood. Matters had fallen away from the glories of 1776 and 1787. "We shall take it for granted, that if the Federal Government may not still be pronounced, as we were all once taught to consider it, a perfect model of political wisdom, the glory of our own land, the consoling hope and example of all other lands, it is, at least, better than any substitute for it, *as yet* thought of by the few, the very few persons amongst us who had avowed themselves its enemies *in all events*." As it was hard to sustain a viable popular government, it was foolish to propose innovations that might jeopardize that rara avis. Washington had legislated too much in the last fifteen years, a fault shared by all, for the federal government worked best when it did least. As William Ellery Channing, "that great man whose genius has formed an aera in the literary history of his country," had explained, the purposes of the government were best when negative. It was a splendid instrument for defense "against fraud and force" but a poor device for initiative because intended only to bind loosely together states whose variety had been the occasion for the confederation. "We conceive that not only is the government of the United States, limited in its powers to those granted in the Federal Constitution, but that even in the exercise of these, it is bound by the spirit and scheme of a confederacy, as such, to pay greater respect to the separate interests of the parties, than could be required of the rulers of a consolidated empire. . . . Mutual confidence and respect is its only sure support—and we venture to say that whatever reliance some of our politicians may feel in the strength of our Federal System, the day is coming when its great original sin—its centrifugal tendencies—will be acknowledged on all hands, to be its daily besetting danger." Sociology dictated restraint, for "an empire as vast as that of Trajan and the Antonines . . . cannot be governed by a rspresentative assembly, gathered from every part of it, changed in its composition every two years, without information, without experience, unless the objects of the social union be as few and simple, as its structure is vast and multifarious." The more perfectly congressmen represented their constituencies, the more centrifugal would be the discord in Washington. This had been understood by the Founding Fathers, who had amended the confederation by giving force to old powers, not by adding new ones, with the significant exception of the power to regulate commerce. Otherwise, as Legaré the close student of *The Federalist Papers* knew, they had ingeniously hedged power around with inhibitions.[5]

Restraint was political wisdom and fiscal sense to a free trader like Legaré. "The commercial policy of an enlightened age, is the simplest thing imaginable. It consists in doing as little as possible, only now and then adopting restrictive measures to bring other nations to fair terms in a commercial treaty. The policy of a protecting system, on the contrary, is, of all others, the most complicated and perplexing; weighing multifarious interests against each other, calling for the most accurate statistical information, and embarrassing those concerned in the conduct of it, with all the proverbial uncertainties of political arithmetic." The economic progress of the United States since 1787 seemed itself to speak the wisdom of free trade, although it had to be conceded that "the times were most favourable to us," because the "situation of Eurpose from the breaking out of the French Revolution, until the fall of Napoleon, was altogether unprecedented in its history, and the troubles which afflicted the most important portion of the earth, were so many means of aggrandizement to us." Nonetheless the nature of the American union was the more important structural cause of prosperity. If Clay's American System had been adopted in 1790 "with all its necessary accompaniments, of an inquisitorial police, a bloody penal code, and an offensive array of the public force," there would have been "a prodigious difference in the situation, the character and the destinies of this people!" But Legaré opted to discuss the political and constitutional standing of the tariff more than its economic effects, though he did take a sideswipe at George McDuffie's much touted and dubious theory that South Carolina was subsidizing the manufacturers of the North to the tune of some four million dollars a year. "We see nothing in the general state of the country, or in any particular facts brought to light in the discussions of this subject, which goes to shew, that all the political economists in the world have been mistaken in representing taxes upon consumption, as ultimately falling on the consumers; and we are persuaded that our consumption of articles subject to high duties, is only proportioned to our wealth and population—some, perhaps a considerable, deduction being made for the peculiar condition of a portion of the latter [i.e. slaves]."[6]

Alexander Hamilton, "the great father of this system . . . too able a man to resort to a deceptive defence of his own measures," had been candid about the tariff, so Legaré artfully quoted him. "In his report on manufacturers, General Hamilton avows that duties are taxes. He says they *'evidently* amount to a virtual bounty on the domestic fabrics, since by enhancing the charges on foreign articles, they enable the national manufacturers to undersell all their foreign competitors.'" So the question resolved itself into "whether the government of the United States has the constitutional power to impose taxes upon the whole people, for the purpose of raising a *bounty* for a particular class or denomination?" It was a difficult and vexatious matter, and only on balance was he sure that such a tariff was unconstitutional. As text he took the Protest sent by the legislature of South Carolina in 1828 to the Congress—circularly so, since he himself had drafted that Protest. It was true that the first Congress and Hamilton the quasi-monarchist had enacted tariffs to provide revenue, "to render the United States independent of foreign nations *for military and other essential supplies,*" and that secondarily they had served to protect domestic manufactures. And it was also true that many had come to look upon the secondary effect as the primary purpose. "When, in 1816, the war-tariff came to be reduced, it seems to have been universally conceded, that duties, higher than were requisite for the financial arrangements of the country, might be levied on imports, in order to save the great amount of capital previously invested in domestic manufactures. From that to the levying of still greater imposts, with a view to future investments of capital, was a very small step, and it was soon taken. When the burthen, however, became too heavy to be borne with patience, the question was asked, for the first time, by what right it was imposed, and if we are not very much mistaken, the constitutional scruples about that right have been gaining ground every day."[7]

A formidable obstacle to a critic of the tariff was James Madison who, in two letters to James C. Cabell in 1829, had expressed the firm opinion that the tariff of 1828 was proper. With politeness and temerity, Legaré challenged the Founding Father: "The authority of this gentleman, in all matters of constitutional law, is so deservedly high, that we felt very much shaken in our opinions when we heard of this. Fortunately, however, Mr. Madison did not give his decision without reasons, and it is a settled rule that when a judge condescends to argue, his decree is no further good than as it is supported by his logic." Legaré took his stand upon the distinction between the constitutional right of the federal government to tax only to sustain itself in the fulfillment of the obligations enumerated in the constitution—for, upon Hamilton's convenient hint, he took the tariff to be a form of taxation—and its unconstitutional wish to use the secondary effects of its taxation for "national" purposes. "The distinction attempted to be set up between *national* objects and objects *not* national, in the exercise of this supposed right to spend the monies of the United States upon projects connected with none of the enumerated powers, must ever be quite unsatisfactory. According to our rule, it is very easy to define a national object. You have nothing to do but to look into the federal covenant and see if the government have any authority to undertake the thing at all. If it have, then it may lay out money upon it as a matter of course." But the American System argued that "*exclusively of all the enumerated objects of the Constitution,*" some measures were "national by their great utility," not in their character, but by their effects. To say that "a road is not national as long as it is confined to a single State" but is "if it pass through two, three, four, &c." was "a mere vulgar abuse of language." For "a *bona fide* military road made *flagrante bello*, would be national, if it were only ten miles or one mile long, because it were in that case, a means of accomplishing an object specified in the Constitution." "We venture to affirm, that if Congress have power to aid in constructing the greatest work of the kind in this country—the Ohio and Chesapeake Canal for instance—there is not a creek or a cross road in the land, which it may not take under its superintendence." Any improvement could be national: "Where one part is benefited and no part injured, the *whole*, of course benefited; so that no man who looks beyond the definitions of the Constitution itself, can stop short of an universal, unrestrained, indiscriminate expenditure of the public money." Fortunately, Jackson's Maysville veto was "fatal . . . to the whole system of internal improvements," even though the President "reserved the question as to the more important (or, as they are miscalled, *national*) projects." Madison himself, in *The Federalist* No. 41 and in the Virginia Resolutions of 1798, had seen the matter in the same light. The American system bade fair to imitate the concept of eminent domain, that "despotism in disguise."⁹

Yet Madison claimed that the prerogative resided in the power of the federal government to regulate commerce. Legaré objected that the relevant clause read not merely to "regulate commerce" but to "regulate commerce *with foreign nations* and *between* the States and *with* the Indian tribes," a much more restricted conveyance of power. The protection of manufactures was not an enumerated power—wisely so, in view of the principles of free trade. As Legaré ironically inquired, was it not "unaccountable in theory, how the prophetic formers of the Constitution—the pretended fathers of the American System—should have left the encouragement of manufactures, to depend almost exclusively upon the manner in which another great interest of the country should be regulated—should leave them, as it were, absolutely dependent upon what they could pick up casually and indirectly, by the liberality of that interest, or by cunning contrivances of their friends to defraud and circumvent it?"⁹

Above all, it would not do to make a distinction between the objects of a power and the power itself: objects were themselves the essence of means. To do so was to betray the trust of the Constitution—here Legaré recurred to the image of government as a legal trust, its officers the executors of the terms. The federal government was supreme, but only in its limited sphere. To say this was not to be paranoid or unreasonably restrictive. Fresh occasion might breed fresh consideration. "We are aware that in the *bona fide* exercise of its transcendent prerogatives a great latitude of discretion, must necessarily be allowed to the Federal Government. We say again, that we have no wish to curtail its usefulness—that we would not even impair its legitimate splendours—'the plumage, (as Junius happily expresses it) which adorns the royal bird.'" If, for example, Haiti should fall into the hands of a dangerous power, it would be well and proper for the government to purchase or subdue the island, and money would be needed to do so. Common sense was antecedent to constitutional quibbling. The American system was, above all, not sensible. [10]

The article had begun with pessimism but ended with optimism. "A great change is now visibly taking place in public opinion. Every omen is favourable. The recent exercise of the *veto* did immense good by merely arresting the profligate and demoralizing expenditure of the public money, and honestly appropriating it to the payment of the national debt. But it had produced an effect vastly more important than this. It has arrested the attention of the people—it has awakened the minds of men—it has sanctified the past efforts of this and of other Southern States in defence of those principles, upon which, and upon which alone, the success of our great experiment in society depends." [11]

In 1830 there was ground for optimism, though not unmixed. The Unionists triumphed in that year's Charleston elections; Calhoun was embroiled in the domestic politics of the Jackson administration and losing; McDuffie's forty-bale theory was increasingly subject to refutation, and his attempts to reform the tariff had been rebuffed by the House of Representatives. On the other hand, by late in the year there were signs that the radicals might rally to defeat the moderates. Stephen Miller was elected to the Senate over William Smith, who had come out against a convention. The state legislature, by a bare majority, endorsed a call for a convention, though a two-thirds vote was required for action. But Legaré's efforts in the press and journals during the late summer had been a plausible effort at influence on behalf of a Unionist party in need of intellectual ballast. If Calhoun's Fort Hill letter had provided the radicals with a theory, Legaré's writings had offered an intellectual alternative, as well as an accurate prediction of the military impasse that nullification, *pace* Calhoun, would create by 1833. [12]

Legaré, though he could not suppress passion, strove for detachment. He was the scholar-politician, gravely citing Vattel to expose the errors of the nullifiers upon matters of international law, hauling out old cases of Lord Coke to exemplify the limitations upon even a royal prerogative, granting to his opponents such concessions as seemed proper, distributing in grams the measures of political and constitutional justice. This was neat but too subtle for as brutal a conflict as the nullification crisis became. Success or failure would hinge upon the mobilization of emotion and the organization of voters. Legaré was adept at neither, though 1831 was to nudge him closer to tugging at the Unionist heartstrings of his constituents.

Although 1830 had seen him re-elected to the state assembly at the head of the Charleston delegation, he was to duck away from politics in the session of that year. James Louis Petigru had decided to resign as the state's attorney general and suggested that Legaré would be a fit replacement, his election "a positive encouragement to learning." Appointment rested with the state assembly, and November provided a heated contest. There were four candidates on the first ballot: Legaré, Memminger, Holmes, and Wilson. Legaré stood for the less aggressive of the Unionists and for erudition, the latter not entirely to his advantage, for the claim that he was too fancy to be a good lawyer revived to bedevil matters. Christopher Memminger, a German emigré, was also a Unionist; he was six years Legaré's junior, though a member of the Charleston bar from the same year, and much later he was to be Charleston's most prominent urban reformer and the Confederacy's Secretary of the Treasury. Isaac Holmes, though Legaré's closest friend, was a hard-line nullifier. About the fourth and least, Wilson, we know little. Memminger led on the first ballot with 51 votes; Legaré came second with 43, Holmes third with 38, and Wilson last with 26 (4 votes being scattered). The advantage rested decisively with the Unionists, though it is not clear whether party considerations were yet a factor. On the second ballot the elimination of Wilson and doubts that Holmes could carry the election worked to Legaré's advantage. Matters then stood, Legaré 72, Memminger 62, Holmes 26. At this point radical support crystallized and moved to Legaré. According to the Charleston *Courier*, "In this election, expectation was greatly excited, for at the third balloting, party feelings entered warmly into the matter, as the Convention party very generally took up Legaré, in opposition to Memminger, and a push was made against the latter, on account of his political principles. Had party spirit been out of the question, the election (it is considered on all hands) would have terminated in favor of Memminger." Here Legaré reaped the benefit of having balanced criticism of the American system against criticism of the theory of nullification, as he seemed to the radicals the lesser of two evils. This turn of events ought not to have pleased him, especially if—politics aside—so inconsiderable a younger figure as Memminger would indeed have been preferred. The final vote gave Legaré 80, Memminger 70. Legaré himself, puzzlingly, was to inform Jesse Harrison that "since you left this country I have been made Attorney General of this State—a high office, which was conferred upon me in a very flattering manner."[13]

The prime advantage and disadvantage of the position was that it removed Legaré from the center of events. Before the election he had

been a member of the crucial Committee on Federal Relations. Now
he occupied an apolitical office. As he had observed to the legislature
in his manifesto letter, election would remove him "immediately from
the political contention which now agitates and divides" the state,
since such a post should "be as far as possible exempt from the
suspicion of personal or party bias, and those prejudices which are
the inevitable lot of every politician." He insisted that the move
would not significantly defraud those who had sent him to Columbia,
"because my vote on the great political question of the day will not be
lost to my constituents—a majority of two thirds of the whole
Legislature being necessary to the call of a Convention." True to this
position, he began to refuse invitations to Unionist meetings. His
judgment was more technically correct, in the short run, than pres-
cient. It began to be bruited about that Legaré lacked political
courage. Yet it was a calculated move, which anticipated his later
departure for Belgium. In renouncing his seat, he was to explain to
Alfred Huger in 1834, "I wished to husband my resources for better
days, for it is a great mistake in a public man to suffer himself to be
*used up* by unavailing and feeble efforts made *mal à propos. . . .* To spit
against such a wind, is, as Franklin or some other sage says, just to
spit in one's own face."[14]

The difficulty was emotional. He had so long stood in the forefront
of criticism of the tariff, so many of his friends were radicals—
Holmes, Hayne, Preston—that he could not put himself fully into
the lists against them. As he observed in 1831, "Differing as I do with
many of my most earnest and most respected friends of the other side
. . . . I have to a great degree sympathized with them in their
feeling." Even in the polemic of his letters as "A Plain Man," he felt
obliged to confess that the nullifiers were "our friends—for they are,
in purpose and in feeling, our friends." His sense of the injustice of the
tariff balanced against his fear of the unknown, of anarchy and civil
war. A certain timidity led to Unionism, for it was the known quality.
"How could one who deeply felt the injustice of the tariff, answer it to
his conscience, if it came to a fight, to take part with the oppressor,
merely because his victim felt his wrongs too keenly?" He did not
know the answer. "The truth is, that by far the most difficult problem
that can be proposed to a good man is, how far he is bound to submit
to those who abuse or have usurped the government, in order to serve
his country—or to abandon and even to embarrass the service of the
country, in order to defeat and to overthrow her domestic tyrants."
Wryness at self became necessary, as the question was "far more

desirable to discuss in the conduct of others, than to have to decide for ourselves in our own."[15]

The best commentary upon Legaré the politician, scrutinized by the challenge of nullification, was to come after his death in an article by Bartholomew Carroll for the *Southern Quarterly Review*. It is worth quoting at length: "In feeling he was with the dominant party [the nullifiers], yet in principle and on reason, he was with the opposition. But even with his own party, he was never found heart-going and strong. If ever a time presented itself, when the orator or the statesman was called on to take his place, it was then. The field of glory was before him,—patriotism called upon him to ascend the stage—and his partisans, with loud cries and cheering, were before him to warm his bosom with the noblest inspiration. He ascended the stage, but not with a firm and self reliant step; he required to be encouraged and handed up to his place,—he spoke with confidence and on conviction, but not with daring boldness. He was willing to suffer for his principles,—aye, to die a martyr for them,—but not to battle for them, and pull down destruction on the heads of his enemies, though he fell under the ruin. His friends urged him along to the contest. Not that he wanted courage, but he looked back and saw personal friends on the other side,—he could not forget that they had been linked with him in political brotherhood, and was unable to bring himself up to that desperate daring, which, as Jeremy Taylor so picturesquely describes it, 'growing impatient at wrongs, rather than suffer them, makes a man cut the cable and dissolve each hope; leave the ship and leap into the sea; hug a wave and die in its embraces.' It was the want of this kind of moral courage, at times so necessary to the success of a measure, that never permitted Mr. Legaré's friends, during a political storm, to place him as the pilot at the helm, nor when a doubtful battle was to be fought, for principle or for right, to trust him as the sword or shield of his party."[16]

This was harsh, but close to just. Its fault as a criticism lay in applying to Unionism the criteria of radicalism. Nullification was the daring measure, requiring the talents of temerity. Unionism was the emotion of foreboding, the instinct educated by the lesson of the French Revolution that energies mobilized for good might unexpectedly precipitate evil in the body politic. Yet Legaré knew his own faults. In writing of D'Aguesseau in early 1832, he assessed himself. Saint-Simon had accused the Chancellor of indecisiveness, and Legaré sympathized with D'Aguesseau: "That he should be perplexed by the tortuous policy of a gang of political libertines—that he should be

embarrassed by a perpetual conflict between the right and the expedi-
ent, and should be often at a loss to determine how far his duty as a
subject and a minister (under a despotism) called upon him for the
sacrifice of his private feelings and opinions . . . is not at all to be
wondered at." Yet Saint-Simon had been right. Overfastidiousness
was imperfection, even as it had causes: the "habit of discussing most
questions *pour et contre* for nearly thirty years—the delicacy of a most
scrupulous conscience—the very fertility of his mind and the forecast
that presented to it all possible consequences of 'coming events,'
together with the uncertainty inherent in the nature of political
subjects."[17]

Only once did Legaré emerge from the shell of the state attorney-
general's office. On the 4th of July, 1831, Unionists and nullifiers
held competing extravaganzas in Charleston, each to claim the legacy
of the Revolution. The nullifiers marched off to the Circular Church
on Meeting Street, where, having passed beneath a modern Doric
portico, they heard Robert Hayne. The Unionists gathered at the
Scotch Church on the corner of Meeting and Tradd Streets, where,
having passed beneath a modern Tuscan portico, they heard William
Drayton. In the evening the Unionists reassembled for their banquet;
a "Union Bower" had been erected at the corner of Meeting and
George Streets. Even the proceedings' historian appeared puzzled by
the aesthetic enthusiasm of the occasion: "The lot and building in
which the party dined were decorated with a taste at once showy and
becoming. Festoons of evergreens encircled the pillars, which,
though we cannot exactly consider or designate them as 'Corinthian
columns,' were, nevertheless, very neat and substantial. The hickory,
entwined with the palmetto and the pine, were conspicuous as
appropriate emblems in illustrating the pride and strength of our
country; and from the archways, one of which being appropriated to
each individual, were suspended shields bearing the names of . . .
many . . . who had distinguished themselves in the cause of liberty in
the fields and on the shores of Carolina. Transparencies of Washington, Hancock, Franklin and others, encircled with boughs and
luxuriant foliage, hung at the upper end of the vast hall. In the front of
the building the eye was attracted to the novel appearance in our
streets of a palmetto and hickory tree, transplanted in full bloom from
the soil in which they originally grew, and waving in that of the
adoption as freshly as they ever did before. The front of the building
was decorated with two full-rigged frigates, manned and armed,
mounting each fifty-two guns, and one rakish-looking and elegant

tender—all perfect models of naval architecture. These were each surmounted by a broad transparent archway, over the centre of which appeared illuminated the words, 'Don't give up the ship!'" Amid such architectural presages of the exclamation marks and underlinings with which Queen Victoria emphasized her epistolary convictions, the Unionists staggered through orations, letters from absent friends, an ode upon "Our Union," 24 official and 128 volunteer toasts. The regular toasts were each accompanied by fitting airs. "The People of South Carolina: They *will* preserve the Union—*peaceably* if they can" was matched with "Home, Sweet Home." Charles Carroll of Carrollton, the last of the Signers, was remembered by "The Last Rose of Summer." The American System was damned by "'Tis All But a Dream." Calhoun was enjoined openly to declare his political principles by "Let Every Pagan Muse Be Gone." "The entertainment was abundant," it was observed, "and . . . the wines were excellent."[18]

No doubt, Legaré might have reflected as he rose to give the main oration of the evening, there had been not a few upon the Bema who had insufficiently watered their wine. He restated and simplified the arguments he had deployed elsewhere. In particular, and perhaps not wisely for so large and clamorous an assembly, he chose to concentrate on the problem of international law: if—as the radicals claimed—South Carolina retained her sovereignty, did that fact resolve her problem with the tariff? Vattel and Grotius agreed that it did not, for then the Union would be but a league of nations agreeing merely by treaty. It was axiomatic among the civilians that for one party to disavow one clause of a treaty disallowed all clauses for all parties. In short, the alternative to nullification for the other states was enforcement of the treaty by arms or dissolution of the Union. The people should not be misled by the nullifiers' soothing words about a state veto as a peaceful solution. It meant war or it meant disunion.[19]

Yet the predominant and opening tone of the speech was less stirring than melancholy, almost pouting: not a call to arms, but a lament that he should be forced into the forage of civil war. "It is melancholy to think of the change which has been made in the feelings and opinions of some of the best and ablest men among us, by this pernicious [American] system—to reflect that alienation and distrust, nay, in some instances, perhaps, that wrath and hostility now possess those bosoms which were but a few years ago warmed with the loftiest and the holiest enthusiasm for the government of their own and their fathers' choice. The authors of this policy are indirectly responsible for this deplorable state of things, and for all the consequences that may grow out of it. They have been guilty of an inexpiable offence against their country. They found us a united, they have made us a distracted people." They had made the Union "a subject of controversy among very enlightened men." Nonetheless, the tariff did not explain everything. You could not blame it for the "misfortunes spring[ing] from the barrenness of the earth, or the inclemency of the seasons, or the revolutions of commerce, or a defective system of domestic and rural economy." "The decay and desolation which are invading many parts of the lower country—the fall in the price of our great staple commodity—the comparative unproductiveness of slave labor" were only slightly connected with the tariff. "Yet I do not wonder at the indignation which the imposition of such a burthen of taxation has excited in our people in the present unprosperous state of their affairs. I have sympathized and do sympathize with them too deeply to rebuke them for their feelings, however improper I deem it to be to act upon such feelings, as recklessly as some of their leaders would have them do."[20]

This was not a steeling for war, or a drawing of a line in the dust. Enemies that are merely "improper" are nearly friends. The tone of reserve was more marked, though not necessarily more evident to this audience on that July night, than the routine and honest declaration, "The country calls upon every individual, however humble he may be, to take his post in this mighty conflict. Sir, I obey that paramount command, and be it for weal or be it for woe, be it for glory, or be it for shame, for life and for death, here I am."[21]

That Legaré was not ready to fight is evident by the fact that he did not. In the spring of 1832, he was offered and accepted the position of American chargé d'affaires in Brussels. It was true that the crisis had slumped, awaiting the congressional session of 1832 to reveal what Washington might choose to amend in the tariff, and the elections of 1832 to resolve the stalemate between nullifiers and Unionists in the South Carolina legislature. It would be idle to imagine that the six years of the nullification crisis saw all at a constant state of moral excitement and vigilance. Normal life and considerations went on, and the time had come when Legaré relished the prospect of a stay in Europe. His years of writing for the *Southern Review* had all but exhausted his stock of intellectual reserves. He needed a break from politics constant since 1820, and writing incessant since 1828. He wanted to rehabilitate his health. It was not clear in the early months of 1832 that what did come to pass—the sweeping defeat of the Unionists, the Convention, the test oath controversy, the marshalling of rival militia—would come to pass. The odds favored the status quo, the indecisive stalemate. It was with anguish, from Belgium, that Legaré came to realize his miscalculation. He had resolved, after the nullifiers' triumph in the convention of 1832, that a military crisis between the Union and South Carolina would compel his return from Europe, and he poured out his angered frustration in a screed to William Cabell Rives, so heated that he delayed sending it for three months. Elsewhere he offered himself the consolation of the "only thing worth repeating from history . . . Brutus' apostrophe at Philippi," in the account of Appian, which even years before he had read with tears: "I am no longer useful to my country if such is the temper of these men."[22]

That is the best face of his decision. The worst, made later by his political enemies, is that he ran out on his party and chose the ease of Europe and embassy festivities over the hard life of his own state's crisis. Why did he leave? The sharpest reason was that nullification broke Legaré's political world. From the ideologue of a consensus he became the orator of a Unionist party badly organized, harassed from power, futile. From a tidy world that had advanced him so evenly, so pleasantly, he passed over into another, slippery, ominous, apocalyptic. The elite of Charleston, to which as politician and lawyer he belonged, found itself diminished of influence by mobilizing nullifier voters and politicians. Charleston, once so warm and appreciative, became the embodiment of uncertainty. With friends splitting from friends, houses from houses, conversation and society grew strained. In Paris, Legaré was to remark a similar degeneration, the price of social and political division, and point the moral: "The truth is that no nation in the world can live perpetually in the midst of civil broils and military adventures, such as France has passed or rather *not* yet passed thro' without degenerating into a horde of Tartars. Only see what Gov. Hamilton & nullification had done, before I left home, to degrade & corrupt to the core the admirable society of our sweet little Charleston." No longer sure where he stood in a society once his safe refuge, he chose exile. The emigré lives in, but need not morally rely upon, the society he is visiting. Belgium offered a gratifying release, a suspension.[23]

Yet the decision to accept the legation reached further than even Legaré realized. He had been offered the job not just because he was schooled in European ways or because it pleased the Jackson administration to reward a Unionist and displease Calhoun, but also because he had tentatively established a place in the estimation of Washington. While pleading cases before the Supreme Court in 1829, he had especially attracted the attention of Edward Livingston. Livingston had been the civilian codifier of Louisiana law, and in this he and Legaré shared a powerful interest. Livingston had become Secretary of State and was able to dispense patronage to his new, young and learned friend. By more than Livingston had Legaré been admired, and in 1829, in the flush of being generally well regarded, he had mused, "I hope I shall be very much in the way of promotion hereafter." In 1832, traveling north to catch his ship to Le Havre and dodging the great cholera epidemic in New York, he expatiated to his mother on his new course. "During the leisure, or rather vacancy of a long voyage, I have thought a great deal of you & felt many a throe of anxiety about our future destinies. But upon the whole, as I acted from the best motives, so I think I came to the *wisest* conclusion, even in a worldly point of view. I shall not give up my knowledge of the *law*, & I have no doubt I shall gain prodigiously by my experience & intercourse with the world under new & interesting circumstances. It is true that the game I play has its hazards & that I suffer a positive & great evil in my absence from you, but those whose career is of a certain kind, cannot look to be exempt from such things & if they be not attended with other evils, one has reason to thank God that his usefulness to the world has not been more prejudicial to himself." To accept a federal office, to become—as he was to joke to Isaac Holmes—"one of the 'mercenaries' (Isn't that the word?) of the general government," was to strike out in a new direction, away from South Carolina. He never quite found his way back.[24]

8

Europe

To Jesse Harrison, Legaré elaborated his plans to learn German, to visit August von Schlegel in Bonn, to study "nine or ten hours a day regularly—not forgetting *my Coke-Litt{leton}* which I shall carry with me—for I have no idea of forgetting my law." To William Cabell Rives, the departing American Minister in Paris, he confessed his motives: "German, Greek & the Civil Law—these with Lord Coke & the Court will engross my time and save me from the blue devils. . . . If our *great* country should not be doomed to perish before our eyes in the *present* squall, I trust I shall have an opportunity of doing her some service nearer home & in a way more agreeable to myself."[1]

These plans Legaré kept, even holding to the ineradicable melancholy that attended him from the moment his ship sailed from New York to Le Havre. "I am here alone & desolate," he wrote to his sister Mary, "in a small party (about a dozen, almost all of them French & Spaniards) of entire strangers. I am going into a country where I have no acquaintance & the step I am taking condemns me to a sort of solitude (most probably) for the rest of my days." Thirty-five, alone, going abroad for several years, he felt the regrets of an exile mingling with the forebodings of a reluctant bachelor. He was worried about his country, concerned at the unhappiness of his mother and sister at his going, and alarmed at the cholera that, harassing New York, might have stepped on to the *Henri Quatre* with him. His fear was not

misplaced. "The day after we got to sea, one man was taken ill of it &
the next day, two more. They were all sailors. A little girl in the cabin
was at the same time seized with strange pains & a fever, but without
any symptoms of the pestilence. The captain only mentioned to us
that there was one case. That was enough to alarm us all very much,
but had we known how the fact really stood, we should have been
miserable. I remember some years ago reading a piece in some
magazine or other of which the title was *'The Fever Ship.'* It purported
to be a description of the raging of the yellow fever on board a British
vessel which lay becalmed somewhere among the West Indian Islands.
It was an appalling picture, & the idea of seeing it realized in our case,
almost unnerved me for a few moments." Fortunately, the winds
proved brisk, and Legaré beguiled his anxiety by reading a play a day
of Sophocles, Aeschylus, and Euripides from a copy of the Greek
dramatists purchased in Philadelphia. Nonetheless, he was pleased to
enter the English Channel, which augured the pleasures of Europe
with a bright sky, clear blue water, a gentle south wind, and the
cleaving grace of a multitude of sail. [2]

In Le Havre he dallied: watching a performing monkey in the
streets that danced, fenced, and answered questions with signs;
observing the celebrations that attended the Feast of the Assumption
and the birthday of Bonaparte; hiring a cabriolet to take him high
above the city for a view. By chance he came across Senor Augustin De
Latamendi, who had in 1828 lectured to the male Academy of the
South Carolina Society upon the utility of the modern languages and
had assisted Legaré with his Spanish, but was now reduced to destitution. He would briefly make a usefully trilingual clerk at the rate of
$230 a year. [3]

In Paris Legaré stayed for four weeks to consult with Rives, to
revisit his old haunts, to fathom the new politics in Europe. He
returned to the theater and the opera to be enchanted by the gentle
delicacy of Taglioni's dancing, to be impressed by the force of Mars'
comic acting, to be struck by Meyerbeer's new opera *Robert Le Diable,*
which romantically echoed the forceful demons of Manfred. Rives
took him out to the chateaux of Neuilly, where Louis Philippe was
holding his bourgeois court. This was a visit of consequence to Legaré,
since the King's daughter had just married Leopold, the new King of
the Belgians. The French were a crucial diplomatic and military
support of the new nation whose rebellion and birth the Dutch wished
still to throttle. To fathom Belgium, Legaré had to understand
France, though he was later also to understand that Belgium was

itself, not a sort of inferior France. Rives brought him to the King at eight, after dinner and coffee, ushering him into a modest salon where courtiers in citizens' dress were scattered informally around. The King sat in conversation with François Guizot, and the Queen plied her needlework at a large circular table of daughters and ladies-in-waiting. Ten days later Legaré returned to dine in a small party of just forty at table, all but the aides-de-camp and soldiers informally dressed, some of the ladies in hats of ostrich feathers. He spoke mostly with the Queen, because Judith Rives had fared better in that liaison than had her husband with the King. Legaré's strongest impression was of the amiable domesticity of the court, unintimidating and comfortable. His strongest fear was that the new French monarchy was unstable. The Duchesse de Berry had landed in April and found her way to the Vendée, there to fail in making a Legitimist revolution but to succeed in exciting much concern. Republicans had not resigned themselves to the Orleanists, and there had been a series of riots and insurrections, of which that in Lyons in 1831, where 15,000 workers fought the National Guard and 600 were casualties, was only the most dramatic example. It was little wonder that in conversation with Legaré the King's sister, Princess Adelaide, spoke in a court whisper "with great anxiety" about public affairs. Not only South Carolina brought Legaré regrets and forebodings: "I had I know not what melancholy feelings come over me, as I contemplated this scene in which the sweet & peaceful interests of domestic life, in its highest felicity & virtue, were strongly mingled with the anxieties of political intrigue & the perils of a revolutionary crisis."[4]

Paris itself, rich in his memory, was disappointing, worrying. "The everlasting revolutions—never ending, still beginning, fighting still & still destroying," he wrote, quoting Dryden's "Alexander's Feast," "—the perpetual dread of them with all their fearful & unforeseen results—the confusion of all distinctions, the contempt of all authority, the savage rudeness & ferocity of jacobinism on the one hand, & the stern necessity, on the other, of controlling & crushing it by the power of the sword—these causes have spread a gloom over the whole face of things in that once frivolous & light hearted capital, & made the French a people, resembling absolutely in nothing but their invincible vanity, what they are described to have been in former times." Incivility and *tristesse* were the new mark, agreed by all foreign visitors with whom Legaré conferred. The spectacle of mustachioed soldiers in red pantaloons elbowing women into gutters, the fact of the government's prosecuting for libel the editors of hostile newspapers, led him to speculate that the capacity for a government of laws was exclusively Anglo-Saxon. Yet even that hope was insecure, with unrest behind him in America and stories of mayhem in England over the Reform Bill greeting him in conversation. Still, an American expected political chaos in Europe; it was part of the relaxation of a visit. As Henry Nott, himself married to a Belgian, observed to Legaré, "Every man feels here [in America] as if he were in his night gown & slippers & does not care a damn for anyone. When we go to Europe tis like visiting the theatre. We see the show, & then wish to be again at home."[5]

From Paris, Legaré traveled via Compiègne and Douai to Brussels, with a copy of Chateaubriand's *Génie du Christianisme* and an American general as companions. John Wool, who had been sent by Andrew Jackson to inspect European military establishments, looked over the fortifications at Douai with Legaré as the interpreter for his bawling voice (later, he was to preside as a Union general over the "Department of Virginia"). Reaching Brussels, Legaré temporarily settled himself into the Hotel de Bellevue, scouted the chances of renting a house, and presented his credentials to the interim Minister of Foreign Affairs, General Albert Goblet D'Aviella, and to the King. His diplomatic mission was not complicated, nor was it to prove onerous. In the summer of 1830, following the July Revolution of France, Belgium had rebelled against the union with Holland that the Congress of Vienna had enforced in 1815. The union had not worked well, for it had joined a Catholic and industrializing country to a Protestant monarch, a large national debt, and a bureaucracy partial to Protestant Dutch over Catholic Belgians. William I had attempted to crush the revolution by force and failed. The French under Louis Philippe and the British under Palmerston, by the protocols of London on 20 December 1830, intervened to stabilize and protect the independence of Belgium. A king was found and elected who met the approval of Belgium, France, and Britain: Leopold of Saxe-Coburg-Gotha was the widower of Princess Charlotte, George IV's only daughter, the uncle of the future Queen Victoria and soon to be the son-in-law of Louis Philippe by marriage to the Princess Louise-Marie. Elections were held, and a constitutional monarchy was established, but it was to be 1839 before Holland accepted the *fait accompli*. There were running disputes over boundaries, the settlement of the national debt, the navigation of the Scheldt, the status of Antwerp. Just twelve days after Leopold's accession in August 1831, the Dutch had invaded, only to be expelled by a French army of 50,000 men and a British naval squadron, sent by Palmerston to caution Dutch and French alike. By the Treaty of XXIV Articles of 15 November 1831, a settlement of contentious issues was arrived at by Britain, France, Russia, Prussia, and Austria, and by Belgium, which had resisted certain terms of the original Protocols. But the Dutch remained obdurate and refused to abandon Antwerp, which, even after Legaré's arrival, was under siege and was only to capitulate in mid-December 1832. Legaré could hear bursting shells from the windows of his Brussels apartments.[6]

In all this, the emissary of the American government played a minor part. In 1830 the American chargé d'affaires at The Hague, Auguste Davezac, had responded favorably to the suggestion of the new Belgian Foreign Minister, Felix-Armand de Muelenaere, that fresh diplomatic and commercial arrangements needed to be established between Belgium and the United States. A Belgian consul arrived in New York in December 1831. Davezac was the brother-in-law of Secretary of State Edward Livingston, who advised Andrew Jackson and the Senate of the desirability of an American chargé in Brussels. The presentation of Legaré's credentials marked the formal recognition of Belgium by only the third foreign power, after Britain and France. A commercial treaty needed negotiation, for trade between the United States and Belgium—chiefly through Antwerp, itself an important entrepôt for trade with the German states beyond—was not inconsiderable. But negotiations took place not in Brussels and through Legaré but in Washington through the State Department and the Belgian envoy, Baron Desiré de Behr. Legaré's role was symbolic, his presence an earnest of the American government. His duties were light: to see to the affairs of American citizens in Belgium (the issue of reparations for damage to property in Antwerp loomed large); to issue and confirm passports; to report on Belgian conditions by sending back newspapers, watching the parliamentary debates, talking with the Ministry, keeping his ear to the ground. All this was done with his customary zeal and thoroughness. His dispatches were precise if discursive, informative about Belgium but reflective of the general European situation in which the affairs of Belgium were more than usually embroiled. Observing all this, Legaré became cynically conscious of the new balance of power instigated at Vienna in 1815, "the new Public Law of Europe, by which the monopoly of war seems likely to be secured to the great powers in their quality of *Armed Judges.*" If he had a fault as a diplomat, it was the impatience of a proud intellect, unaccustomed to dissent and prone to bullying Belgian officials less conversant with the principles of international law.[7]

In fact, the treaty between the United States and Belgium was not to be consummated in Legaré's time; foundering upon the refusal of the Belgians to accept the American interpretation of freedom of navigation for neutrals at sea. The Americans, building upon the hard experience of the Napoleonic Wars, wished neutral trade to be exempt from seizure. "Free ships shall make free goods" was the American wish, convenient to its interests. But Britain, patron of the Belgians, saw matters otherwise, and the Belgian government was in no position to quarrel with the ministers of His Britannic Majesty. Far off in Washington, Behr was foolishly to accept the American interpretation without realizing its implications, and his own government was obliged to disavow the draft treaty initialed in 1833. Matters thereafter drifted until a new treaty was ratified in the United States in 1840, signed by Leopold but rejected by the Belgian Assembly. A definitive treaty was not mutually ratified until 1845. A crucial element in this diplomacy was the preference of successive Belgian governments for a protectionist policy and the wish of the American government that its own exports benefit from the ease of free trade. Adding to confusion was slowness of communications. It took dispatches about two months to get from Brussels to Washington, rather less in returning with following winds; three months for a cycle of letters was usual. Adding to slowness was incompetence. Legaré was more zealous in informing Washington of events than Washington was in informing him. He heard of the first treaty and the offending clause about free goods and free ships, only by chance from the British minister. It had been ratified by the Senate on 9 February 1833, sent by Livingston on March 13, and reached Brussels in the first week on May. The British minister had lodged his protest with the Belgian government on February 23, six weeks before Legaré knew there was occasion for dispute. Inefficiency mandated drift.[8]

Fortunately, diplomatic miracles had not been Legaré's expectation and were not to be his lot. He had come for education, travel, and society; in Brussels he came to terms with himself as a thinking, social, and political animal. The anxious ambition that tinged his earlier writing and political life was subdued into a more realistic discipline, a settling-down for the long haul.

He found himself comfortably established, his salary sufficient without being munificent. He received $4,500 per annum, with an additional equivalent sum to pay for the purchase of such diplomatic attire as a watch and chain, a ring, and—as he noted to his mother with amused pleasure—"a court dress . . . . a blue coat richly embroidered in the collar, shirts & cuffs—painted over with a band or slip of gold lace down the outside seam, cocked hat & sword." His salary translated into 26,000 francs a year, and he was able to rent from an Englishman an agreeable house, including furniture, for just 5,000 francs. It stood upon the Boulevard du Régent, which was bounded on one side by the city wall and on the other by private houses of elegant pretension that commanded a view of the adjacent countryside. Standing back from the boulevard behind a garden protected by a neat iron railing, the house was three stories high, excluding the servants' garrets, with ten rooms high-ceilinged and stylish. Near were the royal palace, the residence of the British Ambassador, and the park. For comfort, Legaré employed a valet, a footman, a chambermaid who doubled as laundress, a cook, and a coachman to tend the carriage that cost 350 francs a month to hire. Dinner was usually supplied by a nearby restaurant for a mere three francs a day when, intermittently, he was obliged to dine at home. Yet his hopes of saving money rapidly evaporated with the expanding demands of his "taste for luxury & show," and he soon sighed for the 52,000-franc salary of a Minister Plentipotentiary. By late 1833 he was obliged to move to a smaller house, which, though more expensive in rent, required a lesser establishment. By late 1835 he had dwindled to renting an apartment in a hotel.[9]

Mornings he could spend in private study before turning to correspondence or the business of the legation. Afternoons were for more reading or visiting. Dinner was about five o'clock, often followed by a carriage ride in the cool evening air along the Allée Verte and through the forest around the city. Later, there were evening receptions or small parties. Brussels was a city of modest but decided amenities, no abrupt transition from the provincial accomplishments of Charleston. It was to prove a favorite haunt of Americans as the nineteenth century progressed, for it offered a certain commercial bustle, a European society without the aristocratic arrogance and hard social lines that disquieted the American in Vienna or London. Even as late as immediately before the First World War, Albert Jay Nock was to find it the pleasantest spot in Europe: a place of subtle unobtrusive beauties that slowly and amiably yielded their secrets to the visitor, a center of competent culture intelligently fostered. Brussels well suited the emigré in search of a still point. In Legaré's time it was unsettled by the immediate problem of establishing independence, but the tone of

VUE DU CHEMIN DE FER
et de l'Allée verte à Bruxelles,
et passage du remorqueur qui peut trainer par sa force trente à trente-cinq Berlines, Diligences,
Char à bancs et Wagons, ce qui peut contenir 700 à 1000 personnes.

The Allée Verte, Brussels.

society was remarkably even. The court was unpretentious and accessible, with Leopold bringing the brisk common sense and stiff rectitude of Coburg, and Marie-Louise adding the sentimental domesticity of Orleans. The city offered a various society, notable for the number of dispossessed emigrés taking refuge from revolutions and coups elsewhere: Legitimists and Bonapartists from France, liberals from recently Austrian Italy, fleeing revolutionaries from Poland. And it was a favorite spot for passing travelers, especially the British landing at Ostend, pausing at Brussels, and moving on to the Rhine and Italy beyond. Indeed, with the temporary derangement of the local *noblesse,* the English community offered social leadership. [10]

At the head of society was Prince Auguste d'Arenberg, at whose round table Legaré would dine at least once and sometimes three times a week, before the Prince died in September 1833 at the age of eighty. The Prince was an embodiment of the *ancien régime,* a favorite in his youth of Marie Antoinette, a patron of Madame de Staël on her fussing travels, a mocking abserver of an age whose degeneration he defined and defied. Antediluvian in politics, sometimes morose but usually gay and confiding, well read, reminiscent, attentive to the political and scandalous affairs of the day, he kept an exclusive but generous table ladened with silver, champagne, and the delicacies of the best chef in Brussels, and circled by half a dozen serving men, two valets, and the ghosts of an older Europe. Being so lofty, D'Arenberg never dined out but permitted the world to come to him. Of Legaré, the anxious student of revolutionary memoirs, he became fond and would spin absorbing tales of the old Queen and of how *The Marriage of Figaro,* once a stimulation to liberty, now fell dully upon the ears of a jaded generation. He would kindly mock the American and remark that he had never before in all his life met a traveling American save once, twenty years ago in Vienna—speaking with the air of a man who by chance had strolled along the boulevard, seen an uninteresting display by a performing flea, and walked on. Legaré he excepted from this judgment of the New World, for, as he once remarked with the graceful condescension of an old man whose arms bore many quarterings and whose roots were in the Enlightenment, "men of learning . . . belong to no country." [11]

The large English community was led by Sir Robert Adair, with whom Legaré maintained a friendship not entirely proper for the American legate with the British minister. Adair was the old Whig, the experienced diplomat to whom Palmerston had entrusted the delicate and important mission to Brussels and "from whom,"

Thomas Moore had noted, "one gets, now and then, an agreeable *whiff* of the days of Fox, Tickell, and Sheridan." Adair had once been Ambassador to Constantinople, where (surely of interest to Legaré) he had looked to the visiting Byron by showing him the sights, the mosques, the Sultan, before sharing a boat and a firman to Greece. The long political exile of the Whigs had given Adair less employment than anecdote, so he was prone to reminiscence, one of the amusements of Holland House, and liked to instruct a younger generation with confident stories of the great and powerless days of Whiggery. Charles Greville remembered in his diary a trip back from Windsor and a Privy Council in 1828: "[Adair] told me a great many things about Burke, and Fox, and Fitzpatrick, and all the eminent men of that time with whom he lived when he was young. He said what I have often heard before, that Fitzpatrick was the most agreeable of them all, but Hare the most brilliant. Burke's conversation was delightful, so luminous and instructive." When Adair flattered Legaré that certain of the Charlestonian's writings were equal to Burke's, the flattery carried weight, even if Adair's first meeting with the Irishman had been unhappy: "[Burke] was very passionate, and Adair said that the first time he ever saw him he unluckily asked him some question about the wild parts of Ireland, when Burke broke out, 'You are a fool and a blockhead; there are no wild parts in Ireland.' He was extremely terrified." "An honester English statesman never lived," Legaré judged, "and few abler public men are to be found any where. I have been frequently struck at the great precision, perspicuity and force of his dispatches." Not brilliant but shrewd, Adair was a good soldier in a Whig army long ragtag and gaudy, now suddenly distinguished and powerful.[12]

In the van of Brussels' formidable regiment of emigré women were the Hastings ladies: Lady Charlotte Fitzgerald, sister of the first Marquis of Hastings, enlightened, old, soon to die, kept alive by quantities of laudanum and brandy that might have felled a horse; Lady Flora Mure Campbell, Countess of Loudoun in her own right and widow of the first Marquis of Hastings, a proud but pleasant dowager; Lady Sophia Hastings, daughter of the Marquis, sensible and well-informed, an invalid whom her mother took care to keep from draughty windows; Lady Adelaide Hastings and Lady Selina Hastings, sisters to Sophia, sweet and obliging, barely turned twenty; and Lady Flora Hastings, a writer of gentle verse. The late Marquis had been habitually extravagant and left his family badly off, for which they paid the price of occasional residence in Brussels. But he had amply bequeathed the memory of an impetuous military career in America, Europe, and India. The former Lord Rawdon had aided French royalists in Britanny in 1793, made a sortie into Belgium in 1794, and fought the Gurkhas in India in 1815 in his office of Governor-General, which he held from 1812 to 1822 with much zeal and a certain financial ingenuity. But Hastings as consolidator of British power in India and procurer of Singapore paled in Legaré's interest beside Hastings as commander of British forces in South Carolina in 1780–81, victor over Nathaniel Greene at Hobkirk's Hill, martinet and executioner of Isaac Hayne in Charleston. The irony was sweet to Legaré, as he flirted with the daughers of the demon. [13]

Outside Brussels in the castle of Gaesbeck lived the Marchese Guiseppe Arconati Visconti, a liberal exiled from Milan by the Austrians, his ancestral coffers sequestered, his living maintained by a fortunate inheritance in Belgium of some 50,000 francs a year. His wife Costanza was notable for taking snuff in large quantities and for being, as Legaré ambiguously noted, "*very* amiable." Gaesbeck was a magnet for emigré Italians, chief among them Giovanni Arrivabene, lately expelled from Mantua, political economist, student of the Belgian working classes, translator of James Mill into Italian and Nassau Senior into French. Senior himself, bursting with the erudition of free trade and Blue Books, passed through Brussels, where he engaged Legaré in mutually agreeable and earnest discourse. "We reason high," Legaré noted with satisfaction of conversation with a man he considered "very intelligent and unobtrusive," the ancestor of generations of Treasury mandarins. [14]

Then there were the Poles. In Paris, Legaré had met Prince Adam Czartoryski, the leader of Polish nationalism in exile, and so came recommended to the smaller but no less frantic band in Belgium. Legaré would go to dine at the French Ambassador's, where he might find Colonel Prozynski playing the pianoforte and "half a dozen young Poles, fine fellows, full of grace and spirit. . . . all interchanging lamentations on their hard fate." Legaré dabbled in Polish literature and was especially moved by the poetry of Adam Mickiewicz. This note in his diary for 24 September 1833 conveys his sympathy with and his sense of the revolutionary emigré's absurdity: "My Poles engage in a political conversation with one another, which they keep up with the greatest animation until past 10 o'clock. . . . The principal interlocuteurs were M. Plater and a young gentleman, just returned from a mad expedition to Poland, where *he* escaped by miracles, but some of his companions suffered death, after the cruel-

lest torture. This young man raves like a maniac when he speaks of the
*retrograde* system of '11 Mars,' and prophecies the downfall of Louis
Philippe. Count Plater talked very much like a man of sense, and,
being a Pole, like a philosopher." In August of the same year, Legaré
had made a domation to the "Association for Promoting the Instruction of Young Polish Exiles," which Czartoryski, Mickiewicz, and
Plater had helped to found in order to preserve "the Polish Youth,
obliged to wander in foreign lands" from the dangers of losing touch
with their "national mode of life." It was a cause likely to excite
Legaré's sympathy, especially as Czartoryski's political creed was a
species of oligarchic liberalism not unlike Legaré's own. [15]

To this fare was added the salt of visitors. Lady Charlotte Greville,
"La Coquette Gentille," came: mother of the diarist, daughter of the
third Duke of Portland (twice a dull but reasonable First Lord of the
Treasury), and a widow; a thorough woman of the world, attractive
even at sixty, of whom General Goblet observed to Legaré, "she has, in
her day, made *many* men *happy* before, and *happier* than you," and
among those thus happily serviced had been the Duke of Wellington.
The Earl of Stanhope came: proclaiming the ruin of his country in the
Chaos of Reform; insisting that his countrymen had grown effeminate, perhaps because of vaccination which had—he punned in the
worst of English traditions—made them "de-Jennerated"; and telling
the improbable story of Lord Grey's constantly seeing a vision of
Brissot's head, freshly guillotined, dripping blood and gore. The good
Lord was, as Legaré noted, "a little 'cracked', north-north-west or so."
Fanny Trollope came, fussing along with her son Henry: she, having
exhausted the profits of *Domestic Manners of the Americans* (the book
whose vulgarity, Legaré decided in his more pompous vein, made it
impossible for the chargé to meet her, though he avidly listened to
gossip), now seeking a quick piece of hack work upon the Low
Countries; he, gaily astonishing dinner parties by telling how in
America he had once killed an Indian for just looking at him, being
believed more often than he deserved. Prince Louis de Rohan came:
playing whist with Legaré; complaining of the King of the French,
who had stripped him of his fortune and obliged exile; between
lamentations dipping snuff from an exquisite box; reminding Legaré
of the fallen condition of a Huguenot house. Assorted Americans
came, like Charles Stuart Perry of Alabama, whom Legaré had met at
a dinner for Stephen Miller in a bare country inn in distant Lancaster,
South Carolina. All these came and more, bringing news, gossip,
insight from half the world, though after the first two years the pace

slackened. D'Arenberg died, the Hastings women left, the diplomatic corps rotated; as Legaré's first fresh taste for society diminished,
he took more to his solitary books and travel outside Belgium.[16]

One of his greatest pleasures was the women of Brussels, more in
and of society than the ladies of Charleston, who were expected to
cultivate a retiring and winning purdah. Brussels provided ladies who
could speak of politics with decisiveness, who were an influence as
much as an adornment. Years before, writing from Edinburgh,
William Campbell Preston had frowned at this European laxity: "The
manners of the women—always the surest index of society, are open
prompt & independent. They join in conversation familiarly—talk
unhesitatingly on most subjects and obviously consider a stranger as
entitled to some slight advances. . . . I confess I think there is rather
too much forwardness in the manners of the ladies. A young lady
meeting a young male acquaintance in the street shakes hands & stops
to talk with him—nor do the most respectable hesitate to walk thro'
the town or call at almost all hours. This may be all well enough to the
age of reason—but either my prejudice or my pride—makes me like
to see woman with a shyness which requires the first advance and a
sense of imbecility which requires to be sustained and protected."
While Legaré did like his young women to have sweet and bashful
airs, he took great pleasure also in the ripened knowledge of a Lady
Charlotte Greville, whose retirements had been to bed rather than to
giggling silence.[17]

There are only scraps by which to understand the question of Legaré
and women. There are no love letters among his papers. His sister
Mary, guardian of his literary remains, took to scratching out references to his amorous endeavors and tearing off sheets of incriminating
news. He remained a bachelor, though not because he was misogynist.
"I love music—next to women—of all things in this world," he once
wrote in his diary, whereupon his sister altered the eager multiplicity
of 'women' to the chaste vagueness of 'woman.' His letters somewhat
(those we have, after all, are mainly letters to his mother and sister)
and his diaries greatly are full of his absorption in the female charms of
a salon: the tone of a woman's voice, the color of her eyes, the length of
her eyelashes, the wit of her conversation. The malformation of his
body gave occasion for the rumor that he was impotent, but this was
apparently untrue. Nor was he opposed to marriage; he felt public
men should wed. He had had one youthful disappointment, a
Charleston girl who would have made "the prettiest little mother of a
family imaginable," for whom, "if I thought *she* really felt any

attachment to me, I might perhaps endeavour to prevail upon myself to forget I have been a Parisian & submit to the yoke that so many other people support through life with better or worse grace as it pleases God." At least twice more he came close to being wed, and occasionally he would cast an envious eye upon the marriages of his friends and launch into raptures about the inestimable gift of connubial bliss. In 1829, he wrote to his mother from Washington, apparently when his marriage proposal was being considered by a Charleston lady: "The uncertainty (not very great, I hope) which hangs over that matter makes it distracting to me. McDuffie, who I believe (don't mention it) is to marry Miss Singleton in the spring, tells me he is in just the same state of mind, dying to get home and quite unfit for any business or exertion . . . . How full of importance for me is this crisis of my existence, more so for *me*, I think, than a similar one could be for anybody else, such is the extreme sensitiveness and gloominess of my character." The lady, it seems, said no.[18]

Then there was the matter of young Anne Bronson. She was the sister of Oliver Bronson, a physician in Connecticut, an old friend at whose family home near Fairfield Legaré had spent pleasant days before embarking for Le Havre in 1832. It would appear he had early an eye for her. Indeed he had had occasion to reproach himself for mildly unchivalrous behavior in exciting and then disappointing her expectation of a marriage proposal, with the excuse that she had cast her net for more than him. "My experience in such matters has led me to doubt very much whether as much mischief is done to women generally by such things as is supposed," he reflected defensively. "I have hardly ever known one suffer deeply, whose chance for another object was not a very bad one. Then there are so many hypocritical & heartless coquettes by profession, that a man of honor who thinks himself in duty bound to prosecute a suit because he has made an impression, may chance to find him self the victim of a most unnecessarily nice conscience." In the autumn of 1835, Anne Bronson passed through Brussels and became reacquainted with Legaré, who promptly went to share a week's excursion along the Rhine and Aix-la-Chapelle. "Something has passed between me and A.B.," he cautiously told his sister, adding that she must keep the secret even from their mother. Two months later he was bolder. "I have just received a letter from her brother-in-law who is travelling with her (at Geneva) & two others from her brother *Oliver*, who is just about to embark at New York with his wife, to come & join her. I think from the appearances of

things now, the matter may almost be considered as *settled—except* so
far as it may be disturbed or even broken off on the question of
*residence,* for that horrible slave excitement has just come up in time to
add immensely to the difficulties already connected that point."
Could she or would she live in Charleston? Could he bring himself to
live elsewhere in America? The matter was to be settled when the
Bronsons reunited in Paris with Legaré in November. To his mother he
hinted that Paris seemed to jeopardize matters, emphasizing especially the influence that abolitionism (the question of censoring the
mails for abolitionist literature was just then agitating both American
and European opinion) had had—to his own surprise—upon the
proposed marriage. To his sister he was more blunt, more confused:
"The affair I told you of is *all off,* so that I am very sorry I was so hasty in
telling you the news & especially that I authorized you to communi-
cate it to Mama. But really after all that had passed & especially after
receiving the letters I mentioned from the two brothers, there did not
appear to be the least room for doubt. It is passing strange! To do all
they could to bring about such an affair—to make me think it
*incumbent* upon me to take the step—& then, to act as if they were
taken completely by surprise. One of the sisters almost—but it is all
over & if they are satisfied with what they have done, I suppose I must
be so too. The truth is from the moment I was fairly committed, I
began to think myself in a *scrape,* owing, among other things, to the
impossibility of reconciling my views for the future with such an
arrangement."[19]

In the Bronson affair is a scant hint, needing careful interpretation.
Legaré was an inveterate flirt and a rare suitor. "Kiss as many of the
girls as will let you in my name," he once urged David McCord. He
was eligible enough as to fortune and prospects, and his mother
(though he had some thought of making her last days pass "as
peacefully & as sweetly as possible" in his care) wished him to marry,
for his childless death would extinguish his line. Yet his proposals of
marriage seem to have been spurned. Certainly his friends looked on
him as an inveterate bachelor, and he had, to be sure, the quirks of a
bachelor: the older he got the more quirky he grew, the more settled in
his ways. But poorer and quirkier men have found wives. The Bronsons' surprise at his presumption of a settled marriage arrangement
may offer a clue, especially if collated with a short story by a friend of
Legaré.[20]

In 1834, Henry Junius Nott published *Novelettes of a Traveller, or,
Odds and Ends from the Knapsack of Thomas Singularity, Journeyman*

*Printer.* The stories were as witty and dry as any South Carolinian might expect of the professor, and worth even now a more than cursory criticism. In one, "Cock Robin," the protagonist is the only son of a widowed mother of respectability and comfortable fortune, who dotes upon her more than usually intelligent son. At school, Robert Wilson—"Cock Robin"—is accomplished and praised. He pores over "poesy and romances, particularly whatever is of a lofty and chivalrous character." Older, he turns to writing for the journals. As Wilson is made to relate, "I found a solace in literature, and pursued it with more energy than ever. Heretofore I had been a reader; my ambition was now to make myself a scholar. As my expenditures in other respects were limited, I had enough to bestow on books. My studies were pursued with ardour, until I acquired a critical knowledge of the ancient and most of the modern languages and their literatures. I tried my hand in different journals, and met with a success that gave me the most flattering anticipations. I was greeted by applause, especially from those whose good opinion I most coveted." One crucial moment in the plot turns upon Wilson's skill in the courtroom. More to the point here, Wilson is a dwarf.[21]

The burden of the story is Wilson's failure with women. In his youth, when his smallness seems delicate and not yet grotesque, he is much petted; the ladies especially like him. Encouraged, not thinking himself an oddity, Wilson mistakes fondness for love, offers marriage, and finds himself abruptly and cruelly rebuked. "Eliza had admired my personal beauty and graces, and Charlotte my intellect and acquirements; yet both shrunk back with horror and contempt from marrying a dwarf." They did so not just with horror, but with amazement that Wilson could think possible the union of a dwarf with an ordinary belle. He becomes morbid and unhappy, a joke in the community, and sinks in his amorous ambition. He tries to marry an old maid, but she jilts him. He tries to marry his serving girl, but their elopement is prevented, and he subsequently discovers that she has been faithless with a local hostler. Frustrated, he becomes a solitary, embittered and reflective.[22]

There is no reason to believe that anything other than the spirit and a few of the circumstances of this story were meant by Nott to portray Legaré; it may be that none of it was thus meant. Yet the spirit, matching so warmly that of Scott's *The Black Dwarf,* itself so admired by Legaré, is instructive. Compare Legaré's comment when he heard of Oliver Bronson's marriage in 1833, "The gloom I was in before is very much *deepened* by this picture of the *only* object I have *earnestly* and constantly aspired to and sighed for, but which seems to be only for others,—*domestic happiness*, 'thou only paradise of man that has survived the fall,'" with Wilson's encomium, "Whatever is balmy in spring, or melting in music, or lovely in the radiance of evening skies, or celestial in poetic images that float through the soul in our happiest moments, seemed to me concentrated in my ideas of female perfection." Compare Legaré's remark about Byron's youthful chagrin at his deformity, "It is vain to say that it argues a weak mind and an ill-regulated temper to be so much affected by what is, in the eye of reason, so trifling. Instinct, especially in youth, when character is forming, is too strong for mere unaided reason," with Wilson's confession, "You will tell me now . . . that it shows weakness of mind to value so highly mere external advantages, and a want of a well regulated disposition to evince so much sensitiveness to remarks from far below me in the noblest gifts of nature. You will tell me, for my consolation, about genius, and attainments, and fame. These are reasonings well enough for my age now, and barely so. But my deep mortifications came at a time when feeling was strong and when reason had hardly been called in for occasional advice. My mortification came too in the midst of joyful hopes and pampered anticipations. The shock was so great that it gave my character an impress that after-reflection might modify, but could not efface." Compare this too with Legaré's characterization of his own adolescence, "*such* a youth, so full of romantic fondness & sensibility & teeming anticipations of the future," and remember the deepening and ingrained melancholy of his maturity.[23]

Failure to marry scarcely ruined Legaré's life. At best it changed the texture of his discontent. He became fond of his nephews and nieces, "for I see no prospects of having any other objects of affection to provide for when I am gone." He found ways to console himself. Some, no doubt, were the customary male diversion. "Should my life ever be written," he once prophesied, "it will be *deplored* that my aversion to marriage betrayed me into many *peccadillos*. Alas! Solomon himself never felt more bitterly than I do, and always have, the vanity and vexation of those wretched substitutes for the interest which man is destined to feel in woman and her virtuous love, on pain of suffering the most desolate *ennui,* and *every* sort of chagrin. Verily, Byron—a second Solomon—never said a better thing, in prose or verse,— 'Pleasure is the severest of moralists.' " Solomon, it may be recalled, "loved many strange women," and certainly Byron did. Whatever Legaré's initiatives in brothels or in keeping mistresses or in exercising the prerogatives of a slaveholder may have been, they are lost to posterity, which he may have preferred and his sister did her best to achieve.[24]

One consolation was the flirtation of the salon. Like many bachelors past the bloom of youth, Legaré enjoyed the company of accomplished married women. He would be gracious, they could be confiding, all in the safe knowledge that flirtation need not reach beyond the salon. His letters to Judith Rives, a correspondence begun in 1832 and continuing well into his later years in Washington, were confessional, sentimental, often written upon paper with laced edges. But his attentions were not confined to the older women; he had a steady line in young and sweet girls. In Brussels he was especially fond of Emma Seymour, the daughter of a neighbor, just eighteen in 1833, *"very,* very pretty,*"* with a talent for painting. But he kept a careful and discerning log of other such who came his way. There was the young English daughter of a naval captain: "Her hair was dressed *à la Grecque,* and this charming simplicity heightened the effect of the fine contrast between its own blackness and her very white cheeks and *gorge."* There was the "very passable" Miss Freke. There was the sister of the Marchesa Arconati, "not pretty, tho' mild and gentle," with "long white eye lashes."[25]

Greatest of these was Lady Flora Hastings, for whom Legaré contracted a genuine affection, perhaps more, that seems to have been reciprocated. She was, he confessed, *"unquestionably* the finest specimen I have met with, *every thing* considered, of *female* character. I would give the world to be united with such a woman, if circumstances (without attending to which, marriage *must* be a failure) permitted it, & should think myself far more blessed than with the possession of a throne." She was tall with a long neck, blue eyes, fair hair, a delicate face framed with curls. She was well read, much traveled, and rather pious, as reflected in her verse. Perfectly mannered, she was accounted by some to be cool and too reserved, by others to be capable of a sharp, even malicious wit. Being twenty-seven years old in 1833, she was the medium between Legaré's tastes for the younger and the older woman. He and she could sit and talk of poetry, of the comparative merits of the nightingale and the mockingbird, of her travels, of their respective Scottish ancestries— for Legaré was a Swinton, and the Hastings family consented to think of him not as an American but as a sort of countryman. It came to be understood even by the court's Grand-Marshal that the chargé and the eldest Hastings daughter liked to be seated together. Nothing could

Lady Flora Hastings, by William Finden, after Hawkins.

come of it, which added to the piquancy. A lady of the bedchamber to
the Duchess of Kent could not marry an American of small fortune
and little rank, especially if she belonged to so resolutely Tory a
family, certainly if she was the daughter of Lord Rawdon. The two met
for a season and went their different ways.[26]

Her way was to prove hard. As a member of the royal household
under Victoria, attached to the Queen's mother and so an object of
suspicion to a queen who hated her mother, she was to be the occasion
of a famous scandal. Lady Flora was often ill. Early in 1839 she
developed a protuberance of the stomach. The Queen and her beloved
Lehzen began to think her pregnant. Lord Melbourne, never one to
think well of a scandalous world when the occasion offered, thought it
possible. The Queen's physician was asked to examine Lady Flora,
who first indignantly refused and then consented. She emerged with a
certificate of virginity and dry satisfaction. The matter seemed settled. But the doctor—not very competent, not eager to run against
the Queen's prejudices, and willing to temporize—confessed privately to Melbourne that perhaps he was wrong, for strange things did
occur. Lady Flora told her brother Lord Hastings of the incident, and
he was outraged. The honor of the family had been impugned, a Tory
family slandered by a Whig Queen. Domestic gossip became en-
tangled with politics, and even the soothing advice of the Duke of
Wellington could not prevent publicity. It was in the newspapers,
even a private letter by Lady Flora to her uncle with a frank account of
the affair. It was all over the Continent. The public took Lady Flora's
side, hissing and insulting Victoria when she went out of the palace.
Reconciliations were attempted and failed, and the Queen cut the
lady-in-waiting. By June, Lady Flora's condition had grown palpably
worse. She had developed a fever; she could not eat; the swelling,
which had abated, returned. "It would," as the Prime Minister
observed, "be very awkward if that woman was to die." Charles
Greville noted, "They are in a great fright lest Lady Flora should die;
because She is very ill, and if She should die the public will certainly
hold an inquest on her body and bring in a verdict of wilful murder
against Buckingham Palace." On the 4th of July she did die. She was
examined and a tumor of the liver was found. Her funeral procession
through London on the way to the docks, where the casket was
embarked for Loudoun Castle, was a scene of great public and melancholy interest. The Queen sent a royal carriage to the procession as a
token of respect and reluctant apology, and it was stoned. All this was
widely reported, even in Charleston, whose *Courier* gave news that

Legaré must have found painful, a fearful postscript to the pleasant evenings of Brussels. [27]

Brussels had been intended for education. It offered three main kinds: the opportunity of observing a government struggling for identity; the chance to read at leisure; the springboard for travel.

Legaré had, for example, an opportunity to observe the interaction between politicized urban unrest and government: in April 1834, from the comfortable vantage point of his apartment windows, he looked down upon a pillage of aristocratic houses, the very spectacle whose force in 1789 had colored his own trepidations about South Carolina. There had remained within Belgium a faction sympathetic to the House of Orange, one viewed with suspicion by both the government and the populace. Early 1834 saw the king of Holland still obdurate in refusing the independence of Belgium and making troop movements on the frontier. His son, the Prince of Orange, had recently visited his cousin the Tsar, who had been unsympathetic to the Belgian Revolution. These omens were worrying. The Orange press had been more than usually violent in its slanders upon the Belgian government and the court, and so matters were ripe for an incident. The occasion for mayhem was an attempt by the Prince of Orange to sell his stud, yet in Belgium and uncertain in its ownership. Among the horses was that which the Prince had ridden with gallantry at Waterloo. To express their continuing loyalty, members of the Orange faction within Belgium decided to get up a subscription list to buy the horses and present them to the Prince. Foolishly, the names of the subscribers were published. They were duly punished and warned by an urban riot, their houses broken into, their wine cellars appropriated.

Legaré was scarcely sympathetic to the Orange faction and had thought them unwise in the extreme. Yet he hated any violation of property rights and was dismayed to see the government acquiesce in the sackings by allowing their soldiers to stand conveniently aside, muskets on shoulders and swords in scabbards, as the rioters went about their business. "I was particularly struck," he reported to Louis McLane, the new Secretary of State, "in looking at the scene that was going on opposite to my house; first, by the comparative smallness of the banditti engaged, not I should say more than one or two hundred, men, women & boys being *actively* employed—secondly, by the extraordinary coolness & deliberation with which they went to work, until they found their way to the wine-cellars—thirdly, at the complete apathy of hundreds of bystanders looking on upon the havoc as they would upon the execution of a legal sentence—fourthly, upon the good understanding that appeared to exist between *some* of the soldiery & the plunderers—while others stood by . . . like so many statues, as if placed there to prevent the interference of the spectators & to see the work well done—fifthly, by the absolute inefficiency of the *few* attempts which *were* made to check this lawless & therefore, alarming force, which set all authority at defiance & delivered up the whole city, during twenty four hours to the discretion of apparently small numbers of ignorant & daring men." Only when the British ambassador protested did the government move, bringing in troops to contain the already flagging energies of the rioters. Briefly the new monarchy had wobbled, not least because there were rumors that these loyalist riots might waken an Orange counterattack, a Dutch intervention, or a republican dissent. Legaré was inclined to think the consequences less apocalyptic. Belgium, he still believed, depended upon the stability of Louis Philippe, then considerable. But it was a lesson. A man who had spent years reviewing the morphology of revolutions saw his opinions confirmed in this hint of an uprising; the thing had been incited by such small motives and carried by such a little band of people, yet was ripe with such large implications. He might have recalled his own words: "Great revolutions in society are often brought about by very slender means. . . . While just men doubt, while wise men deliberate, bold and reckless men decide and do. They lead because they go on—they are believed because they affirm—they intimidate because they boast and threaten—and they are obeyed because they dare to command." It was a reproach to the revolutionary, but it was also a doubt about the efficacy of himself, the man watching from the upper-story window.[28]

As to his reading, it was distinguished by a deepening of what he already knew and a few departures, which marked a concentrating interest in "politics & the history of man, including that of the Church." He read law: Vattel; *Letters on the English Chancery*, edited by Royer-Collard (the main French proponent of Scottish common sense philosophy); a volume of legal philosophy by Eugène Lerminier, an "odd mixture of German rhapsody and *St. Simonian* licentiousness" recommending war as the instrument of civilization. He deepened his understanding of the French Revolution with the latest memoirs and assorted recent meditations: the memoirs of Madame d'Abrantès; De Maistre's *St. Petersburg Dialogues* ("a production of singular originality and power . . . . *tremendous* censure of Voltaire"); the diplomatic correspondence between France and the United States during and after their respective revolutions. He stuck to his classics: Homer, Pindar, Xenophon. He allowed himself to wander into the nonclassical Latin of the Church Fathers: St. Augustine's *Confessions,* "a strange enough composition, to be sure," shocked him not by its candidness but by its bad and diffuse Latin; as for St. John Chrysostom, "I am afraid," he told his mother, "you will not have the pleasure of hearing me hold forth . . . at meetings of the Bible Society. I have no motions of the spirit." He kept up with recent literature: Trelawny's *Adventures of a Younger Son,* "clever but not interesting"; Balzac's *Le Livre Mystique,* too Swedenborgian to be convincing but his *Père Goriot* absorbing; Bulwer Lytton's *England and the English,* whose censure of the English diplomatic corps piqued Sir Robert Adair into an explosion of annoyance. Brussels made it easy to get books. He could borrow them. He could buy them, especially at Summerhauzen's bookshop, the "curious and immense collection of that singular bibliopole" on the Rue de la Madeleine. Legaré was in Europe in the golden age of book buying. Revolutions had dispersed aristocratic and religious libraries, while deflation had cheapened the market so that bibliomaniacs like the great and loony Sir Thomas Phillipps could amass incunabula like postage stamps. Legaré himself, a functional book buyer, brought back to the United States in excess of four hundred volumes. At his death, his library consisted of "some 6,000 volumes."[29]

His greatest gain was to learn German, beginning in June 1833 with lessons from a Mr. Harkan. Legaré got himself a grammar and a pocket dictionary. He bought a German translation of *El Cid,* something familiar in an unfamiliar tongue. He acquired the *Prolegomena to Homer* of Wolf, whose German he found "horribly difficult." By March 1834 he was writing to his sister, "A new excitement for me is German literature, which I am beginning to dive into. The language is hard at first, but by a little perseverance, all its difficulties are soon overcome to one whose mother tongue is English, & who is familiar with the Greek & Latin." By May he was able to add, "I began, yesterday, (for it is quite an epoch in my life,) to read Goëthe's *Faust* in the original, and am happy to find it less difficult than I was led to expect."[30]

It was only natural that such study should have rekindled Legaré's ambition to travel to Germany, a desire stifled by the entertainments of Brussels and reawakened by their slackening. His immediate goal, fulfilled on 23 May 1835, was to visit August von Schlegel in Bonn, after a trip via Aix, the Rhine, and Cologne. Legaré found an elderly gentleman, vain, informal, talkative, hospitable, in slippers and no cravat. They discussed the law with energy. Schlegel proved more the

reformer in legal procedure, being persuaded of Sir James Mackin-
tosh's desire to make jury verdicts a majority decision, with which
Legaré disagreed. But Legaré proved more the romantic in legal
philosophy. "I ask after Hugo and Savigny," he wrote in his journal.
"They do not seem to stand very well in his estimation. Repeats what
somebody said, that the civil law was like scenery in twilight—you
make what you please of it. Savigny, he adds, is of what they call the
*historical* school. I tell him, as I interpret the expression, I am half
inclined to be of that school myself; and ask him what meaning he
attaches to the term. He explains it as being a sort of *legislative necessity,*
by which every age, *nescio quo fato,* makes the laws that suit it. I then
say, all I mean is that the *traditions of a country* must be respected in its
constitutional innovations; otherwise one of two things ensues—
either your constitution is dead-born, as in Belgium now, or every
thing is turned into chaos as by the *Constituent Assembly,* and refer
again to our own history." Schlegel, the veteran enthusiast of the
Revolution's early days, protested that the Assembly had more merit
than was usually accorded to it. Yet the German's philosophical
opinions were deflected by the accidents of personality. Niebuhr,
whose Roman history Legaré so admired, had not been a friend.
Niebuhr, Schlegel explained, "was altogether impatient of contradiction," a vice not confined to the historian. [31]

Visiting Schlegel had been a brief foray. In the spring of 1836,
Legaré went for a longer trip, knowing that he was leaving Europe
soon and inclined to think he would never return. On April 18 he left
Brussels and took his customary route to Aix. Thereafter he went
north to cross the Rhine at Dusseldorf, then east through Elberfeldt,
Kassel, and Magdeburg to Berlin. After a stay of some days in Prussia,
he went south to Dresden, Prague, and Munich before returning to
Belgium via Frankfort. He was gone just over a month on this more
than brisk excursion. He took care to keep a diary of his progress. In
places he was surprised by primitiveness, the paucity of change since
the Thirty Years War in villages with "the most miserable, dirty,
ragged collection of huts that can be conceived—houses built of wood
frames filled up with clay and most of them decaying and dilapidated," reminiscent of slave dwellings in his own country. Elsewhere,
as in Elberfeldt, he was taken aback by new industrial towns entered
on macadamized roads, possessed of "all the freshness and life of an
American town in one of the new states." Prussia impressed him by its
omnicompetent bureaucracy and efficiency, so alien to an American. [32]

Everywhere Legaré found echoes and embodiments of his reading and tastes. The skeptical proponent of the Reformation stood before the tomb of Luther in Wittenberg, impressed by the gravity of the spectacle if amused by the daunting enthusiasm of the tomb's attendant beadle, with whom he conversed in Latin. The newly accomplished German linguist rode through the Brockenberg, the seat of Faust's witches, and put his hand into the ponderous gauntlet of Count Tilly, the destroyer of Magdeburg, and thought of Schiller's *Wallensteins Lager.* The critic of the Enlightenment had the satisfaction of examining Frederick the Great's library at Sans Souci and noting that the king's library contained classics, not in the original but in French translations. The lover of landscape was enchanted by mountains and woods at midnight and bored by the barrenness of the March of Brandenberg. The student of the opera had the misfortune to witness a bad performance of *The Barber of Seville* in Berlin. The aficionado of painting viewed the Raphaels and Correggios of Dresden. The diplomat conversed with the Prussian Foreign Minister, with the added bonus that Joseph Ancillon was also a philosopher, an eager conversationalist whose respect for Legaré had been fashioned by the flattering reports of the Prussian envoy to Belgium. The fastidious snob was harassed by innkeepers, uncomfortable beds, and impertinent waiters. The romantic had the sites of ruined castles. The secular man resisted tales of miracles told by guides, while the doubting quasi-aristocrat found an explanation in rank: "It seems he [Frederick the Great] died in an armed chair. My valet swore to me the clock points now to the very hour at wh. he died—for it went down as the breath left his body. Always some marvel for the vulgar."[33]

In Dresden, Legaré met George Ticknor, then wintering with his family. Ticknor much eased Legaré's brief introduction to Dresden society by taking him to the Gallery, to dinner with the British minister, to an acquaintance with Moritz Retzsch the engraver. Ticknor has left a snapshot in his journals of Legaré, busying himself through central Europe, that is worth a full quotation: "May 4.—Mr. Legaré left us this evening. . . . We were sorry to part from him, for he is a man of very agreeable as well as remarkable powers, and he has literally been the whole of each day with us. . . . His conversation is very rich, and was truly refreshing to us, after having been so long without the pleasure of good, solid English talk. He is a good scholar, with a good and rather severe taste; a wise and deep thinker, who has reflected a great deal, and made up his opinions on a great number of subjects; and a politician who sees the weakness and defects of our government, and the bad tendencies of things among us, as clearly as any person I have ever talked with. He seems to belong to the Jackson party, only from the circumstance that he was of the Union party in South Carolina; for his views are quite too broad and high for any faction, and he is as far from being a Democrat as any man in the United States. We have few men like him, either as scholars, thinkers, or talkers. I knew him very well at Edinburgh in 1819, and thought him then an uncommon person; but it is plain he has taken a much higher tone than I then anticipated."[34]

This rekindled a friendship that would be resumed in the United States and only ended by Legaré's death. The two men had a natural sympathy, though they were very different. They shared social and political conservatism, European travel, a taste for allusive conversation, the habit of gentlemanly writing. But Ticknor had the less sharp mind, the less tactile sensibility; he was more purely the abstracted man of letters, living only for his study and the drawing room. It is instructive to compare Legaré's and Ticknor's accounts of a meeting with Ancillon. Legaré is long, precise; he duplicates the conversation's point and counterpoint, and chronicles even the menu. Legaré sought the sympathy of men of worldly affairs. "Find M. Ancillon *very* agreeable, clever, enlightened and *well read,* with great douceur and kindness of manner, and an ardent *love* of talk—for I know my *own* by instinct. . . . Talk of history. I remark that to write or even to appreciate history, perfectly, one must have lived in the world and even been engaged in public affairs. M.A. assents, but the literary men, cry out against what so trenches upon the privileges of their caste." Ticknor saw Ancillon and the foreign minister's need for scholarly relaxation and discourse differently: "The duty [Ancillon had been tutor to the Crown Prince], he said, lasted fifteen years, and was succeeded, eight years ago, by the duty of being Minister for Foreign Affairs, a burthen over which he groaned this morning . . . telling me what a *rafraichissement* it was to escape from it, sometimes, an hour in the morning, and read a Latin or Greek book. I thought this affected, and in bad taste; but he talked well, and made phrases which, I am sure, pleased himself. . . . he asked me to come next day after tomorrow afternoon, between five and six o'clock, 'pour causer un peu,' which I thought rather an idle business for a Minister of State." This betrays the difference between Legaré's experience of affairs and Ticknor's observation of them, between a man schooled in a culture that prized edifying leisure and a man taught to abhor idleness. Nonetheless, Boston and Charleston could find sympathy enough.[35]

Legaré traveled from many motives. One was his aesthetic participation in the old and still useful tradition of the Grand Tour. He looked at paintings, heard music, and visited buildings, and did so mainly in the hope of being moved, of being surprised into a tumult of mixed emotions. The more experienced and the cooler his discrimination, the more severe he felt was the scrutiny of his examination. In fact, Legaré was easily moved. Contemporary artists and musicians had freshly discovered the usages of emotion and were bombarding unaccustomed eyes and ears with ruthless offerings. Romanticism having grown older, audiences grew hardened and developed ways of resisting by making distinctions between evocation and melodrama. But it was not easy to look upon the first and premier ballerina of romantic persuasion, Maria Taglioni, and not feel moved. It was hard not to hear Rossini's *William Tell* overture, played by a massed orchestra in the open air of Brussels, and be unimpressed. A Paris opera in 1832 could be surprisingly effective: *"Robert le Diable* is a masterpiece of musical composition, which puts Meyerbeer upon an equality with Rossini, and it is got up at Paris with all the pomp and splendor of their unrivalled opera. The subject is a fine one, and gives a sort of epic, religious grandeur and solemnity to the whole exhibition, which recalls the sacred music and gorgeous though gloomy display of the Romish service, in one of their glorious old Gothic cathedrals. The scene, especially, in which Count Robert's father, Bertram, (the devil in human form,) contends for the soul of his son with Alice, the depository of Robert's departed mother's fatal secret and last injunctions, is admirably executed . . . . I never felt so much *interested* in an opera before—I mean so rationally interested, for you know I have always been excessively in love with that charming *spectacle."* Legaré could give no higher praise than to compare Meyerbeer's work to a Gothic cathedral come to life and singing, for few have visited so many cathedrals with such enthusiasm.[36]

Legaré went to Gothic churches and cathedrals in every town he visited, preferably during mass, preferably when the edifice was still in the hands of luxuriant Catholicism and not abandoned to the bare iconoclasm of Protestantism. Antwerp remained his favorite: "It is an immense edifice, which was building during the whole of the fifteenth century, the period of Antwerp's greatest commercial prosperity, and when, indeed, it was the great centre of European business and capital. Its spire, which is upwards of 460 feet high, is one of the most beautiful remains of that sort of architecture extant; and the interior is distinguished by the grandeur of its effect, owing to its vastness, the immense height of the roof, the colossal magnitude of its

pillars, and the perfect simplicity of its style. Judge for yourself what
an impression a building 500 feet long, 230 wide, and 360 high,
presenting the most imposing Gothic forms, consecrated to religion,
resounding with the voice of Christian thanksgiving and supplica-
tion, and adorned with the masterpieces of genius [three paintings by
Rubens]—must make." He wanted a church to humble him; thus he
rated Cologne cathedral lower than Antwerp because it was smaller
and less austere, and awe was dissipated. Lower yet he considered
Liège, whose cathedral, though "a beautiful building," was "not by
any means so vast and imposing as that of Antwerp, but highly
ornamented, and having a striking air of neatness and elegance,—
epithets that seem not quite in character with such a structure, and yet
are applicable to it."[37]

In painting, Legaré inclined to the vivid and emotive. The Antwerp Museum had Rubens' *Descent from the Cross,* the original mini-
ature, from which that in the cathedral was copied. Legaré's
enthusiasm betrays his visual taste: "This . . . is the most delicious
piece (of colouring, especially) I ever saw. If an angel had laid on the
colours, or drawn the shapes, they could not have been brighter or
more exquisite. Two of the Marys at the foot of the cross, with their
golden locks and soft, silken drapery, are perfectly celestial. . . . I
have no idea that the art can go beyond this vision of beauty in delicacy
or vividness of tints." Likewise he was struck by the "frightful power"
of Rubens' *Breaking of the Legs* in the cathedral. "One of [the thieves],"
he explained, "in his terror at the approaching blow, has torn one of his
feet loose from the nail with which it has been fastened to the cross,
and the contortions of his body in its agony, as well as the hyena grin
upon his face, while the blood is trickling from his perforated instep,
makes you almost imagine the wretch howling in anguish and despair
before your eyes." Yet to the turbulence of Rubens he almost preferred
the greater stillness of Van Dyck's religious painting. Of Van Dyck's
*Christ on the Cross,* also in the Antwerp Museum, he wrote "[It] is all
that it should be,—except the cursed little Cupid at the foot of the
cross, so utterly out of place. But the Redeemer himself, as he sleeps in
deep, majestic repose upon that instrument of ignominious punish-
ment, henceforth the symbol of universal triumph and immortal
hopes,—one feels that it is the crucifixion of a God! Then the *mater
dolorosa,* pale, fainting, almost dead with grief, as she supports herself
upon the fatal tree, and embraces *His* feet. Yet, how gentle a form of
womanhood in its devotedness—how graceful and beautiful in her
world—forgetting woe. The outstretched arms of the only other

The Descent from the Cross, by Rubens.

person in the piece—the noble air and attitude as of prophetic inspiration addressing its prayers, not unmixed with imprecations, to the omnipotent sufferer. Then the heavens veiled in darkness and the troubled sky." Reluctantly he discriminated in favour of Rubens: "[Van Dyck] certainly wants the invention, boldness, strength and colouring of Rubens, and may be considered as, upon the whole, an inferior genius. But then there is so much grace and soberness,—such a 'rapture of repose',—and I know not what indescribable classical sweetness about his *forms,* that I yield a very hesitating, reluctant assent to the opinion of better judges, who give the palm to Rubens." Legaré fitted painting into the literary aesthetics that he had so much pondered. Thus "Vandyke is the Sophocles of painters, and bears the same relation to Rubens as that pure Attic artist to the gigantic, though rude, author of the Prometheus and the Agamemnon," Aeschylus.[38]

America offered little opportunity for viewing great painting in the days before the aesthetic pillaging of Europe; so Legaré had to take his chances as travel offered. He became an amateur connoisseur of painting and of galleries. It was natural that, living in Belgium and traveling in northern Europe, he acquired a more intimate knowledge of a Rubens than of the painters of the Italian Renaissance, although Dresden and the Louvre gave him a sampling of Raphael, Da Vinci, and others. Even so, his discriminations of the Flemish school had the full weight of leisured examination and reexamination in museums, in private houses and in churches, whereas without traveling beyond the Alps, his feel for the Italians was thinner and more derived. But art criticism was in its infancy and gave litle guidance beyond the bare elucidation of Lessing's *Laocoon,* Reynolds, or Winckelmann. Galleries were just beginning to extract historical and aesthetic order out of the potpourri that jumbled the walls of eighteenth-century museums, so Legaré was delighted to find the Berlin Museum recently and rationally disposed. "The ground floor is appropriated to the statuary. The picture gallery if I may use the expression is arranged on a new principle . . . . They [the pictures] are divided into a great number of different compartments, intended to illustrate the diversity of schools and the progress of the art—Venetian, Flemish, etc. In this point of view the gallery is extremely interesting to an amateur, and the collection very precious, as it is very extensive." Dresden too had arranged its paintings into schools and nationalities, and offered besides an incomparable quantity and quality of artists, especially Raphael, of whom Legaré was very fond.[39]

Germany had been a consciously intellectual venture, which was to bear fruit in Legaré's writings of the late 1830s. Paris and London were returns to the familiar: the former often visited from Brussels, the latter the object of a brief excursion in June 1834. The main objects in going to London were to attend a great festival of Handel's music held in Westminster Abbey, to consult a doctor about "a sort of chronic malady" of the stomach and kidneys (the immediate symptom of his "wretched *gouty* constitution"), and to exorcise the blue devils. But stepping out from the Clarendon Hotel, he had an opportunity to use the social and diplomatic connections of Brussels. Adair gave him letters to Palmerston, Lord Lansdowne, Lord Grey, Lord Holland, and Brougham. Lady Westmoreland gave him a letter for her daughter-in-law, Lady Jersey. Of his political conversations there is no record. It is known he attended a ball given by the Duke of Wellington. Of his encounter with the great lioness of London society, the Iron Duchess of Almack's, there is his own account. Feeling unwell and doubtless taking pleasure in his perversity, he obtained a ticket of admission to Almack's and disdained to go: "I was fatigued, sleepy and unwell," he explained to his sister, "and, besides, really have too little curiosity about such things now, to put myself at all out of the way to enjoy them." But he did accept Lady Jersey's invitation to call at three o'clock. "Her house struck me as very fine, accustomed as I am to palaces; but I was more engrossed with her than with her *entourage,* a part of which, I ought not to forget to mention, was the Earl of Roslyn. She asked me whom and what I was desirous of seeing, and was liberal in her offers of services, etc. I rose to go away—she rose also, and said 'Here's a fine picture', leading the way into an adjoining room. As she passed, she stopped to say something to me, and fixed her somewhat hawkish eyes on mine with a gaze fixed and intense: she looked, or rather glanced, then, into a mirror at her side, and then went on. I had thus a fair opportunity of surveying the whole person of this great dictator of the fashionable world of London; and think now I understand, what once appeared to me mysterious enough, the secret and the character of her domination over men's and women's minds." What he saw he declined to explain to a sister. What Charles Greville saw was a remarkable lack of pride in one surrounded by sycophants, benevolence rather than sensuality, correctness rather than imagination, a woman powerful by being good-naturedly less than one might expect and fear. Yet perhaps Legaré saw the lingering attractions of the Prince Regent's mistress.[40]

Eventually Legaré tired of Europe. He lacked the constitution of the permanent emigré, the willingness either to live aside from the world around or to become part of it. He liked his America and South Carolina too well. "I am *essentially* & by blood & bone, a *domestic* man. I do not believe any human being ever was created more liable to home sickness or *nostalgia* than I am," he told Alfred Huger. Guilt had attacked him with intensity as letters came from his friends detailing the deepening crisis of nullification; that had abated. Nullification was compromised, as Petrigu told him with cynical exactness. Peace in South Carolina had been declared, if not quite established, which made it possible for him to go home. Yet nullification and Brussels had altered Legaré's relationship to home, had killed whatever capacity for optimism he had once possessed, had hardened his heart against wishing and expecting too much of himself and his state. His ambition, he took to declaring, was dead. Europe had given him philosophical detachment, and the chance for reading had enhanced his capacity for detachment. Or so he told himself, and perhaps he was right. It was a bleaker Legaré who returned to the United States in 1836. He had told his sister, in the spring of 1835, of this consolidated fortress in his spirit: "The love of art or of science, that is to say, the love of beauty & truth, when it becomes an engrossing, habitual, passionate feeling is worth more than all the gifts of fortune. There is one of its good effects which I have never seen pointed out, though it is impossible to overrate its importance. It elevates one's sense of one's own dignity, & at the same time, makes you feel that it is a dignity which the world can neither give nor take away. Thus it mitigates, if it does not entirely cure, the worst of all the diseases of our fallen nature (I know that forbidden tree is called 'the tree of *knowledge, ce pendent*)— that, indeed, by which it fell, as angels did before us—a craving, restless, self-tormenting *ambition.*" Pride and boredom, ambition and insecurity, the vices of his character had been identified if not mastered. Europe had settled the lines of his life by interceding a consoling and informing moment.[41]

Yet his life had to be resumed. An embassy, he knew, "is an episode in one's political existence"; 1836 saw him, as he often noted, fast approaching his fortieth birthday, his hair turning gray, his "fine showy teeth" going. He was weary of "comfort . . . faring sumptuously, sleeping softly, wearing fine linen," and pined for a renewed life of "active usefulness." He had no great confidence in his own efficacy, though he knew his talents. He was unsure about the destiny of his country, though certain that the future of South Carolina was to be declension. He feared disunion at a time when, as he knew from recent experience, from dinner with Palmerston and many evenings of parrying European disdain, this was "the age of *great* empires." Uncertainty about what to expect had detained him in Europe, yet he had to go home. There would always be the bar upon which to fall back. There would be literature, though that was not a profession. As for politics, it defied augury. Still, he packed up his goods in twenty-three boxes: his cellar, linen, plate, books, harness, odds and ends. Having first visited London and Loudoun Castle, not yet the tomb of Lady Flora Hastings, he took the risk of a homecoming.[42]

9

Charleston

Few homecomings have been more flattering. Legaré was elected to Congress from the district of Charleston, though under odd circumstances. The incumbent was Henry Pinckney, the former editor of the nullifying Charleston *Mercury*, the heir to a great political name, the lieutenant of Calhoun. In 1836, Calhoun had resolved that Pinckney needed expulsion from Congress for dissent over the issue of slavery. Late in the previous year, the House of Representatives had begun to debate the problem of antislavery petitions, then becoming a cataract. The old practice had been to table the divisive petitions without comment. Calhoun, James Henry Hammond, William Campbell Preston, Waddy Thompson, and Francis W. Pickens—the majority of the South Carolina delegation—decided upon the merits of change. Congress should refuse even to receive the petitions on the ground that such documents countenanced unconstitutional action. Foolishly, and with Van Buren's guidance, Pinckney offered differing resolutions to the House: the memorials should be received and referred automatically to a special committee with instructions to report that Congress ought not to interfere with slavery. The crux lay with the District of Columbia. Few imagined that Congress could abolish slavery in the states, but the District, over which Congress had suzerain powers, was another matter. Pinckney's resolutions asserted not the incompetence of Congress to abolish slavery in the District but

Eastern View of the City of Charleston, by William Keenan (1838).
Courtesy, Carolina Art Association/Gibbes Art Gallery

the inexpediency. Calhoun and most of Pinckney's constituents felt inexpediency to be a frail and temporary reliance. So anathema was pronounced upon the erring congressman, successful in Washington but to be defeated in Charleston. Backed by Van Buren, Pinckney was to refuse Calhoun's demand for an acquiescent outer darkness and decide to run again. This defiance scrambled the already bemused politics of Charleston. Pinckney the nullifier sought out the votes of Unionists eager to defy Calhoun, and managed to pick up the endorsement of the Charleston *Courier.* The nullifiers ran Isaac Holmes. Calhoun was worried at this turn of events, for Pinckney threatened unexpected strength against Holmes, an obedient but lightweight candidate. Yet in Pinckney's bid for Unionists lay Calhoun's solution. The senator went to the Unionist leaders and offered a compelling bargain: pick your own man; I will back him, and withdraw Holmes, if he is right on the question of slavery. The Unionists, led by Petigru and Alfred Huger, decided upon Legaré, orthodox on abolition and so long an exile that he offended few. Moreover, in the old days Legaré had inhabited a shadowy region between Unionism and nullification, a region that now might carry the election.[1]

So the thing was arranged, while Legaré dallied in the North almost until the eve of the election, and Petigru counseled him upon a contest that proved as close as a hundred votes. "The Nullifiers are betting on your election," Petigru advised on September 6, "and everything shows that the contest will be narrowed down to you and Pinckney, and that the friends of H. [Holmes] will ultimately rally on you if they see no chance of carrying the election, and at all events we shall get as many Nullification votes as Pinckney will take away. But I think you should come as soon as you get this letter. . . . Come home and let us do the thing neatly and well." Legaré's successful margin was provided by the country vote. In Charleston, with the aid of the Irish, the mechanics, and the Methodists, Pinckney carried the day and was to rebuild his political fortunes by taking control of the city government. As for Legaré, he looked upon success with his usual diffident fussiness. "I see I have been announced for Congress," he told his mother. "I own I am not *satisfied* at being placed in that situation—public life has no rewards here—but if they think I can do good is it fit that I should shrink from my post? & one too, for which all my studies have been calculated to fit me?" Such a temperament did not go unnoticed. Joel Poinsett, from the standpoint of Van Buren's War Department, observed in 1837; "Legaré is as a matter of course with the conservatives; but is anxious to be regarded as an administration man. He will fly off ever & anon but on the whole will I think go right after he has been here another session. He made a favorable impression as to talents & acquirements; but is regarded as an unstable man in politics."[2]

For a man of delicate sensibilities and uncertain political ambitions, Washington was no bargain but a roughhouse, brown with mud and tobacco juice, "a vile place—very dear, hot, stupid & sickly." Installed in the seats of power, Legaré was unimpressed. "The House goes on sluggishly with its business, or rather doesn't go on at all," he recounted during 1837. "Interminable speaking on every subject, coarse language & conduct, quarrelling & billingsgate—such are the pleasures of this vast *Cavern,* into which I enter every day with feelings akin to those we may imagine a traveller to have experienced in descending into the shades of Dante's Inferno—bating, however, all curiosity to keep one alive. I detest & loathe it, & more & more the more accustomed I become to it, or rather the less accustomed, for I do not become accustomed to it at all. It is horrible to be forced into association with people that do not suit us or whom we do not suit." There were a few compensations. He found a congenial lodging at Mrs. Ulrick's on the corner of G and 15th Streets. William Cabell Rives was now a Senator from Virginia, a messmate, and had become a closer friend. The alliance was founded upon old sympathies: Rives had been a student of James Ogilvie and a classmate of Francis Walker Gilmer; he had been a friend of William Campbell Preston in Richmond in 1814; he had opposed both nullification and the tariff; he had been a diplomat; he had suffered from severe digestive complaints. But the Virginian inhabited a loftier plane of politics than Legaré. Judith Rives had once consented to call upon Peggy Eaton, and her husband had flourished in his friendship with Martin Van Buren. Rives and Van Buren had opposed Biddle's Second Bank of the United States together, and Rives had entertained serious but thwarted hopes of inheriting the Vice-Presidency when Van Buren moved up to assume the General's mantle. The President-elect had offered Rives the War Department, but the Virginian had wished for the State Department, at which John Forsyth had a tenure endorsed by Jackson. This soured matters, worsened by the heated rivalry of Thomas Hart Benton and Rives over leadership of congressional Democrats and financial policy. Benton was the hardest of hard-money men, who rejoiced in Jackson's 1836 Specie Circular and pressed Van Buren not to abandon the policy just because the economy was panicking into depression in 1837. Rives too advised the President, but to opt for government regulation of state banks and soft money, a situation that would best answer Virginia's needs. By the spring of 1837, Benton had persuaded the President and Rives had persuaded Congress, so matters were stalemated. Rives was delicately poised between being a conservative Democrat at odds with the administration and becoming a Conservative hazarding independency or, what he wished to avoid, being drawn into the orbit of the Whigs.[3]

Amid the fussy tediousness of patronage, Legaré found issues to engage his interest. The question of slavery had brought him to Washington, and he did not violate the bargain of his election. John Quincy Adams presented antislavery petitions by the cartload, and Legaré voted them into oblivion, even though unpersuaded that his Southern allies were sound. "I see a storm brewing, & when I look at the pilots who are expected to guide us thro' its perils—my heart sinks within me." Calhoun, Legaré mistrusted. "Brougham pretends to know everything," he was to hazard the comparison; "Calhoun would have you believe he knows nothing (as indeed he does know but little, but that little is everything to him) [.]" In 1838, Legaré entered this judgment to George Bryan: "Poor Calhoun! Nature certainly gave him great parts & experience has helped him: but his intellectual organization is radically defective & he wants *science*. His glance is quick & penetrating—but not *broad*. He is a French head—an *homme à système* as the Gauls call it—He comes to his conclusions always by the high *priori road,* & bends all facts to suit them. If you could make him President, I would advise you to do so—it would cure him of his maladies forever. He would exercise power, I have no doubt, magnanimously & even wisely—but he *will* have it—*or,* make poor So. Carolina sweat for it!—at least, if keeping her always in *hot water* will do it."[4]

As for his opponent, John Quincy Adams, Legaré felt him to be a controversialist, unfit for and dangerous in power. "A sophist in reasoning, a cynic in language, a buffoon in action & gesticulation, without self control, without manners, scolding like a fish-woman, raging at times like a fury of hell, snapping like a wounded serpent at everything about him, at friend & foe, what a picture is this of the old age of a man who for sixty years has been charged with the most important interests of mankind, & has been exercising the most exalted functions of government." For all that, Legaré reflected from his seat in the House, "It is still a singular spectacle, as the world goes, to see a man verging upon eighty, wrestling with the youth of a second generation beneath him, with *more* than their keenness of emulation, & struggling for promotion in this world as if it contained no grave." In his turn, Adams first reacted unfavorably to Legaré. On 2 October 1837 he noted in his diary, "Legaré, of Charleston, an orator of the South Carolina school—flashy and shallow." Two weeks later, Adams had discerned the man inside the representative: "Legaré has not the ideal form of an orator—short, thick, with a head disproportioned in size to his body; a fattish, ugly, but intelligent face, dark complexion, and slightly limping left foot; but his voice is strong; his enunciation distinct, though rapid; his action not grace-ful, but energetic; his intonations alternately high and low; and his command of language copious and ornamental. He is . . . rather of the English than the American school, and will surely rank among the distinguished orators of the nation."[5]

The year 1837 brought a depression to complicate the perennial issue of government and the banks, and Legaré's first session produced the monster Sub-Treasury scheme: a treasury not a treasury, a bank not a bank. The new President's message to Congress called for laws to bankrupt banks that had suspended specie payment, to postpone disbursement of the Treasury's surplus to the states, to issue Treasury notes to meet immediate government needs, to allow the government to keep its own receipts in its own Treasury, to establish an Indepen-dent Treasury whereby the "collection, safe-keeping, transfer and disbursement of the public money" would be through government agents and not through banks. This was designed to contract the intervention of government in the economy and to abolish the influ-ence of the "pet banks" upon government, thus steering between the Scylla and Charybdis of the Jacksonian political economy, the over centralization of Biddle's Bank of the United States, and the under-centralization of innumerable small banks inflated by government deposits. As always with Van Buren, this was ingenious. Yet when Congress gathered to consider the measures, the fate of the admin-istration's solution was doubtful. From the Democrats had defected a number of independents, to whom Rives of Virginia and Nicholas Tallmadge of New York offered conservative but vigorous leadership. There promised to be a countervailing defection from the Whigs. Van Buren agreeing to a full resumption of specie payments upon Treasury notes by 1841, Calhoun would throw the support of nullifiers, those temporary Whigs, to the Sub-Treasury. Thereby Calhoun would return to the Jacksonians, the party whose Vice President he had been for less than four improbable years. This bargain might be bad economics, deflationary in the midst of a recession, but perhaps excellent politics.[6]

Legaré, a good economist but an indifferent politician, chose to defy Calhoun, the Atreus of South Carolina politics who served up his own lieutenants as hors d'oeuvres. He rose on October 13 to address the issue of the Sub-Treasury. It was to be his most elaborate congressional address, perhaps his best political speech. Certainly he felt it to have been. "I never spoke so well in my life," he told his mother. Even Adams was impressed: "Legaré . . . delivered one of the most eloquent speeches, of two hours, ever pronounced in that hall." Legaré felt that his life had prepared him for the occasion, and with justice, for he deployed the reading and experiences of recent years: the tariff crisis, classical scholarship, European travel and conversation, reading, all fused into a vision of political economy of service to the moment.[7]

He began conventionally enough. The depression was a lesson to be deciphered and learned. He noted briefly that informed British opinion was divided on banking policy, though united on the intrinsic desirability of a paper currency system. But the United States had special difficulties in arriving at a rational economic policy as a result of having a federal system in which power was divided and limited—a point Van Buren, the old Jeffersonian, had reminded the Congress of and Legaré had often endorsed. Still, power—however vexed and dispersed—needed in this crisis to be deployed: "The task is an immensely difficult one—but it must be undertaken, and it must be *done.*" Yet the President was rushing things. Congressmen were being asked to pass upon a novel and precipitate measure, without any opportunity for thought or consultation with constituents. On that ground alone, Legaré was inclined to vote against the administration.[8]

Nonetheless, he felt it right to discuss the general principles of political economy. One principle he opposed was that bleak Jacksonian preference for austere republican virtue. "It may be true that luxury, according to the old saw, is the ruin of States, and that sumptuary and agrarian laws are necessary to maintain your true Spartan discipline," he drily observed. "But I am excessively disinclined to try any such experiment upon my constituents; at least without receiving an express instruction, to that effect, from them. I am afraid they have no taste for black broth—that Spartan discipline will be irksome, and even revolting to them." To the contrary, Legaré observed, the leading feature and hope of modern civilization was the evaporation of black broth. International commerce was promoting a rising "standard of comfort," reconciling populations to their governments and governments to one another. War was not abolished, human nature being unabrogated, but wars were diminishing. "During my last residence of four years abroad," Legaré remarked and remembered, "I saw sufficient grounds of quarrel to have led, under the old order of things, to twenty wars, as spreading and bloody as the Thirty Years' War, or the Seven Years' War—and yet these threatening differences passed harmlessly away, cloud after cloud dissolved as it rose above the horizon, leaving the sky more serene than before."[9] This was not the consequence of increased enlightenment so much as of technology. "It is the STEAM-ENGINE—in its two-fold capacity of a means of production and a means of transport—the most powerful instrument by far of pacification and commerce, and therefore of improvement and happiness that the world has ever seen; which, while it increases capital, and multiplies beyond all imagination the products of industry, brings the most distant people into contact with one another—breaks down the barriers which exclusive legislation would oppose to the freedom of mercantile exchanges—effaces all peculiarities of national character, and promises, at no distant period, to make the whole Christian world, at least, one great family." To this change the South was making a signal contribution. The combination of cheap cotton and modern machinery was clothing the world's ragged, giving them self-esteem, exciting their desire to further affluence, and so encouraging the mechanisms of commerce. In 1819, Legaré had traveled over the country between Liège and Spa, finding there only beauty and wildness. He returned in 1835 to witness "mills and factories, begrimed with the smoke and soot of steam-engines; its romantic beauty deformed, its sylvan solitudes disturbed and desecrated by the sounds of active industry, and the busy hum of men." This mixed blessing had been brought about by an emigré English iron founder. What the steam engine and commerce helped to foster, and what John Cockerill in Flanders had exemplified, was a shift in energies and in spirit. What must then be considered was the effect of the Sub-Treasury upon the spirit of modern society, the probable tendency of the plan to enrich or enfeeble moral energy. Legaré did not doubt that opinion created reality, as fully as reality created opinion.[10]

Still there were technical matters that needed brief consideration. A few months before, Legaré confessed, he had been greatly opposed to the government demand for the use of specie in revenue collections, because gold and silver prices had been exceptionally high. Those prices having diminished, he was less strenuously though still opposed. By harping upon specie and by hoarding specie, the government made the paper currency of both sound and unsound banks suspect to the public without differentiation. While the federal government lacked the outright power to regulate the currency, still it exercised an influence upon the marketplace which ought to be deployed to strengthen the responsible and weaken the incompetent banks. "We can do much, if we cannot do everything." In the short run, during a deflationary depression, it was prudent temporarily for banks to suspend specie payments. In the long run, the only sure test of financial responsibility was the conversion of paper into specie. Convertability was a restraint upon the irresponsibly expansive and thus inflationary bank, not an iron law. But it was the moral obligation of government to inhibit inflation, a social evil especially harmful to those living on fixed incomes.[11]

What of the second dimension of the Sub-Treasury, the provision that government agents should themselves receive, hold, and disburse funds? On this score, Legaré was uneasy. Did it not merely transfer from the Bank of the United States to the government the vice of overweening influence and power? Had not the fall of Rome been assisted by the evils of a shortage of specie, a depreciating currency, a centralizing treasury at the bidding of a military despotism? Herder, Adam Smith, and Plutarch were not too gravely cited to alarm his congressional listeners with an ancient ghost. More seriously, Legaré turned to the objections of those who, with some justice, felt that an extensive credit system led to fluctuations in the currency and to attendant dislocations and uncertainties. To some extent, he took pleasure in observing, Congress had created the problem for itself. Had not the Treasury surplus created problems, and was that not the result of an unnecessarily high tariff? That aside, too much was made of fluctuations, a problem insoluble by an insistence upon specie. Speculation, the wise or unwise hazard of credit, proceeded from moral, not physical, causes. "Some people seem to think that an expansion in the circulating medium must always be attended with a sudden rise in prices and a spirit of extravagant speculation. But it is not so. . . . these two things have in fact very seldom coincided . . . speculation depends, in the first instance, upon moral causes wholly unconnected with the state of the currency; and, although an abundance of money may, and does aggravate the evil where it exists, yet, by itself, it never leads to any excitement." The South Sea Bubble had occurred in a year, 1721, when the currency of England was metallic and small. Trade cycles had psychological as well as monetary motives, the "perpetual round of quiescence—improvement—increasing confidence—prosperity—excitement—over-trading—convulsion—stagnation—pressure—distress—ending in quiescence again." For bank issues were a small part of the fabric of credit. In 1825 mercantile paper to the extent of $600,000,000 was negotiated in London, yet the Rothschilds received in two months only $1,500,000 in actual bills, and the combined circulating paper of the Bank of England and the country banks was not over $30,000,000. "It is *commercial credit* and private loans, that at such periods encourage and sustain those great and perilous operations—not banks, not bank notes, not redundant currency, strictly so called."[12]

The problems of control ran deep. The economy was grown international, insusceptible to the control of individual governments. The American economy had been boosted in 1832 by a flight of capital from England during the excitement over the Reform Bill, and was being deflated by a shortage of Mexican and Latin American bullion. No Southerner needed reminder that the fate of Charleston's economy might be and frequently was settled in Liverpool. Yet the problem ran even deeper in a country, the United States, where land was so abundant and landowners so little attached to place. "In periods of great excitement, it is not merely the products of our industry that we sell, it is not simply the annual income of the land and labor of the country that is exchanged, but the very soil itself, the whole country with all that it contains, is in the market. This, to the extent to which it is carried, is a peculiarity of our people. Sir, I do not mention this as a very prepossessing or honorable *trait* in our character—I mention it simply as a *fact*. We have no local attachments, generally speaking—nothing bears the *pretium affectionis* in our eyes. If an estate, a residence in town, a country seat, rises a little beyond what we are accustomed to think its value, it is sold without any hesitation. Accordingly, there is in such times a capacity for absorbing an expanded currency in this country, greater perhaps, in proportion than was even known in any other country."[13]

Was there any evidence that prosperity was diminished by a paper currency and an extensive credit system? There was one country where there was virtually no specie and where paper was everywhere, yet "a country, which has made greater progress, within the period mentioned, than any other in Europe, with an agriculture second (if second) only to that of Flanders, with a flourishing commerce, with manufactures of the greatest extent and the most exquisite refinement—whose cities have almost kept pace with ours." Scotland was evidence for the efficacy of credit, but England and the United States more so. England was (here Legaré weighed his words carefully in an American assembly) unprecedented in the achievement of a prosperous commercial society: "I say nothing of her recent achievements on the land and on the sea; of her fleets, her armies, her subsidised allies. Look at the Thames crowded with shipping; visit her arsenals, her docks, her canals, her railways, her factories, her mines, her warehouses, her roads, and bridges; go through the streets of that wonderful metropolis, the bank, the emporium, and the exchange of the whole world." And the United States? Legaré claimed the privilege of a returned wanderer, astonished at transformation. New York was doubled, the West explored and conquered by men and steamboats. At the root of the wealth of both countries was not credit alone but the spirit that made credit and risk possible. "Whoever heard of CREDIT in a despotism, or an anarchy?" he asked. "It implies *confidence*—confidence in your self, confidence in your neighbor, confidence in your government, confidence in the administration of the laws, confidence in the sagacity, the integrity, the discretion of those with whom you have to deal; confidence, in a word, in your destiny, and your fortune, in the destinies and fortune of the country to which you belong; as, for instance, in the case of a great national debt." Paradoxical as it might seem, debt was vital to a modern society: "Our people have been enriched by debt." It was the mark of energy, the tumultuous enlivenments of a democracy. The more advanced a culture, the more it could rely upon the symbolism of a paper currency, and the less it needed specie—itself a symbol, yet cumbersome and inconvenient. For what was a bank but a convenience, part of the division of labor in a modern society? What was the point of making a convenience inconvenient and restricted, especially when economics was becoming a science? When the population of the United States was growing and the supply of specie was stagnant or declining, was it sensible to curtail the facilities of trade and credit? And what would have been the economic history of the Union if specie had been the unvarying principle since 1789?[14]

It was objected by some that the Sub-Treasury was an experiment and so in keeping with the American spirit. Toward this opinion Legaré was stern. The Constitution was no experiment but merely the old truths under novel circumstances: "The whole constitution of society in the States, the great body and bulk of their public law, with all its maxims and principles—in short, all that is republican in our institutions—remained after the revolution, and remains *now,* with some very subordinate modifications, what it was from the beginning." In matters of governance, experiment was un-American.[15]

There was indistinct logic in the cry against banking corporations. There was danger in a corporation, but not special danger. Private banking houses could exercise as much, if not more, power. Witness the Rothschilds, "a mere private partnership . . . its colossal fortune . . . amassed in little more than a single generation, by an obscure person, born in a corner of the Juden-Strasse of Frankfurt on the Maine, and his four sons." Power was intrinsic to money, and tended always to centralization. As Preston in the Senate had indicated, those who feared such centralization might ponder what might be the consequences of a limited supply of specie, hoarded in New York.[16]

These remarks had censured the pieties of the Jacksonian political economy. After ironic comments about the tariff, Legaré ended on the same note by analyzing the belief that hard money might close social gaps between laboring and moneyed classes, deemed to have been sundered by the fluctuations of a paper currency. On the contrary, inflation tended to favor wage earners over those upon fixed incomes and tended therefore towards equality of condition. "The idea that the poor are to gain by a return to metallic currency is, so far as I know, confined to their friends in this country, whose zeal is certainly greater than their knowledge." There was no natural hostility between labor and capital in the United States, even in the South. "As a southern man, I represent equally rent, capital and wages, which are all confounded in our estates—and I protest against attempts to array, without cause, without a color of pretext or plausibility, the different classes of society against one another, as if, in such a country as this, there *could* be any natural hostility, or any real distinction between them—a country in which all the rich, with hardly an exception, have been poor and all the poor may be rich—a country in which banking institutions have been of immense service, precisely because they have been most needed by a people who all had their fortunes to make by good character and industrious habits." Had not Benjamin Franklin and Roger Sherman, Signers both, been mechanics? A fundamental gulf existed between the mechanics of America and the poor of Europe, whose hovels Legaré had seen in his travels. The class analyses of Europe had no place in the United States, the social conditions and ideology of the two continents being an ocean distinct. To his support, Legaré enlisted the remark of a Charleston mechanic at a recent public meeting, a remark be dubbed "noble beyond all praise." "He said, he wondered what could be meant by addressing, to the industrious classes particularly, all inflammatory appeals against the institutions of the country—as if they were not a part of the community, as much interested in its order and peace, as any other—as if they had no ties of sympathy or connection with their fellow-citizens—above all, as if they had not intelligence and knowledge enough to take care of their own interests, but were reduced to a state of perpetual pupilage and infancy, and needed the officious protection of self-constituted guardians!" With this reproach from the conservative Democrat to the Locofoco, Legaré ended. [17]

The speech was a deliberate success—lucid, persuasive, learned, easy—but a political disaster, though that implication was unclear to the new congressman when he rose to speak, sat down, and found himself the object of flattery in the press. The administration and Calhoun had combined on the Sub-Treasury, but the matter had been rushed upon the attention of Congress, and the price of dissent had not yet been fixed. The price was to be extirpation, but it took nearly a year for that to clarify. The speech moved Legaré decisively toward the Conservatives of Rives and Tallmadge, themselves in motion away from the Democrats and toward the Whigs. Above all, the oration made Legaré uneasy in his relationship to Charleston, a bond ambivalent since nullification. He took care to have the speech printed and distributed in South Carolina, for while Northern newspapers were enthusiastic, those in Charleston were ominously silent about Legaré but full of priase for Calhoun. And of Calhoun's displeasure, there had been immediate evidence. During the Sub-Treasury speech, the senator had come into the House, sat down behind Legaré, and conversed loudly with Dixon H. Lewis of Alabama to distract the orator and his audience. So Legaré felt constrained to warn his friends, especially Alfred Huger, who as Charleston postmaster held a revocable federal office. "I have done my duty conscientiously & do not, for myself, care . . . about consequences, but I will not consent to hurt my friends. So, I tell you, on no account, take any active part in the distribution. Calhoun will never forgive you. He has another hobby—& I have thwarted him. He looked like a demon on the day the vote was taken, when he found the whole [S.C.] delegation except Pickens, going with me." This was to make no mean enemy. [18]

Legaré was due for reelection in October 1838. Early in July of that year, Calhoun pointedly wrote to Joel R. Poinsett, South Carolinian, Unionist, and Secretary of War: "It would be a great misfortune, if the commercial metropolis of the State should be misrepresented on a

William Cabell Rives, by Charles Fenderich.
Courtesy, Virginia Historical Society

question and at a time when she has so much at stake. I had supposed there would be no doubt of opposition to the present incumbent there. Can you say what is intended?" In short, would the administration and the Unionists, conjoined in the single pivotal figure of Poinsett, abandon Legaré? Poinsett's position was awkward. He was an old opponent of Calhoun, but now allied. Legaré had, on all but the Sub-Treasury, been faithful to the administration and had given great support to Poinsett's army reforms. Legaré and Poinsett were friendly: Poinsett admired Legaré's abilities, and the respect was mutual. Christopher Memminger had counseled the advisability of holding on to Legaré, keeping him in "the traces" as "a valuable accession in the show part of evey game." So Poinsett hedged, hoping that others would make the decision for him. And the administration had reason to wonder if in Calhoun they had an ally who could carry his state.[19]

By midsummer of 1838, Petigru was confident that with proper management Legaré could win reelection. Opposition to Calhoun was considerable, for his volte-face had confused and appalled many, not least several of his lieutenants. Preston, Waddy Thompson, and David McCord, all were disaffected. What worried Petigru the most was not Calhoun but Legaré's diffidence. The man had a taste for martyrdom as a reassurance of integrity, a fondness for repining at success. No sooner had Legaré made his Sub-Treasury speech than his thoughts had turned to retirement, and his mind had focused on the vulgar disadvantages of a congressman's lot. He told Huger not to speak of his reluctance and ambivalence, yet it could not be a secret in so small a world as Charleston, and his attitude corroded the support even of his friends. The political advantage of a long clarifying letter in July 1838 on the Sub-Treasury, published in the *Courier* and elsewhere, was dissipated when Legaré refused to return to Charleston for the campaign. It was, as he later acknowledged, his greatest and most extraordinary political mistake, the more so as he had once himself written: "If the representative, whose conduct is impeached, meets the opposition boldly, and encounters and exposes its authors in open discussion, his victory is generally a sure and easy one. If, on the contrary, mistaking the clamours of a few for the voice of the whole, he shrink from the contest . . . what marvel if the majority go . . . [against] him[?][20]

The attractions of the White Sulphur Springs, of staying with the Rives family and dallying with Mary Tallmadge (the senator's daughter, whom he nicknamed the "Madonna"), of visiting Ticknor, of rambling up the Hudson were, it was true, considerable. Legaré did not relish the heat of Charleston, where he had not spent a summer since 1829. In the beginning he did not fear defeat and thought special efforts superfluous. Later he was to be surprised by opposition, hurt, reluctant to dignify slanders upon his name with an energetic response. He found himself paralyzed by uncertainty, by that proud timidity that was his Achilles heel as a politician. All this was complicated by the slowness of communications between him, traveling, and Charleston, where events moved rapidly. Petigru, his most dedicated supporter and the organizer of his successful 1836 campaign, was spending the autumn in New England. His allies were unsure about Legaré, tinged with the suspicion of having been insufficiently zealous during the nullification crisis. Alfred Huger, writing to Poinsett on September 1, provided a chillingly ambivalent endorsement: "Pringle, Bennett & myself have endeavored to keep down opposition to him, because it is difficult & painful for us to forget how long, & in what troubled waters we sailed under the same flag—but during those dreadfull conflicts Swinton received no wounds: while we were traitors and took the penalty *here* for being so—*he* was hardly ever hit, even by a spent shot—nevertheless it is hard to sponge out old recollections, & break up old affinities."[21]

Gradually, opposition coalesced around Isaac Holmes, nullifier and Legaré's closest friend, the man with whom he had "used less disguise than with almost any person besides." Part of Legaré's early confidence had rested on an unwillingness to believe that Holmes would oppose him. In the short run, Poinsett's caginess had seemed to work to Legaré's advantage. John Campbell, a Calhoun supporter, had published under the pseudonym of "Friend to Truth" in the *Southern Patriot* on October 3 the claim that Poinsett and the administration wished for Legaré's defeat; those like Huger and Bennett, insisting upon Poinsett's sympathy for Legaré, were wantonly and dishonorably misrepresenting the Secretary of War. Bennett and Huger, in possession of letters from Poinsett that did speak highly of Legaré, took the dramatic step of calling all interested parties to the City Hall, where their reasons would be explained. This was crushing to Campbell, whose reputation as an honorable man seemed ruined. But the long-run effect was bad, for it drove Poinsett from cover. Letters where Poinsett's dismissal of Legaré was explicit were made public. This revelation rallied opposition to Legaré, for to the Calhounites were added Poinsett Democrats with the incentive of vindicating the Secretary from the suspicion of duplicity. Many had puzzled why

Unionists should support the nullifer Holmes to oust the Unionist Legaré—and thereby elect a man whose Unionist credentials were negligible. It did not seem logical, and many had doubted that this was Poinsett's wish. The Campbell affair cleared away the ambiguity: however improbable, Poinsett did wish it, and therefore many consented to do it, the more so as Legaré did not deign to come home and defend himself. The final poll was crushing: Holmes 1,504 votes, Legaré 854. Legaré was fretfully philosophical, hurt to be defeated as he had been hurt to be maligned as a cosmopolitan renegade, an overly learned dilettante, a political coward, a man "trifling, effeminate, pedantic, nice, sickly." In his letter to Rives announcing his defeat, he quoted a few classical tags so that he might comment acidly: "You see I still quote Greek & Latin privately, which is one of the gravest charges alleged against me by the Jack Cades of the Mercury."[22]

This reversal disenchanted Legaré with his Charleston. Nullification had weakened bonds; electoral defeat came close to breaking them. Vexation was intensified into bitterness. He started to complain that "Charleston never loved me," that his defeat was a proscription, that "they" had once chained him to the *Southern Review.* "You know how many nights & days of laborious thought I have given gratuitously to what *they* represented to me as a work necessary to the interests & honor of So. Carolina," he grumbled to his sister. "My sight was & is seriously impaired by those thankless vigils—& now they ask me tauntingly with what useful undertaking my name has ever been associated." Later, in 1841, he would give jaundiced advice to a young man, Thomas C. Reynolds, about to study in Germany: "I have found my *studies in Europe* impede me at every step of my progress. They have hung around my neck like a dead weight,—and do so to this very day. Our people have a fixed aversion to every thing that looks like foreign education. They never give credit to any one for being *one of them,* who does not take his post in life early, and do and live as they do." This antiintellectualism came not, he felt, from "the merely ignorant, the work people" but from the gentlemen.[23]

So many of his enemies had seemed to survive; so many of his friends had died or been estranged. As a prodigy, Legaré had no doubt mingled with men his senior, and their deaths were to be expected: Stephen Elliott, whom Legaré revered, found dead with an unfinished contribution to the *Southern Review* on his desk; Samuel Prioleau, who had written so engagingly upon the ravages of dyspepsia, Legaré's own familiar ailment; Edward Rutledge, who had beguiled a sickly and half-orphaned child; Thomas Pinckney, who had introduced Legaré to the cadences of Greek. But others, Legaré's contemporaries, had gone prematurely: Henry Junius Nott, Edward Pringle, Elizabeth Pringle, all drowned at sea; Thomas Grimké, an intellectual opponent, eccentric but much loved; Joshua Toomer, who took his own life with unnerving deliberation and rationality; John Gadsden; Jennings Waring; Robert Hayne. By 1840, amid this wreckage, Legaré was to observe, "Another of *my* best friends gone! Charleston is becoming a dismal solitude to me."[24] To friends dead, he had to add friends lost: William Drayton, who had left South Carolina in the wake of nullification; William Campbell Preston, estranged by politics and a proud diffidence; above all, most poignantly, Isaac Holmes, the very man to whom in 1833 Legaré had prayed that his "little circle" of friends might survive, dear dim "Ikey" Holmes who thought it might be nice to have a political standing equal to the wealth he had made from railroads, poor Holmes who lisped that the Sub-Treasury was "wital," poor Holmes the nullifying foot soldier, who crushed Legaré at the polls. "He has been," Legaré explained to Rives, "for twenty years one of my most confidential & devoted friends, & contributed very much to place me where I am. I should have regarded his opposing me, under any circumstances, as a *moral* impossibility—but is there in this sinful world, any such thing? . . . I have *felt* this opposition very much. I am a being, you know, of exclusive habits & so condemned to few intimates at best, on whom I very much depend for sympathy & support. A cruel death—a double shipwreck—deprived me in poor Nott & Pringle of two of these, men who had grown up with me in perfect intimacy from childhood. Holmes was one of the survivors on whom I most counted, & here he is lending himself to my capital enemies. . . . You see that my griefs are not merely those of a politician."[25]

Choosing politics as his vocation, Legaré had taken a hard path against the grain of a sensitive temperament. For 1838 had exposed to all, as 1832 had suggested to some, that Legaré was an indifferent politician, with no stomach for a Jacksonian world. He had received preferment when it had been convenient for others that he be preferred. He never commanded events. He understood, in the abstract, how politics worked, and few Carolinians analyzed it more acutely or better understood how it could be deflected by unreasoning accident and angular passion. But he could not bring himself to labor day in and day out, to ferret out information, to influence, to cajole, to intimate patronage, to use the propaganda of the press, to set loose plug-uglies and bullyboys. He had been genteelly appalled in 1831 when his brother-in-law had boasted of keeping gentlemen drunk for days in order to ensure their votes.[26] Studying oratory, excited by its tense achievement, he conflated the power of words with the power of politics. Meeting opposition, he bridled and delivered a long, erudite, grand, and subtle speech that annihilated his opponents intellectually but changed little politically. Seeing this result, witnessing intellectual superiority untranslated into advancement, he limped back to his solitary learning, wrote acid letters, and waited in discontent until events—at the will of others—turned smiling upon him again.

Like many of his South Carolinian contemporaries, Legaré was uneasy about the great precept of Jacksonian politics: party regularity. He had done his best, more perhaps than he might have admitted to himself, by way of loyalty to Van Buren. But he could not keep it up, and was puzzled to find even a single lapse fatal. Jacob Cardozo, before the 1838 defeat, had emphasized the precept (and the thought had turned Legaré's delicate stomach): "it appears to me that success in public life in the United States depends in a great degree on the surrender of private judgment to the dictation of party. He who enters on a political career must make up his mind if he attach himself at all to party, to sacrifice intellectual independence and freedom of will. If he is not prepared to do this his chances of success, whatever be his ability and intelligence, are much diminished, and less scrupulous men will rise by the pliancy of their principles." Poinsett knew it and wrote with unblushing candor of his repudiation of Legaré: "Intercourse with my political friends left me no longer ignorant of the general opinion of the friends of the administration as to Mr. Legaré's course, and I did not hesitate one moment to sacrifice my personal feelings to what I believed to be my duty to my country and to the administration to which I belong." Gouverneur Kemble of New York, a real politician in a Jacksonian age that perfected the American craft, was to remember Legaré to Poinsett in 1843 and deliver the professional's verdict: "But for his inordinate vanity, he would have been a very useful man, but this rendered him continually the dupe of others."[27]

Much in Legaré's estrangement was personal, but much was social, the plight of his generation. In a small social world like Charleston and South Carolina, crowded with intelligent men ambitious for office and esteem, estrangement was intrinsic. In a culture that prized honor and male friendship but faced politically divisive, volatile, and whirling tensions, alienation that cut to the marrow was everywhere.

It was not just the politically dispossessed like Legaré who felt it, though few in Calhoun's world did not experience dispossession. Even a William Campbell Preston felt it. In old age Preston was to muse to his old ally Waddy Thompson on the cost: "Amidst the struggle of life while it was intense I met with many and most agreeable men at the bar in the Senate, in the court, scholars, orators, men of talents and of spirit, men with whom I thought I had contracted *friendship.* Where are they[?] It was seed sown by the wayside. I ask not of the dead but of the living, where are they? The fowls came and devoured them up."[28]

Defeat had compensations, of which the first was the lame-duck congressional session of late 1838 and early 1839. Legaré's first reaction to his loss had been uncertainty and bitterness, an impulse to abandon Charleston, a shuddering at the imminent prospect of the bar. Reflection brought the puritanical insight that repudiation was a useful check to his pride, which he knew had once been absurdly great and hoped might be diminished with maturity. Washington now brought a pleasing irresponsibility. "I feel like an eagle turned out of a cage," he told his mother, worried at her son's fate and needing reassurance. It was no mean enjoyment to cut Calhoun upon the steps of the Capitol, to shake hands with Poinsett with cold indifference, to be "civil, cold & laconic" towards Van Buren. While he was ironically careful to tend to his constituents in pleading for a new naval yard in Charleston, Legaré could be puckishly his own man.[29]

He spoke against the diplomatic recognition of Haiti, which the abolitionists had contrived as an issue to insinuate their cause past the gag rule. The speech was extempore, Legaré having come into the chamber when the debate was joined, and he spoke with more than usual warmth and less than usual care. He had always feared the consequences of revolution, the eddying into anarchy that a dissolution of the Union might bring. Now he explicitly cast the abolitionists as Jacobins, no novel insight but one that Legaré had always hesitated to use, lest his own Southern passion exacerbate Northern animus. Now he was disposed to be blunt and bleak, with sentiments like these: "As sure as you live, sir, if this course is permitted to go on, the sun of this Union will go down—it will go down in blood—and go down to rise no more. I will vote unhesitatingly against nefarious designs like these. They are treason. . . . Without being, perhaps, a *legitimate* democrat—whether I am or not, God knows; I leave it to the doctors of the school—I have been nursed from my youth in an idolatrous love of that most noble of all forms of polity, republican government, and I have dreamed for my country the highest things

within the reach of humanity—a career of greatness such as the world
has never yet witnessed." But paper visionaries might destroy it;
politicians might meddle it away. While the people might be sensible
if addressed with candor and truth, Legaré wondered whether the
opportunity for candor would be available. Yet this attack upon the
abolitionists came too little and too late to be of political use. Alfred
Huger, who cared nothing and understood less about the Sub-Treasury, had once faulted Legaré for deserting Van Buren and the cause of
slavery: "What signifies to *me,* all the jargon about Whigs & conservatives &c &c if the abolitionists stand between me & the white gate at
Longwood? these are the inquiries that make *me* an administration
man—with *me,* the very foundation of Liberty is Slavery, & I go for
Mr. Van Buren because Mr. Van Buren goes for me." Usually Legaré
was moderate on the politics of slavery. In 1841, his eye again fixed on
the chance of power, he was to deprecate the Senate's rejection of
Edward Everett as American Minister in London because Southerners
knew Everett had uttered abolitionist sentiments. It was unwise to
make a martyr, Legaré thought, but more, "to seize on the equivocal
language of a candidate wishing to get every vote he could pick up, &
put him out of the pale of the commonwealth thereupon, would be
doing a thing so very rigorous that it would inevitably *react."* Later
yet, he was to pronouce the dictum, "Overt acts alone justify interference."[30]

His own electoral case had excited in Legaré a suspicion, touching
an old sensitivity of the republican tradition renewed in the dispute
between Whigs and Jacksonians, of corruption in the land. Had he
not been defeated for the sake of a placeman? Had not executive
influence touched an electorate far beyond the circumscribed jurisdiction of a President? Had not Van Buren been reforming and strengthening a standing army? Had not Samuel Swartout, a government-
appointed collector of the Port of New York, coolly stolen
$1,374,119 over several years? And had not the administration the
gall, the suspicious nerve, to ask the House to set up a committee of
investigation at the dictate of the Speaker, the administration's man,
to tidy away this corruption? And was not the administration persist-
ing in pleading for a Sub-Treasury that would multiply the opportunities of such as Swartout? And were not faction and party, the
sophistry of an insufficiently alert democracy, at the root of all this?
Thus Legaré aired his suspicions to and at Churchill C. Cambreleng of
New York, the government's emissary: "For, sir, without meaning to
intimate in the most distant manner any thing offensive or unkind to

my colleague, he will permit me to confess that I had looked with a painfully anxious interest to the course which he and his friends were going to pursue in this matter—not that I distrusted their honor and integrity, but I did not know how far the fatal sophistry of party had triumphed over their naturally clear heads and elevated characters— that sophistry which is rooting itself so deeply in our political practice, and perverting so fearfullly the opinions of the wisest and best among us, as to threaten nothing less than an entire revolution in the genius and character of our institutions. . . . these strange portents and prodigies of fraud—these spectral terrors of official profligacy, almost unheard of in our previous history, but which so often of late 'visited the glimpses of the moon,' make me fear that 'something is rotten in the state of Denmark.' "[31]

With these comments Legaré took a long step towards the themes of 1840, the election that would salvage his political fortunes. It was a suspicion he did not blush to express to Van Buren himself, when they met at Saratoga Springs in August 1839. "My own opinion, as I told the President to his face," Legaré reported to Rives, "is that *the monarchy* is established—to this he replied that there might be something in it, if he were a man like Gen. Jackson—my answer was the system built up by him, or rather, developed (for it was in the constitution of such a government conducted on party principles) was now strong enough to work in any body's hands. I told him I really had felt comparatively little interest in the Presidential election, but that I had most fervently hoped there would be a decided majority against him in the House—that I opposed the overgrown influence of the Executive, in whose control soever it might be found &c. &c."[32]

But Legaré had failed as a politician by being insufficiently a party man, and his confirming allegiance to Rives and Tallmadge was a continued evasion of party, for the Conservatives had been repelled by Van Buren but still resisted annexation to the Whigs. As late as December 1839, Gouverneur Kemble could entertain hopes that Legaré might restore himself to the administration ranks. But Legaré's desire that Poinsett and Van Buren should yet "feel" him was too strong for recantation, and before Kemble wrote, Legaré had committed himself to the opposition. In April 1839, Legaré refused an invitation to a Clay meeting in Charleston. In June he was pleased to see that Rives was electorally successful in Virginia. Tallmadge made headway in New York. In October, Legaré went to Syracuse and spoke in his "popular style" to an enthusiastic Conservative rally orchestrated by Tallmadge. He felt himself warmed by applause that contrasted agreeably with the mingled bitterness of Charleston, and supplied the excitement the want of which had fatigued him in April.[33] The boyish excitement of the chase overcame much, including a small regard for William Henry Harrison and an old contempt for John Tyler.[34] Excitement came close to overwhelming even the irony of the ambivalent democrat. "Depend upon it, V. Buren's jig is up," he told Rives in December 1839. "If *you* or any of your friends (such as Niles) want any little favor from him [Harrison], put on yr. boots & spurs & via!—en *grand galop,* for depend upon it, the *demos* goes for *North Bend.* I *feel* it in me—it is an oracle I utter. *Deus Vult,* as the crusaders cried." The little favor that crossed Legaré's mind was the Attorney-Generalship of the United States. As he told his sister Mary in October, "Should there ever be a revolution in politics, the chance is I should be (if I *chose*) Attorney Gen. of the United States." And, as he had told Van Buren in August, he expected precisely that: "I had long talk with him last night, in which I told him, as I think, that there will now be a new organization of parties & a *fresh* start."[35]

In the meantime Legaré had to earn a living. The bar was the available means, but he was initially uncertain about where to practice. New York? Boston? To Baltimore he gave the greatest consideration. Yet the needs of his mother and sister Mary were in Charleston, and their property difficult to sell in the aftermath of the Panic of 1837. Over the years he was to lend his mother upwards of $5,000. And there was the problem of Eliza, whose wretched marriage, incessant pregnancies, and financial straits required a mother's attention and a brother's assistance. So Legaré took himself to Charleston, though a lingering disenchantment with the proscribing city kept him away from society at his mother's John's Island residence, a recluse with his books.[36]

Legaré came back to the bar, his reputation and competence formidably enhanced. Charleston had scarcely thrown him out before some repented. William Campbell Preston was to eulogize the legal prodigal: "he returned to the bar with an earnestness of purpose, enhanced by his short congressional career, and he came to it with surpassing brilliancy and power. Animated by a competition which tasked all his resources, he displayed so much learning, ability and eloquence, that the courts in which he appeared expanded into a forum, and became objects of public attraction, to which multitudes flocked as to a theatre, and from which opinions, principles and emotions were propagated through the community." The observation was kind of Preston and almost accurate, though the legacy of Pres-

Eliza Legaré Bryan, by Peter Copmann (1835).
COURTESY, SOUTH CAROLINIANA LIBRARY

ton's and Legaré's political differences might be read in the tart adjective, "short." Legaré was busy; he made money, for the first time in any abundance, though he still complained of being straitened and could not afford the $100 that a copy of his portrait by Edward Marchant would have cost. The 1840 federal census credits him with 42 slaves, though it is likely that many previously credited to his mother were now in his name. And he had one famous and popular case, which stands out among dry financial pleadings for the Bank of South Carolina of an advocate who, in modern times, would be dubbed a corporate lawyer. In *Pell and Wife* v. *the Executors of Ball*, Legaré, Petigru, and DeSaussure argued for the complainants, and Christopher Memminger, Alexander Mazyck, Benjamin Hunt, and James Smith Rhett pleaded for the executors. The case involved death and pathos, the stuff of oratory.[37]

The steamship *Pulaski* had departed Charleston on the morning of June 1838, on its way to New York. It had come from Savannah the day before and was crowded. At Charleston had boarded a Mr. and Mrs. Ball with their adopted daughter Emma and a servant. The boat, as was customary, provided cabins segregated by sex: a ladies' cabin on the main deck at the stern, a gentlemen's after-cabin beneath it and a gentlemen's forward-cabin. Above the ladies' after-cabin was a promenade deck, for breezes on hot Atlantic summer days. The *Pulaski* sailed without incident through the day, and by late evening nearly everyone had retired. About an hour before midnight the starboard boiler exploded. A breach was opened on the starboard side, the center of the main deck was ripped off, and the forward wheelhouse was blown away with the sleeping captain in it. Communication between stem and stern was broken; the ship lurched to port and began to fill rapidly with water and break her back. First to be flooded had been the two gentlemen's cabins before the ship broke completely in two, its halves settling towards the breach at an angle of thirty degrees. All this took some forty minutes. Many died in the first explosion; others drowned in the flooding; some escaped in boats, on wrecked timbers, or on hastily constructed rafts. A few minutes after the first explosion—when the passengers were stunned and quiet, the wheels of the ship had stopped, and the sound of rushing water was mixed with the scrambling attempts of those trying to reach the heights of the promenade deck—Mrs. Ball emerged from the ladies' cabin. She ran towards the breach, came back, and rushed about the starboard gangway, calling out her husband's name in panicked anxiety. A boat was lowered on the starboard side, and several gentlemen clambered down into it; above them appeared a man who threw a coat down to them, said he would return, disappeared, and was not seen again. The next day this black dress coat was examined, found to be of a large size such as would fit Mr. Ball, and had in its pocket a shirt collar on which Ball's name appeared. Neither Ball nor his wife survived the catastrophe.[38]

Their deaths created legal complications. Mr. Ball had left a will, bequeathing his estate to his wife. The necessary question arose, who had died first? If Mr. Ball, the estate had fleetingly passed to his wife and should be settled among her family, the Pells. If Mrs. Ball, her husband had died intestate, and assets would be divided among his family. At stake was a large inheritance as well as several small legacies. The case was pressed not so much from bitter family squabble as from genuine perplexity. The law was unclear: common law was evasive; civil law presumed the survivorship of the husband on the grounds that the stronger survives best. Everything would depend upon the case pleaded before Chancellor Job Johnston, affable, witty, irritable with lawyers but fond of logical niceties and their exposition. He was a judge with whom a lawyer could work, a man susceptible to persuasion and not afraid of being heterodox.[39]

It was a complicated case. The details of the wreck were explained with the aid of a working model of the *Pulaski*. Witnesses were produced to flesh out the narrative. Legal precedents about survivorship were indecisively thrashed out. Memminger, assuming that nothing definite could be proved about who survived whom and that the evidence was circumstantial, depended upon the cloudy logic of the law. To Legaré fell the task of refuting Memminger's law and making something from slim testimony. That Memminger relied upon the civil law redounded to Legaré's advantage, for he could spend much casual and discursive time in showing that the civilians did not conclusively assume the survivorship of a husband. This being so, all that remained to settle a case that had to be settled was testimony. Being small, the evidence had to be produced at the end of a cumulative exposition, so that it might gather weight from the delay. Of the fate of Mr. Ball there was no clear testimony beyond the confusing matter of the coat and collar. It was even unclear whether he had been in the forward or aft gentlemen's cabin. No one had seen him, for no one could identify the man who threw the coat into the small boat as Mr. Ball. All that was unimpeachable was that Mrs. Ball had been seen to rush about the deck, crying for her husband. To this small but pathetic scrap, Legaré moved his argument and his audience. His peroration, evoking the miserable frantic woman, artfully mingling sympathy for her tragedy with partisanship for her posthumous legal cause, and heightened by a sudden turn to the bench to ask if the judge did not feel the justified grief of Mrs. Ball, brought tears to the Chancellor's eyes—and victory: "Upon the narrow theatre of that shattered deck there was enacted a scene, to paint the horror of which all that imagination or poetry could invent of the most pathetic must fail. She called upon the husband on whom she had never before called in vain—upon whose arm she had ever leaned in danger—her stay, her rescue! She called—but he never answered—no, sir, he was dead! he was dead!" This was, as has been shrewdly noted, "an appeal out of the antique tradition of the pathetic proof; it was an appeal to bring a tear, and a wink, to Cicero's eye." It looked back to Cicero, yet forward to Tennyson: "Break, break, break, on thy cold gray stones, O Sea! / And I would that my tongue could utter / The thoughts that arise in me. . . . And the stately ships go on / To their haven under the hill; / But O for the touch of a vanish'd hand, / and the sound of a voice that is still!"[40]

In 1816, Legaré had expressed an ambition that characteristically made allowance for disappointment. "The learning that I would aim at is that of Cicero—a learning that can be instrumental in promoting the purposes of active life, in elevating the man of business into sage, and the mere statement of wholesome truths, into sublime and touching eloquence—and in case there be no demand for our services in practical affairs, can embellish retirement & multiply before us the most refined and elevated enjoyments." Being now disappointed, Legaré went back to his books, a recluse and hard student. "I think of publishing shortly two or three things." The urge to write, dead since the exhaustions of the *Southern Review,* revived and found in his intervening experience much to modify his viewpoint. "I have lately read Greek & German enough to choke ten professors. But as it was all about law & politics, I was (having *renounced* the latter!) profoundly interested in them." Joseph Cogswell, now editing the *New York Review,* offered a forum, payment at five dollars a page (three times the rate for his other contributors), and endorsement of Legaré's interests, "the whole spirit of ancient democracy & as much of the modern as you choose to add." In two years Legaré wrote three long pieces: "New School of the Civil Law: The Origin, History and Influence of Roman Legislation" (October 1839), "Constitutional History of Greece and the Democracy of Athens" (July 1840), and "Demosthenes, the Man, the Statesman, and the Orator" (July 1841). Their interest is great.

They were his first writings since he had learned German and so reflected his considerations upon modern classical scholarship. They ran over old ground with altered nuance and so demonstrated intellectual shifts. They supplied deficiencies in his earlier essays, topics intended but never completed. They embodied thoughts excited by the contemporary American scene. They betray his surprise and pleasure that the interests and mind of the nineteenth century were moving in sympathy with himself. And they were to be his last substantial writings.[41]

Each of the essays began with a bow to German scholarship, demonstrating both Legaré's allegiance and his skepticism. The enthusiast of Demosthenes felt obliged to acknowledge the old masters who had labored in poverty and difficulty to fashion the orator's canon: Jerome Wolf, the "Wolfius" of the sixteenth century, to whom "the modern world is under greater obligations for the advantage of reading Demosthenes in a correct edition, than to any other individual whatever," who had lived a drudging philologist's life that his name and Demosthenes might survive together; Johann Jacob Reiske of the eighteenth century, whose edition of Demosthenes took decades, indigence, and the pawning of his wife's jewelry to subsidize printing costs. There were German contemporaries of Legaré who merited attention for their competing and overlapping studies of Greek oratory and society: Karl Friedrich Hermann, then professor at Marburg, a student especially of Plato but author of *A Manual of the Political Antiquities of Greece;* Anton Westermann of Leipzig, nine years Legaré's junior, whose *Quaestiones Demosthenicae* hazarded opinions about the orator that Legaré found pertinent; Albert Gerard von Bekker, who lived a private scholar at Quedlinberg (through which Legaré had passed in 1836), a man who had diligently interested himself in Demosthenes ever since 1791, when F.A. Wolf had consented to approve of Bekker's dissertation demonstrating the spuriousness of the Oration in the Letter of Philip, and whose *Demosthenes als Staatsman und Redner* of 1815 Legaré had repeatedly and in vain attempted to locate; Wilhelm Waschsmuth of Leipzig, whose four-volume study of the *Public Antiquities of Greece* was parallel and barely superior to Hermann's, though the latter felt himself a disciple; the older and often neglected Johann Friedrich Rietemeier, a pupil of Heyne at Göttingen, whose 1789 study, *Geschichte und Zustand der Sklaverey und Leibeigenschaft in Griechenland,* rare even in Europe, was among the first to suggest a sociology for Greek slavery. All these were among the lesser though important contemporary German scholars to be refuted, weighed, consented to, or mocked.[42]

Others were confessedly giants. Some were too old and familiar to need obeisance: Christian Gottlob Heyne and Johann Heinrich Voss among the founders of German philology; F.A. Wolf, whose skepticism on the Homeric question had been a great engine to move the convoys of German scholarship. But others were more recent and needed assessment and propagation, chief among them Ritter Hugo and Barthold Niebuhr.[43]

Niebuhr, Legaré studied with lengthy conscientiousness, very rarely dissenting, even then with respect for arguments cogent and forceful. Niebuhr combined the qualities of Bentley with the wisdom of Montesquieu ("when Montesquieu is not sacrificing his wisdom to his wit"), all informed by the scholarly advances of the intervening sixty years. Niebuhr had wrought a revolution in the history of public law. "He was, we believe, the first to lay his hand upon that key of the Past—the effect of races upon the revolutions of society, and the character of governments—of which Thierry has since made so striking an application in his History of the Norman Conquest, and his Letters on the History of France." The German was to be prized not for doubts but for discoveries, "not for what he has done to discredit the magnificent romance of Livy (for the barren scepticism of Beaufort was equal to that) but for what only such a combination, as had scarcely ever been seen in any single individual, of immense erudition, unwearied industry, and incessant vigilance of research, with matchless critical sagacity, could have enabled him to accomplish, towards explaining what was obscure, reconciling what was contradictory, completing what was defective, and correcting—often out of his own mouth—what was mistaken, or misstated, in Dionysius of Halicarnassus." Niebuhr was like a lawyer, cross-examining confused and recalcitrant ancient sources to drag out the truth. On occasion he seemed more, a necromancer "raising the dead."[44]

Niebuhr's value was to present a convincing image of Rome the young city, which helped to explain Rome the arbiter of the world. This city, unlike the sunlight youth of Greece, was crowded with the austere mysticism of Etruria, the wars of incessant tribalism, the rigid autocracy of the patriarch, values stern and heroic. Rome's guiding spirit had been discipline and tradition: "If ever there was a people that adhered to establishments; that revered the past, and used it, at once, to awe and to protect the present; that had faith in the wisdom of their ancestors, and none at all in the pretensions of political quacks of all sorts—it was they." In law the Romans were *sui generis,* however much in philosophy and literature they were the disciples of Greece. And Niebuhr's contribution in resurrecting and analyzing this law was incalculable, not least by the discovery in Italy, at his own hands or behest, of precious palimpsests, among them that of Gaius.[45]

Hugo had a different value, less disciplined than Niebuhr but more specific. Hugo had been deeply involved in reediting and reassessing the civilian tradition, restoring the pristine form of the original Roman law by identifying and weeding out the corruptions of Byzantine and medieval editors. Fresh editions of Gaius and Ulpian, as well as the Florentine copy of the Pandects, had shown how wretchedly mangled the civil law had become at the hands of such as the so-called "Gothic Gaius," whose epitome of the Institutes of Gaius had been done at the instruction of Alaric, King of the Visigoths, for the governance of his Roman subjects. By such research it was now possible, with some accuracy, to distinguish the original Roman law from the emendations of Justinian and medieval civil law. Hugo had not only participated in this scholarly revolution but reflected upon it, noting how matters had changed since his youth. "What with new readings of old books and the acquisition of new ones, and what with a deeper study and more critical examination of those long in the possession of civilians, an entirely new aspect has been given to the study of Roman law," Legaré wrote. "Hugo quotes a letter from a friend, (p. 75,) in which, congratulating the present generation upon the change, he declares, that he had taken his degree of Doctor, before he knew who Gaius or Ulpian was—writers now familiar to all his *hearers;* and Hugo confesses as much of himself, in regard to Ulpian and Theophilus." Legaré could point the moral of his own education and experience when he pondered Hugo's lectures. "It is difficult to imagine a greater contrast than that which presents itself to us, in comparing this *Lehr-Buch* of Göttingen lecturer, with what we remember was the *course* of professor of the Civil Law in the University of Edinburgh, just twenty years ago. One who was initiated into this study, as we happened to be, under the old plan of the eighteenth century, with Heineccius for a guide, will find himself in the schools of the present day, in almost another world—new doctrines, new history, new methods, new text-books, and, above all, new views and a new spirit." Heineccius had been good in and for his day, and Gibbon had praised the Halle scholar as the first of guides to the Roman law. But Gibbon stood before the criticism of the nineteenth century rather than embodying it, and Heineccius had worked upon inferior texts with a philosophy at odds with the new canons of historicism. Legaré by zealous reeducation looked fascinated upon "the great dogma . . . of the *historical school,* that, in the matter of government, 'whatever is, is right,' for the time being, and nothing so for all times; that positive institutions are merely provisional; and that every people has, *ipso facto,* precisely those which are best adapted to its character and condition," and reluctantly judged it to be "a great fundamental truth, without a distinct perception of which, history becomes a riddle, and government impossible."[46]

Legaré chose to learn from these Germans. From English scholars he got little except a whiff of incompetence. William Mitford, whose *History of Greece* (1784–1810) held the field until demolished by George Grote, Legaré dismissed as "an able, certainly, but prejudiced and not very learned writer." An author who distrusted republics as anarchies, who thought well of Philip of Macedon, who imagined Greeks incompetent in matters of government, who spoke out belligerently against the institution of slavery would not come recommended to a South Carolinian. In a lengthy critique of Lord Brougham, "that charlatan . . . the English *Calhoun,*" whose *Dissertation on the Eloquence of the Ancients* had argued that Demosthenes would be a failure in the House of Commons and the worse for it, Legaré vented a veritable explosion of irritation. English scholars were undertaking a task analogous to that of Legaré, comprehending antiquity to aid in understanding and refining the usages of modernity. But their scholarship was too slight beside that of Germany.[47]

Yet the Germans had faults. They were unworldly academics, "mere professors, and, of all professors, perhaps the least versed, by any personal observation, in the affairs of war and peace, as they are conducted by captains and politicians," which betrayed itself by insensitivity when judging the practical decisions and actions of the ancients. On balance their sins were venial, not mortal, and Legaré was inclined to temporize. "We do not . . . wish to be understood . . . as entertaining . . . the opinion which a brilliant and eloquent but 'presumptuous and superficial' writer [as Burke described Bolingbroke] has not scrupled to pronounce on all such undertakings of philologists, whose pretensions to write, or even to understand the history of nations, he treats with scorn and ridicule. This sneer, unbecoming as applied to Bentley, for whom it was probably meant, were sheer impertinence, addressed by the author of the 'Letter on the Study of History,' [Bolingbroke] to that class of writers in the Germany of the present day. But it is no injurious detraction from their unquestionable merits to affirm that, however admirable the use they have made of the wisdom of antiquity, there are some of the phenomena of society, in the various shapes and phases it has passed through, which the ancient writers have dealt with in a manner *hitherto* unrivalled by the moderns—Burke himself, not excepted, much less Machiavelli and Montesquieu—and which it is difficult even to appreciate without a considerable experience in public affairs."[48]

Yet reading the Germans meant confronting the intellectual difficulties of historicism, more directly even than when criticizing Schlegel in the *Southern Review*. Historicism fretted Legaré not as a truth of history but as an ethic of political action. It led among the Germans to a glorification of the state, "the pretended claims of state necessity, or the indefeasible sovereign power of society," and this was to be deprecated. More subtly, historicism inculcated "the color of a dark and licentious fatalism." It was a reproach that Legaré, by temperament a gloomy fatalist, was making to himself. He had experienced in the energies of Calhoun the political efficacies of individuality.[49]

Historicism was a problem for the partisan of the civil law. If each culture produced the institutions and customs fitting for itself, how could the legal culture of a single city, Rome, be fitting for the whole world? How could it be useful, as Legaré had always urged, that modern Americans could and should meditate upon ancient law, when ancient society was vanished? There were truths of human nature and truths of social custom, the distinction between *jus gentium* and *jus civile*. It was the value of the new historicism to create a more detailed record of the interaction between the local and the universal: defining how the dialectic of the civil law had altered between the time of Cicero and Gaius, Gaius and Justinian, Justinian and Frederick Barbarossa, Frederick Barbarossa and Pothier. The equity of the civil law, its obedience to the necessities of human nature and instinct, was unvarying. But the forms of the civil law had been legion. So historicism permitted the distinguishing of equity and custom. The Roman law had been most lucid upon a crucial and perennial aspect of human society, the law of property, such that it was plagiarised even by Coke, the embodiment of a common-law tradition most insulated from and contemptuous of the civil law.[50]

But Legaré brought a second argument to the defense of the Roman law, one he had disdained in former years. He used Christianity in a manner conventional for others but puzzling in him; these essays of the late 1830s can be said to betray a new spirit. "In a rude state of society," he argued, "the *jus civile* covers . . . nearly the whole orb of legislation. . . . It is local and exclusive. But, in the progress of civilization, the other element—natural law, or the principles of general equity and reason—gradually occupies and illumines a larger and larger surface, until at length the differences which separate the legal system of foreign states, almost wholly disappear." This Legaré had argued in 1830, but he continued unwontedly, "It is impossible not to perceive this tendency in the actual condition of Christendom. The spirit of a religion, which we consider as the source of the highest and most refined civilization, and as a bond of union among modern nations—which, never interfering directly with the policy of any government, never fails in the long run to influence that of all—of a religion essentially catholic and comprehensive, breathing mercy, justice, equality, fraternity among men—unfavorable to all partial advantages, all exclusive privilege, all marked nationality,—clearly manifests itself in the advances of modern legislation, just as it did in that of Constantine and his successors, especially in that of Justinian. Democracy, in the high and only true sense of that much abused word, is the destiny of nations, because it is the spirit of Christianity."[51]

This turn to thinking of Christianity as the spirit of fraternity and humanity, the "opening to the whole earth of the doors of the temple, hitherto closed upon all but the descendents of Abraham," "the work of the 'Son of Man,' and the apostle of the gentiles," was influenced by the secularized Protestantism of German historicism, which ironically herded him towards the Thomas Grimké whose enthusiasm for the Reformation Legaré had mocked in 1828. Other motives can only be guessed. The aesthetic pleasures of European cathedrals and the harrowing crucifixions of Rubens may have shifted him towards the God of his countrymen. The disappointments of politics and his new isolation may have excited a desire for religious consolation, if only in the nuances of historical and legal explication. Yet his conversion was mild. He mentioned the Son of Man in quotation marks, as though there should be a doubt about divinity, and elsewhere he had defined the greatest value of Christianity as its encouragement of *pudor,* best exemplified in Milton's *Comus.* This was a modest evangelism. Whatever the motive, the effect upon his perception of Rome was marked, for it permitted the bleaker view of early ancient Rome that Niebuhr had sketched. Rome became a darker, more primitive, more barbaric, less Greek city, not only in the days of Tarquin but in the time of Cicero. The discovery of the real Gaius, so severe a jurist, had cast a more benign light upon the civil law of the Christian Justinian. The golden age of Roman jurisprudence was displaced from the pagan third to the Christian fifth century. Justinian became not the last of the Romans but the first of the medieval adapters of the old Roman law, the first in a modifying tradition that Legaré wished to inherit and use.[52]

Cicero had become, by the evidence of his nostalgia for the ancient republic, not a Greek in Roman form but the heir of the superstitious Etruscans, the respecter of the Law of the XII Tables, many of whose terms seemed "savage and strange." Though the full text of those laws was lost, Niebuhr had done enough to show some of their terms and all of their spirit, "and to show how remarkably contrasted it is with the body of jurisprudence collected by Justinian." "We see the rude forms of process, and the cruel modes of execution. We see the despotic authority of the father over the son, who stands to him in the relation of a chattel, of which he has the most absolute disposal, and which does not cease to be his, until he has alienated it three several times. We find libels punished with death, and the *lex talionis* enforced for a broken limb." This meditation partially dispelled the coziness of Legaré's old sympathy for Cicero's Rome and moved him to the bald and censorious observation, almost unthinkable for the Legaré of 1830, that the ancient world was marked by a "deep and disgusting moral depravity." "There was scarcely a great man of Greece whose biography is free from some of those dark stains, which no virtues would now be thought sufficient to compensate, and no glory to conceal. Without citing the examples of such men as Themistocles and Lysander, notoriously, and even for their own times, remarkably unprincipled, however gifted and celebrated men, Plutarch has scarcely a hero who would pass muster as a gentleman now."[53]

Legaré returned to familiar ground with the contemplation and defense of Demosthenes, but with increased heat and different logic. This vivid sense of the moral turpitude of the ancient world altered matters. Now he felt moved to write: "The Athenians were a people steeped in profligacy to the very lips, and wholly without shame or sensibility on subjects of honor. This shocking contrast between the exquisite in art, the polite in diction, the sublime in thought, and occasionally the great and heroical in sentiment, and a tone of manners and topics of discourse often the most low, vicious, brutal and cynical, is one of the most striking peculiarities of the ancient Greek world." This altered the emphasis of his old enthusiasm for Demosthenes, the feeling that the good taste of the Attic audience had demanded sublimity from the orator. Now defense shifted to the talents and ingenuity of Demosthenes himself. Philology and literary criticism displaced sociology, so Legaré moved to examine the or-

atorical devices of the Philippics, which Brougham had singled out
and relied upon as evidence of the theatrical and unreasoning quality
of Greek eloquence. Legaré insisted that Brougham had needed to
differentiate among the various kinds of Greek oratory: the judicial
speech, the eulogy, and such as the Philippics. These last were calls to
action, not calm analyses. "The Philippics are not 'chains of reasoning,' to establish principles of science; they are rapid developments of
practical truths, with a view to immediate action—they are vehement
exhortations to the performance of duty, pressing every topic that can
make it be felt as sacred and imperative." They were, after all,
attempts to persuade Athens of the imminent danger from Philip of
Macedon: "His eloquence is concerned with the future, rather than
the past; it deals in prophecy and conjecture; it encounters danger
with courage; it is sanguine of success in spite of difficulties." They
were meant to inspire fanaticism and, because Philip was a true
enemy, they needed to be judged upon different scales.[54]

The prickliness of Legaré's examination of Demosthenes had a
contemporary motive. Van Buren was Philip to Legaré's Demosthenes
and, just as the Athenian had been criticized for overly impassioned
appeals to the worst instincts of his audience, so Legaré had been wary
of himself for harangues in the wigwams and log cabins of American
Whiggery. The parallel was explicit, for the essay upon Demosthenes
begins: "A new era seems to have occurred in the development of our
democratic institutions. There have been congresses of the sovereigns
in proper person. We have seen multitudes, probably greater than any
addressed by the ancient masters, brought together, by means of the
steam engine, from the most distant parts of our immense territory, to
consult with one another upon the state of the nation, and to listen to
the counsels of men distinguished among us for their influence and
ability. We have seen the best speakers of the country, called for from
all parts of it, compelled to leave their homes however remote—some
of them drawn forth even out of the shades of private life—to advise,
to instruct, and to animate their fellow-citizens, exhausting all their
resources of invention to supply topics, of strength to endure fatigue,
of oratory to command attention, and even of voice to utter and
articulate sound, in order to meet the almost incessant demands made
upon them by a people insatiable after political discussion."[55]

Buoyed by the applause of Whig crowds, called out of his New York
hotel to speak, addressing throngs of Conservatives eager to drive out
the corruptions of the Macedonian of Kinderhook, Legaré found
himself optimistic about the condition of American democracy. He

was listened to in 1840, as he had not been by Charleston in 1838. "It was not one part of the country that was thus awakened and agitated, the commotion was universal," he reflected. "Yet nothing was more remarkable in these stirring scenes than the order, decorum and seriousness which in general distinguished them. These eager throngs listened like men accustomed to inquire for themselves, and to weigh the grounds of their opinions. There was to us, we confess, something imposing and even majestic in such mighty exhibitions of the Democracy." Most of all, he flattered himself, crowds listened most closely to the best speaker, "the best in the proper, critical sense of the word." Once, out of his melancholy, Legaré had believed that the sublimity of Demosthenes was induplicable because Athenian society, now vanished, was the author of that eloquence. Now, out of his cautious optimism, he restrainedly gave to modern Americans the praise he had once reserved for the Agora. This assessment allowed the bleaker side of his view of ancient society, an undertone in 1830, to become almost predominant. Legaré thus ironically left Demosthenes in the position that he himself had occupied in 1830—a man prospering oratorically despite the degenerate world in which he lived, and so dependent upon the inner logics of technique, emotion, and sincerity for his efficacy. Even so, Legaré relied guardedly upon this brave new American world, now made one great Agora by means of the steam engine.[56]

Recent political experiences in Europe and Van Buren's America had sharpened his sense of living through volatile times and deepened his understanding of the usefulness of Greek history. The Greeks had experienced and meditated upon an infinite variety of political forms. It was no accident that the modern world—German, American, and English—should be turning to the Greeks for illumination and precedent. The French Revolution had broken the mold of the European polity and created the new principle of revolution and innovation based upon speculative opinion, a principle for which democracy was an emblem. "Then, for the *first* time, the philosophers of modern Europe had an opportunity of witnessing one of those experiments in political chemistry which were continually occurring in the last days of Greece, as in a laboratory set apart for them. They saw society resolved into its elements, and these elements, like atoms in the void of Epicurus, disengaged, seeking, according to their affinities, new combinations, or too refractory to be reduced into any. They had opened the gates of Chaos." Democracy was becoming the "inevitable condition of modern nations." Tocqueville had made no discovery but merely proclaimed what all already knew. "Absolute equality before the law and the spirit of equality in every thing are the predominant characteristics of the times; and a theory of human rights and social powers, far more levelling than was ever known in Greece, has established iself in the laws of the state and in the opinions of the people. The same causes are producing the same tendencies every-where, and whatever shape the universal democracy that is approach-ing may ultimately take . . . nothing seems to us surer, than that all institutions, bottomed upon distinctions of race or caste, will sooner or later, peaceably or by violence, fall before the progress of commerce and opinion." But the problem of democracy was its plasticity and capacity to assume a republican or a monarchical form. This choice was "the great problem of society," in which "recent experience is far from encouraging," since the monarchical option was often being exercised. "We speak familiarly of monarchy, aristocracy, and democ-racy, as if they were precisely defined and widely distinguished, instead of being susceptible of endless modifications, and running continually into one another." The Greeks had witnessed and defined these kaleidoscopic forms.[57]

Yet—and the "yet" was crucial for Legaré—little of the essences of Greek culture remained. One studied Greece and examined the likes of Aristotle not to learn what modernity was like, not to see it mirrored, but to see by negation what had altered. Five distinctions between the ancient and the modern were important for Legaré: the definition of democracy, the nature of domestic slavery, the place of war in society, the relationship between the individual and the state, the meaning of republicanism.

"We must remark that democracy, [that is, "the enjoyment of perfect numerical equality, recognized as one of the universal, in-alienable rights of man"] never existed at all in antiquity, no more than in modern European history, for the revolutionary governments of France cannot be treated as an exception." Antiquity had devoutly believed in the distinctions of race, nation, and caste: Greek despised barbarian; Athenian scarcely less held Spartan and Corinthian in contempt. Hierarchy was crucial to ancient society, caste being es-pecially embodied in family distinctions. Labor was meanly regarded. From this attitude Christianity had marked a dissent, for it "enjoined and consecrated labor; it made honest poverty honorable; it exalted the humble and lowly. . . . The order of St. Benedict, by establishing a system of free labor, on the principles thus enjoined upon the primitive church, created, as Herder remarks, a new era in Europe."[58]

Likewise, slavery was crucial to the ancient world "not only as an actual institution, but as an essential element of civilized society." Culture was the cultivation of the aristocracy at the expense of the enslaved mass. Boeckh had calculated that in Attica some 95,000 citizens and 45,000 resident foreigners were attended by 365,000 slaves, and in Sparta the disproportion was still greater. These were numbers to astonish even a Southerner, if not a low-countryman. "The Doric race was literally, as has been said of their successors the Turks, *encamped* in the midst of subjugated enemies." This was a despotism unparalleled in modern times, for the problem of modern European society was how to integrate the poor and the laboring classes into government in a way consistent with social order, how to resolve what the Abbé de Lamennais had condemned as the "slavery of the whites." From this problem, America, for a moment that might extend to centuries, was exempted by prosperity. "Is this to be forever so?" Legaré asked with genuine perplexity at Europe's present and America's eventual destiny. "The masses in Europe are called free, yet they every where receive the law, and their destinies and those of their children are in the hands of their task-masters. They are, in truth, with few exceptions, a permanently degraded *caste;* and are, like the Helots, slaves, not of individuals, but of whole communities. On this subject the history of antiquity throws no light. Their philosophers solved the dreadful problem . . . against the majority of mankind, and doomed the mass to serve perpetually for the well-being and improvement of the few." With this conclusion Legaré had dispossessed himself of a crucial element in the proslavery argument, which Thomas Dew had used, plundering Aristotle and quoting Plutarch. Ancient and modern slavery were different.[59]

War was the life of antiquity, whereas in modern times peace had become the rule. Kidnapping, piracy, revolution, disorder, proscription, these were the natural lot of the ancients. The presumption of their inevitability was rooted in the whole fabric of ancient law and ethics: it governed the training of warriors, the practice of infanticide, the rationale of the Olympics, the mechanisms of slavery and ransom. Thucydides recounted atrocities with the utmost coolness and intended no irony. "Cruelty, rapacity, and violence, were the characteristics of all forms of government in antiquity. . . . We refer, for a singular illustration of this reverence for the right of the strongest, to an oration of Isocrates. . . . The old rhetorician had been declaiming against Sparta for her contempt of all laws, and her remorseless spirit of conquest, and exalting, in comparison with it, the more humane

and peaceful conduct of Athens. He had gone so far in his invective
that he felt some remorse for his intemperance—but what was his
surprise when, on consulting a professed partisan of that state, he
found him regarding that declamation as only an artful piece of irony,
and the pretended censures as really the highest panegyric."[60]

In ancient society the individual counted for little save in his
relationship to the state, his place in the armed camp. The modern
notion of a limited government would make no sense to the Greek, for
whom from Pythagoras onwards the state was "a body politic,
organized after the fashion of the natural body, with a variety of
members and faculties varying in dignity, but each indispensable in
its place, and all co-operating to the same end, the health, strength,
and well-being of the whole, under the absolute control of one will
and understanding." In this conception, of which disregard for private property was a symptom, the Greek was Asiatic. Horne Tooke,
who derived the etymology of right, *rectum,* from *regere,* to rule, was
only too correct, for in the ancient world the eminent domain of the
state was absolute and internalized into its morality.[61]

Lastly, the Greeks possessed a fixed theory as to the relationship
between republicanism, population, and space. Commonwealths
could flourish only in cities of limited dimensions, as to both population and extent. "Certain it is," Legaré noted, "that the greatest
philosophers among them would have regarded as something mon-
strous a *republic,* spreading over half a continent and embracing
twenty-six states, each of which would have itself been an empire, and
not a *commonwealth,* in their sense of the word. Aristotle expressly
declares, that the population of a city must not be allowed to increase
beyond a competent number because it would cease to be a state,
(πολις) and would become a nation, (εθνος) unsusceptible of any
thing deserving the name of a polity." Believing this notion, the
Greeks went to great lengths artificially to maintain an equilibrium.
Since a battle could drastically and suddenly affect matters, polyg-
amy, the legitimizing of bastards, the emancipation of slaves, and the
naturalization of aliens were often adopted as necessary social and
political measures. Concomitantly, the problem of the division of
land, balancing a small population against a small territory, "became,
as Niebuhr remarks, the great first principle of ancient political
philosophy and legislation." On this point Legaré took care to refute
Montesquieu, who followed the opinion of Aristotle; he implicitly
endorsed Madison and Hume, who had amended that ancient
wisdom: "One of the great conservative principles of our own republi-

can institutions is the very extensive space over which they spread their benignant influences."[62]

The burden of these reflections differed strikingly from those Legaré had once entertained. Ten years had expelled him from the magic circle of the Charleston elite and set him loose psychologically. Europe had been a useful diversion but a dead end. Charleston had failed him. The Legaré of 1830 would have been appalled at the Legaré of 1840, in and coping with the Agora of Harrison's Whig democracy. Discontented in Charleston, Legaré had found it necessary uncertainly to fashion a new home. His essays upon the ancient world bore the mark of a dimly grasped, perhaps fugitive, contentment with a wider and beckoning ambition, which made possible a distancing from the legacy of the ancients. He needed Demosthenes the less, the more he became the orator of a wide and appreciative audience. In 1830 he had drawn a line between himself and the ancients, and mourned for it. In 1840 he saw the same line but was no longer sure that it was a matter for discontent. He was coming very close to accepting the nineteenth century.

# 10

# Washington

THE NINETEENTH CENTURY did not rush to embrace him back, though Legaré had done yeoman service, written "many rather sharp letters" to conventions and barbecues, spoken with real and simulated passion against the "insolent & intolerable misrule of the Cabal in power," flattered John Tyler, and suppressed doubts about William Henry Harrison. All the while he maintained his defenses against failure. "As times go," he reflected to Rives in June 1840, "I am entirely persuaded that it is not given to any gentleman to aspire to do more than make himself be respected, & acquire what is called *authority* or *consideration* in the community. Power, advancement & all that, may possibly come, but they will be for such a man, mere casualties, & are not to be taken into the account at all." He visited Washington when the tide had turned against Van Buren and listened with interested skepticism to the gossip of those planning Cabinets and office. On these travels Legaré deepened his sense of the uncertainty and indigence of South Carolina, when compared with the prosperities of the Astor House in New York City, or a sumptuous dinner with the Governor in Albany. But his sense of engagement was so fresh, so pleasing, that he could even manage amusement at criticism, as when the Charleston *Mercury* called his "electrifying" speech to the Conservative convention in Syracuse "galvanism wasted upon a dead frog."[1]

Spoils were to be divided. When Charleston Whigs held in December a victory dinner, but for Preston not Legaré, and thereby—or
so Legaré thought—stamped the former as their candidate for the
consideration of the new administration, Legaré's brave sense of
detachment broke: "This movement on their part will probably
destroy entirely any chance I may have stood, & the papers seem to
mention me with the rest, for the place of Atty. Gen." Still, he added,
"that . . . is not robbing me of much, for that chance must have been
extremely small." He knew the jealous energy of his own temperament. "It is a thing I cannot help feeling that after all my sacrifices &
services—both of them undeniable—the few people in Charleston
that call themselves a Harrison party, should exert all the little
strength they have acquired in some degree by my efforts, to destroy
my usefulness as a public man, &, indeed, to drive me utterly from
the public service." Even in victory he could find proscription. It was
a cut, though he went sullenly to the dinner and even allowed himself
to be persuaded to speak. Yet he should not have been surprised. The
Conservatives of Rives and Tallmadge had but shifted their support
from Van Buren to the Whigs, and in keeping their independence,
they had forfeited first claim to office. It was Henry Clay who
presented his voucher to Harrison and had it cashed, not least in
having his close friend John J. Crittenden appointed as Attorney-
General.[2]

So Legaré went back to the familiar: thinking of moving, the law,
the solitudes of Charleston. To Judith Rives, successful in her husband's election to the Senate, he was playfully morose: "What could a
poor *solitaire*, only not an *eremite*, say to you that would not have been
like the skull in an Egyptian festival? I am altogether changed since
you saw me. I don't believe—except one evening at Powers' Irish
characters—that I have had a hearty laugh since my return to Carolina. I read scarcely anything but *law*, & think of nothing but
business." The cliques, the scramblers for Harrison's favor, he
mocked, only to add drily: "It is so ridiculous I almost laugh at my self
when I contrast what was said of some of us five months ago, with
what has *not* been said of *any* of us ever since." He wrote this on 5 April
1841, just a day after William Henry Harrison had expired of pneu-
monia but before the news reached Charleston.[3]

His reaction to the transformation was immediate. Tyler offered a
new prospect, and Legaré wrote to Tallmadge that in case the new
President should need a diplomat, he need not construe Legaré's
failure to solicit office from Harrison as evidence of a permanent

disinclination to public affairs. Might not Tyler be sounded? To Rives he was more candid. Madrid or Berlin would be agreeable, the latter especially to a German scholar. On the vexed issue of the U.S. Bank, which was to become the bone of contention between Tyler and Clay, Legaré was cagey, though inclined towards the necessity of "a general banking institution" to prevent the country's falling tributary to paper currency issued in New York. He had been impressed by the almost unanimous opinion of bankers that such a bank was necessary. But it was a "subject of extreme difficulty with me. . . . On the whole I do not exactly know what I shd. do if I were now in Congress— except *listen*." This was prudent, matters being in flux. But a few more weeks evidenced indecision in Washington and no immediate signs from Tyler of accepting Legaré's soundings. Legaré drew back, having heard that "two gentlemen from this state had been designated by the Secy [of State] for foreign missions & that my name was never mentioned at all. Be it so." Harrison's Cabinet, including Secretary of State Webster, was still in office, so old dissonances were yet relevant. By mid-May, Legaré felt himself "neither here nor there," neither stuck with Charleston nor confirmed of Washington, yet not un- hopeful of a "new formation of parties" that might work to his advantage. He drifted in mingled studiousness and melancholy. "I am making sport," he told Judith Rives, "& yet would you believe it? my heart is *breaking*. I never felt more like despair than at this very moment. I am in one of those moods when I ask myself why was such a being created? to what earthly purpose either for himself or for others? And yet in the calm solitude I have been dwelling in for some months past—studious solitude, only broken by occasional speeches in courts, I have been as nearly happy as a lone man can be."[4]

He watched the growing feuds of Washington in early summer from South Carolina. Clay moved to bend Tyler to his will and, failing, strove then to break him by using Congress to smash a merely accidental President. In July, Legaré traveled briefly through Wash- ington to meet Rives before going on to New York and New England to stay with friends, among them Ticknor, who had urged the *ignobile otium* of Cape Cod. As an unplanned side trip, he went to Lebanon Springs for the first time since 1816. It was a reminder of the passage of twenty-five years, of the death of friends, and of more or less sound health continued. And the visit reminded him that he was yet, as he had been in 1816, an itinerant bachelor: "I met there with a young man a grown up son of one of the *belles* I most admired in '16."[5]

He took up residence in Newport, playing the dispassionate and coy statesman. On August 20 he wrote to Rives, in the midst of the squabbles of Washington, with a feigned disingenuousness that the Virginia senator did not misunderstand: "Will the present Cabinet hold on? I don't see but they may, altho' 'twould certainly not surprise me, to see them disband. But in that event, who would succeed them?" Rives was the key. In Tyler's quarrels with Clay, Rives was virtually the only congressman with whom his fellow Virginian, the harassed but obdurate President, maintained close links. The Conservatives, the uncertain states' rights wing of the victorious coalition of 1840, now proved crucial to Tyler, who felt himself precipitately pressed by an imperious Clay into an economic nationalism that the Virginian had never endorsed and did not want. Two vetoes of bank bills dear to Clay signaled the breach, as palatable to Tyler as to the Kentuckian. Throughout August, Rives and Tyler had discussed the replacement of the Harrison/Clay cabinet, so when everyone but Webster resigned on September 11, a new slate was ready, previously sounded. Legaré, with a flush of pleasure and then a despondency dispelled by action, found himself Attorney-General. [6]

This, he knew, was scarcely to ride in triumph through Persepolis. Tyler was besieged, forced to deepen the turmoils of politics to reap the harvest of a reorganization beneficial to himself and his allies. His Cabinet was full of politically independent lieutenants, over whom a party captain like Webster towered. Abel P. Upshur of Virginia, Walter Forward of Pennsylvania, John C. Spencer of New York, Charles A. Wickliffe of Kentucky were the dispossessed of politics and, being so, had nothing to lose from joining Tyler and just perhaps something to gain. But it was an unusually bright Cabinet of "very *clever* & agreeable men," for both Legaré and Upshur were men of intelligence and learning, and Tyler himself, though scarcely intellectual, maintained links with Virginian ideologists like Thomas Dew and Beverley Tucker. Legaré knew from the first that the game had to be played with nerve and skill, for almost everyone was opposed, and those who flirted with alliance—such as Calhoun—were uncertain. But the possibility that he, an outsider among outsiders, might fashion success by intelligence was a sweet lure to Legaré's pride. [7]

The office of Attorney-General was of ambiguous political influence, a part time job, compensated at a rate half that of ordinary Cabinet members. Its holder was allowed and expected to continue private practice, for the Attorney-General was, to all intents and purposes, a lawyer kept on permanent retainer to advise and represent the government of the United States before the Supreme Court. Some of its holders, notably William Wirt, had striven to remove it from partisan politics—a venture doomed, since the law in a political system so bedeviled by constitutionality and litigation was a necessary adjunct to effective power. But it was an office that might serve as the conscience of an administration, especially one that flattered itself with the mission, so often proclaimed, of calling back the American system to first principles.[8]

The Charlestonian understood that politics was a society and that politicians might be influenced by the salon. Arrived in Washington, sworn to office, having acquired an efficient clerk from Petigru, Legaré resolved to play the game to the hilt. Though a bachelor, he disdained the customary lodgings, took himself a house, decided to move his mother and sister Mary up from South Carolina, and began systematically to liquidate his South Carolina holdings; for he expected to remain, after his office should expire, as a lawyer in Baltimore or Washington. On his last visit to Charleston he was obliged, like a stranger, to stay in a hotel. The outgoing Secretary of War, John Bell of Tennessee, finding himself unnecessarily encumbered with a large house packed with European furniture, proved amenable to Legaré's request to buy the furniture and rent the house: the former coming expensively at some $1,600, and the latter cheaply at $360 for seven months. Amid French bedsteads, a fine mahogany bureau, three slaves sent from Charleston, a housekeeper whose Swiss husband served as messenger, and a torrent of new and complicated legal matters, Legaré set himself up. The rest of the Cabinet, betraying more prudence than nerve, took themselves to lodgings which, Legaré thought, gave "too much the air of *self-distrust* . . . to the whole concern." Legaré's society would be delicate, not pell-mell for rumbustious congressmen from the West, not *"mobs"* but "little dinner parties from time to time," as though Legaré were the Auguste d'Arenberg of the District of Columbia. Yet his concerted illusion did not betray an expectation of permanence. Politics would go on: Tyler would probably not win reelection; Van Buren would likely be the Democratic candidate for President in 1844; Calhoun would plot unsuccessfully; the Whigs would waver and scuffle. "We have a card to play," Legaré told Rives, "if we be pressed & *really* wish to play a magnificent game—which will win for us, more than the stakes on the table—the highest glory—which is to be satisfied with our *four years*. That is decidedly my desire. I go for the honour of such an example, & for administering the govt. on its true principles, without fear, favour or affection. It would make our administration an era in history & give it immortality. I do not think it possible to overrate the effect of such a step in elevating & purifying public opinion."[9]

His social ambitions proved easier to achieve than his political hopes. The White House, as part of the burden of office, went in for mobs: two formal dinners a week during the congressional session, with twenty to forty guests; each night the public rooms open to informal visitors; once a month a grand leveé, when a thousand people might attend. (Charles Dickens once found himself at such a leveé, where the "company was not, in our sense of the term, select, for it comprehended persons of very many grades and classes; nor was there any great display of costly attire: indeed some of the costumes may have been, for aught I know, grotesque enough. But the decorum and propriety of behavior which prevailed, were unbroken by any rude or disagreeable incident," save inescapably the incessant ringing of spittoons.) These Legaré almost never attended, partly because of the crush of his business. Growing affluent as his private practice before the Supreme Court gathered pace with the successes of his public practice (his fee for *Watkins* v. *Holman* was $1,000), he gave evening parties of his own, such as that on 4 February 1842 for the visiting Lord Morpeth. "The rest of the Cabinet except Webster, do very little for society, & the consequence is they are fast losing their consideration here. I am sorry to see it because they are very *clever* & agreeable men, some of them at least. But they will not let people come in contact with them. I was very much amused at my table yesterday, to see how *freely* some of my guests, old Senators &c. drank my good Carolina Madeira. Several of them thus went off merry."[10]

As Attorney-General, Legaré had two main responsibilities: to render opinions to government departments requiring legal advice and to appear before the Supreme Court. Of the former we have abundant published record; of the latter, little but the bare log of fifteen cases.

He was thorough and minute in his opinions. He did decline the entreaties of Cabinet officers to make the Attorney-General a referee between departments, which had been Wirt's custom: "The Attorney General's office is not a Court of Appeals, " he told the Secretary of the Treasury in March 1842. Otherwise he was energetic. Many opinions are not of permanent interest for the student of Legaré. Did distressed seamen have the right to aid from American consuls, under the provisions of the acts of 1792 and 1803? Did the president have the right to set aside the verdict of decades-old courts-martial, if irregularities could be demonstrated? Did the government have the prerogative of establishing post offices in Indian territory? What was the legal definition of a newspaper? Were instructors at West Point entitled to extra compensation? Did the Third Auditor to the Department of War have jurisdiction, under the auspices of the act of 1837, over accounts rendered for horses and other property destroyed? In other opinions speaking to small but significant matters of the day, Legaré displayed no reluctance to enforce federal and presidential power against competing claims. He argued, for example, that New York had no constitutional right to conclude a treaty of extradition with Canada. The President had the right to dismiss an officer from the military without trial, though this power Legaré conceded with reluctance and not without reference to the potential of capricious despotism. Being part of an administration much at odds with Congress, Legaré usefully declined to offer legal advice to congressional committees and asserted the President's right to make *ad interim* appointments while Congress was in recess. For Congress "has only a negative and secondary agency in appointment to office. It has no share of the executive power, properly so called—that is, active, discretionary executive power; it simply controls the head of that department in the choice of its agents. It has no constitutional right to create an interregnum of the government; no such tremendous discretion has been confided to it. It is not responsible to the people for any failure to execute the laws. It cannot be impeached for denying the means of executing them to him who is liable to be judged and punished for a failure to exercise the powers which, in every well-constituted society, must be perpetually and everywhere at work for its protection." This was doctrine of little use to a frustrated Henry Clay and might later have been of service to Andrew Johnson.[11]

Three opinions compel attention, one bearing upon domestic politics, two upon foreign policy. The first, dealing with the collection of duties under the Compromise Tariff Act of 1833, was ironic for the veteran of the tariff wars. That act had called for progressive reductions in the level of duties—gradual during the 1830s, inconveniently abrupt in 1842—down to the level of 20 percent. Government deficits had increased, and in 1842 the national debt stood at $13,500,000. Dropping revenues and rising deficits produced a crisis, even threatened a disaster, since the 1833 act was so badly drafted that it was unclear whether any duties could be collected after 30 June 1842. Congress passed a Whiggish "Little Tariff" in early June, which Tyler vetoed. A second measure was passed and again vetoed. At issue was the Whig desire not only to keep tariffs high but to preserve the distribution to the states of revenues from the sale of public lands. In the meantime, it was vague whether the federal government had the right to continue to collect duties. Arbitration fell to Legaré. He was brisk and decisive, giving the affirmative answer that made Tyler's veto and government plausible. [12]

The second opinion, given in December 1841 and reiterated in January 1842, was of less moment to the processes of American government but bears interest because it demonstrates some of Legaré's views on foreign policy. The Secretary of the Treasury had inquired whether a ship built in the United States, fitted for war, and sold to a foreign belligerent (in this case Mexico) could lawfully sail, or whether its owners were subject to prosecution under the American law of neutrality. Legaré was clear that they were so subject: "The policy of this country is, and ever has been, perfect neutrality and non-interference in the quarrels of others; but, by the law of nations that neutrality may, in the matter of furnishing military supplies, be preserved by two opposite systems, viz:—either by furnishing both parties with perfect impartiality or by furnishing *neither* . . . . this country has seen fit, with regard to ships of war, to adopt the other branch of the alternative—less profitable with a view to commerce, but more favorable to the preservation of a state of really pacific feeling within her borders—she has forbidden all furnishing of them under severe penalties. The memorable act of 1794 consecrated this policy at an early period of our federal history; and that act was only repealed in 1818 to give place to an equally decided expression of the legislative will to the same effect." The decision was technical, but the tone was warm. Neutrality was not merely law but wisdom. [13]

The third opinion was important and vexatious. Webster had remained with Tyler not just for the pleasure of office but also to conclude the difficult and crucial negotiations with Great Britain that would issue in the Webster-Ashburton Treaty of 1842. These negotiations were muddied by the case of the *Creole*, which touched the antislavery sentiment of Great Britain, divided proslavery from antislavery Americans, and affected the law of nations. In so doing, it fell squarely within Legaré's interests and expertise. The *Creole* had sailed from Virginia in October 1841 with a cargo of slaves destined for New Orleans. When the ship was about to enter harbor at Abaco Island in the Bahamas, a portion of the slaves had mutinied, taken control of the vessel, and ordered the captain to proceed to Nassau. There the British authorities, acting in the spirit of the Emancipation Act of 1833 and the Somerset case, had released those slaves not instrumental in the mutiny but held the remaining nineteen until advice should come from London. In the early months of 1842, the ensuing debate seriously jeopardized the greater diplomatic issue of stabilizing Anglo-American relations. The Southern press urged not only extradition to the United States for the nineteen mutineers but compensation to slaveowners for those released by the British. On the latter score, their hopes seemed slim, for the British had consistently freed slaves entering British territory; on the former, matters were more obscure. Under normal circumstances, the ship entering British waters of its own free will, extradition would have been out of the question, for no such agreement existed between the United States and Great Britain. But, the ship entering under duress, how did the issue stand? Webster was reluctant to press the matter, and the Peel ministry eventually decided to release the nineteen, receiving in consequence only mild protest from Webster and the American Minister in London, Edward Everett. [14]

The first diplomatic exchange was over by the time Legaré was asked to give an opinion. He had been drawn into the discussions in Washington between Webster and Ashburton and, first making his views known in conversation, was asked by the British Minister to reduce his standpoint to writing. Technically, the Americans were still pressing for extradition and compensation, and the slave-holding Tyler was especially touchy on the matter. Both Webster and Everett, being mildly antislavery, were not overly concerned. Ashburton was irritated at being held up by a minor and peripheral matter, delaying him in a steamy Washington July. Legaré took up a moderate position that skirted briefly the issue of slavery and instead took ground upon the technicalities of international law. He did reiterate his old belief, stated in the *Southern Review*, that the "relation of master and slave exists even now in most countries, and was until recently as universal as that of parent and child, husband and wife, guardian and ward. In the New Testament the only word for servant, with scarcely an exception, is *slave*." Slavery did touch the law of property and status. But the nub of the matter was that the *Creole* had entered British waters under duress and thus did not fall within the jurisdiction of British municipal law. "The principle is, that if a vessel be driven by stress of weather, or forced by *vis major*, or, in short, be compelled by any overruling necessity to take refuge in the ports of another, she is not considered as subject to the municipal law of that other, so far as concerns any penalty, tax, or incapacity that would otherwise be incurred by entering the ports; provided she do nothing further to violate the minicipal law during her stay. The comity of nations, which is the usage—the common law of civilized nations, and the breach of which would now be justly regarded as a grave offence—has gone very far on this point." The judgment was supported with citations from Coke, Sir William Scott, Martens, Vattel, and the Code Napoleon. This position, moderately taken up on the principles of international comity, was eventually to be endorsed by the arbitration of 1853, which awarded $110,330 to the owners of the liberated slaves. In the immediate context of 1842, the opinion helped in both vindicating the American position and moving Tyler towards accepting a moderate compromise, jammed into the treaty. Legaré himself was pleased with that pact and sent a letter of honest congratulations to the dinner held in Ashburton's honor in New York in September 1842. Its tone echoes Legaré's characteristic desire for international sympathy brought about by commerce, and his distaste for the sacrifice of common sense to metaphysics: "If I do not greatly overrate the importance of this event, it will mark an era in the history of diplomatic intercourse and of public law. The mere etiquette, the unmeaning mystery and mummeries of negotiations were dispensed with, and questions in which the peace of the world and the independence of nations were deeply concerned, have been discussed with the calm and sober reason, the strict and searching analysis, the gravity, directness and simplicity of purpose, that belonged to the severest judicial investigation." No doubt he had witnessed the urbane facility with which Webster and Ashburton, having resolved upon the necessity of avoiding war and achieving a settlement, had concluded the negotiations even against the claims of their own governments and constituents. [15]

Legaré appeared before the Supreme Court of the United States on fifteen occasions in 1842 and 1843, in eleven cases as Attorney-General, in four as a private attorney. For the United States, his record was seven cases won to four lost; for his private clients, he carried three cases and can be said to have effected a draw in the fourth. Six of the official cases, and all his losses, were concerned with Florida land claims, a perennial nuisance for Attorneys-General and the court. By law all land claims decided against the United States by Florida courts were automatically appealed to the Supreme Court. They were seldom interesting, sometimes only perfunctorily contested by the government. [16]

None of Legaré's cases proved of great constitutional moment. *Wood* v. *U.S.* helped to clarify the government's right to prosecute an importer whose invoices had first been cleared by customs but subsequently demonstrated to be fraudulent. *U.S.* v. *Eliason* allowed the federal government to be reimbursed by an army officer who had been overpaid under regulations subject to misinterpretation. *U.S.* v. *William Murphy et al.* endorsed the proposition that the victim of a robbery could be a witness in the ensuing prosecution, even though by exaggerating the scale of the robbery he might be said to have an improper interest. *Williams* v. *U.S.* made clear that a President, in delegating authority, could not be held directly responsible for the dubious actions of his underlings. *Jewell's Lessee et al.* v. *Jewell et al.* bore upon the nice question of the legal definition of a marriage but was chiefly remarkable for applying familiar legal doctrines to the case of a Jewish common law marriage. *U.S.* v. *Eckford's Executors*, while it involved no new law, was of special interest to Legaré, the old enemy of Van Buren, for it settled the legal liability of Samuel Swartout, the embezzling collector of the Port of New York. *Watkins* v. *Holman et al.* decided a complicated land claim in Mobile, to the enrichment of Legaré's clients and himself. That his performance in the court was efficient, eloquent, and erudite, there is no reason to doubt. Legaré kept a proud record of compliments received, from Chief Justice Roger Taney, from Justice Joseph Story, just as he took pleasure in vanquishing his legal peers, among them his predecessor Crittenden.[17]

But his desires went beyond mere success in gaining favorable verdicts. Joseph Story recognized the measure of this ambition. "I had looked to see him," the Justice observed in eulogy a few days after Legaré's death, "accomplish what he was so well fitted to do,—what, I know, was the darling object of his pure ambition—to engraft the Civil Law upon the jurisprudence of the country, and thereby to expand the Common Law to greater usefulness and a wider adaptation to the progress of society." Legaré toyed in the spring of 1842 with spending part of the following summer making an annotated translation of Heineccius on the Institutes, "as an introduction to the study of the Civil Law." Nothing came of it. Story reminisced that "his arguments before the Supreme Court were crowded with the principles of the Roman Law wrought into the texture of the Common Law with great success." "Crowded" is too strong, but it is true that almost alone of lawyers before the court, Legaré cited the civil law. In the Mobile case he deployed the Institutes, Heineccius, and Grotius to argue that the law of alluvion, affecting the formation of new land by alluvial deposits, applied only to possession and should not be allowed

The Supreme Court, restored to its antebellum appearance,
in the basement of the Capitol.
Courtesy, Architect of the Capitol

to apply to land newly created by the river after the initial definition of ownership. In *Williams* v. *U.S.* he glancingly referred to Justinian. In the Swartout case he cited Domat's Public Law, as well as Pothier on the law of obligations. In the Jewell case he recurred to Pothier. Yet these were small if useful flourishes in arguments that were obliged to rest firmly upon the common law, upon Westminster Hall, Kent's *Commentaries* and the precedents of American courts. Story did remember Legaré's capacities as a common lawyer, yet went too far: "I may say of him, having seen his mastery of both systems of jurisprudence—that he walked with them triumphantly, the one in one hand, and the other in the other hand, in the path of a great jurist." Legaré was too good a practicing lawyer to do other than keep the civil law in his pocket, to be produced for emphasis. Yet it is difficult (though probably necessary) to repress the speculation that Legaré, if he had lived to practice decades more and to occupy a seat on the Supreme Court, almost his natural destination, matters might have gone otherwise with the status of the civilians in American constitutional law. [18]

The law kept him professionally busy, yet politics was the stuff of Washington. Legaré, by being in the executive branch, by being committed to a President bedeviled by Congress, by representing the government in court, and—though he would have blushed to admit it—by temperament, found himself launched upon a strengthening of presidential prerogatives. He began to feel the power of patronage. [19] Calhoun, repelled by Clay and drawn to the Virginian Tyler, drifted towards the administration, and Legaré managed a stiff reconciliation. By May 1842, Petigru was reporting to his daughter, "It is said by people from Washington that Mr. Calhoun and Mr. Legaré are becoming cronies." Legaré occasionally permitted himself to hope that Tyler might prosper, as he did when Webster, with a great speech in Boston, inhibited temporarily the movement of New England opinion away from the administration; its effect was such that even Ticknor, who regularly counseled Legaré upon the futility of the Tyler cause, was given occasion for doubt. He did his best in the Cabinet and came to be almost Tyler's best man. Yet he kept a little aloof, careful to remain the useful technician, and seems to have taken the greatest pleasure in skirmishes against political and administrative corruption. Petigru observed in January 1842, "The Ministry seem to look forward with all the complacency of passengers in a new coach; taking it for granted that they will arrive at their inn in good time, and quite unconcerned as to who will take their places in the next stage. It is the getting out, which is likely to be disagreeable, and about that they seem to think very little." Of Tyler's ambition this was poor forecasting, but less so of the Attorney-General.[20]

In 1842, Legaré had been drawn into foreign policy. He advised Webster in the negotiations with Ashburton; he corresponded with Lewis Cass over the problems of the Quintuple Treaty which—an old concern of American diplomacy and the former chargé in Brussels— raised questions about the right of search on the high seas, especially and inevitably by the British. As Minister to France, Cass had interfered undiplomatically in matters strictly the concern of Webster and of Edward Everett in London. In this Legaré encouraged Cass and helped to secure Cabinet endorsement of Cass's protest. "But as from the very first moment I heard of that treaty & especially, as soon as I heard it read," he wrote to Cass in April 1842, "I regarded it in the very light to which it has presented itself to you, as a most signal attempt on the part of the great maritime powers, to foist a new & pregnant innovation into the law of nations, & to subject the flags of all other countries to her own, you will easily conceive the very particular pleasure with which *I* heard of your bold, able & effective interposition on behalf of your government & country." For Legaré was sympathetic to those reforms, expressed by Upshur in the Navy Department as they had previously been expressed by Poinsett in the War Department, that strengthened the American military and so disposed the country towards a more expansionist foreign policy. Though he lacked the rhetoric, Legaré did not entirely avoid the substance of the ideology of Manifest Destiny. He moved in sympathy with Tyler and Upshur in casting covetous eyes upon Texas and, farther still, to the Pacific, to Hawaii, and to China beyond.[21]

With such policies Webster was uncomfortable and by early 1843 was disposed to cut loose from schemes he did not approve and an administration he felt to be doomed. Tyler, casting about for a replacement, offered the State Department to Legaré. It must have been tempting, the summit for a former diplomat and a student of foreign policy. Yet Legaré declined, preferring instead to retain the post of Attorney-General. The refusal says much about his estimate of Tyler's future. As he explained to Rives, to accept was "out of the question for many reasons—of which one very weighty one is that I do not choose to give up my present place & practice in the Supreme Court—just at the moment that the latter *promises* as well as it does." This was a cold blooded calculation about prospects beyond 1845. Still, Legaré took over Webster's duties informally from as early as

January 1843, and on May 5 accepted *ad interim* appointment as Secretary of State, without forfeiting the Attorney-Generalship.[22]

He found an inefficient State Department, partly because Webster had been less than energetic or completely competent, especially in his latter days. In April, Legaré had had to redraft a dispatch in which Webster's exposition of the legal basis of a government policy had been imprecise and weak. "The God-like, I find," he told Rives, "*entre nous*, both morally & intellectually, needs a good deal of *prompting*, or he doesn't *act* well." After barely a month in office, he felt obliged to comment, "There are prodigious abuses to be rooted out, pollutions to be wiped away & a general indolence, incapacity & want of a conscientious sense of duty, to be thoroughly corrected." This confirmed his old impression, gained from Brussels, that in the State Department "truth is less told & tolerated . . . than in any court in Europe." In his office as Attorney-General, the work load had been great—during the Supreme Court session of 1843 he averaged a legal opinion a day—but the staff, Legaré and his clerk alone, had been efficient. The State Department was a wider and lazier field where he had little discretion, it being the focus of a pandemonium of patronage and he but *ad interim*.[23]

There is little to record of Legaré as Secretary of State, in office for just six weeks. He wrote dispatches to clear the way for Caleb Cushing's China mission to open trade links, a purpose with which Legaré was markedly in sympathy. He had occasion to advise the American Minister to Holland that there was no legal recourse to the federal government for those in Amsterdam holding debts from American states and individuals that recent financial difficulties had placed in hazard. But he suggested that they might rest easy, for Legaré was sure the American economy was mending rapidly along with the government's finances. He instructed Edward Everett to protest vigorously at a violation of American rights by the Royal Navy, engaged upon police duties on the West African coast. He showed himself especially concerned, the more so with the Cushing mission pending, at the unexpected military seizure of the Sandwich Islands by an enterprising but unauthorized British naval force. His discursive dispatch to Everett shows the temperament of his informal imperialism. He protested at the "revolting usurpation" by a power otherwise sanctimonious about international justice, particularly on the slave trade, before going on: "It is well known that our settled policy is the strictest non-intervention in what does not immediately concern us, that we accept Governments *de facto* as Governments *de jure*, and that above all, we have no wish to plant, or to acquire, colonies abroad. Yet there is something so entirely peculiar in the relations between this little commonwealth and ourselves, that we might even feel justified, consistently with our own principles, in interfering by force to prevent its falling into the hands of one of the great Powers of Europe. These relations spring out of the local situation, the history, and the character and institutions of the Hawaiian Islands. . . . If the attempt now making by ourselves, as well as by other Christian Powers, to open the markets of China to a more general commerce, be successful, there can be no doubt but that a great part of that commerce will find its way over the Isthmus. In that event it will be impossible to overrate the importance of the Hawaiian group as a stage in the long voyage between Asia and America." Even in the short run they were significant for the whaling trade. "It seems doubtful whether even the undisputed possession of the Oregon territory and the use of the Columbia river, or indeed any thing short of the acquisition of California (if that were possible) would be sufficient indemnity to us for the loss of those harbors." Here, as in domestic politics, his taste for influence inclined to outrun his belief in restraint. Indeed, this dispatch proved the founding document of the eventual American annexation of Hawaii.[24]

May and June 1843 found Legaré *in medias res*: powerful, busy, discursive, not sanguine of continued power but content with passing influence and sure of making his mark, the greatest balm to his proud temperament. He had, it was true, suffered domestic reverses. In the summer of 1842 his sister Eliza had died, battered with continual pregnancies and the worries of an incompetent husband. In the autumn, assisted by this grief, his mother had faltered. This turn moved Legaré to his only extended tribute to her, though his whole life had marked his love and devotion. "I have just left the bed side of my poor mother, whose precious life I fear is fast ebbing away," he told Rives on 28 October 1842. "She has just had a paroxism which is not yet passed, & I do not know but that I may be summoned within twenty four hours to attend her in her dying moments. O God, how desolate the prospect is of a world in which such a chasm is to remain forever more unfilled. Tho' death at the age of 71 & upwards is certainly in the order of nature, yet this dearly beloved friend was so distinguished, up, even to a twelvemonth ago when I took leave of her in Charleston, by vigour & activity, both of body & mind, her high & decided moral character seemed still so prepared for every trial & every struggle which might be still in reserve for her, that I never once thought of the chance of my surviving her." She lingered until New Year's Day, 1843. And Legaré himself had been ill, in March of 1842, with stomach pains so severe it is said he observed to his sister Mary that "if it pleased God, he would rather die than again encounter such to live."[25]

Nonetheless, power, its pleasant dance of speculation and action, contented him. On June 12, not long back from a brief trip to Charleston and about to go to Boston, he bubbled away to Rives about the future: "For parties, it seems to me as yet a jumble. You see Calhoun carries Georgia (unanimously in the *committee*) & there are movements in his favour in the West. The sage of Kinderhook, I think, has seen his culminating point, & is now rapidly on the decline. If Calhoun were not a Southern man, he wd. be the lucky man, past all doubt. As it is *quare*, for I have, any time these last ten years, regarded the election of a Southron as a very remote contingency. If a Westn. candidate for the V. Presidency, who could carry Ohio wd. join stocks with him they wd. probably be elected, but the deuce is that no candidate who is pretty sure of carrying Ohio, will condescend to be vice president. As to the old Whig candidate, I really do not think he stands much chance, as things are now. The country is not distressed enough—that is, though straitened for money, bankruptcy has done its worst, & banks somewhat *au rabais*. Then whatever—but I am interrupted & let fall the curtain."[26]

There was to be a great celebration in Boston on Saturday, June 17, to mark the sixty-eighth anniversary of the Battle of Bunker Hill and to dedicate its completed monument. The President and Cabinet were to attend, Webster was to speak, there were to be marches, banners, dinners, pomp. Legaré had not much wished to go, being busy in Washington, and had skipped the antecedent progress of Tyler through New York and New England. He traveled up to Boston at the last moment, leaving open on his desk a copy of *Coke's Reports*, and arrived on the Friday morning, to take rooms at the Tremont House and visit friends in the early evening. He had felt ill, not unusual for him, and took the precaution of turning away his heaped plates at the Mayor's dinner. He retired to bed, to be seized at one o'clock on Saturday morning with severe abdominal pains. Dr. Thomas, the President's physician and staying at the same hotel, was summoned. With the advice of Legaré, the student of his own complaints, Thomas resorted to the remedies that in the attacks of the previous two years had proved efficacious against the pain and constipation. Enemas and laxatives offered bare relief, and Saturday—though it saw Legaré absent from the festivities of Bunker Hill—gave no cause for great alarm. Early Sunday morning brought no change, but Thomas felt it wise to summon a prominent local physician, Jacob Bigelow. The Bostonian found Legaré suffering intermittent pain but with a strong pulse, no sensitivity about the abdomen, no nausea, no flatulence. Bigelow suggested opiates, but Legaré declined on the seasoned logic that old remedies would work. Yet two doses of Epsom salts laced with senna and hyoscyamus, followed by enemas, brought no improvement. Worryingly, the enema tubes would travel no further than the entrance to the sigmoid flexure, which connects the rectum to the colon.[27]

At six on the Sunday evening they moved him to the house of George Ticknor, which stood at the corner of Park and Beacon Streets, overlooking Boston Common and an avenue of elms. They took him through the hall, up the staircase, and past the library. They gave him a warm bath, at which he expressed relief and satisfaction. They dosed him with laudanum, which bought sleep for intervals. The early morning of Monday found him much the same, the pain even a little less, but with new symptoms that increased ominously during the morning. His abdomen grew tender and flatulent, his blood pressure rose from the 60 of Saturday morning to 80 by nine o'clock and 100 at noon. By this time Dr. Thomas had gone to attend the President, himself indisposed, and Bigelow called in a Dr. Warren. The physicians grew anxious and resolved to act. They leeched his abdomen. They rubbed in croton oil, a drastic purgative. They stuck in more tubes. They tried to remove the obstruction by inflating him with a bellows. They twice injected tobacco. His blood pressure rose to 140.[28]

All of Monday, Legaré retained the composure of a veteran in the wars of his own body. Like a brisk lawyer he settled his affairs, sent on dispatches to the President, made his will. He left everything to his sister Mary except a small legacy of $1,000 to a nephew and $500 to Petigru, "for a purpose which I shall mention to him," a phrase that suggests Legaré was unconvinced of his coming death. During Monday night he was restless, often getting up in the belief that he could evacuate his bowels in the close stool. By the early morning he had worsened. They offered him a glass of water, but he waved it aside, saying it contained ants. They told him it was an illusion and, being a rational man, he put out his hand for the glass but missed it, said a few incoherent words, leaned back. Ticknor was holding him, until

Park Street, Boston; Ticknor's house to the left.
COURTESY, LIBRARY OF THE BOSTON ATHENAEUM

Bigelow told the historian to put Legaré down. Ticknor protested that he was not tired, until he realized that it was unnecessary to console a corpse. [29]

# Abbreviations

In the notes and the following checklist of *Southern Review* contributors, references to materials that are cited in the bibliography have been shortened; others appear in full when first cited. The page numbers given for Legaré's essays and speeches are to the original publication, with the frequent exception of those reprinted in the two volumes of his *Writings* edited by his sister. All manuscripts whose location is not otherwise specified can be assumed to be in the Legaré Papers at the South Caroliniana Library. These abbreviations have been commonly used:

| | |
|---|---|
| AG/NA | Department of Justice Letters, National Archives |
| Belgium/ NA | Dispatches to and from the Belgian legation, National Archives |
| LC | Library of Congress |
| PHS | Historical Society of Pennsylvania |
| PRO | Public Record Office, England |
| *SCHM* | *South Carolina Historical Magazine* |
| SCHS | South Carolina Historical Society |
| SCL | South Caroliniana Library |
| *SR* | *Southern Review* |
| *Writings* | *Writings of Hugh Swinton Legaré* |

# Contributors to the *Southern Review*

N<small>OT THE SMALLEST PROBLEM</small> in writing about Hugh Legaré is establishing his canon. Since many of his essays appeared anonymously in the *Southern Review*, this means sorting out his own contributions from those of others. As there is no adequate published checklist of that periodical, it seems useful—not only on Legaré's account—to compile one.[1] Estimates of Legaré's contributions have varied. Rhea offers little guidance. Christophersen claims no less than 36 essays as Legaré's, often in cases where the evidence is not impressive. If my own attributions are correct, this number can be reduced to 25, excluding "Percival's Clio," the only case in which I am genuinely doubtful whether the author is or is not Legaré.

There is a variety of sources upon which to base attributions: contemporary correspondence, memoirs, eulogies, annotations in surviving sets of the periodical, reprintings. These enable us to settle authorship for most pieces, though far from all. When I consider an attribution virtually certain, I have italicized the author's name after the essay's title. The following abbreviations are used to indicate recurring sources of the attribution given.

Shand: a letter, now in the Charleston Library Society, from Peter J. Shand of Trinity Church, Columbia, S.C., to Whitefoord Smith, dated 26 July 1869, which contains a list of attributions and explains, "I have lately seen in Mr. Barnwell's [Robert Barn-

---

[1]Early efforts are fragmentary: see Edward R. Rogers, *Four Southern Magazines* (Charlottesville, 1902); Guy A. Cardwell, "Charleston Periodicals, 1795–1860" (Ph.D. diss. Univ. of North Carolina, 1936), 388–93; Elizabeth Steele Bearden, "The Southern Review" (M.A. thesis, Columbia Univ., 1925).

well of South Carolina College] private library a copy of the 'Southern Review' embracing all but one volume. I find in it the name of the Author appended to almost every article. This was done, as Mr. B. thinks, by the late Bishop Elliott who, after his Father's death was associated I believe with Hugh Legaré in the management of the work, & the information thus furnished you may rely upon as authentic."

Snowden: a list, printed in the Columbia *State*, 30 November 1924, by Yates Snowden. It came, Snowden claimed, from a clipping of the Charleston *Courier* "in the 1840s." The clipping has vanished, and a search in the *Courier* has failed to unearth the original. This does not in itself prove the list spurious, as Snowden may have misremembered the date or newspaper, or just guessed at the provenance of a stray clipping. Nonetheless, until the original is found, this source must be treated with caution. (This list, by the way, is identical to the one made available to researchers in the SCL.)

Trapier: a set of *SR* issues, catalogued as copy 3, now in the SCL, that once belonged to B.F. Trapier. It has attributions which, judging by Trapier's signature, seem to be in his handwriting.

Clariosophic: an incomplete set with attributions, presented by Stephen Elliott, Jr., to the Clariosophic Society of the South Carolina College, now in the SCL.

Euphradian: an incomplete set with attributions, formerly belonging to the Euphradian Society of the South Carolina College, now in the SCL.

*Writings*: essays reprinted in the second volume of Legaré's *Writings*, with the publisher's note (p. 5), "The reprint of this and the following articles, from the 'Southern Review' is made from a bound copy of that work, which belonged to Mr. Legaré, and which was revised by him, as indicated by frequent notes, penned or pencilled by him, on the margin or at the foot of the several numbers." This set is no longer extant.

LaBorde: attributions in Maximilian LaBorde, *History of the South Carolina College* (Columbia, 1859).

Elliott: attributions in James Moultrie, *An Eulogium on Stephen Elliott, M.D. & L.L.D.* (Charleston, 1830).

Lectures: a list in Thomas Cooper, *Lectures on the Elements of Political Economy*, (2d ed. (Columbia, 1830).

Arkansas: an incomplete set with attributions, formerly belonging to Drayton Grimké-Drayton, now in the University of Arkansas Library, Fayetteville.

Thornwell: attributions in James Henley Thornwell, "Memoir of Dr. Henry," *Southern Quarterly Review*, n.s., 1 (April 1856): 189–206.

Cooper: Thomas Cooper to Parker, 21 Feb. 1829, Cooper MSS, SCL.

### VOLUME I, NUMBER 1, FEBRUARY 1828

1. "Classical Learning," 1–49. *Hugh Swinton Legaré. Writings*; Trapier; Arkansas; Euphradian; Shand.
2. "Principles of Agriculture," 49–70. *Thomas Cooper.* Cooper; Trapier; Shand; LaBorde; Arkansas; Snowden; Euphradian; Lectures.
3. "Execution of Colonel Isaac Hayne," 70–106. *Robert Young Hayne.* Shand; Trapier; Arkansas; Snowden; Euphradian; "Life, Character and Speeches of the Late Robert Y. Hayne," *Southern Quarterly Review* 8, (Oct. 1845): 508.
4. "Geometry and the Calculus," 107–34. *James Wallace.* Shand; Trapier; Arkansas; LaBorde; Euphradian; Snowden.
5. "Gall on the Functions of the Brain," 134–59. *Thomas Cooper.* Cooper; Lectures; Shand; Trapier; Snowden; LaBorde; Arkansas; Euphradian.
6. "Scott's Life of Napoleon Bonaparte," 159–92. *Stephen Elliott, Sr.* Elliott; Shand; Trapier; Snowden; Arkansas; Euphradian.
7. "Political Economy—Rent," 192–218. *Jacob N. Cardozo.* Shand; Trapier; Euphradian; Snowden; Arkansas; Melvin L. Leiman, "The Economic Ideas of Jacob N. Cardozo," in B.F. Kiker and Robert J. Carlsson, eds., *South Carolina Economists: Essays on the Evolution of Antebellum Economic Thought* (Columbia, 1969), 19.
8. "Colonization Society," 219–34. *William Harper.* Shand; Trapier; Arkansas; Snowden; Euphradian.
9. "Geology and Mineralogy of North Carolina," 235–61. Snowden and Euphradian have Thomas Cooper, although it is mentioned in neither Cooper nor Lectures. Shand, Trapier, and

Arkansas have Stephen Elliott, Sr., although it is not in Elliott. On balance, I incline to Elliott, since Cooper himself did not claim the piece and already had two essays in this number.

10. "The Talisman," 262–71. Shand has "contributed from New York"; Snowden and Arkansas have "Dr. Nelson of New York."

### VOLUME I, NUMBER 2, MAY 1828

1. "On the Constitution of the United States," 273–320. *Stephen Elliott, Sr.* Elliott; Shand; Trapier; Euphradian; Snowden.

2. "Niebuhr's Roman History," 320–41. *Robert Henry.* Shand, Trapier, Thornwell, Snowden, and Euphradian have Henry; Holmes, "Writings of Legaré," 345, has Legaré; Legaré himself, in "Cicero de Republica," 228, observes that he has examined the early history of Rome in an earlier piece and a footnote identifies this occasion as "Southern Review, No. II, Art. 2." Here is an apparently irreconcilable conflict. The attributions for Henry are impressive, and he is known to have commenced a translation of Niebuhr. On the other hand, while Holmes carries less weight, Legaré himself carries much. Yet the author of this essay could read German, an accomplishment of Henry but not of Legaré until 1833. Moreover Legaré notes (*Writings*, II, 502) that he was not to read the prologomena to Niebuhr's history until 1832. I infer therefore that the footnote in *Writings*, 228, is a misprint for "Southern Review, No. II, Art. 4,"—i.e., "Roman Literature"—or else Legaré simply misremembered the number of his article.

3. "Begin's Therapeutics," 342–57. *Thomas Cooper.* Lectures; Shand; Trapier; LaBorde; Euphradian; Snowden.

4. "Roman Literature," 358–410. *Hugh Swinton Legaré. Writings*; Legaré to Jesse B. Harrison, 26 Aug. 1830, Harrison Papers, LC; Shand; Trapier; Euphradian.

5. "Life of Wyttenbach," 410–42. *Henry Junius Nott.* Shand; Trapier; Euphradian; Snowden; LaBorde; William Elliott to Ann Elliott, 6 Dec. 1828, Elliott-Gonzales Papers, Southern Historical Collection.

6. "Percival's Clio—Number III," 442–57. Shand, Trapier, Euphradian, and Snowden have Legaré. This seems dubious, though not impossible. Some of its sentiments and its style are not inconsistent with Legaré, yet the cavalier dismissal of August von Schlegel does not seem consistent with what is known

of Legaré's views elsewhere, and the tone of the prose is a touch jejune.

7. "Butler's Life of Hugo Grotius," 457–78. Snowden has Thomas S. Grimké, but Trapier and Euphradian have Colonel [William] Drayton. A.S. Salley, once librarian of the University of South Carolina (in a list of attributions drawn from Shand, an incomplete set in Salley's possession, and a clipping from the Charleston *Courier* "around 1840"—presumably the same used by Snowden—cited in Bearden, "The Southern Review,") suggests Baron Wallenstein of the Austrian Embassy in Washington.

8. "On the Monitorial System of Education," 478–503. Trapier has "Griscom," while Shand ventures "from New York." There was a John Griscom, then professor of chemistry at the New York Institution, in Edinburgh at the same time as Legaré and therefore a likely candidate: see Andrew Hook, *Scotland and America: A Study of Cultural Relations 1750–1835* (Glasgow, 1975), 176.

9. "Crafts' Fugitive Writings," 503–29. *Hugh Swinton Legaré. Writings*; Shand; Trapier; Euphradian; Snowden.

## VOLUME II, NUMBER 3, AUGUST 1828

1. "Irving's Life of Columbus," 1–31. Snowden has Legaré; Euphradian has Stephen Elliott, Jr.; an odd copy in the SCL, of unknown provenance (catalogued as copy 5), has William Howland; Trapier, Arkansas, and Elliott have Stephen Elliott, Sr. It is certainly not Legaré for the style is not his, but much more the elder Elliott's. But see Number 13, Article 8, below.

2. "Origin of Rhyme," 31–72. *Thomas S. Grimké*. Trapier; Arkansas; Snowden; James H. Smith, *Eulogium on the Life and Character of Thomas S. Grimké* (Charleston, 1835), 31.

3. "Kent's Commentaries," 72–113. *Hugh Swinton Legaré. Writings*; Trapier; Arkansas; Euphradian.

4. "Travels in the South of Russia," 114–52. *Stephen Elliott, Sr.* Elliott; Trapier; Arkansas.

5. "Malaria," 152–92. *Samuel Dickson*. Trapier; Arkansas; Snowden.

6. "Flint's Valley of the Mississippi," 192–216. *Samuel Prioleau*. Trapier; Arkansas; Snowden.

7. "The Fair Maid of Perth," 216–63. *Hugh Swinton Legaré*. Tra-

pier; Arkansas; Snowden; Euphradian; Holmes, "Writings of Legaré," 345; Johnston, "Legaré," 425.

8. "Scott's Life of Napoleon Bonaparte," 263–90. *Stephen Elliott, Sr.*, Elliott; Trapier; Arkansas; Snowden.

9. "The Omnipresence of the Deity," 290–302. *Hugh Swinton Legaré.* Trapier; Euphradian; Arkansas; Snowden; Johnston, "Legaré," 425.

### VOLUME II, NUMBER 4, NOVEMBER 1828

1. "Religion of the Aboriginal Americans," 305–48. *John England.* Trapier; Snowden; reprinted in *Works of the Right Rev. John England*, ed. I.A. Reynolds (Baltimore, 1849), IV, 462–84.

2. "American Naval History," 349–83. *Robert Young Hayne.* Trapier; Snowden; "Hayne," *Southern Quarterly Review* 8: 508; Hayne to Samuel L. Southard, 30 Oct. 1828, Southard Papers, Princeton, quoted in Harold D. Langley, "Robert Y. Hayne and the Navy," *SCHM* 83 (Oct. 1982): 319.

3. "Sparks' Life of John Ledyard," 383–408. Trapier has "Mr. Tucker of the Virginia University," i.e., George Tucker. This article is not mentioned in the bibliography of Robert C. McLean, *George Tucker: Moral Philosopher and Man of Letters* (Chapel Hill, N.C.; 1961), but this is not decisive negative evidence, since McLean would probably not think to look for a Tucker piece in the *Southern Review.*

4. "Views of Nature," 408–31. *Stephen Elliott, Sr.* Trapier; Snowden; Elliott.

5. "The Federal Constitution," 432–54. Trapier and Snowden have James McCord.

6. "Pollok's Course of Time," 454–70. *Hugh Swinton Legaré.* Trapier; Snowden; Legaré to Jesse B. Harrison, 3 Nov. 1828.

7. "Internal Improvements," 470–91. *Stephen Elliott, Sr.* Trapier; Snowden; Elliott.

8. "The Roman Orators," 491–540. *Hugh Swinton Legaré.* Trapier; Euphradian; Snowden; Holmes, "Legaré," 345; Legaré to Jesse B. Harrison, 3 Nov. 1828.

9. "Georgia Controversy," 541–82. Trapier and Snowden have William Drayton.

10. "The Tariff," 582–619. Trapier and Snowden have George McDuffie.

VOLUME III, NUMBER 5, FEBRUARY 1829

1. "Law of Tenures," 1–31. *Hugh Swinton Legaré*. Shand; Trapier; Euphradian (although it is worth noting that the ascription here is in pencil and a different handwriting from the annotations elsewhere).

2. "Romances of the Baron de la Motte Fouqué," 31–63. *Robert Henry*. Shand; Trapier; Euphradian; Snowden; Thornwell; La-Borde.

3. "Court of Chancery," 63–77. *James Louis Petigru*. Shand; Trapier; Euphradian; Snowden.

4. "Life of Erasmus," 77–124. *Henry Junius Nott*. Shand; Trapier; Euphradian; Snowden; LaBorde.

5. "Brown's Philosophy of the Human Mind," 125–56. Snowden, Euphradian, and E. Brooks Holifield, *The Gentleman Theologians: American Theology in Southern Culture, 1795–1860* (Durham, 1978), 230, have Samuel Gilman. Shand has the "Reverend Mr. Annan of Baltimore,"

6. "Origin of Rhyme," 156–92. *Thomas S. Grimké*. Shand; Snowden; Trapier; Euphradian; Smith, *Grimké*, 31; Number 3, Article 2, above.

7. "Travels of the Duke of Saxe-Weimar," 192–207. *Hugh Swinton Legaré*. *Writings*; Euphradian; Johnston, "Legaré," 425; Trapier.

8. "Higgins' Celtic Druids" 207–25. *Thomas Cooper*. Cooper; Lectures; Shand; Trapier; Euphradian; LaBorde; Snowden.

9. "Walsh's Narrative" 225–60. Snowden and Euphradian have James McCord; Shand, Trapier, and Elliott have Stephen Elliott, Sr. Elliott seems more likely, given both his taste for travel literature and the more reliable sources for the ascription.

VOLUME III, NUMBER 6, MAY 1829

1. "Franklin's Narrative," 260–88. Shand and Trapier have Stephen Elliott, Sr., though it is not in Elliott.

2. "Cambridge Course of Mathematics," 289–308. Shand and Trapier have Jasper Adams; Euphradian has James Wallace.

3. "Stuart's Commentary on the Hebrews," 308–29. Snowden has James Wallace, improbably; Shand and Trapier have Samuel Dickson.

4. "On the Manufacture of Sugar," 329–52. *Stephen Elliott, Sr.* Shand; Elliott; Trapier; Snowden; Euphradian.

5. "Goethe's Wilhelm Meister," 353–85. *Robert Henry*. Trapier; Thornwell; LaBorde; Euphradian; Snowden.
6. "Memoirs of Dr. Parr," 385–415. *Henry Junius Nott*. Shand; Trapier; Euphradian; Snowden.
7. "Modern Gastronomy," 416–30. *Thomas Cooper*. Lectures; Shand; Trapier; Euphradian; LaBorde; Snowden.
8. "Law and Lawyers," 431–50. Trapier and Snowden have Samuel Prioleau.
9. "Liberty of the Press—Sedition Law of '98," 450–67. Snowden and Euphradian have Samuel Prioleau; Trapier is hard to read but seems to say, "Georgia."
10. "The Disowned—Tales of the Great Saint Bernard," 467–507. *Hugh Swinton Legaré*. *Writings*; Johnston, "Legaré," 425; Trapier; Euphradian.

### Volume IV, Number 7, August 1829

1. "Higgins' Celtic Druids," 1–46. *Thomas Cooper*. Trapier; Arkansas; LaBorde; Number 5, Article 8, above.
2. "Hoffman's Legal Outlines," 47–69. *Hugh Swinton Legaré*. Shand; Trapier; Arkansas; Euphradian; Legaré to Mary Legaré, 24 Aug. 1835.
3. "The Fine Arts," 70–86. *Charles Fraser*. Shand; Trapier; Arkansas; Euphradian; Alexander Moore, "A Checklist of Published Works by Charles Fraser," in David Moltke-Hansen, ed., *Art in the Lives of South Carolinians: Nineteenth-Century Chapters* (Charleston, 1979), AM-11.
4. "Education in Germany," 86–123. *Stephen Elliott, Sr.* Shand; Elliott; Trapier; Euphradian; Thornwell, "Free School System of South Carolina," *Southern Quarterly Review*, n.s., 2 (Nov. 1856): 158; odd volume in SCL.
5. "Abbot's Letters from Cuba," 123–36. Trapier has "Courtenay."
6. "Cicero de Republica," 136–76. *Hugh Swinton Legaré*. *Writings*; Shand; Legaré to Jesse B. Harrison, 26 Aug. 1830; Legaré to mother, 4 Nov. 1832; Trapier; odd volume in SCL.
7. "Travels in China," 176–207. Shand and Trapier have Henry Junius Nott.
8. "Dyspepsia," 208–41. *Samuel Prioleau*. Shand; Trapier; Euphradian; odd volume in SCL.
9. "Heber's Sermons," 241–60. Shand, Trapier, and Euphradian

have Legaré, which is impossible because of style and subject matter.

## VOLUME IV, NUMBER 8, NOVEMBER 1829

1. "Sismondi's Political Economy," 261–85. Arkansas has James H. Smith; Shand has James S. Smith. Since James Hervey Smith was later to change his name to James Smith Rhett, I take Shand to be an understandable slip and this to be by James Hervey Smith. For a further discussion, see Michael O'Brien, ed., *All Clever Men, Who Make Their Way* (Fayetteville, Ark., 1982), 29–32.
2. "Cuba," 285–321. *Stephen Elliott, Sr.* Shand; Elliott.
3. "Hall's Travels in North America," 321–69. *Hugh Swinton Legaré.* Shand has Stephen Elliott, but it is in *Writings*, and Legaré claims it in Legaré to Pierce Butler, 26 June 1838, reprinted in Charleston *Courier*, 20 July 1838.
4. "Novels—Devereux," 369–405. Shand has James Hamilton.
5. "Influence of Chivalry upon Literature," 405–33. Shand has Edward M. Michaelowitz.
6. "Sir Walter Raleigh," 433–66.
7. "Classification of Plants," 466–98. *Stephen Elliott, Sr.* Elliott; Shand; Snowden.
8. "Anne of Geierstein," 498–522. *William Elliott.* Shand; Stephen Elliott, Jr., to William Elliott, 1 Oct. 1829, Elliott-Gonzales Papers, Southern Historical Collection.

## VOLUME V, NUMBER 9, FEBRUARY 1830

1. "Grammar of the Hebrew Language," 1–24. Snowden and a copy in the possesion of Merrill G. Christophersen have Stephen Elliott; Shand, a copy in the SCHS (these two may be identical sources, as the latter seems to have belonged to Robert Barnwell, from whom Shand obtained his ascriptions), and Thornwell to W.H. Robbins, 12 Feb. 1830, quoted in Benjamin M. Palmer, *The Life and Letters of James Henley Thornwell, D.D., L.L.D.* (Richmond, 1875), 67, have Edward Michaelowitz. Though evidence (see Number 11, Article 2, below) of Michaelowitz as a plagiarist makes this piece suspicious, nonetheless he did teach Hebrew at the South Carolina College.
2. "Raymond's Political Economy," 25–62. Snowden and Christo-

phersen copy have Stephen Elliott; Shand has the Rev. Mr. Annan of Baltimore.

3. "Early Spanish Ballads," 62–99. *Hugh Swinton Legaré. Writings*; Shand; Johnston, "Legaré," 425; Euphradian; Christophersen copy.

4. "Jefferson's Memoirs," 100–38. Snowden, Euphradian, and Christophersen copy have Stephen Elliott [Sr.].

5. "Paul Louis Courier," 139–70. *Henry Junius Nott*. Shand; Snowden; Christophersen copy; LaBorde; Palmer, *Thornwell*, 68; Euphradian; SCHS copy.

6. "The Navy," 170–206. Snowden, Christophersen copy, and Euphradian have William Drayton. Shand, SCHS copy, and Langley, "Hayne and the Navy," 326, have Robert Hayne.

7. "The Wept of Wish-ton-Wish," 207–26. *Hugh Swinton Legaré*. Snowden, Euphradian, and Christophersen copy have Legaré. Shand has John A. Stuart, as does SCHS copy (which, as noted above, may be identical to Shand), although Legaré's name was first written in and then crossed out, to be replaced by Stuart. I incline strongly to Legaré.

8. "The Anatomy of Drunkenness," 226–49. Shand has James Hamilton.

VOLUME V, NUMBER 10, MAY 1830

1. "Bourienne's Memoirs," 257–95. Shand and Elliott have Stephen Elliott, Sr.

2. "Sir Philip Sidney's Miscellanies," 295–318. *Hugh Swinton Legaré. Writings*; Shand; Euphradian; Christophersen copy; Snowden.

3. "Ancient and Modern Oratory," 319–37. Shand has Jacob N. Cardozo.

4. "Etymology," 337–81. Shand and Euphradian have Edward Michaelowitz.

5. "Bentham's Judicial Evidence," 381–426. *Thomas Cooper*. Shand; LaBorde; Snowden; Christophersen copy; Euphradian.

6. "Heber's Life of Jeremy Taylor," 426–62. Snowden and Christophersen copy have Stephen Elliott. Shand and Euphradian have Stephen Elliott, Jr. Given the provenance of the Shand list and the younger Elliott's Episcopalian career, the latter is more likely.

7. "Lord Byron's Character and Writings," 463–522. *Hugh Swinton Legaré. Writings*; Shand; Euphradian; Christophersen copy.

## VOLUME VI, NUMBER 11, AUGUST 1830

1. "Agrarian and Education Systems," 1–31. *Thomas Cooper.* Shand; Arkansas; Clariosophic; LaBorde; second copy in SCHS formerly belonging to John B. Moore.
2. "History of Greek Literature," 32–61. Clariosophic has Edward Michaeolowitz. It is, in fact, a plagiary of and translation by Michaelowitz of passages from Johann F.L. Wachler, *Handbuch der Geschichte der Literatur* (Frankfurt-am-Main, 1822–24), as noted in *SR* 7 (August 1831): 518, which confesses the discovery of assorted Michaelowitz plagiarisms.
3. "Memoires d'un Pair de France," 61–91. Shand and Clariosophic have Samuel Prioleau.
4. "Ben Jonson's Works," 91–116. *William Elliott.* Shand; Arkansas; Clariosophic; Stephen Elliott, Jr., to William Elliott, 27 July 1830.
5. "Physiologie des Passions," 116–40. *James Hervey Smith.* Shand has James S. Smith; Arkansas has James H. Smith; Clariosophic has J. Rhett. As argued in Number 8, Article 1, above, this points to James Hervey Smith.
6. "Debate on Mr. Foot's Resolution," 140–98. *James Hamilton.* Shand; Moore copy, SCHS; Arkansas; Clariosophic; Stephen Elliott, Jr., to William Elliott, 27 July 1830; Thomas Cooper, *Consolidation* (Columbia, 1830), 25, 31.
7. "Hall's Familiar Letters of Milton," 198–206. *Stephen Elliott, Jr.* Shand; Clariosophic; Stephen Elliott, Jr., to William Elliott, 27 July 1830.
8. "The American System," 206–54. *Hugh Swinton Legaré.* Shand; Arkansas; Stephen Elliott, Jr., to William Elliott, 27 July 1830; Legaré to Stephen Miller, 5 Aug. 1830; Clariosophic; Thornwell to George F. Holmes, 9 Oct. 1856, in Palmer, *Thornwell*, 405.

## VOLUME VI, NUMBER 12, NOVEMBER 1830

1. "Mental Development" 265–83. Clariosophic has Thomas Cooper, which is unlikely, since two other essays in this number are almost certainly by Cooper.
2. "Geology," 284–307. *Thomas Cooper.* Shand; LaBorde; Clariosophic; Stephen Elliott, Jr., to William Elliott, 27 July 1830.

3. "Memoires of Josephine," 307–57. Shand and Clariosophic have Samuel Prioleau.

4. "History of Greek Literature," 358–79. Michaelowitz plagiary of Wachler: see Number 11, Article 2, above.

5. "Social Life of England and France," 379–409. *Thomas Cooper.* Shand; Clariosophic; Snowden; Christophersen copy; LaBorde.

6. "Florida," 410–20.

7. "The Tribunal of Dernier Resort," 421–513. Shand and Clariosophic have Robert J. Turnbull.

8. "Griesbach's New Testament," 513–48. Shand and Clariosophic have the Rev. Alston Gibbes.

(No issue of the *Southern Review* was published in February 1831.)

### VOLUME VII, NUMBER 13, MAY 1831

1. "Byron's Letters and Journals," 1–42. *Hugh Swinton Legaré.* Shand; *Writings*; Clariosophic.

2. "Beranger's Poems," 42–67. Shand has Theodore Sedgwick of New York, but see Number 15, Article 4, below.

3. "The Life and Times of Daniel De Foe," 68–101. Shand and Trapier have Henry Junius Nott.

4. "Murat's Letters on the United States," 102–20. *Samuel Prioleau.* Shand; Trapier; Snowden.

5. "History of the Fine Arts," 121–59. Michaelowitz plagiary of passages from Johann Dominick Fiorillo, *Geschichte der zeichnenden Künste von ihrer weiderauflebung bis auf die neusten Zeiten* (Göttingen, 1798–1808): see Number 11, Article 2, above.

6. "Steam Engine and Rail-Roads," 159–91. *James Wallace.* Shand; Trapier; LaBorde.

7. "The Siamese Twins," 192–213. *Hugh Swinton Legaré.* Shand; Trapier; Clariosophic.

8. "Irving's Voyages and Discoveries of the Companions of Columbus," 214–46. Trapier and Shand have Stephen Elliott, presumably meaning the younger Elliott, as the elder had died in 1830. If it is the younger Elliott, this might strengthen the case for his authorship of Number 3, Article 1 (otherwise much confused).

9. "The Family Library," 247–59. Shand, Trapier, and Clariosophic have Legaré. I doubt this very much, for reasons of style.

## Volume VII, Number 14, August 1831

1. "Jeremy Bentham and the Utilitarians," 261–96. *Hugh Swinton Legaré*. *Writings*; Shand; Clariosophic; Legaré to Jesse B. Harrison, 12 March 1832; Stephen Elliott, Jr., to William Elliott, 31 Aug. 1831.
2. "Operation of Poisons," 297–319. Shand and LaBorde have Thomas Cooper.
3. "French Novels," 319–68. *Henry Junius Nott*. Shand; Thornwell to A.H. Pegues, 1 Oct. 1831, in Palmer, *Thornwell*, 87.
4. "Theory of Association in Matters of Taste," 368–91. Shand has James H. Simmons.
5. "Codification," 391–412. *Hugh Swinton Legaré*. Shand; *Writings*; Clariosophic; Palmer, *Thornwell*, 87.
6. "Small-Pox, Variolid Diseases, and Vaccine," 412–35. Shand has Samuel Dickson.
7. "American Literature," 436–59. Shand suggests Edward Johnston; Legaré to Rives, 3 Dec. 1840, Rives Papers, LC, indicates that at least one contribution was made to the *Review* by Johnston, and this is the only essay to which his name has been linked. Moreover, it is in the "Scriblerian" vein, which Legaré speaks of as characteristic of Johnston's piece.
8. "Woolrych's Life of Judge Jeffreys," 459–85. *Henry Junius Nott*. Shand; LaBorde; Clariosophic.
9. "Waterhouse's Junius," 486–517. *Robert Henry*. Shand; Thornwell; Palmer, *Thornwell*, 87; LaBorde; Stephen Elliott, Jr., to William Elliott, 31 Aug. 1831.

## Volume VIII, Number 15, November 1831

1. "United States Bank," 1–41. *Thomas Cooper*. Trapier; Snowden; LaBorde; Charleston *Courier*, 28 May 1841.
2. "Cyril Thornton," 42–69. Trapier has "Colonel Drayton,"
3. "Cuvier's Theory of the Globe," 69–88.
4. "Delavigne's Poems," 88–114. Trapier has Nott. The author of this observes that he has written on Beranger earlier (i.e., Number 13, Article 2). This suggests authorship either by Theodore Sedgwick (which seems unlikely) or by Nott, who therefore wrote the Beranger essay, a probability since Nott regularly wrote upon French literature for the *Review*.
5. "Remarks on Canal Navigation and on the Resistance of Fluids," 114–53. *James Wallace*. Trapier; Snowden; LaBorde.

6. "A Year in Spain," 154–71. Snowden has Nott.
7. "Distribution of Wealth," 171–92. *Thomas Cooper*. Trapier; Snowden; LaBorde.
8. "Peninsular Campaigns," 192–212. Trapier has "Colonel Drayton."
9. "Indirect Taxation," 213–60. Snowden has Robert Turnbull.

### VOLUME VIII, NUMBER 16, FEBRUARY 1832

1. "The Public Economy of Athens," 265–326. *Hugh Swinton Legaré. Writings*; Legaré to Jesse B. Harrison, 12 March 1832.
2. "Griffin's Remains," 326–44. Snowden has Legaré. But Legaré to Thomas Bee, c. Sept. 1831, asks Bee to write this, and Legaré to Harrison, 12 March 1832, suggests that only articles 1 and 5 are by Legaré.
3. "Life of Mary Queen of Scots," 345–82.
4. "Cooper's Bravo," 382–99. Snowden has Legaré. Edd Winfield Parks, *Ante-Bellum Southern Literary Critics* (Athens, 1962), 274, rightly points out that the author of this appears to have been in Italy, which Legaré had not. In addition, it is not quite Legaré's style. The essay even seems to suggest a personal acquaintance with Cooper. My suspicion is that the author is Henry Cruger, a friend of both Legaré and Cooper, newly returned from seeing Cooper in Europe. Cruger was a young Charleston lawyer who was soon to abandon the city for New York; the essay has a famous lament for Charleston's decline. See James Franklin Beard, ed., *The Letters and Journals of James Fenimore Cooper* (Cambridge, Mass., 1960), I, 417–24.
5. "D'Aguesseau," 399–443. *Hugh Swinton Legaré*. Snowden and LaBorde have Nott, but *Writings* and Legaré to Harrison, 12 March 1832, confirm Legaré.
6. "Bryant's Poems," 443–62. Snowden has Legaré, which for style is not impossible. But Legaré to Harrison, 12 March 1832, seems to rule it out.
7. "English Civilizaiton," 462–91. *Jesse Burton Harrison*. Legaré to Harrison, 24 April 1832; reprinted in Fairfax Harrison, ed., *Aris Sonis Focisque, Being a Memoir of an American Family, the Harrisons of Skimino* (n.p., 1910), 301–36.
8. "Political Economy," 492–511. There are no suggestions as to the author of this, but its appendix (pp. 511–15) is by Legaré: see Legaré to Harrison, 24 April 1832.

# Notes

## PREFACE

1. Rhea, *Charleston Intellectual,* spent much time explaining how important was the *Southern Review,* how unimportant and indigestible was Legaré's thought.

2. Legaré, "Sir Philip Sidney's Miscellanies," 336; Lord Acton, "Political Causes of the American Revolution," in *Essays on Freedom and Power,* ed. Gertrude Himmelfarb (New York, 1948), 203. Acton's library in Cambridge contains a well-marked set of Legaré's works. In 1858, Acton wrote to Richard Simpson, "I find a very good paper against the Benthamites in the works of a very accomplished American, Legaré, which I daresay you will be glad to see when you tackle Mill Junr." Later he added, "Legaré is 'cute, but he might be deeper." See *The Correspondence of Lord Acton and Richard Simpson,* ed. J.L. Altholz and D. McElrath (Cambridge, 1971), I, 35, 53.

3. The only previous extended consideration of Legaré's thought is Edd Winfield Parks, *Ante-Bellum Southern Literary Critics* (Athens, Ga., 1962), 23–50, 268–76. It may be worth noting that I have excluded historiographical discussions from this study, since, if space is at a premium, they are most dispensable.

4. Legaré, "Travels of Saxe-Weimar," 167; "A Character of King Charles II," in *Halifax: Complete Works,* ed. J.P. Kenyon (Harmondsworth, 1969), 247.

## 1. YOUTH

1. Johnston, in *Writings,* I, vi; Mary Legaré, "Memoir," 4; Rhea, *Charleston Intellectual,* 13.

2. Mary Legaré, "Memoir," 3; Mrs. Eliza C.K. Fludd, *Biographical Sketches of the Huguenot Solomon Legaré, and of His Family* (Charleston, S.C., 1886), 10–12.

3. Ibid.; Charles W. Baird, "Legaré genealogy," Charleston Library Society; Legaré to C.R. King, 9 Feb. 1838; Legaré to sister, 16 June 1833.

4. Baird, "Legaré genealogy"; Johnston, in *Writings*, I, vii; E. Milby Burton, *South Carolina Silversmiths, 1690–1860* (Charleston, S.C., 1942), 105–106.

5. Burton, *South Carolina Silversmiths*, 106–10; Fludd, *Solomon Legaré*, 41–42.

6. Legaré to mother, 16 March 1835.

7. Mary Legaré, "Memoir," 4–5.

8. Johnston, *Writings*, I, viii: "We are in possession of few particulars beyond his early death."

9. Mary Legaré, "Memoir," 5; Fludd, *Solomon Legaré*, 131.

10. Will of Thomas Legaré, 9 Sept. 1798, Charleston Wills, S.C. State Archives.

11. Johnston, in *Writings*, I, x; Mary Legaré, "Memoir," 7.

12. Peter Razzell, *The Conquest of Smallpox: The Impact of Inoculation on Smallpox Mortality in Eighteenth Century Britain* (Firle, 1977), 1–6.

13. Ibid., 6–25, 42.

14. Ola Elizabeth Winslow, *A Destroying Angel: The Conquest of Smallpox in Colonial Boston* (Boston, 1974), 94–111; David Ramsay, *History of South-Carolina* (Newberry, S.C., 1858), II, 45; Ramsay to Joshua E. White, 22 July 1802, in Robert L. Brunhouse, ed., "David Ramsay, 1749–1815: Selections from his Writings," *Transactions of the American Philosophical Society*, n.s., 55 (Aug. 1965): 153–54; Mary Legaré, "Memoir," 6. Thomas Legaré died on 9 Feb. 1801 ("Inscriptions from the Circular Church," *SCHM* 29 [Oct. 1928]: 313).

15. Mary Legaré, "Memoir," 6–7.

16. Johnston, in *Writings*, I, viii; Mary Legaré, "Memoir," 12; Benjamin F. Perry, *Reminiscences of Public Men*, vol. III of *The Writings of Benjamin F. Perry*, ed. Stephen Meats and Edwin T. Arnold (Spartanburg, S.C., 1980), 38. It may be relevant that according to a modern member of the Legarés, the family is prone to short legs, even without the intervention of illness.

17. I am grateful to Dr. Charles Chalfant of the University of Arkansas for this diagnosis, which seems a better explanation than Linda Rhea's suggestion of infantile paralysis; see *Cecil: Textbook of Medicine*, ed. Paul B. Beeson et al., 15th ed. (Philadelphia, 1979), 255–59, 2103–04.

18. James L. Petigru to Legaré, 6 Sept. 1836, in Carson, *Petrigru,* 185.

19. William J. Grayson, *James Louis Petigru: A Biographical Sketch* (New York, 1866), 102; Carroll, "Sketch," 360. Harriet Horry Rutledge, just nine or ten in 1841, wrote to her mother of this habit of Legaré's: "Yesterday Mr. Legaré came and read Manfred to Aunt Holbrook. He sometimes swells his voice so that it frightens me and then brings it down so sweet and low that it's a pleasure to hear him" (Harriet Horry Rutledge to mother, 24 June 1841, H.H. Rutledge Papers, Duke University; I am grateful to Steven Stowe for this quotation).

20. Legaré, "Lord Byron's Character and Writings," 373–75.

21. Mary Legaré, "Memoir," 8; Johnston, in *Writings,* I, x–xi; Legaré to sister, 25 Jan. 1836. It might be remembered that encomia to domesticity, so frequent in his letters, can partly be explained by the large share of his extant correspondence taken up by letters to his mother and sister. The tone of his letters to male friends, of which fewer survive, is more rumbustious.

22. Johnston, in *Writings,* I, xii; Mary Legaré, "Memoir," 8.

23. "History of the Diocess of Charleston," in *The Works of the Right Rev. John England,* ed. I.A. Reynolds (Baltimore, Md., 1849), III, 251.

24. Mary Legaré, "Memoir," 8; Johnston, in *Writings,* I, xii; Legaré, "Lord Byron's Character and Writings," 377.

25. Mary Legaré, "Memoir," 9.

26. "Mitchell King," in John Belton O'Neall, *Biographical Sketches of the Bench and Bar of South Carolina* (Charleston, S.C., 1859), I, 347–77; "The Abiel Abbot Journals: A Yankee Preacher in Charleston Society, 1818–1827," ed. J.H. Moore, *SCHM* 68 (July 1967): 126–27.

27. Johnston, in *Writings,* I, xv.

28. Thomas Legaré to Moses Waddel, 6 March 1798, Moses Waddel Letterbook, LC; Ralph M. Lyon, "Moses Waddel and the Willington Academy," *North Carolina Historical Review* 7 (July 1931): 284–99.

29. Lyon, "Willington," passim; Johnston, in *Writings,* I, xvi–xx.

30. Augustus Baldwin Longstreet, *Master William Mitten* (Macon, Ga., 1864), 72, quoted in Lyon, "Willington," 292.

31. Mary Legaré, "Memoir," 11.

32. Daniel Walker Hollis, *South Carolina College* (Columbia, S.C., 1951), 31–32.

33. Patrick Scott, "Jonathan Maxcy and the Aims of Early Nine-

teenth-Century Rhetorical Teaching," *College English* 45 (Jan. 1983): 21–30; on the issue of Scottish thought and American education, see Douglas Sloan, *The Scottish Enlightenment and the American College Ideal* (New York, 1971).

34. Hollis, *South Carolina College*, 32, 47.

35. Ibid., 43, 44, 75, 62–63; Johnston, in *Writings*, I, xxii.

36. Preston, *Eulogy*, 7; Johnston, in *Writings*, I, xxxiv–xxxv; Hayne, "Legaré," 130.

37. Legaré, "The Disowned," 189–90; Legaré to mother, 25 Nov. 1814; Legaré, "Classical Learning," 49–50.

38. Legaré to sister, 4 Nov. 1814, quoted in Mary Legaré, "Memoir," 18; Christophersen, "Legaré," 59–70.

39. Cf. Legaré, "Hall's Travels," 274: "Lawyers . . . have had and ever must have . . . [an] ascendency in all free countries"; Mary Legaré, "Memoir," 14. The subtlety and range of King's advice can be gauged from King to David Johnson, 1 Aug. 1836, reprinted in O'Neall, *Bench and Bar*, I, 367–77; his specific advice on books often parallels Legaré's tastes, though as this was written later, it may be as much evidence of Legaré's influence on King as vice-versa.

40. Albert Simons and Samuel Lapham, eds., *The Early Architecture of Charleston*, 2d ed. (Columbia, S.C. 1970), 99–213.

41. On the context of Charleston, see George C. Rogers, Jr., *Charleston in the Age of the Pinckneys* (Norman, Okla., 1969), and David Moltke-Hansen, "The Expansion of Intellectual Life: A Prospectus," in Michael O'Brien and David Moltke-Hansen, eds., *Intellectual Life in Antebellum Charleston* (Knoxville, Tenn., 1986); Legaré to Henry Middleton, 23 June 1820, Middleton MSS, SCHS; "Charleston," in *Miscellaneous Writings of the Late William Crafts* (Charleston, S.C., 1828), 309.

42. Charles S. Watson, *Antebellum Charleston Dramatists* (Tuscaloosa, Ala., 1976), 1–47.

43. Moltke-Hansen, "Expansion."

44. James Hervey Smith, *Eulogium on the Life and Character of Thomas S. Grimké* (Charleston, S.C., 1835); Carson, *Petigru*; Theodore D. Jervey, *Robert Y. Hayne and His Times* (New York, 1909); Mary Legaré to Mrs. Yeadon, 21 May 1857 (copy in Chisholm Papers, SCL) mentions that Legaré once wrote a "Treatise on Ennui" and quotes from a poem "On Ennui" written in 1826–27, which reads:

> Non Hanno Speranza di morte,
> Hast thou ever felt the sorrow;
> That knows no cause, that sheds no tear?

That dreads to see another morrow,
Rise on the world so dark and drear?

The craving void, the aching heart,
The objectless existence,
Where health and strength make no resistance.
Hast thou, when twilight's come . . .

45. Richard Beale Davis, "The Early American Lawyer and the Profession of Letters," in *Literature and Society in Early Virginia, 1608–1840* (Baton Rouge, La., 1973), 290–91; "Stephen Elliott," Charleston *Courier,* 30 March 1840.

46. Legaré to F.W. Gilmer, 24 Aug. 1816, Gilmer Papers, University of Virginia; James S. Gilliam, "Journal kept . . . during a tour through some of the Northern states," 42, Virginia State Library, Richmond.

47. Legaré to Gilmer, 1 Oct. 1816, Gilmer Papers, University of Virginia.

48. Mary Legaré, "Memoir," 12, 22; Carroll, "Sketch," 359. Preston, *Eulogy,* 25, notes that Legaré "accumulated an immense mass of common-place books," no longer extant, except for some notes from 1822 upon Mosheim's *Ecclesiastical History* and Grotius' *De Jure Belli et Pacis,* and an earlier set on Roman history.

49. Anna Wells Rutledge, *Artists in the Life of Charleston,* 2d ed. (Columbia, S.C., 1980), 151, 159, 240; the inscription of Eliza Legaré Bryan's tomb is reproduced in *SCHM* 29 (Oct. 1928): 312–13; Mary Legaré, "Memoir," 22.

50. Johnston, in *Writings,* I, xxxviii.

51. Davis, "Early American Lawyer," 290.

52. Legaré to mother, 24 June 1818, in *Writings,* I, xxxix–xli; Preston, *Eulogy,* 9–10; Mary Legaré, "Memoir," 14; Legaré to Henry Middleton, 25 March 1835, in *Writings,* I, 230.

53. *The Reminiscences of William C. Preston,* ed. M.C. Yarborough (Chapel Hill, N.C., 1933), 43–50; Washington Irving, *Journals and Notebooks,* ed. Walter A. Reichart and Lillian Schlissel (Boston, 1981), II, 92–162.

54. *Reminiscences of Preston,* 53–65; cf. Elizabeth Suddaby and P.J. Yarrow, eds., *Lady Morgan in France* (Newcastle, 1971), 149–94.

55. Preston, *Eulogy,* 10; fragment of a letter [1819?]; Carroll, "Sketch," 358.

56. *Reminiscences of Preston,* 65–66; Legaré to sister, 4 Aug. 1833.

57. Mary Legaré, "Memoir," 19.

58. The best introduction is A.J. Youngson, *The Making of Classical Edinburgh, 1750–1840* (Edinburgh, 1966).

59. D.B. Horn, *A Short History of the University of Edinburgh, 1556–1889* (Edinburgh, 1967), 121–32, 109, 107.

60. [J.G. Lockhart] *Peter's Letters to His Kinsfolk,* 3rd. ed. (Edinburgh, 1819), I, 191, 196–97.

61. Charles Coulston Gillespie, *Genesis and Geology* (Cambridge, Mass., 1951), 73–79; Henry Cockburn, *Memorials of His Time,* ed. K.F.C. Miller (Chicago, 1974), 256, 338–39; Legaré, "Classical Learning," 36: this tribute is virtually identical in language to those Legaré tendered to Serra and Stephen Elliott.

62. "Sir John Leslie," *Dictionary of National Biography,* ed. S. Lee (London, 1909), XI, 984–86; Preston to M. O'Connor, 4 Dec. 1818, Preston Papers, SCL.

63. Legaré to sister, Christmas Day 1818; Washington Irving to Preston, 13 July 1852, in Irving, *Letters,* ed. R.M. Alderman et al. (Boston, 1982), IV, 312; Sir Alexander Grant, *The Story of the University of Edinburgh* (London, 1884), II, 366. Preston misremembers this Irving as David Irving, the biographer of George Buchanan, though—as the *DNB* notes that Irving took in private pupils in the civil law—there is a slim chance that Preston is right.

64. Peter Stein, "Law and Society in Eighteenth-Century Scottish Thought," in N.T. Phillipson and Rosalind Mitchison, eds., *Scotland in the Age of Improvement* (Edinburgh, 1970), 148–68; Douglas Young, *Edinburgh in the Age of Sir Walter Scott* (Norman, Okla., 1965), 47, 49.

65. Patrick Scott, "Two South Carolinians in Scotland," 5, makes this useful point: this unpublished talk to the Robert Burns Society of the [S.C.] Midlands was kindly lent by the author.

66. Preston, *Eulogy,* 12; Preston to O'Connor, 4 Dec. 1818, Preston Papers, SCL.

67. Preston, *Eulogy,* 11, 13; there is a marked lack of writing about Heineccius, but see the articles on him in the *Encyclopedia Britannica* (11th ed.) and in the *Biographie universelle: ancienne et moderne* (Paris, 1856), XIX, 59–60, both of which are based upon his son's memoir, Johann Christian Heineccius, *Memoria Ioh. Gottl. Heineccii,* which prefaces the *Omnia Opera,* and see also Duncan Forbes, *Hume's Philosophical Politics* (Cambridge, 1975), 3ff, 27, 31f, 38n, 43f, 47, 51–54, 72n; Johann Gottlieb Heineccius, *A Methodical System of Universal Law,* trans. George Turnbull (London, 1763), I, 8–11, 48–49, II, 8–17, 63–72, 86–107; Jane Rendall, *The Origins of the Scottish Enlightenment* (New York, 1978), 24–25; Walter Scott to William Clerk, 6

Aug. 1790, in *The Letters of Sir Walter Scott, 1787–1807*, ed. H.J.C. Grierson (London, 1932), 11; *Boswell in Holland, 1763–1764*, ed. F.A. Pottle (New York, 1952), 49.

68. Dugald Stewart, *Dissertation: Exhibiting the Progress of Metaphysical, Ethical and Political Philosophy*, ed. Sir William Hamilton (Edinburgh, 1854), 448–49; Stewart was in Devon for his health during Legaré's time in Edinburgh.

69. Preston, *Eulogy*, 11; Preston to O'Connor, 4 Dec. 1818, Preston Papers; Cockburn, *Memorials*, 259–60; Andrew Hook, *Scotland and America: A Study in Cultural Relations, 1750–1835* (Glasgow, 1975), 185–93, 222.

70. *Reminiscences of Preston*, 96–102, 129; Hillard, *Life of Ticknor*, I, 162–74, 273–82.

71. Preston, *Eulogy*, 13; George Shepperson, ed., "Thomas Chalmers, The Free Church of Scotland, and the South," *Journal of Southern History* 17 (Nov. 1951): 517–37; Alexander Munro, quoted in John Clive, "The Social Background of the Scottish Renaissance," in Phillipson and Mitchison, *Scotland*, 232. Legaré was later to censure his sister Mary as "so very exclusive and even *bigoted* a Presbyterian" (Legaré to sister, 4 Aug. 1833).

72. Carroll, "Sketch," 351; Lockhart, *Peter's Letters*, III, 267–73.

73. Legaré, "German Diaries," 110; Legaré to mother, n.d. [1819].

74. Hillard, *Life of Ticknor*, I, 281–82; Youngson, *Classical Edinburgh*, 235–56; Lockhart, *Peter's Letters*, I, 268; ibid., II, 196–97, 174–94.

75. Legaré to mother, 15 Feb. 1819, in *Writings*, I, xlviii; Irving to Preston, 13 July 1852, in Irving, *Letters IV*, 312; Legaré, "Lord Byron's Character and Writings," 358–59. Legaré was distantly related to Scott, whose maternal grandmother's sister was a Mrs. Margaret Swinton: see J.G. Lockhart, *Memoirs of the Life of Sir Walter Scott, Bart.*, abridged ed. (London, 1888), 445.

76. Nathan Sargent, *Public Men and Events* (Philadelphia, 1875), II, 87, only mentions "a Greek professor from Oxford," whom I take to be Gaisford (see *Dictionary of National Biography*, VII, 810–12, and Hugh Lloyd-Jones, *Blood for the Ghosts: Classical Influences in the Nineteenth and Twentieth Centuries* [London, 1982], 81–102); Legaré to mother, n.d. [1819]. The Archbishop is not named by Legaré but can be identified in William Jowett, *Christian Researches in Syria and the Holy Land in 1823 and 1824* (London, 1825), 23, 105, and in the *New Catholic Encyclopedia* (New York, 1967), XIII, 902. Jarweh went on in

1820 to assume the Patriarchate as Peter Ignatius VII, and his reign until 1851 saw a mitigation of the struggle between Jacobites and Catholics.

77. Legaré to mother, 30 June 1819; fragment of an 1819 journal.

78. John Tyler, "The Dead of the Cabinet," *Southern Literary Messenger* 23 (Aug. 1856): 81–84.

79. Legaré to Judith Rives, 26 April 1833, Rives Papers, LC.

## 2. POLITICS

1. Johnston, in *Writings,* I, li; Legaré "Roman Literature," 96, 97; Legaré to Henry Middleton, 23 June 1820, Middleton MSS, SCHS. Under the terms of Thomas Legaré's will, Legaré was entitled (with due compensation to his sisters) to sell that portion kept in trust for Solomon Legaré's children: that is, "that part of the plantation or tract of land which I bought from the heirs of John Raven Mathewes not herein before given to my daughter Mary" (Will of Thomas Legaré, 9 Sept. 1798, Charleston Wills, S.C. State Archives).

2. Johnston, in *Writings,* I, liii–lv; Legaré to Jesse B. Harrison, 2 April 1829, Harrison Papers, LC; Story, "Tribute."

3. Christophersen, "Legaré," 113–14.

4. Legaré, "Roman Orators," 532; Wilbur Samuel Howell, *Eighteenth-Century British Logic and Rhetoric* (Princeton, N.J., 1971), 549; Hugh Blair, *Lectures on Rhetoric and Belles Lettres,* 14th Amer. ed. (New York, 1826), 271.

5. Legaré, "Crafts' Fugitive Writings," 157; Legaré, "Roman Orators," 510; Legaré, "Classical Learning," 10; Nott to Legaré, 7 May 1831, Nott Papers, SCL. The only extant draft of a Legaré essay, that on "Roman Literature," shows that he took his own advice about careful revision.

6. Christophersen, "Legaré," 390–449, is useful on Legaré's forensic style; Charleston *Courier,* 20 Jan. 1842; Story, "Tribute"; Carroll, "Sketch," 348.

7. Carroll, "Sketch," 349.

8. Rhea, *Charleston Intellectual,* 84–85. Merrill G. Christophersen, "The Earliest Law School in the South," *South Carolina Law Quarterly* 7 (1955): 375–78, claims the Forensic Club was an abortive law school.

9. Johnston, in *Writings,* I, li; 1820s map of John's Island by Kinsey Burden [Legaré's uncle], Maps and Muniments, SCHS; Mary Legaré, "Memoir," 31; William W. Freehling, *Prelude to Civil War:*

*The Nullification Controversy in South Carolina, 1816–1836* (New York, 1965), 1–133; on Hamilton, cf. Legaré, "Official Defalcations," 345, and "The American System," 234; Nott to Legaré, 7 May 1831, Nott Papers, SCL.

10. Christophersen, "Legaré," 101–04; Camden *Journal,* 6 Sept. 1828; Freehling, *Prelude,* 144–47.

11. Freehling, *Prelude,* 145–46; *Southern Patriot,* Oct. 2–5, 1821; Legaré's authorship is attested by James Hamilton, in a letter to the Charleston *Courier,* 23 Aug. 1830.

12. Christophersen, "Legaré," 114; Petigru to Legaré, 1 Aug. 1834, reprinted in Carson, *Petigru,* 156; Legaré, "Classical Learning," 7; Legaré to Jesse B. Harrison, 3 Nov. 1828, Harrison Papers, LC; Legaré, "Cicero de Republica," 231–32; George C. Rogers, Jr., "South Carolina Federalists and the Origins of the Nullification Movement," *SCHM* 71 (Jan. 1970): 28.

13. Legaré, "Oration of 1823," 257–59.

14. Ibid., 259–60. Cf. "Conciliation with America," in *Burke: Select Works,* ed. E.J. Payne (Oxford, 1876), I, 183; the reader will recognize here the faint outline of the argument in Bernard Bailyn, *The Ideological Origins of the American Revolution* (Cambridge, Mass., 1967), itself neo-Whiggish.

15. Legaré, "Oration of 1823," 260–63. Like most Charlestonians, Legaré was influenced by the interpretations of David Ramsay.

16. Ibid., 263–69.

17. Ibid., 269; Legaré, "Classical Learning," 11; Legaré to mother, 9 Sept. 1834; "The Spirit of the Sub-Treasury," 284–85. Cf. William R. Taylor, *Cavalier and Yankee: The Old South and American National Character* (New York, 1961), 98–99, on the typicality of such sentiments in the 1820s.

18. John Oliver Killens, ed., *The Trial Record of Denmark Vesey* (Boston, 1970); Freehling, *Prelude,* 53–61; Federal Census of 1820, South Carolina, Charleston District, 33 (naturally, the number may have shifted by 1822).

19. Philip M. Hamer, "Great Britain, the United States, and the Negro Seamen Acts, 1822–1848," *Journal of Southern History* 1 (Feb. 1935): 3–28; Donald G. Morgan, *Justice William Johnson: The First Dissenter* (Columbia, S.C., 1954), 192–202.

20. Christophersen, "Legaré," 123–28; Legaré to Isaac Holmes, 8 April 1833, in *Writings,* I, 215; Legaré to sister, 14 Aug. 1834, in *Writings,* I, 254; "Elkison's Case" MS, SCL.

21. "Elkison's Case" MS, SCL.

22. Hamer, "Negro Seamen Acts," 11–28.

23. Freehling, *Prelude,* 116–21; Christophersen, "Legaré," 149–52.

24. Freehling, *Prelude,* 115–19; Alfred Huger to Joel R. Poinsett, 24 Nov. 1825, Poinsett Papers, PHS.

25. Quoted in Robert J. Turnbull, *The Crisis* (Charleston, S.C. 1827), 72.

26. Legaré to Eliza Bryan, 1 Aug. 1834; Christophersen, "Legaré," 158.

27. Jacob Cardozo, *Reminiscences of Charleston* (Charleston, S.C., 1866), 36.

28. Reprinted in Rhea, *Charleston Intellectual,* 236–38.

29. James Moultrie, Jr., *An Eulogium on Stephen Elliott, M.D. & LL.D.* (Charleston, S.C., 1830); "Stephen Elliott," Charleston *Courier,* 30 March 1840.

30. David Ramsay, *The History of the American Revolution* (Philadelphia, 1789), *The History of the Revolution of South-Carolina, from a British Province to an Independent State* (Trenton, N.J., 1785), *The History of South-Carolina* (Charleston, S.C., 1809); Stephen Elliott, *A Sketch of the Botany of South Carolina and Georgia* (Charleston, S.C., 1821–24); *Miscellaneous Writings of the Late William Crafts* (Charleston, S.C., 1828); Thomas Bee, *Omnium Gatherum* (Charleston, S.C., 1821), rebuked in *Omnium Botherum* (Charleston, S.C., 1821) and remembered in S.G. Stoney, ed., "The Memoirs of Frederick Adolphus Porcher," *SCHM* 47 (Jan. 1946): 45–46.

31. His remark, "They have succeeded here in harnessing me to their Review," suggests Legaré was drawn into the venture latterly (Legaré to Jesse B. Harrison, 3 Nov. 1828).

32. On Kennedy, see Legaré to Rives, 29 Oct. 1839, Rives Papers, LC.

33. Charleston *Courier,* 17 Aug. and 22 Oct. 1840. He did once toy with joining Frederick Grimké in Ohio (Legaré to mother, 24 Dec. 1838), but disdain for the West was more characteristic: see Legaré to mother, 21 Sept. 1835, in which he observes, "As to the Western country, it has grown up much too fast for its own good, or for ours, & nothing surprises me that happens there in the way of murder & violence."

34. Legaré to Rives, 14 April 1841, Rives Papers, LC: "As another clever impostor we had here by name Michaelowitz said pungently enough of Dr. Cooper & his universal attainments—on somebody asking what was C's *fort*—'I don't know exactly, replied M—but I

suppose it is *politics,* for I know nothing about that'"; on McCord, see
Legaré to sister, 15 April 1835.

35. "Origin of Trial by Jury," *Southern Quarterly Review* 6 (July
1844): 251; Holmes to Daniel K. Whitaker, 19 Sept. 1843, Holmes
Papers, LC, is an emotional defense of Legaré, which Holmes drafted
but never sent; Francis Lieber to Madame Françoise Lieber, 13 Oct.
1839, Lieber Papers, SCL, suggests translating Legaré's "Origin of
Roman Legislation" into German; "A Fable for Critics," in *Edgar
Allan Poe: Essays and Reviews*, ed. G.R. Thompson (New York, 1984),
819; Hayne, "Legaré", 134-35.

36. Cf. Joseph J. Ellis, *After the Revolution: Profiles of Early American
Culture* (New York, 1979); Lawrence Friedman, *Inventors of the Prom-
ised Land* (New York, 1975); and Arthur H. Shaffer, *The Politics of
History: Writing the History of the American Revolution, 1783-1815*
(Chicago, 1975).

37. Peter Stein, "The Attraction of the Civil Law in Post-Revolu-
tionary America," *Virginia Law Review* 52 (April 1966): 403-34,
discusses Legaré.

38. I have expanded upon this in "Politics, Romanticism and
Hugh Legaré: 'The Fondness of Disappointed Love,'" in O'Brien and
Moltke-Hansen, eds., *Intellectual Life in Antebellum Charleston.*

39. Legaré to Judith Rives, 22 June 1839, Rives Papers, LC.


3. MANNER

1. Legaré to Rives, 3 Dec. 1840, Rives Papers, LC, when Legaré
was recommending Johnston for a professorship at the University of
Virginia, observes, "I know him pretty well—& esteem his talents
highly. He writes *very* cleverly, as I judge from an article he gave us for
the So. Review—in the Scriblerian vein—& some other things. He
has a passion for letters & a capacity for them, which I think will carry
him far." See [Johnston], "American Literature," *SR* 7 (Aug. 1831):
436-59. The original plan was for the volume to be prefaced with
sketches of Legaré by various hands: Preston on the early life, Mitchell
King on the Charleston bar, George Bryan on state politics, Stephen
Elliott, Jr., on the writings, and Rives on the later diplomatic and
national career. Later, Mary Legaré thought of asking "Trescot,"
presumably William Henry Trescot, to write the biographical sketch
but seems to have been talked into Johnston by Preston (Johnston was
Preston's cousin: see E.W. Johnston to Preston, 26 May 1841, Preston
Family Papers, Virginia Historical Society). It is likely that Johnston

drew upon fragments gathered under the auspices of the first plan. See Mary Legaré to Rives, 6 Dec. 1844, Rives Papers, LC; Preston to Mary Legaré, 25 Nov. 1844, Preston Papers, SCL; Mary Legaré to P.H. Hayne, 27 July 1878, Hayne Papers, Duke University.

2. On this, see Legaré, "German Diaries," in O'Brien, ed., *All Clever Men*, 89–124; Mary Legaré was later to say she had little hand in the editing and, if she had, would have suppressed the Brussels Diary; Mary Legaré to P.H. Hayne, 27 July 1878, Hayne Papers, Duke.

3. John W. Rooney, Jr., *Belgian-American Diplomatic and Consular Relations, 1830–1850* (Louvain, 1969), 45.

4. Mary Legaré to Hayne, n.d. [1878], Hayne Papers, Duke. Preston did suggest the inclusion of some of the opinions: Preston to Mary Legaré, 25 Nov. 1844, Preston Papers, SCL. However, Volume II was published in 1845, Volume I in 1846.

5. Hayne, "Legaré," 156.

6. "Note by the Publishers," in *Writings*, I, 101; Legaré to Judith Rives, 26 April 1833, Rives Papers, LC; MS on John Quincy Adams; Legaré to Gouverneur Kemble, 21 Dec. 1839; Legaré to Joseph Story, 7 March 1842, Story Papers, Clements Library, University of Michigan; Legaré to Jesse B. Harrison, 2 April 1829, Harrison Papers, LC.

7. Legaré, "Classical Learning," 17; his commentary on ancient historians is later to be found in Legaré, "Constitutional History of Greece," 380ff; Legaré, "Hall's Travels," 254.

8. Legaré, "The Disowned," 215; "Jeremy Bentham," 481.

9. Legaré, "Cicero de Republica," 224; Legaré, "Hall's Travels," 275.

10. Legaré, "The Fair Maid of Perth," 216–17.

11. Legaré, "Hall's Travels," 267.

12. Legaré, "Classical Learning," 51; Legaré, "Crafts' Fugitive Writings," 164; Legaré to Alfred Huger, 21 Nov. 1835, in *Writings*, I, 224.

13. Legaré to mother, 22 Dec. 1832, notes that he had declined Auguste d'Arenberg's offer to translate a Legaré essay into French for publication, though he did once toy with republishing some of his essays in England, as an experiment to gauge the validity of praise from his English friends in Brussels: (Legaré to [mother?], Feb. 1834; Legaré to mother, 4 Nov. 1832). But he does seem to have been pleased at the thought that his classical scholarship might have found favor in Germany: Legaré to Jesse B. Harrison, 26 Aug. 1830, Harrison Papers, LC, notes, "by the bye, that gentlemen [Edward Michaelowitz of the South Carolina College] mentioned to me what

was so flattering to my self-love, that I can scarcely deem it true—which is, that Professor Schutz (is it?) of Heidelberg had done me the honor of alluding to some opinions of mine advanced in an article on 'Roman Literature'. . . . in very favorable terms. I think there must be some mistake about it, as it exceeds all credibility that a German professor of eminent learning should see any thing to admire in the speculations of a 'young lawyer' in So. Carolina."

14. Legaré, "Hall's Travels," 255. Legaré was so reticent on his first trip to Europe that one suspects sensitivity about his deformity was especially inhibiting; by the 1830s he had grown more assured, but he shared the gentlemanly pride that had led Preston to decline a chance to attend Byron's Venetian levees, as well as the curiosity that made Preston notice the poet passing in his gondola.

15. Legaré to Jesse B. Harrison, 3 Nov. 1828; Legaré, "Hall's Travels," 254; Legaré, "Roman Literature," 83; Legaré, "Jeremy Bentham," 449–50; Legaré, "Lord Byron's Character and Writings," 357; Legare, "Siamese Twins," 192; Legaré, "Cicero de Republica," 242.

16. Legaré, "Demosthenes," 477; Legaré, "Roman Literature," 101; Legaré, "Cicero de Republica," 244.

17. Legaré, "Jeremy Bentham," 448–62; Legaré, "Saxe-Weimar," 170; Legaré, "Classical Learning," 30; Legaré, "Jeremy Bentham," 465. Philadelphia *Ledger,* 22 June 1843 (clipping in the W.G. Chisholm Papers, SCL) notes that "irony was his great forte, but he was less successful with repartee, and still less fortunate in reading character."

18. Legaré, "Byron's Letters and Journals," 425; Legaré, "Classical Learning," 51, 25.

19. Legaré, "Crafts' Fugitive Writings," 150; Legaré, "The Public Economy of Athens," 522.

20. Legaré, "Classical Learning," 14.

21. Legaré, "Lord Byron's Character and Writings," 410; Legaré, "German Diaries," 107; Legaré to Alfred Huger, 15 Dec. 1834, in *Writings,* I, 218.

22. Legaré, "Kent's Commentaries," 134; Legaré, "Hall's Travels," 284; Legaré, "Roman Literature," 97; Legaré to Jesse B. Harrison, 3 Nov. 1828.

23. Legaré, "Classical Learning," 40, 31, 32, 33; Legaré, "Hoffman's Legal Outlines," 54.

24. Legaré, "Jeremy Bentham," 465–66, 479; Legaré, "Classical Learning," 44–45, 31; cf. Thomas Jefferson to William Short, 31

Oct. 1819, on the philosophy of Epicurus, reprinted in *The Portable Thomas Jefferson*, ed. Merrill D. Peterson (New York, 1975), 564–67; see also, on Jefferson and Scottish philosophy, Garry Wills, *Inventing America: Jefferson's Declaration of Independence* (New York, 1978), and Henry F. May, *The Enlightenment in America* (New York, 1976).

25. Richard Foster Jones, *Ancients and Moderns: A Study of the Rise of the Scientific Movement in Seventeenth-Century England*, 2d ed. (St. Louis, 1961); Legaré, "Classical Learning," 29, 9.

26. Legaré, "Jeremy Bentham," 463.

27. Legaré to Jesse B. Harrison, 12 March 1832, Harrison Papers, LC: he especially liked Channing's essay on Napoleon, reprinted in *The Works of William E. Channing, D.D.* (Boston, 1881), 522–59; Legaré, "Cicero de Republica," 244; Legaré, "Classical Learning," 49.

28. Legaré, "Classical Learning," 42; Legaré, "Kent's Commentaries," 107–09; Nicholas T. Phillipson, "Culture and Society in the 18th Century Province: The Case of Edinburgh and the Scottish Enlightenment," in Lawrence Stone, ed., *The University in Society* (Princeton, N.J., 1974), II, 407–48; Rendall, *Origins of the Scottish Enlightenment*, 24–25; Leonard Krieger, *The Politics of Discretion: Pufendorf and the Acceptance of Natural Law* (Chicago, 1965), 258.

29. Legaré, "Law of Tenures," 18; Legaré, "Classical Learning," 41–42; Gladys Bryson, *Man and Society: The Scottish Inquiry of the Eighteenth Century* (Princeton, N.J. 1945), 85–86, 106; Donald R. Kelley, *Foundations of Modern Historical Scholarship: Language, Law, and History in the French Renaissance* (New York, 1970); cf. Legaré, "Roman Literature," 67, with "Origin of Roman Legislation," 504–08.

30. Legaré, "Roman Literature," 54; Legaré, "The Public Economy of Athens," 503; Legaré, "Cicero de Republica," 242; Legaré, "Law of Tenures," 19.

31. Legaré, "Hall's Travels," 268; Legaré, "Lord Byron's Character and Writings," 390–91.

32. Legaré "Classical Learning," 22, 24, 25.

33. Ibid., 33–34, 8, 30–31; Legaré, "Jeremy Bentham," 469; M.H. Abrams, *Natural Supernaturalism: Tradition and Revolution in Romantic Literature* (New York, 1971), passim; Legaré to mother, 9 Sept. 1834, confesses a lack of religious instinct; Alexander Everett to wife, 25 June 1840, Everett Papers, Massachusetts Historical Society (I am grateful to Jane and William Pease for bringing this letter to my attention).

34. Legaré to Thomas White, 10 May 1838.

35. Legaré, "D'Aguesseau," 591; Legaré, "Cicero de Republica," 253.

36. August von Schlegel, "Abriss von den europäischen Verhältnissen der deutschen Literatur," quoted in René Wellek, *A History of Modern Criticism: 1750–1950* (New Haven, Conn., 1955), II, 38; Legaré "Saxe-Weimar," 168; Legaré, "Early Spanish Ballads," 299–300; Bryson, *Man and Society,* 78–113.

37. Legaré, "Classical Learning," 32, 48; Legaré, "Hoffman's Legal Outlines," 49–58; Bryson, *Man and Society,* 53–77; cf. Josiah C. Nott, *Two Lectures on the Natural History of the Causasian and Negro Races* (Mobile, Ala., 1844), with Legaré's amusement at Monboddo on the Etruscans in "Roman Literature," 61.

38. Legaré, "Byron's Letters and Journals," 426–28.

39. Ibid., 428–29.

40. Ibid., 430–31; Wellek, *History of Modern Criticism,* II, 59.

41. Legaré, "Byron's Letters and Journals," 431–32.

42. Ibid., 432–33.

43. Ibid., 435, 440.

44. Ibid., 439, 441–42.

45. Ibid., 443, 437; Legaré, "Lord Byron's Character and Writings," 380; cf. Adam Smith, *The Theory of Moral Sentiments,* 10th ed. (London, 1804), I, 33.

## 4. ANTIQUITY

1. On the general subject of American classicism, see John W. Eadie, ed., *Classical Traditions in Early America* (Ann Arbor, Mich., 1976); Meyer Reinhold, ed., *The Classick Pages: Classical Reading of Eighteenth-Century Americans* (University Park, Pa., 1975); H. Trevor Colbourn, *The Lamp of Experience: Whig History and the Intellectual Origins of the American Revolution* (Chapel Hill, N.C., 1965); Meyer Reinhold, *Classica Americana: The Greek and Roman Heritage in the United States* (Detroit, 1984). See also "Ancient History and the Antiquarian" and "Gibbon's Contribution to Historical Method," in Arnaldo Momigliano, *Studies in Historiography* (London, 1966), 1–55.

2. Legaré, "Hall's Travels," 277; Charles Cotesworth Pinckney, *Life of General Thomas Pinckney* (Boston, 1895), 23, 218, 222–25.

3. Legaré, "Classical Learning," 15, 7; Legaré, "Cicero de Republica," 217–18; on the other hand, like Basil Gildersleeve later, Legaré could be harsh on the general standard of Northern scholarship: "The Irvings & Coopers and Percivals & id omne genus . . . won't do. . . . I think very little *entre nous* of those Northern smatterers": Legaré to Jesse B. Harrison, 3 Nov. 1828: cf. Gildersleeve, "The Necessity of

the Classics," in Michael O'Brien, ed., *All Clever Men, Who Make Their Way* (Fayetteville, Ark., 1982), 417–19.

4. Carl Diehl, *Americans and German Scholarship, 1770–1870* (New Haven, Conn., 1978), 49–100; Jesse Burton Harrison, "English Civilization," in O'Brien, ed., *All Clever Men,* 79–88; U. von Wilamowitz-Moellendorff, *History of Classical Scholarship,* trans. A. Harris (Baltimore, Md., 1982), 108.

5. Diehl, *Americans and German Scholarship,* 6–27; John Edwin Sandys, *A History of Classical Scholarship* (Cambridge, 1906–08), III, 7, 32.

6. Legaré, "The Public Economy of Athens," 503, 502, 504.

7. Charles E. McClelland, *State, Society, and University in Germany, 1700–1914* (Cambridge, 1980), 101–49; Thomas S. Grimké, *An Address on the Character and Objects of Science* (Charleston, S.C., 1827). For other contemporary defenses, cf. *Selected Writings of Sydney Smith,* ed. W.H. Auden (New York, 1956), 258–71, and George Bancroft, "The Utility of Classical Learning," *North American Review* 19 (July, 1824): 125–37.

8. Legaré, "Classical Learning," 8, 22–50.

9. Bryson, *Man and Society,* 91; Legaré, "Classical Learning," 40–41; W.H. Bruford, *Culture and Society in Classical Weimar, 1775–1806* (Cambridge, 1962), 389–425; Leonard Krieger, *Ranke: The Meaning of History* (Chicago, 1977), 1–31.

10. Bryson, *Man and Society,* 41–52; Isaiah Berlin, *Vico and Herder: Two Studies in the History of Ideas* (New York, 1976), 150; Legaré, "Early Spanish Ballads," 320–21; Abrams, *Natural Supernaturalism,* 141–312. For an application of this pattern to Walter Scott, who mingled Ferguson and romanticism, see Avrom Fleishman, *The English Historical Novel: Walter Scott to Virginia Woolf* (Baltimore, Md., 1971), 37–101.

11. Legaré, "Classical Learning," 29; Legaré, "Early Spanish Ballads," 322; Legaré, "Roman Literature," 52–55, 84–85; Legaré, "Byron's Letters and Journals," 424.

12. Richard Lounsbury, *"Ludibria Rerum Mortalium:* Charlestonian Intellectuals and Their Classics," in O'Brien and Moltke-Hansen, eds., *Intellectual Life in Antebellum Charleston*; the tradition of comparing Demosthenes and Cicero was as old as Plutarch and as recent as Hugh Blair, but Legaré confessed that "no comparison of them that I have ever seen having satisfied me, I thought I might as well come out with my own view of their styles & merits" (Legaré to Jesse B. Harrison, 3 Nov. 1828).

13. Legaré, "Classical Learning," 24, 43, 44.

14. The generation of 1776, on the other hand, disliked Athens and tended to prefer Sparta: see Meyer Reinhold, "Eighteenth-Century American Political Thought," in R.R. Bolgar, ed., *Classical Influences on Western Thought, A.D. 1650–1870* (Cambridge, 1979), 228.

15. Legaré, "Classical Learning," 46–47; Legaré, "Roman Literature," 57.

16. Legaré, "Roman Orators," 520–22.

17. Legaré, "Roman Literature," 52–54, 77–78; Howell, *Eighteenth-Century British Logic and Rhetoric,* 440–691.

18. Legaré, "Roman Orators," 527–31.

19. Ibid., 532–33, 537–38.

20. Johann Gottfried von Herder, *Reflections on the Philosophy of the History of Mankind,* ed. Frank E. Manuel (Chicago, 1968), 177–79; Legaré, "Cicero de Republica," 244–50.

21. Legaré, "Cicero de Republica," 250–52; Legaré, "The Public Economy of Athens," 528; cf. William Sumner Jenkins, *Pro-Slavery Thought in the Old South* (Chapel Hill, N.C., 1935), 137, and Thomas Dew, "Republicanism and Literature," in O'Brien, ed., *All Clever Men,* 164–70.

22. Legaré, "The Public Economy of Athens," 517–18; Freehling, *Prelude,* 219–59.

23. Legaré, "The Public Economy of Athens," 557.

24. Legaré, "Roman Literature," 100–101; Legaré, "Jeremy Bentham," 463.

25. Legaré, "Jeremy Bentham," 464, 472–74, 476–77; Legaré, "Cicero de Republica," 235, 240. Nonetheless, Legaré spent much of the summer of 1829 reading through Plato with the aid of Dietrich Tiedemann's edition, *Dialogorum Platonis argumenta, exposita et illustrata* (Biponti, 1786), though this does not justify the puzzling belief of George Frederick Holmes and Edward Everett that Plato was Legaré's "favorite": Legaré to Jesse B. Harrison, 26 Aug. 1830, Harrison Papers, LC; Holmes, "Writings of Legaré," 338; Everett, "Remarks on the Death of Legaré," clipping, New York *Evening Post* [1843].

26. Legaré, "Roman Literature," 77–80.

27. Ibid., 84.

28. G.P. Gooch, *History and Historians in the Nineteenth Century,* rev. ed. (London, 1952), 14–23, 43–49; Berlin, *Vico and Herder,* 158–61; J.G.A. Pocock, *The Machiavellian Moment: Florentine Political*

*Thought and the Atlantic Republican Tradition* (Princeton, N.J., 1975), esp. 333–552.

29. Legaré, "Roman Literature," 55–57.

30. Ibid., 60–93.

31. Ibid., 93–95.

32. Ibid., 96–97.

33. Ibid., 101, 73; Legaré, "Lord Byron's Character and Writings," 408; Legaré, "Cicero de Republica," 233–34, 242. The judgment of "tous ces garçons là" is apparently taken from Scaliger: cf. Basil L. Gildersleeve, *Essays and Studies: Educational and Literary* (Baltimore, Md., 1890), 8.

34. Legaré, "Cicero de Republica," 242–44.

35. Ibid., 244–53.

36. Legaré, "Roman Orators," 493.

37. Ibid., 524–25, 527–40, 510.

38. Ibid., 514; Legaré, "Cicero de Republica," 229–31.

## 5. BELLES LETTRES

1. Legaré, "Early Spanish Ballads," 300, 304; Legaré, "Roman Literature," 55.

2. Legaré to Lady Colleton, 19 June 1830, Colleton Family MSS, SCL; Legaré, "Early Spanish Ballads," 333, 317–18, 313–14.

3. Legaré, "Roman Literature," 57–58.

4. Legaré, "Early Spanish Ballads," 300.

5. Beatrice Corrigan, ed., *Italian Poets and English Critics, 1755–1859* (Chicago, 1969), 1–31; Legaré, "Sir Philip Sidney's Miscellanies," 349; Legaré, "Classical Learning," 37.

6. Legare, "Sir Philip Sidney's Miscellanies," 349–50.

7. Ibid., 349; Legaré, "The Disowned," 187; Legaré, "Pollok's Course of Time," 456.

8. Legaré, "Early Spanish Ballads," 303, 304–305; Legaré, "Sir Philip Sidney's Miscellanies," 337–38.

9. Legaré, "Sir Philip Sidney's Miscellanies," 335, 336, 350.

10. Ibid., 338–39.

11. Ibid., 339–41.

12. Legaré, "The Siamese Twins," 196; Legaré to sister, 16–17 May 1835; Legaré, "Lord Byron's Character and Writings," 410; Legaré, "Classical Learning," 44.

13. Legaré, "Classical Learning," 34.

14. Frederick Porcher, "Modern Art," in O'Brien, ed., *All Clever*

*Men,* 317; Legaré, "Pollok's Course of Time," 456, 457; Legaré, "Lord Byron's Character and Writings," 407; Legaré, "Hall's Travels," 265. On the subject of Milton's reputation, see Joseph A. Wittreich, Jr., ed., *The Romantics on Milton* (Cleveland, 1970), and Marilyn Butler, *Romantics, Rebels, and Reactionaries: English Literature and Its Background, 1760–1830* (New York, 1982), 122.

15. Legaré, "Lord Byron's Character and Writings," 384; Wellek, *History of Modern Criticism,* II, 252–58, 29; Legaré, "Roman Literature," 77–78, 84; Legaré, "The Siamese Twins," 196; Legaré, "The Omnipresence of the Deity," 292; Legaré, "Pollok's Course of Time," 454; Legaré, "D'Aguesseau," 597.

16. Legaré to Thomas White, 10 May 1838; Legaré, "Hoffman's Legal Outlines," 58; Legaré, "Classical Learning," 19; Legaré, "Lord Byron's Character and Writings," 408; Legaré to sister, 28 March 1836; Legaré to C.R. King, 9 Feb. 1838.

17. Legaré, "D'Aguesseau," 584; Legaré, "Cicero de Republica," 253.

18. Legaré, "Lord Byron's Character and Writings," 408, 363; Legaré, "Roman Literature," 77; Legaré, "Byron's Letters and Journals," 419, 435; Legaré, "Roman Orators," 525; Legaré, "German Diaries," 115; Legaré, "Classical Learning," 39.

19. Legaré, "Classical Learning," 31; Legaré, "The Disowned," 206, 204; Legaré, "D'Aguesseau," 579; Legaré, "Sir Philip Sidney's Miscellanies," 335; Legaré, "Pollok's Course of Time", 458, 459.

20. Cf. John D. Hart, *The Oxford Companion to American Literature,* 4th ed. (New York, 1965), 466–67, and John R. Welsh, "An Early Pioneer: Legaré's *Southern Review,*" *Southern Literary Journal* 3 (Spring 1971): 83; Legaré, "German Diaries," 115.

21. Legaré, "Constitutional History of Greece," 394; Legaré, "Sir Philip Sidney's Miscellanies," 349; Legaré, "Roman Literature," 61; Legaré, "Cicero de Republica," 226, 251; Legaré, "Codification," 489; Legaré, "Origin of Roman Legislation," 509, 542; Legaré, "Roman Orators," 519; Legaré's "Early Spanish Ballads," 315.

22. Legaré, "Byron's Letters and Journals," 435–36; "Roman Literature," 70; Wellek, *History of Modern Criticism,* II, 216; Legaré, "Lord Byron's Character and Writings," 387–88, 391–92.

23. Legaré, "Lord Byron's Character and Writings," 358–59; Legaré, "The Fair Maid of Perth," 216–17. Cf. Rollin G. Osterweis, *Romanticism and Nationalism in the Old South* (New Haven, Conn.) 1949), 41–53.

24. Legaré, "Lord Byron's Character and Writings," 373–75;

Legaré, "The Fair Maid of Perth," 241; Walter Scott, *The Black Dwarf* (London, 1897), ix and passim; cf. Robert C. Gordon's view in *"The Bride of Lammermoor: A Novel of Tory Pessimism,"* in D.D. Devlin, ed., *Walter Scott: Modern Judgements* (London, 1969), 139, and Scott's own, cited in A.O.J. Cockshut, *The Achievement of Walter Scott* (New York, 1969), 19.

25. Scott, *Black Dwarf,* 111–12.

26. Byron to Murray, 9 May 1817, in *'So Late into the night': Byron's Letters and Journals,* ed. Leslie A. Marchand (Cambridge, Mass., 1976), V, 220.

27. Legaré, "Lord Byron's Character and Writings," 358.

28. Legaré, "Jeremy Bentham," 466; Legaré, "The Disowned," 187; Legaré, "Byron's Letters and Journals," 411.

29. Legaré, "Lord Byron's Character and Writings," 359–60 and passim; Legaré, "Byron's Letters and Journals," 412.

30. Legaré, "Lord Byron's Character and Writings," 359, 385, 366, 358, 410, 379.

31. "Moore's Life of Lord Byron," [*Edinburgh Review,* June 1831] in *Lord Macaulay's Essays and Lays of Ancient Rome* (London, 1889), 159; Legaré, "Lord Byron's Character and Writings," 379, 400–401, 376; Mozart was his sister Mary's favorite composer: Legaré to sister, 16–17 May 1835. An anonymous reviewer in the Charleston *Courier* (22 May 1830) was much offended by Legaré's strictures and declined to think the case for Byron's immorality proven.

32. Legaré, "Lord Byron's Character and Writings," 360, 379; Legaré, "Byron's Letters and Journals," 438.

33. Legaré, "The Disowned," passim; Legare, "The Siamese Twins," 192; Legaré, "The Disowned," 205; Legaré to Thomas White, 10 May 1838.

34. Legaré, "Kent's Commentaries," 102, 103; Legaré, "Hall's Travels," 255–56; Legaré to sister, 16–17 May 1835.

35. Legaré, "The Wept of Wish-ton-Wish," 224–26.

36. Legaré, "Crafts' Fugitive Writings," 142, 147, 149.

37. Ibid., 151, 155, 157.

38. Charleston *Courier,* 7 May 1828.

## 6. SOCIETY

1. Legaré, "German Diaries," 120.

2. Legaré, "Kent's Commentaries," 104, 114–16.

3. Legaré, "Lord Byron's Character and Writings," 376–77;

Bryson, *Man and Society,* 141–42; cf. "Virtue," in *The Works of William Paley, D.D.,* ed. E. Paley (London, 1838), III, 20–26; D.H. Meyer, *The Instructed Conscience: The Shaping of the American National Ethic* (Philadelphia, 1972), 61–86.

4. Legaré, "Hoffman's Legal Outlines," 60–61. This standpoint seems much influenced by James Dalrymple, himself indebted to Hobbes: see Peter Stein, "Law and Society in Eighteenth-Century Scottish Thought," in Phillipson and Mitchison, eds., *Scotland,* 149–50.

5. Legaré, "Kent's Commentaries," 103, 104.

6. Ibid., 110.

7. Legaré, "D'Aguesseau," 562–63; Legaré, "Codification," 487–89.

8. Legaré, "Codification," 489–90.

9. Legaré, "Roman Orators," 510; "Codification," 490.

10. Legaré, "D'Aguesseau," 586–87.

11. Legaré, "Kent's Commentaries," 107–08, 109. *Jus gentium* was, in fact, used in two senses. Less usually, as here by Legaré, quoting Gaius in the *Institutes,* it was employed "as synonym for the philosophical ius naturale, conceived as an ideal and universally valid set of precepts" (*Oxford Classical Dictionary,* ed. N.G.L. Hammond and H.H. Scullard, 2d ed., [Oxford, 1970], 559). More usually and practically, *jus gentium* referred to "those legal habits which were accepted by the Roman law as applying to, and being used by, all the people they met, whether Roman citizens or not" (John Crook, *Law and Life of Rome* [Ithaca, 1967], 29). A law open to citizens and noncitizens alike naturally evolved largely through trade; hence much of Roman commercial law was embodied in the *jus gentium.*

12. Legaré, "Kent's Commentaries," 120–22.

13. Ibid., 105, 106.

14. Legaré, "D'Aguesseau," 567, 578, 581. Legaré was not alone in his enthusiasm: cf. "Biographical Sketch of Chancellor D'Aguesseau," *Carolina Law Journal* 1 (Oct. 1830), 151–77.

15. Legaré, "D'Aguesseau," 580.

16. Ibid., 561–62.

17. Legaré, "Law of Tenures," 5–16.

18. Ibid., 16–19, 3; Legaré, "Codification," 484. Legaré's account of feudalism and Magna Carta conforms to that of David Hume in his *History of England;* on the customary skepticism of the Scots to Magna Carta, see J.W. Burrow, *A Liberal Descent: Victorian Historians and the English Past* (Cambridge, 1981), 11–35.

19. Legaré, "D'Aguesseau," 560–61; Legaré, "Kent's Commentaries," 110–11.

20. Legaré, "Codification," 491–93; Legaré, "Crafts' Fugitive Writings," 148–49.

21. Legaré, "D'Aguesseau," 587, 561.

22. Charles M. Cook, *The American Codification Movement: A Study of Antebellum Legal Reform* (Westport, Conn., 1981); Donald J. Senese, "Legal Thought in South Carolina, 1800–1860," Ph.D. diss., University of South Carolina, 1970, 78, 80, 77.

23. Legaré, "Codification," 500, 492, 494, 498.

24. Alexander Everett to wife, 25 June 1840, Everett Papers, Massachusetts Historical Society. Another was Legaré's contemporary, Frederick Grimké: cf. Grimké, *The Nature and Tendency of Free Institutions,* ed. J.W. Ward (Cambridge, Mass., 1968).

25. Legaré, "Hall's Travels," 277–79; Legaré, "Crafts' Fugitive Writings," 148; Legaré, "Classical Learning," 12; Legaré to mother, 21 July 1834.

26. Legaré, "Classical Learning," 5–6; Legaré, "Hoffman's Legal Outlines," 56; Legaré, "Saxe-Weimar," 166–67.

27. Legaré, "Kent's Commentaries," 124–25.

28. Ibid., 125–26.

29. Legaré, "Hoffman's Legal Outlines," 64–65.

30. His standpoint was much influenced by the case *Shanks et al.* v. *Dupont et al.* (3 Peters 242) that Legaré argued before the Supreme Court in 1829, which hinged upon the problem of alienage. Thomas Scott of South Carolina had died intestate in 1782, leaving two daughters, Ann and Mary, who had been born before 1776 as British citizens. Mary Scott married a citizen of South Carolina and died in 1802, entitled to half her father's estate. Ann Scott married a British officer in 1781, when the British had temporarily retaken Charleston, and moved to England in 1782, where she died in 1801. Her five children sued for their share of Thomas Scott's estate under the terms of the Jay Treaty of 1794, which had guaranteed the holdings of British subjects in the United States. The case turned upon whether Ann Scott was a British or an American subject. Legaré, pleading for the defendants in error, "insisted, that the decree of the state court [which had disallowed the claims of Ann Scott's children] ought to be affirmed, because Mrs. Shanks was an American citizen, capable of holding by the laws of South Carolina; so that there was no interest or title in her, to which the ninth article of the treaty of 1794, by which the titles of British subjects, holding lands in this country, were saved

from the disabilities of alienage, could in any wise attach." Legaré lost the case, with Joseph Story writing the majority opinion. The matter obviously gave Legaré much pause, as he worries the issue in "Kent's Commentaries," 118–19.

31. Legaré, "Hoffman's Legal Outlines," 65–69; Legaré, "Kent's Commentaries," 125; Bryson, *Man and Society,* 39, 103.

32. Legaré, "Hall's Travels," 268; Legaré, "Kent's Commentaries," 102; Legaré, "Hall's Travels," 268.

33. Legaré, "German Diaries," 100; Legaré, "Hall's Travels," 268–69. Later, Legaré was to criticize Tocqueville for being too systematic, in making democracy explain everything in American society: "Bankruptcy, and the Bank Bill," 440.

34. Legaré, "Kent's Commentaries," 103. Nonetheless, he refused to talk to Frederick Marryat when the Englishman visited White Sulphur Springs on a book-making expedition (Legaré to sister, 25 Aug. 1838).

35. Legaré, "Saxe-Weimar," 168.

36. Legaré, "Hall's Travels," 261, 259.

37. Ibid., 262, 261; Legaré, "The Disowned," 181–84.

38. Carroll, "Sketch," 360; Legaré, "German Diaries," 118; Legaré to sister, 28 June 1834, in *Writings,* I, 240.

39. Legaré to mother, 8 July 1832; "Of Love and Marriage," in David Hume, *Essays: Moral, Political and Literary* (London, 1903), 552–57; Legaré, "Roman Literature," 78–79 (these remarks parallel those of John Millar, in *Observations Concerning the Distinction of Ranks in Society* [London, 1771], 71–72); Legaré, "The Disowned," 204; Legaré to Colonel Aspinwall, 12 Oct. 1832, Joline Collection, Huntingdon Library.

40. Legaré, "Hall's Travels," 257–58.

41. Ibid., 266–67, 269; Legaré to Pierce Butler, 26 June 1838, in Charleston *Courier,* 20 and 21 July 1838.

42. Legaré, "Kent's Commentaries," 123–41. He was later to be equally critical about stinginess in the American diplomatic corps (Legaré to Edward Livingston, 16 April 1833, Belgium/NA).

43. Legaré, "Hall's Travels," 271–72.

44. Legaré, "Kent's Commentaries," 123–24, 126–33.

45. Ibid., 124; Legaré, "Hall's Travels," 297.

46. Legaré, "Hall's Travels," 283.

47. Ibid., 284–85.

48. Ibid., 286–88.

49. Ibid., 287, 288–89; Legaré to mother, 26 Jan. 1835.

50. Legaré, "Hall's Travels," 292–93.

51. Ibid., 295; Legaré, "Lord Byron's Character and Writings," 380.

## 7. CENTRIFUGAL TENDENCIES

1. Legaré to mother, 24 Jan. 1829; Legaré to Stephen Elliott, Jr., 14 April 1839, Legaré Papers, Duke University.

2. Robert M. Weir, "'The Harmony We Were Famous For': An Interpretation of Pre-Revolutionary South Carolina Politics," *William and Mary Quarterly* 26 (Oct. 1969): 473–501; Mark D. Kaplanoff, "Making the South Solid: Politics and the Structure of Society in South Carolina, 1790–1815," Ph.D. diss., University of Cambridge, 1980; Legaré to Barnwell Smith, 25 Oct. 1831.

3. Freehling, *Prelude,* 130–31, 158–59; Christophersen, "Legaré," 173–74, claims Legaré's authorship of the protest, although I cannot find the letter he cites (Legaré to mother, 15 Dec. 1828) in the place, the "Chisholm Papers" (now the Legaré papers at SCL), he mentions: Legaré to mother, 8 March 1829. John Marshall to Legaré, 21 Sept. 1829, is flattering while defending David Hoffman from Legaré's strictures.

4. Jane H. Pease and William H. Pease, "The Economics and Politics of Charleston's Nullification Crisis," *Journal of Southern History* 47 (Aug. 1981): 335–62. The MSS of the articles from which this discussion is drawn are in the Legaré papers. Legaré indulged in the sport of anonymity by writing to the governor of South Carolina, Stephen Miller, on 5 August 1830: "Who are writing for the 'Journal' under signatures of 'Jefferson' & a 'Plain Man'? Those pieces will do good." It may be relevant that Legaré once wrote from Paris, "I am determined to be a very plain man for *some time to come,* whatever I might be here" (Legaré to sister, n.d. [July, 1819]).

5. Legaré, "The American System," 206–12.

6. Ibid., 213–16.

7. Ibid., 217–22.

8. Ibid., 222–29, 230.

9. Ibid., 229–34.

10. Ibid., 235–44; cf. Heineccius, *Methodical System of Universal Law,* II, 91: "It is from the end of a society that we must judge of the means, and of the rights and duties of its members."

11. Legaré, "The American System," 254.

12. Freehling, *Prelude,* 177–218.

13. Petigru to Joseph D. Pope, 18 Nov. 1830, Petigru Papers, SCL; Charleston *Courier,* 30 Nov. 1830; Legaré to Jesse B. Harrison, 24 Jan. 1832.

14. Christophersen, "Legaré," 191; Legaré to Alfred Huger, 15 Dec. 1834, in *Writings,* I, 216.

15. Christophersen, "Legaré," 192; "Plain Man" MSS; Legaré to Alfred Huger, 15 Dec. 1834, in *Writings,* I, 216; "D'Aguesseau," 584.

16. Carroll, "Sketch," 354.

17. "D'Aguesseau," 594.

18. "Celebration of the Fifty-Fifth Anniversary of American Independence by the Union State Rights Party," reprinted in Henry D. Capers, *The Life and Times of C.G. Memminger* (Richmond, Va., 1893), 37–105; Freehling, *Prelude,* 223–24.

19. Legaré, "Speech Before the Union Party," 270–79.

20. Ibid., 271–72.

21. Ibid., 271.

22. Legaré to Edward Livingston, 26 Nov. 1832, Belgium/NA; Legaré to Rives, 28 Jan., 5 Jan., 16 April, 1833, Rives Papers, LC; Legaré, "Classical Learning," 50; Appian, *The Civil Wars,* IV, 131.

23. Legaré to sister, 13 Oct. 1832.

24. William B. Hatcher, *Edward Livingston: Jeffersonian Republican and Jacksonian Democrat* (Baton Rouge, La., 1940), 245–88; Legaré to mother, 8 March 1829; Legaré to mother, 17 June 1832; Legaré to Isaac Holmes, 8 April 1833, in *Writings,* I, 207.

## 8. Europe

1. Legaré to Jesse B. Harrison, 24 April 1832, Harrison Papers, LC; Legaré to Rives, 19 Sept. 1832, Rives Papers, LC.

2. Legaré to sister, n.d. [July 1832]; Legaré to mother, 13 Aug. 1832.

3. Legaré to mother, 13 Aug. 1832; Charleston *Courier,* 28 Feb. 1828. Latamendi, after failing to regulate Legaré's household affairs and, without authority, styling himself secretary to the chargé, left after a few months (Legaré to mother, 22 Dec. 1832).

4. Legaré to sister, 5 May 1833, in *Writings,* I, 225; Legaré to Isaac Holmes, 2 Oct. 1832, in *Writings,* I, 202–07; Legaré to Rives, 19 Sept. 1832, Rives Papers, LC; Legaré to mother, 6 Sept. 1832; Legaré to sister, 13 Oct. 1832; Frederick B. Artz, *Reaction and Revolution, 1814–1832* (New York, 1934), 270–76; Legaré, "German

Diaries," 119; Gordon Wright, *France in Modern Times, 1760 to the Present* (Chicago, 1960), 148–50.

5. Legaré to sister, 13 Oct. 1832; Legaré to Isaac Holmes, 2 Oct. 1832, in *Writings,* I, 202–07; Nott to Legaré, 7 May 1831, Nott Papers. SCL.

6. Legaré to Rives, 19 Sept. 1832, Rives Papers, LC; Henri Laurent, "Les debuts de la mission de Hugh Swinton Legaré, chargé d'affaires des États-Unis à Bruxelles (septembre-decembre, 1832)," *Bulletin de la Commission Royale D'Histoire* (Jan. 1937): 37–38; "John Wool," *Dictionary of American Biography,* ed. D. Malone (New York, 1943), XX, 513–14; Legaré to mother, 26 Sept. 1832; Legaré to Edward Livingston, 26 Sept. 1832, Belgium/NA; Rooney, *Belgian-American Relations,* 20–44; Legaré to [sister?], 6 Dec. 1832; Legaré to Edward Livingston, 1 April 1833, Belgium/NA.

7. Rooney, *Belgian-American Relations,* 32–34, 52–80; Legaré's irrelevance can be gauged by the paucity of references to the American in Sir Robert Adair's correspondence with Palmerston: see Foreign Office Papers, Group 10/13, 14, 24, 25, 31, 32, 33, 37, PRO; Legaré to Louis McLane, 6 Oct. 1833, 23 March 1834, Belgium/NA.

8. Rooney, *Belgian-American Relations,* 52–80; Robert Adair to Lord Palmerston, 26 Feb. 1833, Foreign Office Papers, Group 10/24, PRO; later, however when France and the United States became embroiled over the indemnity question, Legaré was able to offer advice and intelligence to the State Department (Legaré to John Forsyth, 15 Jan. 1835, Belgium/NA).

9. Legaré to mother, 30 June 1832; Rooney, *Belgian-American Relations,* 56; Legaré to sister, 13 Oct. 1832; Laurent, "Legaré," 39, however says that Legaré's address was 9 rue des Sablons, which seems to mistake the Boulevard du Régent for the rue de la Régence, which does intersect the rue des Sablons: se G. Des Marez, *Guide Illustré de Bruxelles* (Brussels, 1928), I, 261. Legaré found servants, instead of slaves, a great vexation, as they were inclined to petty robberies, drunkenness, and liaisons (Legaré to mother, 22 Dec. 1832; Legaré to [mother?], Feb. 1834; Legaré to sister, 3–4 March 1834; Legaré to mother, 24–25 Nov. 1835.

10. Legaré, "Diary of Brussels," 1–100, passim; Albert Jay Nock, *Memoirs of a Superflous Man* (New York, 1943), 153–58; Frances Trollope, *Belgium and Western Germany in 1833* (London, 1834), 67.

11. Legaré to mother, 4 Feb. 1833; Legaré," Diary of Brussels," 4–5, 6, 20, 43, 93; Legaré to Isaac Holmes, 8 April 1833, in *Writings* I, 212.

12. *Memoirs, Journal and Correspondence of Thomas Moore,* ed. Lord John Russell (London, 1856), VII, 216; Legaré, "Diary of Brussels," 16, 81; *'In My Hot Youth': Byron's Letters and Journals,* ed. Leslie A. Marchand (Cambridge, Mass., 1973), I, 236, 239, 242, 243, 256; Charles Greville, *A Journal of the Reigns of King George IV and King William IV,* ed. Henry Reeve (New York, 1887), I, 115; Legaré to mother, 4 Nov. 1832.

13. Legaré, "Diary of Brussels," 2, 7, 30; Legaré to mother, 10 May 1833; Legaré to sister, 3–4 March 1834; *Dictionary of National Biography,* ed. L. Stephen and S. Lee (London, 1908), IX, 117–22.

14. Legaré, "Diary of Brussels," 73, 94, 99, 100; S. Leon Levy, *Nassau W. Senior, 1790–1864* (New York, 1970), 78, 305–06; see also Nassau Senior to Legaré, 28 Jan. 1840.

15. Legaré to Mr. Niles, 2 Jan. 1833, Legaré Miscellaneous MSS, LC; Legaré, "Diary of Brussels," 32–33, 87, 95; pamphlet, enclosed in Legaré to Louis McLane, 15 Aug. 1833, Belgium/NA; M. Kukiel, *Czartoryski and European Unity* (Princeton, N.J., 1955).

16. J. Steven Watson, *The Reign of George III, 1760–1815* (Oxford, 1960), 243; Legaré, "Diary of Brussels," 56, 12–16, 46, 49, 84; Elizabeth Longford, *Wellington: The Years of the Sword* (London, 1969), 448; Legaré to sister, 2 May 1834, in *Writings,* I, 238.

17. Preston to O'Connor, 4 Dec. 1818, Preston Papers, SCL.

18. Legaré to sister, 25 Nov. 1832, and Oliver Bronson to Legaré, 18 Dec. 1832, for example, are both defaced; Legaré, "German Diaries," 108; Legaré to sister, n.d. [July, 1819]; Legaré to mother, 24 Jan. 1829. William Garnett Chisholm seems to have been exercised on the matter of Legaré's sexual potency, as Yates Snowden to Chisholm, 18 Feb. 1930, Chisholm Papers, SCL, contains this vigorous if belated evidence: "Professor Ramage [of the University of the South, who wrote a piece on Legaré for the *Sewanee Review* in 1902] asked me if it was true that Hugh S. Legaré was *impotent?* I consulted Mr. W. Mazyck Porcher, who knew Mr. Legaré, Col. Henry E. Young (of R.E. Lee's staff) & U.S. Dist. Judge C.H. Simonton & I received from those gentlemen, *convincing evidence* that H.S.L. was *not impotent!*" It is hard to say what would constitute convincing evidence, except a bastard, which might explain Legaré's mysterious legacy of $500, left to Petigru to handle.

19. Legaré to mother, 8 July 1832; Legaré to sister, 25 Nov. 1832; Legaré to sister, 1 Aug. 1834; Legaré to sister, 24 Aug. 1835; Legaré to sister, 19 Oct. 1835; Legaré to mother, 24–25 Nov. 1835; Legaré to sister, 10 Dec. 1835.

20. Legaré to David McCord, 29 March 1825; Legaré to mother, n.d. [1818]; [Charles Fraser?] to Legaré, 10 June 1833.

21. Henry Junius Nott, *Novelettes of a Traveller; or, Odds and Ends from the Knapsack of Thomas Singularity, Journeyman Printer* (New York, 1834), II, 5–7, 11–12, 25, 61–65.

22. Ibid., 30 and passim.

23. Legaré, "Diary of Brussels," 52–53; Nott, *Novelettes of a Traveller,* 82–83; Legaré, "Lord Byron's Character and Writings," 374; Nott, *Novelettes of a Traveller,* 83; Legaré to Judith Rives, 26 April 1833, Rives Papers, LC. On the other hand, a differing candidate for Nott's satire is Alexander Pope.

24. Legaré to sister, 26 Feb. 1833; Legaré, "Diary of Brussels," 53. He certainly felt that vice was eventually punished, for "all vice is a violation of some law of nature & nature is never offended in vain—Be assured that sheer self love preaches virtue" (Legaré to [?], 19 Aug. 1834). There is one very small hint of a liaison. When leaving for Brussels in 1832, he sent to his law partner George Eggleston a letter and $100. Eggleston replied, "The person to whom I am to make the paymt. of $100, has not called or sent for it—the letter you enclosed me was delivered—should she be in need, I will pay her according to your wishes, the further sum of $100" (Eggleston to Legaré, 7 July 1832). Mills Thornton not implausibly suggests to me that when Henry Nott (cited in ch. 2) spoke in 1831 of Legaré as having "fattened on a Moor" like Desdemona, a slave mistress may have been implied.

25. Legaré to mother, 10 May 1833; Legaré, "Diary of Brussels," 8, 9; Legaré, "German Diaries," 99.

26. Legaré to sister, 4 Aug. 1833; Legaré, "Diary of Brussels," 45–46, 54, 55, 64, 73; Legaré to sister, 28 March 1836; Lytton Strachey, *Queen Victoria* (Harmondsworth, 1971), 43, 70.

27. The best account of the Hastings scandal is Elizabeth Longford, *Queen Victoria: Born to Succeed* (New York, 1964), 94–124; Roger Fulford, ed., *The Greville Memoirs* (New York, 1963), 165–66; Charleston *Courier,* 27 July 1839.

28. Legaré to Louis McLane, 10 April 1834, Belgium/NA; Legaré to sister, 2 May 1834; Legaré, "D'Aguesseau," 592. Sir Robert Adair was inclined to think responsible "Italians & other refugees from all Countries . . . of late most active & indefatigable in disseminating their doctrines among the populace" (Adair to Palmerston, 11 April 1834, Foreign Office Papers Group 10/32, PRO).

29. Legaré to sister, 2 May 1834; Legaré, "Diary of Brussels," 3, 7, 11, 28, 52, 64, 78, 79, 81, 82; Legaré to mother, 28 Dec. 1835;

Legaré, "German Diaries," 114, 116; A.N.L. Munby, *Portrait of an Obsession: The Life of Sir Thomas Phillipps* (New York, 1967), 15–16; Legaré to sister, 28 March 1836; Winfield Scott to William Campbell Preston, 18 July 1843, Preston Family Papers, Virginia Historical Society.

30. Legaré, "Diary of Brussels," 34, 44, 55, 62, 63; Legaré to sister 3–4 March 1834; Legaré to sister, 2 May 1834, in *Writings,* I, 237.

31. Legaré, "German Diaries," 98–104.

32. Ibid., 104–24.

33. Ibid., passim; Legaré, "Journal of the Rhine," 139–42.

34. Hillard, *Life of Ticknor,* I, 488–89.

35. Legaré, "German Diaries," 119; Hillard, *Life of Ticknor,* 496–97; cf. David B. Tyack, *George Ticknor and the Boston Brahmins* (Cambridge, Mass., 1967).

36. Legaré to Isaac Holmes, 2 Oct. 1832, in *Writings,* I, 203; Legaré, "German Diaries," 113; Legaré, "Diary of Brussels," 97; Legaré to sister, 5 May 1833, in *Writings,* I, 225.

37. Legaré to sister, 5 May 1833, in *Writings,* I, 225–26; Legaré, "German Diaries," 97; Legaré to sister, 14 Aug. 1834, in *Writings,* I, 254.

38. Legaré, "Journal of the Rhine," 106; Legaré to sister, 5 May 1833, in *Writings,* I, 226–27.

39. Legaré, "German Diaries," 115–16; Legaré, "Journal of the Rhine," 141.

40. Legaré to mother, 21 July, 9 Sept. 1834; Legaré to sister, 21–28 June 1834, in *Writings,* I, 238–41; Charles Greville, *A Journal of the Reigns of King George IV and King William IV,* ed. Henry Reeve (New York, 1887), I, 11.

41. Legaré to Alfred Huger, 12 May 1835; Mitchell King to Legaré, 5 May 1833; Petigru to Legaré, 24 April 1834, in Carson, *Petigru,* 137–39; Petigru to Legaré, 15 Dec. 1834, in Carson, *Petigru,* 167–71; Legaré to sister, 16–17 May 1835.

42. Legaré to Judith Rives, 26 April 1833, Rives Papers, LC; Legaré to Alfred Huger, 21 Nov. 1835, in *Writings,* I, lll; Legaré to sister, 16–17 May 1835; Legaré to mother, 11 Sept. 1835; Legaré to sister, 28 March, 14 April 1836; Legaré to mother, 10 June 1836, 3 Aug. 1834, 22 Sept. 1836.

## 9. Charleston

1. Charles M. Wiltse, *John C. Calhoun: Nullifier, 1829–1839* (Indianapolis, Ind., 1949), 280–86, 293–94; Drew Gilpin Faust, *James Henry Hammond and the Old South: A Design for Mastery* (Baton Rouge, La., 1982), 165–85; Alfred Huger to J.R. Poinsett, 27 Aug. 1836, Poinsett Papers, PHS; Petigru to Legaré, 26 Aug. 1836, Petigru Papers, LC. Thomas Bennett was first opposed to Legaré but permitted himself to be persuaded (Legaré to mother, 22 Sept. 1836).

2. Petigru to Legaré, 6 Sept. 1836, in Carson, *Petigru,* 184–85; Legaré to mother, 10 Sept. 1836; Poinsett to Campbell, 17 Oct. 1837, in "Poinsett-Campbell Correspondence," ed. S.G. Stoney, *SCHM* 42 (Oct. 1941): 165.

3. Legaré to mother, 5 Feb. 1835; Legaré to sister, n.d. [1837]; Raymond C. Dingledine, "The Political Career of William Cabell Rives," Ph.D. diss., University of Virginia, 1947, 9, 10, 20, 78, 91, 104–05, 108, 205–06, 258–82; John H. Moore, "Judith Rives of Castle Hill," *Virginia Cavalcade* 13 (Spring 1964): 30–35; John M. McFaul, *The Politics of Jacksonian Finance* (Ithaca, N.Y., 1972), 178–209; James Rogers Sharp, *The Jacksonians versus the Banks: Politics in the States After the Panic of 1837* (New York, 1970), esp. 215–73.

5. Legaré to sister, n.d. [1837]; Legaré to Rives, 14 April 1841, Rives Papers, LC; Legaré to George S. Bryan, 11 Aug. 1838; the assessment of Calhoun is repeated and elaborated in "Bankruptcy, and the Bankrupt Bill," 447; the phrase "high priori road" is from *The Dunciad,* IV, 471: "We nobly take the High Priori Road, And reason downward, til we doubt of God"—a reproach from Pope to Hobbes, Spinoza, and Descartes.

5. MS., "John Quincy Adams"; *Memoirs of John Quincy Adams,* ed. Charles Francis Adams (Philadelphia, 1876), IX, 388, 405.

6. Bray Hammond, *Banks and Politics in America: From the Revolution to the Civil War* (Princeton, N.J., 1957), 450–99; Wiltse, *Calhoun: Nullifier,* 343–61.

7. Legaré to mother, 13 Oct. 1837, Miscellaneous MSS, New York Historical Society; *Memoirs of John Quincy Adams,* IX, 404.

8. Legaré, "Spirit of the Sub-Treasury," 280–82.

9. In this view, he had been influenced by conversations in Brussels with a Mr. Bates, an American prominent in the House of Baring (Legaré to mother, 26 Oct. 1834).

10. Legaré, "Spirit of the Sub-Treasury," 282–86. Nonetheless, Legaré believed "man is a warlike animal by nature" and felt, oddly,

that "had I lived in Europe & nothing prevented me, I should certainly have been a soldier" (Legaré to sister, 25 Nov. 1832).

11. Legaré, "Spirit of the Sub-Treasury," 287–92.

12. Ibid., 292–98.

13. Ibid., 298–301.

14. Ibid., 302–15. Yet Legaré himself hated to be in debt, and part of his disenchantment with South Carolina lay in seeing about him increasing indebtedness and ruin. Nonetheless, he was to plead in 1840 for a more expeditious and "modernized" bankruptcy law.

15. Ibid., 315–16.

16. Ibid., 316–17.

17. Ibid., 317–21.

18. Legaré to Alfred Huger, 28 Oct. 1837.

19. John C. Calhoun to Joel R. Poinsett, 4 or 14 July 1838, in *The Papers of John C. Calhoun,* ed. Clyde N. Wilson (Columbia, 1981), XIV, 390; Legaré to Rives, 12 Oct. 1838, Rives Papers, LC; statement by Poinsett on Legaré, 15 Oct. 1838, Gilpin/Poinsett Papers, PHS; Christopher Memminger to Poinsett, 13 Dec. 1837, Gilpin/Poinsett Papers, PHS.

20. David J. McCord to Waddy Thompson, 19 June 1838, McCord Papers, SCL; Petigru to Legaré, 7 May 1838, Petigru Papers, SCL; Petigru to Legaré, 1 June 1838, in Carson, *Petigru,* 197–98; Petigru to Waddy Thompson, 19 Oct. 1838, Thompson Papers, SCL; Legaré to mother, 13 Oct. 1837; Legaré to Alfred Huger, 28 Oct. 1837; Legaré to Pierce Butler, 26 June 1838, in Charleston *Courier,* 20 July 1838; Legaré to Rives, 12 Oct. 1838, Rives Papers, LC; Legaré, "Hall's Travels," 270–71.

21. Legaré to Judith Rives, 28 June 1838, Rives Papers, LC; Legaré to Waddy Thompson, 13 Aug. 1838; Legaré to mother, 15 Aug. 1838; Legaré to sister, 25 Aug. 1838; Legaré to Judith Rives, 25 Aug. 1838, Rives Papers, LC; Legaré to sister, 10 Sept. 1838; Legaré to Alfred Huger, 23 Sept. 1838, Paul Hamilton Hayne Papers, Duke University; Legaré to mother, 25 Sept. 1838; Alfred Huger to Poinsett, 1 Sept. 1838, Poinsett Papers, PHS.

22. Legaré to Isaac Holmes, 2 Oct. 1832, in *Writings,* I, 203; Joseph Johnson to Poinsett, 4 Oct. 1838, Poinsett Papers, PHS; Edward McCrady to Poinsett, 6 Oct. 1838, Poinsett Papers, PHS; copy of "Friend to Truth" to *Southern Patriot,* 4 Oct. 1838, Poinsett Papers, PHS; Edward McCrady to Poinsett, 9 Oct. 1838, Poinsett Papers, PHS; "Kinloch," in Charleston *Courier,* 13 Aug. 1838; Legaré to Rives, 12 Oct. 1838, Rives Papers, LC.

23. Legaré to Judith Rives, 19 Oct. 1838, Rives Papers, LC; Legaré to sister, 10 Sept. 1838; Legaré to sister, 12 Oct. 1838; Legaré to Thomas C. Reynolds, 6 Feb. 1841, in *Writings,* I, 236.

24. Legaré, "Stephen Elliott," Charleston *Courier,* 30 March 1840; [Samuel Prioleau] "Dyspepsia," *SR* 4 (Aug. 1829): 208–41; Legaré to sister, 25 Jan. 1836; Legaré to mother, 25 Sept. 1838; Legaré to Rives, 5 Oct. 1838, Rives Papers, LC; Legaré to Alfred Huger, 15 Dec. 1834, in *Writings,* I, 216–19; Legaré to mother, 4 Nov. 1832; Legaré to sister, 10 Oct. 1839; Legaré to mother, 27 Sept. 1840.

25. Mitchell King to Legaré, 5 May 1833, Legaré to Isaac Holmes, 8 April 1833, in *Writings,* I, 215; Petigru to Legaré, 12 Nov. 1838, in Carson, *Petigru,* 200–201; Legaré to Rives, 5 Oct. 1838, Rives Papers, LC.

26. Legaré to sister, 15 April 1835.

27. Jacob Cardozo to Legaré, 5 Sept. 1838; statement by Poinsett on Legaré, 15 Oct. 1838, Gilpin/Poinsett Papers, PHS; Gouverneur Kemble to Poinsett, 29 June 1843, Gilpin/Poinsett Papers, PHS.

28. Preston to Waddy Thompson, 28 Aug. 1855, Preston Papers, SCL.

29. Legaré to sister, 12 Oct. 1838; Legaré to mother, 25 Oct. 1838; Legaré to mother, 24 Dec. 1838; Legaré to sister, 11 Jan. 1839; Legaré to Judith Rives, 30 Dec. 1838, Rives Papers, LC; Legaré, "Southern Naval Depot," 329–37.

30. Legaré, "Recognition of Hayti," 322–28; Huger to Poinsett, 1 Sept. 1838, Poinsett Papers, PHS; Legaré to Rives, 20 Aug., 2 Sept.,1841, Rives Papers, LC.

31. Legaré, "Official Defalcations," 338–53.

32. Legaré to Rives, 16 Aug. 1839, Rives Papers, LC.

33. Legaré to Rives, 14 April 1839, Rives Papers, LC; Gouverneur Kemble to Legaré, 8 Dec. 1839, Charles L. Chandler Papers, Southern Historical Collection; Legaré to mother, 24 Dec. 1838; Rives to Legaré, 18 June 1839; Legaré to Judith Rives, 22 June 1839, Rives Papers, LC; Legaré to Rives, 3 Oct. 1839, Rives Papers, LC; Charleston *Courier,* 29 Oct. 1839; Legaré to Rives, 17 April 1839, Rives Papers, LC.

34. Cf. Legaré to Judith Rives, 26 April 1836, Rives Papers, LC, which speaks of Tyler's "longwinded & empty balderdash."

35. Legaré to Rives, 20 Dec. 1839, Rives Papers, LC; Legaré to sister, 31 Oct. 1839; Legaré to Rives, 16 Aug. 1839, Rives Papers, LC.

36. Legaré to sister, 12 Oct. 1838; Legaré to mother, 24 Dec. 1838; Legaré to mother, 20 Feb. 1839; Legaré to Judith Rives, 22

June 1839, Rives Papers, LC; Will of Mary Swinton Legaré, 22 Oct. 1842, Charleston Wills, S.C. State Archives; Legaré to Gouverneur Kemble, 9 June 1839, Chandler Papers, Southern Historical Collection.

37. Preston, *Eulogy,* 20; Legaré to mother, 27 Sept. 1840; Federal Census of 1840, South Carolina, Charleston District, p. 94.

38. Christophersen, "Legaré," 397–402; Charleston *Courier,* 7 Feb. 1840.

39. Capers, *Memminger,* 179–82; *Writings of Benjamin F. Perry,* II, 442–46.

40. Charleston *Courier,* 7 Feb. 1840; Johnston, in *Writings,* I, lxvi; Alfred Huger to Paul Hamilton Hayne, 27 Jan. 1871, Hayne Papers, Duke University; Lounsbury, *"Ludibria Rerum Mortalium";* Alfred Lord Tennyson, "Break, Break, Break," lines 1–4, 9–12.

41. Legaré to Francis Walker Gilmer, 1 Oct. 1816, Gilmer Papers, University of Virginia; Legaré to Judith Rives, 22 June 1839, Rives Papers, LC; Joseph Cogswell to Legaré, 24 April 1839.

42. Legaré, "Demosthenes," 445–49, 472, 474, 479, 482; Legaré, "Constitutional History of Greece," 367–73, 430; M.I. Finley, *Ancient Slavery and Modern Ideology* (London, 1980), 35–39; Sandys, *History of Classical Scholarship,* III, 14–18, 162, 163, 232.

43. Legaré, "Demosthenes," 450; Legaré, "Origin of Roman Legislation," 504.

44. Legaré, "Origin of Roman Legislation," 504–06.

45. Ibid., 506–09.

46. Ibid., 509–14; Edward Gibbon, *The Decline and Fall of the Roman Empire,* ed. J.B. Bury (London, 1909), IV, 47ln.

47. Legaré, "Constitutional History of Greece," 380; Legaré to Rives, 14 April 1841, Rives Papers, LC; Frank M. Turner, *The Greek Heritage in Victorian Britain* (New Haven, Conn.: 1981), 192–213; Legaré, "Demosthenes," 454–72. In addition to Turner's sober and useful book, see the elegant if episodic Richard Jenkyns, *The Victorians and Ancient Greece* (Cambridge, Mass., 1980).

48. Legaré, "Constitutional History of Greece," 372–73.

49. Legaré, "Origin of Roman Legislation," 511.

50. Ibid., 514–25; on Coke, see J.G.A. Pocock, *The Ancient Constitution and the Feudal Law* (Cambridge, 1957), 56–69.

51. Ibid., 525–27.

52. Legaré, "Constitutional History of Greece," 422–23; Legaré, "Origin of Roman Legislation," 525–30; Legaré to Thomas White, 10 May 1838; cf. Legaré, "Classical Learning," 40n.

53. Legaré, "Origin of Roman Legislation," 540–41; Legaré, "Constitutional History of Greece," 439.

54. Legaré, "Demosthenes," 476, 463–64.

55. Ibid., 443.

56. Legaré to mother, 14 Sept. 1840; Legaré to mother, 27 Sept. 1840; Legaré, "Demosthenes," 443–44.

57. Legaré, "Constitutional History of Greece," 373–78, 425.

58. Ibid., 425–28.

59. Ibid., 428–31.

60. Ibid., 431–34.

61. Ibid., 434–49.

62. Ibid., 440–42.

## 10. WASHINGTON

1. Legaré to Preston, 18 July 1840, Miscellaneous MSS, Bancroft Library, University of California, Berkeley; Legaré to "Friends of Harrison and Reform," 12 June 1840, Legaré MSS, LC; Legaré to Mssrs. Atkinson et al., 24 June 1840; Legaré to Messrs. Griffin et. al., 22 July 1840, Connaroe Collection, PHS; Legaré to Messrs. Winthrop et al., 7 Aug. 1840; Legaré to Rives, 5 June 1840, Rives Papers, LC; Legaré to mother, 14 Sept. 1840; Legaré to Rives, 22 Aug. 1840, Rives Papers, LC. On Legaré's place in the 1840 campaign, see Robert G. Gunderson, *The Log-Cabin Campaign* (Lexington, Ky., 1957), esp. 6, 75, 158, 163, 187, 199–200.

2. Legaré to Rives, 3 Dec. 1840, Rives Papers, LC; Charleston *Courier,* 9 Dec. 1840; Glyndon G. Van Deusen, *The Jacksonian Era, 1828–1848* (New York, 1959), 152.

3. Legaré to Judith Rives, 5 April 1841, Rives Papers, LC.

4. Legaré to Nicholas Tallmadge, 8 April, 1841, Tallmadge MSS, Historical Society of Wisconsin; Legaré to Rives, 14 April 1841, Rives Papers, LC; Legaré to Nicholas Tallmadge, 26 April 1841, Tallmadge MSS., Historical Society of Wisconsin; Legaré to Judith Rives, 14 May 1841, Rives Papers, LC.

5. Van Deusen, *Jacksonian Era,* 153–58; George Ticknor to Legaré, 16 June 1841, in Hillard, *Life of Ticknor,* II, 196–97; Legaré to Rives, 2 July 1841, Rives Papers, LC; Legaré to mother, 11 Aug. 1841.

6. Legaré to Rives, 20 Aug. 1841, Rives Papers, LC; Van Deusen, *Jacksonian Era,* 157; Dingledine, "Rives," 399–403; Legaré to mother, 13 Sept. 1841; Daniel Webster to Legaré, 15 Sept. 1841, AG/NA.

7. Oliver P. Chitwood, *John Tyler: Champion of the Old South* (New York, 1939), 269–89; Legaré to sister, 5 Feb. 1842.

8. Albert Langeluttig, *The Department of Justice of the United States* (Baltimore, Md., 1927), 1–26; Leonard D. White, *The Jeffersonians: A Study in Administrative History, 1801–1829* (New York, 1951), 336–46.

9. Legaré to mother, 3 Oct. 1841; Legaré to sister, 9 March 1842; Charleston *Courier,* 22 April 1843; Legaré to Rives, 12 Nov. 1841, Rives Papers, LC; Petigru to William Elliott, 6 Oct. 1841, in Carson, *Petigru,* 206.

10. Charles Dickens, *American Notes for General Circulation* (New York, 1868), 165; Charles Dickens to Albany Fonblanque, 12 [and 21?] March 1842, in *The Letters of Charles Dickesn,* ed. Madeline House, Graham Storey, and Kathleen Tillotson (Oxford, 1974), III, 115–21; Robert Seager II, *and Tyler too: A Biography of John & Julia Gardiner Tyler* (New York, 1963), 174; Legaré to mother, 22 Oct. 1841; Legaré to sister, 5 Feb. 1842. Morpeth was pleased with both the dinner and Legaré—"the best scholar, and the most generally accomplished man, I met in all the Union"—especially with Legaré's admiration of Alexander Pope ("Travels in America," in J.J. Gaskin, ed. *The Vice Regal Speeches and Addresses, Lectures and Poems of the Late Earl of Carlisle, K.B.*[Dublin, 1865], 406–407). Legaré seems also to have entertained Sir Charles and Lady Lyell (Ticknor to Legaré, 2 Jan. 1842, in Hillard, *Life of Ticknor,* II, 197).

11. Legaré to John Spencer, 20 Oct. 1841, AG/NA; Legaré to Walter Forward, 11 March 1842, AG/NA; Benjamin F. Hall, ed., *Official Opinions of the Attorneys General of the United States* (Washington, 1852), III, 683, 685–87, IV, 19–20, 29–30, 10–13, 139, 16, III, 661–62, IV, 1–2; Legaré to J.A. Tomlinson, 14 Dec. 1841, AG/NA; Hall, ed., *Official Opinions,* III, 673–76.

12. F.W. Taussig, *The Tariff History of the United States,* 8th rev. ed. (New York, 1931), 110–14; Chitwood, *Tyler,* 293–304; Hall, ed., *Official Opinions,* IV, 56–68; Legaré to Franklin Dexter, 23 Oct. 1842, Legaré MSS., LC. Legaré suffered personally from the crisis, as his salary went unpaid for several months (Legaré to sister, 7 April 1842).

13. Hall, ed., *Official Opinions,* III, 738–48.

14. Howard Jones, *To the Webster-Ashburton Treaty: A Study in Anglo-American Relations, 1783–1843* (Chapel Hill, N.C., 1977), 78–85.

15. Ibid., 145–52; Legaré to Daniel Webster, 29 July 1842, Webster-Healy Papers, Massachusetts Historical Society; Hall, ed.,

*Official Opinions*, IV, 98–105; Legaré to Messrs. James D.P. Ogden et al., 29 Aug. 1842, in *Niles National Register* 63 (17 Sept. 1842): 37.

16. The six Florida cases were *U.S.* v. *Heirs of Clarke and Atkinson* (16 Peters 228), *U.S.* v. *Hanson* (16 Peters 196), *U.S.* v. *Low et al.* (16 Peters 162), *U.S.* v. *Miranda* (16 Peters 153), *U.S.* v. *Breward* (16 Peters 143), *U.S.* v. *Acosta* (1 Howard 24).

17. *Wood* v. *U.S.* (16 Peters 342); *U.S.* v. *Eliason* (16 Peters 291); *U.S.* v. *William Murphy et al.* (16 Peters 203); *Williams* v. *U.S.* (1 Howard 290); *Jewell's Lessee* v. *Jewell et al.* (1 Howard 219); *U.S.* v. *Eckford's Executors* (1 Howard 250); *Watkins* v. *Holman et al.* (16 Peters 25); Legaré to mother, 17 Jan. 1842; Legaré to mother, 29 Jan. 1842; Legaré to sister, 5 Feb. 1842. See also *Kelsey and McIntyre* v. *Hobby and Bond* (16 Peters 269), and *Bowman et al.* v. *Wathen et al.* (1 Howard 189).

18. Story, "Tribute to Legaré"; Legaré to Joseph Story, 7 March 1842, Story Papers, Clements Library, University of Michigan; 16 Peters 49; 1 Howard 292; 1 Howard 254; 1 Howard 228.

19. Marvin R. Cain, "Return to Republicanism: A Reappraisal of Hugh Swinton Legaré and the Tyler Presidency," *SCHM* 79 (Oct. 1978): 264–80, which overstates Legaré's importance; among many examples of the exercise of patronage, notable are Legaré to Waddy Thompson, 21 Oct. 1841, Waddy Thompson Papers, LC, which helped to secure the Mexican mission for Thompson; Joseph Cogswell to Legaré, 9 March 1842, which acknowledges Legaré's part in Cogswell's appointment as secretary to Washington Irving in Madrid (though Cogswell subsequently decided against acceptance).

20. Petigru to Jane Petigru North, 19 May 1842, in Carson, *Petigru,* 216; Calhoun offered Legaré politic congratulations when the latter became *ad interim* Secretary of State (Calhoun to Legaré, 7 June 1843, Miscellaneous Letters of the Department of State, National Archives); George Ticknor to Legaré, 2 Oct. 1842, in Hillard, *Life of Ticknor,* II, 210; Legaré to Rives, 6 Oct. 1842, Rives Papers, LC; Cain, "Return to Republicanism" 273–75, 277–79; Petigru to Susan Petigru, 14 Jan. 1842, Petigru Papers, LC.

21. Legaré to Daniel Webster, 2 March 1842, 5 August 1842, Webster-Healy Papers, Massachusetts Historical Society; Legaré to Lewis Cass, 5 April 1842, Lewis Cass Papers, Clements Library, University of Michigan; Jones, *To the Webster-Ashburton Treaty,* 75–78.

22. Irving H. Bartlett, *Daniel Webster* (New York, 1978), 184–85; Cain, "Return to Republicanism," 278; Legaré to Rives, 2 April 1843, Rives Family Papers, University of Virginia. The British

Minister in Washington was pleased by Legaré's appointment, though he underestimated the South Carolinian's wariness of Britain: "The appointment of Mr. Legaré is probably the most fortunate and satisfactory that could at present have been made. . . . I have long known Mr. Legaré, and have formed a high opinion both of his character and of his abilities. Having been employed under the administration of General Jackson on diplomatic service in Europe, he is well acquainted with foreign affairs; and I believe his appointment will be generally acceptable to all Powers who have to treat with the United States. Four years ago, when Mr. Legaré was member in Congress from South Carolina, he distinguished himself by several very eloquent speeches, in praise of British institutions, and in favor of the closest and most friendly alliance between the United States and Great Britain" (Henry S. Fox to the Earl of Aberdeen, 12 May 1843, Foreign Office Papers, Group 5/392, PRO).

23. Legaré to Rives, 6 April 1843, 12 June 1843, Rives Family Papers, University of Virginia; Legaré to sister, 16–17 May 1835.

24. Legaré to Henry Ledyard, 17 May 1843, Diplomatic Instructions of the Department of State, Microcopy 77, Roll 54 (France), National Archives; Legaré to Ambrose Baber, 17 May 1843, ibid., Roll 101 (Italy); Legaré to Christopher Hughes, 12 June 1843, ibid., Roll 123 (Netherlands); Legaré to Edward Everett, 13 June 1843, ibid., Roll 74 (Great Britain); Ralph S. Kuykendall, *The Hawaiian Kingdon, 1778–1854: Foundation and Transformation* (Honolulu, 1938), 200; Harold W. Bradley, *The American Frontier in Hawaii: The Pioneers, 1789–1843* (Stanford, Calif., 1942), 454–55.

25. Legaré to Rives, 6 Oct., 28 Oct. 1842, Rives Papers, LC; Charleston *Courier,* 7 Jan. 1843; Johnston, in *Writings,* I, lxxi.

26. Legaré to Rives, 12 June 1843, Rives Papers, LC.

27. Letter to the editor, *Law Reporter,* 12 July 1843, in Chisholm Papers, SCL; Charleston *Courier,* 21 June 1843; Legaré to Rives, 12 June 1843, Rives Papers, LC; Jacob Bigelow, " Case of Strangulated Intestine, from Rotation of the Sigmoid Flexure—with Remarks," *Boston Medical and Surgical Journal,* reprinted in Charleston *Courier,* 19 July 1843, which contradicts Rhea's speculation that he died of appendicitis.

28. Hillard, *Life of Ticknor,* I, 387–88; Bigelow, "Strangulated Intestine."

29. Bigelow, "Strangulated Intestine"; Hillard *Life of Ticknor,* II, 212–13. The autopsy seven hours later showed that "externally the limbs were very rigid, and there was much lividity about the head and

back. The abdomen was greatly distended. On laying it open the cavity seemed nearly filled by the sigmoid flexure of the large intestine, which extended across the abdomen into the right hypochondrium, and was in a state of such distension, that its external circumference was in one place fifteen inches. It had a dusky green color, as if commencing gangrene, but there seemed to be no softening, nor diminution of the natural polish. The two extremities of the flexure connected with the colon above, and the rectum below, were felt to be twisted together about the mesentery as an axis, into a firm cord or neck, about an inch in diameter; and on being carefully untwisted, the whole included portion was found to have made two turns, or two entire revolutions upon itself. There was no line of demarcation between the healthy and strangulated portions, nor was there any appearance externally of old disease about this part. The small intestine and the colon were moderately distended, but the rectum was rather contracted. The cavity of the peritoneum contained a small quantity of turbid reddish fluid, and in one place there was recent lymph upon the small intestine, but there were no other appearances of inflammation. Owing to the state of the body and the place of examination, the intestine was not opened, and no farther dissection made" (Bigelow, "Strangulated Intestine"). It is not impossible that the immediate cause of death was not the twisted sigmoid flexure but peritonitis, occasioned by the physicians puncturing the intestine in the course of their ministrations.

# Select Bibliography

THIS LISTING is intended only to indicate the chief sources, by and on Legaré, upon which this study is based; for more general secondary sources, the reader is referred to the notes.

### WRITINGS AND SPEECHES OF HUGH LEGARÉ

"The American System." *SR* 6 (Aug. 1830): 206–54.

"Arbitrement of National Disputes." Report of the Committee on Foreign Affairs, House of Representatives, 13 June 1838. In Charleston *Courier*, 28 June 1838 [*Writings*, I, 354–66].

"Bankruptcy, and the Bankrupt Bill." *New York Review* 7 (Oct. 1840): 440–75.

"Border Troubles." MS in Legaré Papers, SCL.

"Byron's Letters and Journals." *SR* 7 (May 1831): 1–42 [*Writings*, II, 411–48].

"Cicero de Republica." *SR* 4 (Aug. 1829): 136–76 [*Writings*, II, 216–53].

"Classical Learning." *SR* 1 (Feb. 1828): 1–49 [*Writings*, II, 5–51].

"Codification." *SR* 7 (Aug. 1831): 391–412 [*Writings*, II, 482–501].

"Constitutional History of Greece." *New York Review* 7 (July 1840): 1–85 [*Writings*, I, 367–442].

"Crafts' Fugitive Writings." *SR* 1 (May 1828): 503–29 [*Writings*, II, 142–65].

"D'Aguesseau." *SR* 8 (Feb. 1832): 399–443 [*Writings*, II, 559–98].

"Demosthenes, the Man, the Statesman, and the Orator." *New York Review* 9 (July 1841): 1–70 [*Writings*, I, 443–501].

"Diary of Brussels." *Writings*, I, 1–100.

"The Disowned—Tales of the Great St. Bernard." *SR* 3 (May, 1829): 467–507 [*Writings*, II, 180–215].

"Early Spanish Ballads: Charlemagne and His Peers." *SR* 5 (Feb. 1830): 62–99 [*Writings*, II, 299–333].

"The Fair Maid of Perth." *SR* 2 (Aug. 1828): 216–63.

"German Diaries." In Michael O'Brien, ed. *All Clever Men, Who Make Their Way: Critical Discourse in the Old South* (Fayetteville, Ark., 1982), 92–124 [this is edited from the extant MS, and is thus a corrected version of passages in "Journal of the Rhine," corresponding to *Writings*, I, 108–39].

"Hall's *Travels in North America.*" *SR* 4 (Nov. 1829): 321–69 [*Writings*, II, 254–98].

"Hoffman's Legal Outlines." *SR* 4 (Aug. 1829): 47–69.

"Jeremy Bentham and the Utilitarians." *SR* 7 (Aug. 1831): 261–96 [*Writings*, II, 449–81].

"John Q. Adams." MS in Legaré Papers, SCL.

"Journal of the Rhine." *Writings*, I, 103–51.

"Kent's Commentaries" *SR* 2 (Aug. 1828): 72–113 [*Writings*, II, 102–41].

"Law of Tenures." *SR* 3 (Feb. 1829): 1–31.

*Letter from the Hon. Hugh S. Legaré on the probable effects of the Sub-Treasury policy on the specie clasue, to His Excellency, Pierce Butler, Governor of South Carolina* (Washington, 1838).

"Letter to Hugh Mercer et al., 13 July 1840." Charleston *Courier*, 11 Aug. 1840.

"Letter to the Editors." Charleston *Courier*, 1 April 1841.

"Lord Byron's Character and Writings." *SR* 5 (May 1830): 463–522 [*Writings*, II, 356–410].

"Mississippi Election." Speech in the House of Representatives, 2 Oct. 1837. In *Register of Debates in Congress* (Washington, 1837), XIV, 1178–90.

"Nullification." Camden *Journal* 24, 31 July; 7, 14, 21, 28 Aug.; 4, 18 Sept. 1830 [MS in Legaré Papers, SCL].

"Official Defalcations." Speech in the House of Representatives, 15 Jan. 1839. In Charleston *Courier*, 7, 8, 11 Feb. 1839 [*Writings*, I, 338–53].

*Official Opinions of the Attorneys General of the United States*, ed. Benjamin F. Hall (Washington, 1852), III, 657–751; IV, 1–183.

"The Omnipresence of the Deity." *SR* 2 (Aug. 1828): 290–302.

"On Internal Improvements in South Carolina." Camden *Journal*, 6 Sept. 1828.

"On 'One of the People,' by James Hamilton, Jr." *Southern Patriot,* 2–5 Oct. 1821.

"Oration of the 4th of July, 1823." *Writings,* I, 257–69.

"Origin, History, and Influence of Roman Legislation." *New York Review* 5 (Oct. 1839): 269–334 [*Writings,* I, 502–58].

"Pollok's *Course of Time.*" *SR* 2 (Nov. 1828): 454–70.

"Producers and Consumers" *SR* 8 (Feb. 1832): 511–15.

"The Public Economy of Athens." *SR* 8 (Feb. 1832): 265–326 [*Writings,* II, 502–58].

"Recognition of Hayti." Speech in the House of Representatives, 18 Dec. 1838. *Writings,* I, 322–28.

"Remarks on giving the President additional powers for the defense of the United States against invasion." Speech in House of Representatives, 1 March 1839. In *Congressional Globe,* 25th Cong., 3rd sess., vol. VII: 283, 285–86.

"Roman Literature." *SR* 1 (May, 1828): 358–410 [*Writings,* II, 52–101].

"The Roman Orators." *SR* 2 (Nov. 1828): 491–540.

"The Siamese Twins." *SR* 7 (May 1831): 192–213.

"Sir Philip Sidney's Miscellanies." *SR* 5 (May 1830): 295–318 [*Writings,* II, 334–55].

"Southern Naval Depot." Speech in the House of Representatives, 11 Jan. 1839. In *Writings,* I, 329–37.

"Speech at the Log Cabin, Richmond, Va." In Charleston *Courier,* 24 Nov. 1840.

"Speech before the Union Party, 4th July 1831." *Writings,* I, 270–79.

"Speech on the bill making appropriations for preventing and suppressing Indian hostilities." House of Representatives, 4 June 1837. In *Congressional Globe,* 25th Cong. 2d sess., volume VI: 564–65.

"Speech to the Conservative Meeting," Syracuse, N.Y., 23 Oct. 1839. In Charleston *Courier,* 29 Oct. 1839.

"Spirit of the Sub-Treasury." Speech in the House of Representatives, 13 Oct. 1837. In *Congressional Globe,* 25th Cong., 1st sess., vol. V: 236–45 [*Writings,* I, 280–321].

"Stephen Elliott." Charleston *Courier,* 30 March 1840.

"Travels of the Duke of Saxe-Weimar." *SR* 3 (Feb. 1829): 192–207 [*Writings,* II, 166–79].

"Treasury Notes." Speech in the House of Representatives, 6 Oct. 1837. In *Register of Debates in Congress* (Washington, 1837), XIV: 1311–18.

"Washington Day Speech," St. Philip's Church, Charleston, 14 Feb. 1832. In Charleston *Courier,* 24 Feb. 1832.

"The Wept of Wish-ton-Wish." *SR* 5 (Feb. 1830): 207–26.

*Writings of Hugh Swinton Legaré.* 2 vols. Ed. Mary Legaré. Charleston, 1845–46.


## MANUSCRIPT SOURCES

*South Caroliniana Library, University of South Carolina, Columbia.*
Albert Case MSS; William Garnett Chisholm Papers; Colleton Family MSS; Charles Fraser Papers; E.A. Green MSS; Mitchell King Papers; Hugh Swinton Legaré Papers; Francis Lieber Papers; David J. McCord Papers; Robert Mills Papers; Henry Junius Nott Papers; James Louis Petigru Papers; William Campbell Preston Papers; Joel R. Poinsett Papers; John C. Schulz MSS; Waddy Thompson Papers; Thompson-Jones Family Papers.

*National Archives, Washington, D.C.*
Record Group 59, General Records of the Department of State: Instructions, Belgium, 1832–70 (Microcopy 77, Roll 19); Dispatches from U.S. Ministers to Belgium, 1832–43 (Microcopy 6, Roll 2); Notes to Belgium legation in the United States, 1834–74 (Microcopy 6, Roll 5); Miscellaneous Letters, 1843 (Microcopy 179, Rolls 101, 102, 103); Domestic Letters, 1842–44 (Microcopy 40, Roll 31); Instructions, 1801–1906 (Microcopy 77) to Austria (Roll 13), Brazil (Roll 23), Chile (Roll 35), China (Roll 38), Colombia (Roll 44), Denmark (Roll 50), France (Roll 54), German States (Roll 65), Great Britain (Roll 74), Italy (Roll 101), Mexico (Roll 111), the Netherlands (Roll 123), Spain (Roll 142), Special Missions (Roll 152), Sweden and Norway (Roll 156), Texas (Roll 161), Turkey (Roll 162), the Two Sicilies (Roll 170), Venezuela (Roll 171).

Record Group 60, General Records of the Department of State: Letters sent by the Department of Justice, General and Miscellaneous, 1818–58 (Microcopy 699, Roll 2).

*Library of Congress, Washington, D.C.*
Jesse Burton Harrison Papers; George Frederick Holmes Papers; Hugh Swinton Legaré Miscellaneous MSS; Alden Partridge MSS; James Louis Petigru Papers; William Cabell Rives Papers; Waddy Thompson Papers; John Tyler Papers.

*Southern Historical Collection, University of North Carolina, Chapel Hill*
Charles L. Chandler Papers; Elliott-Gonzales Papers; Franklin Elmore Papers; William Lowndes Papers; William Porcher Miles Papers.

*Historical Society of Pennsylvania, Philadelphia*
Cadwalader Collection; Connaroe Collection; Dreer Collection/ American Lawyers; Dreer Collection/Presidents; Etting Papers/ Administrations; Gratz Collection/15th Administration; Joel R. Poinsett Papers; Joel R. Poinsett Papers in the Henry D. Gilpin Collection.

*South Carolina State Archives, Columbia*
Charleston Wills; Inventories; Memorials.

*University of Virginia, Charlottesville*
Charles Augustus David Papers; Francis Walker Gilmer Papers; Benjamin Huger Papers; McGregor Collection; Rives Family Papers.

*Massachusetts Historical Society, Boston*
Alexander Everett Papers; Edward Everett Papers; Webster-Healy Papers.

*Perkins Library, Duke University, Durham, North Carolina*
Armistead Burt Papers; Paul Hamilton Hayne Papers; Hugh Swinton Legaré MSS; Waddy Thompson MSS.

*Huntington Library, San Marino, California*
J.L. Graham Collection; Joline Collection; Francis Lieber Collection; Rhees Collection.

*Clements Library, University of Michigan, Ann Arbor*
Lewis Cass Papers; Lucius Lyon Papers; Joseph Story Papers.

*New York Historical Society, New York*
Miscellaneous MSS; Murray Family MSS.

*South Carolina Historical Society, Charleston*
Maps and Muniments; Middleton MSS.

*Charleston Library Society, Charleston, South Carolina*
Shand Letter; Charles W. Baird, "Legaré Genealogy."

*Dartmouth College, Hanover, New Hampshire*
Daniel Webster Papers.

*Historical Society of Wisconsin, Madison*
Nicholas P. Tallmadge Papers.

*Amistad Research Center, Dillard University, New Orleans, Louisana*
Schooner Case Collection.

*Bancroft Library, University of California, Berkeley*
Miscellaneous MSS.

*Virginia Historical Society, Richmond*
Preston Family Papers.

*Virginia State Library, Richmond*
James S. Gilliam Journal.

*Public Record Office, Kew, England*
Foreign Office Records (Group 10):
    Letters from Sir Robert Adair, 1832–35 (Files 13, 14, 24, 25,
    31, 32, 33, 37); Letters from H. Lytton Bulwer, 1836 (File 41);
    Letters from George H. Seymour, 1836 (Files 42, 43).
Foreign Office Records (Group 5, Series II):
    Letters from Henry S. Fox, 1843 (Files 391, 392).

SECONDARY SOURCES

Carroll, Bartholomew R. "Sketch of the Character of the Hon. Hugh
    S. Legaré." *Southern Quarterly Review* 4 (Oct. 1843): 347–62.
    (Portions of this are reproduced in *The Charleston Book,* ed. W.G.
    Simms [Charleston, 1845], 266–71.)
Carson, James Petigru. *Life, Letters and Speeches of James Louis Petigru:
    The Union Man of South Carolina.* Washington, D.C. 1920.
Christophersen, Merrill G. "A Rhetorical Study of High Swinton
    Legaré: South Carolina Unionist." Ph.D. diss. Univ. of Florida,
    1954.
Hayne, Paul Hamilton. "Hugh Swinton Legaré." *SR* 7 (Jan. 1870):
    123–58.
Hillard, George S., ed. *Life, Letters and Journals of George Ticknor.* 2
    vols. Boston, 1876.
Holmes, George Frederick. "Writings of Hugh Swinton Legaré."
    *Southern Quarterly Review* 10 (April 1846): 321–61.
Johnston, Edward W. "Biographical Notice." In *Writings of Hugh
    Swinton Legaré,* I, v–lxxii.
Johnston, Edward W. "Life and Labors, Literary, Professional and
    Public, of Legaré." *American Whig Review* 2 (Oct. 1845): 416–30.

Laurent, Henri. "Les débuts de la mission de Hugh Swinton Legaré, chargé d'affaires des États-Unis à Bruxelles (septembre-decembre 1832)." *Bulletin de la Commission Royale Histoire* (Brussels, 1937), 3–75.

Legaré, Mary. "Memoir of Hugh Swinton Legaré." Legaré Papers, SCL.

Parks, Edd Winfield. "Hugh Swinton Legaré: Humanist." In *Ante-Bellum Southern Literary Critics*. 23–50, 268–76. Athens, Ga., 1962.

————. "Legaré and Grayson: Types of Classical Influence on Criticism in the Old South." In *Segments of Southern Thought*, 156–71. Athens, Ga., 1938.

Parrington, Vernon L., "Hugh Swinton Legaré—Charleston Intellectual." In *The Romantic Revolution in America, 1800–1860*, 114–24. New York, 1927.

Preston, William Campbell. *Eulogy on Hugh Swinton Legaré*. Charleston, 1843.

Ramage, Burr J. "Hugh Swinton Legaré." *Sewanee Review* 10 (Jan. 1902): 43–55; 10 (April 1902): 167–80.

Rhea, Linda. *Hugh Swinton Legaré, A Charleston Intellectual*. Chapel Hill, N.C., 1934.

Rives, William Cabell. "Hugh S. Legaré." *Southern Literary Messenger* 9 (Sept. 1843): 570–74.

Scott, Patrick Craig. "Two South Carolinians in Scotland During Edinburgh's Golden Age: Hugh Swinton Legaré and William Campbell Preston." Talk given to the Robert Burns Society of the Midlands, 23 March 1980 (MS. in the author's possession).

Simms, William Gilmore. "Life and Writings of Hugh Swinton Legaré." *Southern Literary Messenger* 12 (April 1846): 252–54.

Story, Joseph. "Tribute to the Memory of Mr. Legaré." Boston *Daily Advertiser*, 30 June 1843.

# Index

*A Character of Hugh Legaré* was composed into type on a Linotron 202 digital phototypesetter in eleven point Garamond No. 3 with one point of spacing between the lines. Garamond No. 3 was also selected for display. The book was designed by Frank O. Williams, composed by Typecraft Company, printed offset by Thomson-Shore, Inc., and bound by John H. Dekker & Sons. The paper on which the book is printed embodies acid-free characteristics designed for an effective life of at least three hundred years.

The University of Tennessee Press
Knoxville